Bayard Taylor

By-Ways of Europe

Bayard Taylor

By-Ways of Europe

ISBN/EAN: 9783743353671

Manufactured in Europe, USA, Canada, Australia, Japa

Cover: Foto ©ninafisch / pixelio.de

Manufactured and distributed by brebook publishing software (www.brebook.com)

Bayard Taylor

By-Ways of Europe

Entered according to Act of Congress, in the year 1869, by
G. P. PUTNAM AND SON,
in the Clerk's Office of the District Court for the Southern District of New York.

DEDICATED

TO MY FRIEND OF MANY YEARS,

HORACE GREELEY.

CONTENTS.

	PAGE
A Familiar Letter to the Reader	7
A Cruise on Lake Ladoga	21
Between Europe and Asia	59
Winter-Life in St. Petersburg	85
The Little Land of Appenzell	113
From Perpignan to Montserrat	145
Balearic Days, I.	171
Balearic Days, II.	197
Catalonian Bridle-Roads	227
The Republic of the Pyrenees	259
The Grande Chartreuse	293
The Kyffhäuser and its Legends	307
A Week on Capri	335
A Trip to Ischia	365
The Land of Paoli	391
The Island of Maddalena; with a Distant View of Caprera	419
In the Teutoburger Forest	449

how or why it was written is my own secret;" or, to take the reader frankly into his confidence, and brave the ready charge of vanity or over-estimation of self, by the free communication of his message. Generally, the latter course is only to anticipate the approval which is sure to come in the end, if there is any vitality in an author's work. To most critics the personal gossip of an acknowledged name is delightful: posthumous confidences also somehow lose the air of assertion which one finds in the living man. Death, or that fixed renown which rarely comes during life, sets aside the conventionalities of literature; and the very modesty and reticence which are supposed to be a part of them then become matters of regret. So there are transitions in life which seem posthumous to its preceding phases, and the present self looks upon the past as akin, indeed, but not identical.

During the past twenty-two years I have written and published ten volumes of travel, which have been extensively read, and are still read by newer classes of readers. Whatever may be the quality or value of those works, I may certainly assume that they possess an interest of some kind, and that the reader whom I so often meet, who has followed me from first to last (a fidelity which, I must confess, is always grateful and always surprising), will not object if, now, in offering him this eleventh and final volume, I suspend my rôle of observer long enough to relate how the series came to be written.

The cause of my having travelled so extensively has been due to a succession of circumstances, of a character more or less accidental. My prolonged wanderings formed no part of my youthful programme of life. I cannot disconnect my early longings for a knowledge of the Old World from a still earlier passion for Art and Literature. To the latter was added a propensity, which I have never unlearned, of acquiring as much knowledge as possible through the medium of my own experience rather than to accept it, unquestioned, from anybody else. When I first set out for Europe I was still a boy, and less acquainted with life than most boys of my age. I was driven to the venture by the strong necessity of providing for myself sources of education which, situated as I was, could not be reached at home. In other words, the journey offered me a chance of working my way.

At that time, Europe was not the familiar neighbor-continent which it has since become. The merest superficial letters, describing cities, scenery, and the details of travel, were welcome to a very large class of readers, and the narrative of a youth of nineteen, plodding a-foot over the Old World, met with an acceptance which would have been impossible ten years later. I am fully aware how little literary merit that narrative possesses. It is the work of a boy who was trying to learn something, but with a very faint idea of the proper method or discipline; who had an immense capacity for wonder and enjoyment, but not much power, as yet, to discriminate between the important and the trivial, the true and the false. Perhaps the want of development which the book betrays makes it attractive to those passing through the same phase of mental growth. I cannot otherwise account for its continued vitality.

Having been led, after returning home, into the profession of journalism, the prospect of further travel seemed very remote. I felt, it is true, that a visit to Greece, Egypt, and Syria was desirable in order to complete my acquaintance with the lands richest in the history of civilization; and I would have been quite willing to relinquish all chance of seeing more of the world, had that much been assured to me. I looked forward to years of steady labor as a servant of the Press; but, being a servant, and by necessity an obedient one, I was presently sent forth, in the line of my duty, to fresh wanderings. The "New York Tribune" required a special correspondent in California, in 1849, and the choice of its editor fell upon me. After performing the stipulated service, I returned by way of Mexico, in order to make the best practicable use of my time. Thus, and not from any roving propensity, originated my second journey.

When, two years later, a change of scene and of occupation became imperative, from the action of causes quite external to my own plans and hopes, my first thought naturally, was to complete my imperfect scheme of travel by a journey to Egypt and the Orient. I was, moreover, threatened with an affection of the throat, for which the climate of Africa offered a sure remedy. The journey was simply a change of position, from assistant-editor to correspondent, enabling me to obtain the strength which I sought, without giving up the service on which I relied for support. How it came to be extended to Central Africa is partly explained by the obvious advantage of writing from a new and but partially explored field; but there were other influences acting upon me which I did not fully comprehend at the time, and cannot now describe without going too deeply into matters of private history. I obeyed an instinct, rather than followed a conscious plan.

After having completed my African journeys, I traversed Palestine, Syria, and Asia Minor, and finally reached Constantinople, intending to return homewards through Europe. There, however, I found letters from my associates of "The Tribune," insisting that I should proceed speedily to China, for the purpose of attaching myself to the American Expedition to Japan, under Commodore Perry. I cannot say that the offer was welcome, yet its conditions were such that I could not well refuse, and, besides, I had then no plan of my own of sufficient importance to oppose to it. The circumstances of my life made me indifferent, so long as the service required was not exactly distasteful, and in this mood I accepted the proposition. Eight months still intervened before the squadron could reach China, and I determined to turn the time to good advantage, by including Spain and India in the outward journey. Thus the travel of one year was extended to two and a half, and instead of the one volume which I had premeditated, I brought home the material for three.

It would be strange if an experience so prolonged should not sensibly change the bent of an author's mind. It was not the sphere of activity which I should have chosen, had I been free to choose, but it was a grateful release from the drudgery of the editorial room. After three years of clipping and pasting, and the daily arrangement of a chaos of ephemeral shreds, in an atmosphere which soon exhausts the vigor of the blood, the change to the freedom of Oriental life, to the wonders of the oldest art and to the easy record of impressions so bright and keen that they put themselves into words, was like that from night to day. With restored health, the life of the body became a delight in itself; a kindly fortune seemed to attend my steps; I learned something of the patience and fatalistic content of the races among whom I was thrown, and troubled myself no longer with an anxious concern for the future.

I confess, too, that while floating upon the waters of the White Nile, while roaming through the pine forests of Phrygia or over the hills of Loo-Choo, I learned to feel the passion of the Explorer. Almost had I eaten of that fruit which gives its restless poison to the blood. It is very likely that, had I *then* been able to have marked out my future path, I might have given it the character which was afterwards ascribed to me.

I will further confess that the unusual favor with which those three volumes of travel were received, — perhaps, also, the ever-repeated attachment of "traveller" to my name, and that demand for oral report of what I had seen and learned, which threw me suddenly into the profession of lecturing, with much the sensation of the priest whom Henri Quatre made general by mistake, — I will confess, I say, that these things did for a time mislead me as to the kind of work which I was best fitted to do. I did not see, then, that my books were still a continuation of the process of development, and that, tried by a higher literary standard, they stopped short of real achievement. My plan, in writing them, had been very simple. Within the limits which I shall presently indicate, my faculty of observation had been matured by exercise; my capacity to receive impressions was quick and sensitive, and the satisfaction I took in descriptive writing was much the same as that of an artist who should paint the same scenes. I endeavored, in fact, to make words a substitute for pencil and palette. Having learned, at last, to analyze and compare, and finding that the impression produced upon my readers was proportionate to its degree of strength upon my own mind, I fancied that I might acquire the power of bringing home to thousands of firesides clear pictures of the remotest regions of the earth, and that this would be a service worth undertaking.

With a view of properly qualifying myself for the work, I made a collection of the narratives of the noted travellers of all ages, from Herodotus to Humboldt. It was a rich and most instructive field of study; but the first result was to open my eyes to the many requirements of a successful traveller — a list which increases with each generation. I was forced to compare myself with those wanderers of the Middle Ages, whose chief characteristic was a boundless capacity for wonder and delight, but, alas! this age would not allow me their naïve frankness of speech. Moreover, I had now discovered that Man is vastly more important than Nature, and the more I dipped into anthropological and ethnological works, the more I became convinced that I could not hope to be of service unless I should drop all other purposes and plans, and give my life wholly to the studies upon which those sciences are based. But the latter lay so far away from my intentions — so far from that intellectual activity which is joyous because it is spontaneous — that I was forced to pause and consider the matter seriously.

A writer whose mind has been systematically trained from the start will hardly comprehend by what gradual processes I attained unto a little self-knowledge. The faculties called into exercise by travel so repeated and prolonged, continued to act from the habit of action, and subsided very slowly into their normal relation to other qualities of the mind. They still continued to affect my plans, when I left home, in 1856, for another visit to Europe. It will, therefore, be easily understood how I came to combine a winter and summer trip to the Arctic Zone with my design of studying the Scandinavian races and languages: the former was meant as a counterpart to my previous experiences in tropical lands. This journey, and that to Greece and Russia, which immediately followed, were the receding waves of the tide. While I was engaged with them I found that my former enjoyment of new scenes, and the zest of getting knowledge at first-hand, were sensibly diminished by regret for the lack of those severe preparatory studies which would have enabled me to see and learn so much more.

I never thought it worth while to contradict a story which, for eight or nine years past has appeared from time to time in the newspapers — that Humboldt had said of me: "He has travelled more and seen less than any man living." The simple publication of a letter from Humboldt to myself would have silenced this invention; but I desisted, because I knew its originator, and did not care to take that much notice of him. The same newspapers afterwards informed me that he had confessed the slander, shortly before his death. I mention the circumstance now, in order to say that the sentence attributed to Humboldt was no doubt kept alive by the grain of truth at the bottom of it. Had Humboldt actually said: "No man who has published so many volumes of travel has contributed so little to positive science"—he would have spoken the truth, and I should have agreed with him. But when, during my last interview with that great student of Nature, I remarked that he would find in my volumes nothing of the special knowledge which he needed, it was very grateful to me when he replied: "But you paint the world as we, explorers of science, cannot. Do not undervalue what you have done. It is a real service; and the unscientific traveller, who knows the use of his eyes, observes for us always, without being aware of it." Dr. Petermann, the distinguished geographer, made almost the same remark to me, four or five years afterwards.

I should have been satisfied with such approval and with certain kindly messages which I received from Dr. Barth and other explorers, and have gone forward in the path into which I was accidentally led, had I not felt that it was diverging more and more from the work wherein I should find my true content. I may here be met by the threadbare platitude that an author is no judge of his own performance. Very well: let me, then, be the judge of my own tastes! On the one hand there was still the temptation of completing an unfulfilled scheme. Two additional journeys — one to the Caucasus, Persia, and the more accessible portions of Central Asia, and the other to South America — would have rounded into tolerable completeness my personal knowledge of Man and Nature. Were these once accomplished, I might attempt the construction of a work, the idea of which hovered before my mind for a long time — a *human* cosmos, which should represent the race in its grand divisions, its relation to soil and climate, its varieties of mental and moral development, and its social, political, and spiritual phenomena, with the complex causes from which they spring. The field thus opened was grander than that which a mere "tourist" could claim: it had a genuine charm for the imagination, and even failure therein was more attractive than success in a superficial branch of literature.

On the other hand, I began to feel very keenly the demoralizing influence (if one may apply such a term to intellectual effort) of travel. The mind flags under the strain of a constant receptivity: it must have time to assimilate and arrange its stores of new impressions. Moreover, without that ripe knowledge which belongs to the later rather than the earlier life of a man, the traveller misses the full value of his opportunities. His observations, in many respects, must be incomplete, and tantalize rather than satisfy. While he grows weary of describing the external forms of Nature and the more obvious peculiarities of races, he has little chance of following the clews to deeper and graver knowledge which are continually offered to his hands. Where, as in my case, other visions, of very different features, obscured for a time but never suppressed, beckon him onward, he must needs pause before the desultory habit of mind, engendered by travel, becomes confirmed.

It was easy for me, at this "parting of the ways," to decide which was my better road. While I was grateful for the fortune which had led me so far, and through such manifold experience, I saw that I should only reach the best results of what I had already gained, by giving up all further plans of travel. The favor with which my narratives had been received was, in great measure, due to a reflection in them of the lively interest which I had taken in my own wanderings,— to an appetite for external impressions which was now somewhat cloyed, and a delight in mere description which I could no longer feel. My activity in this direction appeared to me as a field which had been traversed in order to reach my proper pastures. It had been broad and pleasant to the feet, and many good friends cried to me: "Stay where you are — it is the path which you should tread!" yet I preferred to press onward towards the rugged steeps beyond. It seemed to me that the pleasure of reading a book must be commensurate with the author's pleasure in writing it, and that those books which do not grow from the natural productive force of the mind will never possess any real vitality.

The poet Tennyson once said to me: " A book of travels may be so written that it shall be as immortal as a great poem." Perhaps so: but in that case its immortality will be dependent upon intellectual qualities which the traveller, as a traveller, does not absolutely require. The most interesting narrative of exploration is that which is most simply told. A poetic apprehension of Nature, a sparkling humor, graces of style — all these are doubtful merits. We want the naked truth, without even a fig-leaf of fancy. We may not appreciate all the facts of science which the explorer has collected, but to omit them would be to weaken his authority. Narratives of travel serve either to measure our knowledge of other lands, in which case they stand only until superseded by more thorough research, or to exhibit the coloring which those lands take when painted for us by individual minds, in which case their value must be fixed by the common standards of literature. For the former class, the widest scientific culture is demanded: for the latter, something of the grace and freedom and keen mental insight which we require in a work of fiction. The only traveller in whom the two characters were thoroughly combined, was Goethe.

Should I hesitate to confess that to be styled "a great American traveller," has always touched me with a sense of humiliation? It is as if one should say "a great American pupil;" for the books of travel which I have published appear to me as so many studies, so many processes of education, with the one advantage that, however immature they may be, nothing in them is forced or affected. The journeys they describe came, as I have shown, through a natural series of circumstances, one leading on the other: no particular daring or energy, and no privation from which a healthy man need shrink, was necessary. Danger is oftener a creation of one's own mind than an absolute fact, and I presume that my share of personal adventure was no more than would fall to the lot of any man, in the same period of travel. To be praised for virtues which one does not feel to be such, is quite as unwelcome as to be censured for faults which are not made evident to one's self.

If I wish that these volumes of mine were worthier of the opportunities granted to me, at least I do not regret that they were written. Hardly a week passes, but I receive letters from young men, who have been stimulated by them to achieve the education of travel; and, believing as I do that the more broad and cosmopolitan in his views a man becomes through his knowledge of other lands, the purer and more intelligent shall be his patriotic sentiment — the more easily he shall lift himself out of the narrow sphere of local interests and prejudices — I rejoice that I have been able to assist in giving this direction to the minds of the American youth. It is hardly necessary to say that I had no such special intention in the beginning, for I never counted beforehand on the favor of the public: but the fact, as it has been made manifest to me, is something for which I am exceedingly grateful.

In this volume I have purposely dropped the form of continuous narrative, which, indeed, was precluded by the nature of my material. The papers it contains, each devoted to a separate By-way of Europe, were written at various times, during two journeys abroad, within the past five or six years. I employed the intervals of other occupation, from time to time, in making excursions to outlying corners of the Old World, few of which are touched by the ordinary round of travel. Nearly all of them, nevertheless, attracted me by some picturesque interest, either of history, or scenery, or popular institutions and customs. Such points, for instance, as Lake Ladoga, Appenzell, Andorra, and the Teutoburger Forest, although lying near the frequented highways and not difficult of access, are very rarely visited, and an account of them is not an unnecessary contribution to the literature of travel. A few of the places I have included — St. Petersburg in winter, Capri and Ischia — cannot properly be classed as "By-ways," yet they form so small a proportion of the contents of the volume that I may be allowed to retain its title. Being the result of brief intervals of leisure, and the desire to turn my season of recreation to some good account, the various papers were produced without regard to any plan, and each is meant to be independent of the others. If I had designed to present a tolerably complete description of *all* the interesting By-ways of Europe, I must have included Auvergne, Brittany, the Basque provinces of Spain, Friesland, the Carpathians, Apulia, Croatia, and Transylvania.

In laying down the mantle of a traveller, which has been thrown upon my shoulders rather than voluntarily assumed, I do not wish to be understood as renouncing all the chances of the future. I cannot foresee what compulsory influences, what inevitable events, may come to shape the course of my life: the work of the day is all with which a man need concern himself. One thing, only, is certain; I shall never, from the mere desire of travel, go forth to the distant parts of the earth. Some minds are so constituted that their freest and cheerfulest activity will not accompany the body from place to place, but is dependent on the air of home, on certain familiar surroundings, and an equable habit of life. Each writer has his own peculiar laws of production, which the reader cannot always deduce from his works. It amuses me, who have set my household gods upon the soil which my ancestors have tilled for near two hundred years, to hear my love of home questioned by men who have changed theirs a dozen times.

I therefore entreat of you, my kindly reader, that you will not ascribe my many wanderings to an inborn propensity to wander, — that you will believe me when I say that culture, in its most comprehensive sense, is more to me than the chance of seeing the world, — and, finally, that you will consider whether I have any legitimate right to assume the calling of an author, unless I choose the work that seems fittest, without regard to that acceptance of it which is termed popularity. If you have found enough in my former volumes of travel to persuade you to accompany me into other walks of literature, I shall do my best to convince you that I am right in the conclusions at which I have arrived. If, believing me mistaken, you decide to turn away, let us at least shake hands, and, while I thank you for your company thus far on my way, still part as friends!

BAYARD TAYLOR.

CEDARCROFT, *September*. 1868.

A CRUISE ON LAKE LADOGA.

"Dear T.,—The steamboat Valamo is advertised to leave on Tuesday, the 26th (July 8th, New Style), for Serdopol, at the very head of Lake Ladoga, stopping on the way at Schlüsselburg, Konewitz Island, Kexholm, and the island and monastery of Valaam. The anniversary of Saints Sergius and Herrmann, miracle-workers, will be celebrated at the last named place on Thursday, and the festival of the Apostles Peter and Paul on Friday. If the weather is fine, the boat will take passengers to the Holy Island. The fare is nine rubles for the trip. You can be back again in St. Petersburg by six o'clock on Saturday evening. Provisions can be had on board, but (probably) not beds; so, if you are luxurious in this particular, take along your own sheets, pillow-cases, and blankets. I intend going, and depend upon your company. Make up your mind by ten o'clock, when I will call for your decision. Yours,

"P."

I laid down the note, looked at my watch, and found that I had an hour for deliberation before P.'s arrival. "Lake Ladoga?" said I to myself; "it is the largest lake in Europe—I learned that at school. It is full of fish; it is stormy; and the Neva is its outlet. What else?" I took down a geographical dictionary, and obtained the following additional particulars: The name *Lad'oga* (not *Lado'ga*, as it is pronounced in America) is Finnish, and means "new." The lake lies between 60° and 61° 45' north latitude, is 175 versts—about 117 miles—in length, from north to south, and 100 versts in breadth; receives the great river Volkhoff on the south, the Svir, which pours into it the waters of Lake Onega, on the east, and the overflow of speed to her and her passengers. The latter, in spite of the rain, thronged the deck, and continually repeated their devotions to the shrines on either bank. On the right, the starry domes of the Smolnoi, rising from the lap of a linden-grove, flashed upon us; then, beyond the long front of the college of *demoiselles nobles* and the military store-houses, we hailed the silver hemispheres which canopy the tomb and shrine of St. Alexander of the Neva. On the left, huge brick factories pushed back the gleaming groves of birch, which flowed around and between them, to dip their hanging boughs in the river; but here and there peeped out the bright green cupolas of some little church, none of which, I was glad to see, slipped out of the panorama without its share of reverence.

For some miles we sailed between a double row of contiguous villages — a long suburb of the capital, which stretched on and on, until the slight undulations of the shore showed that we had left behind us the dead level of the Ingrian marshes. It is surprising what an interest one takes in the slightest mole-hill, after living for a short time on a plain. You are charmed with an elevation which enables you to look over your neighbor's hedge. I once heard a clergyman, in his sermon, assert that "the world was perfectly smooth before the fall of Adam, and the present inequalities in its surface were the evidences of human sin." I was a boy at the time, and I thought to myself, " How fortunate it is that we are sinners!" Peter the Great, however, had no choice left him. The piles he drove in these marshes were the surest foundation of his empire.

The Neva, in its sudden and continual windings, in its clear, cold, sweet water, and its fringing groves of birch, maple, and alder, compensates, in a great measure, for the flatness of its shores. It has not the slow magnificence of the Hudson or the rush of the Rhine, but carries with it a sense of power, of steady, straightforward force, like that of the ancient warriors who disdained all clothing except their swords. Its river-god is not even crowned with reeds, but the full flow of his urn rolls forth undiminished by summer and unchecked beneath its wintry lid. Outlets of large lakes frequently exhibit this characteristic, and the impression they make upon the mind does not depend on the scenery through which they flow. Nevertheless, we discovered many points, the beauty of which was not blotted out by rain and cloud, and would have shone freshly and winningly under the touch of the sun. On the north bank there is a palace of Potemkin (or Pòtchómkin, as his name is pronounced in Russian), charmingly placed at a bend, whence it looks both up and down the river. The gay color of the building, as of most of the *datchas*, or country-villas, in Russia, makes a curious impression upon the stranger. Until he has learned to accept it as a portion of the landscape, the effect is that of a scenic design on the part of the builder. These dwellings, these villages and churches, he thinks, are scarcely intended to be permanent: they were erected as part of some great dramatic spectacle, which has been, or is to be, enacted under the open sky. Contrasted with the sober, matter-of-fact aspect of dwellings in other countries, they have the effect of temporary decorations. But when one has entered within those walls of green and blue and red arabesques, inspected their thickness, viewed the ponderous porcelain stoves, tasted, perhaps, the bountiful cheer of the owner, he realizes their palpable comforts, and begins to suspect that all the external adornment is merely an attempt to restore to Nature that coloring of which she is stripped by the cold sky of the North.

A little further on, there is a summer villa of the Empress Catharine — a small, modest building, crowning a slope of green turf. Beyond this, the banks are draped with foliage, and the thinly clad birches, with their silver stems, shiver above the rush of the waters. We, also, began to shiver under the steadily falling rain, and retreated to the cabin on the steward's first hint of dinner. A *table d'hôte* of four courses was promised us, including the preliminary *zakouski* and the supplementary coffee — all for sixty *copéks*, which is about forty-five cents. The *zakouski* is an arrangement peculiar to Northern countries, and readily adopted by foreigners. In Sweden it is called the *smörgås*, or "buttergoose," but the American term (if we had the custom) would be "the whetter." On a side-table there are various plates of anchovies, cheese, chopped onions, raw salt herring, and bread, all in diminutive slices, while glasses of corresponding size surround a bottle of *kümmel*, or cordial of carawayseed. This, at least, was the *zakouski* on board the Valamo, and to which our valiant captain addressed himself, after first bowing and crossing himself towards the Byzantine Christ and Virgin in either corner of the cabin. We, of course, followed his example, finding our appetites, if not improved, certainly not at all injured thereby. The dinner which followed far surpassed our expectations. The national *shchee*, or cabbage-soup, is better than the sound of its name; the fish, fresh from the cold Neva, is sure to be well cooked where it forms an important article of diet; and the partridges were accompanied by those plump little Russian cucumbers, which are so tender and flavorous that they deserve to be called fruit rather than vegetables.

When we went on deck to light our Riga cigars, the boat was approaching Schlüsselburg, at the outlet of the lake. Here the Neva, just born, sweeps in two broad arms around the island which bears the Key-fortress — the key by which Peter opened this river-door to the Gulf of Finland. The pretty town of the same name is on the south bank, and in the centre of its front yawn the granite gates of the canal which, for a hundred versts, skirts the southern shore of the lake, forming, with the Volkhoff River and another canal beyond, a summer communication with the vast regions watered by the Volga and its affluents. The

Ladoga Canal, by which the heavy barges laden with hemp from Mid-Russia, and wool from the Ural, and wood from the Valdaï Hills, avoid the sudden storms of the lake, was also the work of Peter the Great. I should have gone on shore to inspect the locks, but for the discouraging persistence of the rain. Huddled against the smoke-stack, we could do nothing but look on the draggled soldiers and *mujiks* splashing through the mud, the low yellow fortress, which has long outlived its importance, and the dark-gray waste of lake which loomed in front, suggestive of rough water and kindred abominations.

There it was, at last, — Lake Ladoga, — and now our prow turns to unknown regions. We steamed past the fort, past a fleet of brigs, schooners, and brigantines, with huge, rounded stems and sterns, laden with wood from the Wolkonskoi forests, and boldly entered the gray void of fog and rain. The surface of the lake was but slightly agitated, as the wind gradually fell and a thick mist settled on the water. Hour after hour passed away, as we rushed onward through the blank, and we naturally turned to our fellow-passengers in search of some interest or diversion to beguile the time. The heavy-bearded peasants and their weather-beaten wives were scattered around the deck in various attitudes, some of the former asleep on their backs, with open mouths, beside the smoke-stack. There were many picturesque figures among them, and, if I possessed the quick pencil of Kaulbach, I might have filled a dozen leaves of my sketch-book. The *bourgeoisie* were huddled on the quarter-deck benches, silent, and fearful of sea-sickness. But a very bright, intelligent young officer turned up, who had crossed the Ural, and was able to entertain us with an account of the splendid sword-blades of Zlatáoust. He was now on his way to the copper mines of Pitkaranda, on the northeastern shore of the lake.

About nine o'clock in the evening, although still before sunset, the fog began to darken, and I was apprehensive that we should have some difficulty in finding the island of Konewitz, which was to be our stopping-place for the night. The captain ordered the engine to be slowed, and brought forward a brass half-pounder, about a foot long, which was charged and fired. In less than a minute after the report, the sound of a deep, solemn bell boomed in the mist, dead ahead. Instantly every head was uncovered, and the rustle of whispered prayers fluttered over the deck, as the pilgrims bowed and crossed themselves. Nothing was to be seen; but, stroke after stroke, the hollow sounds, muffled and blurred in the opaque atmosphere, were pealed out by the guiding bell. Presently a chime of smaller bells joined in a rapid accompaniment, growing louder and clearer as we advanced. The effect was startling. After voyaging for hours over the blank water, this sudden and solemn welcome, sounded from some invisible tower, assumed a mystic and marvelous character. Was it not rather the bells of a city, ages ago submerged, and now sending its ghostly summons up to the pilgrims passing over its crystal grave?

Finally a tall mast, its height immensely magnified by the fog, could be distinguished; then the dark hulk of a steamer, a white gleam of sand through the fog, indistinct outlines of trees, a fisherman's hut, and a landing-place. The bells still rang out from some high station near at hand, but unseen. We landed as soon as the steamer had made fast, and followed the direction of the sound. A few paces from the beach stood a little chapel, open, and with a lamp burning before its brown Virgin and Child. Here our passengers stopped, and made a brief prayer before going on. Two or three beggars, whose tattered dresses of tow suggested the idea of their having clothed themselves with the sails of shipwrecked vessels, bowed before us so profoundly and reverently that we at first feared they had mistaken us for the shrines. Following an avenue of trees, up a gentle eminence, the tall white towers and green domes of a stately church gradually detached themselves from the mist, and we found ourselves at the portal of the monastery. A group of monks, in the usual black robes, and high, cylindrical caps of crape, the covering of which overlapped and fell upon their shoulders, were waiting, apparently to receive visitors. Recognizing us as foreigners, they greeted us with great cordiality, and invited us to take up our quarters for the night in the house appropriated to guests. We desired, however, to see the church before the combined fog and twilight should make it too dark; so a benevolent old monk led the way, hand in hand with P., across the court-yard.

The churches of the Greek faith present a general resemblance in their internal decorations. There is a glitter of gold, silver, and flaring colors in the poorest. Statues are not permitted, but the pictures of dark Saviours and saints are generally covered with a drapery of silver, with openings for the head and hands. Konewitz, however, boasts of a special sanctity, in possessing the body of Saint Arsenius, the founder of the monastery. His remains are inclosed in a large coffin of silver, elaborately chased. It was surrounded, as we entered, by a crowd of kneeling pilgrims; the tapers burned beside it, and at the various altars; the air was thick with incense, and the great bell still boomed from the misty tower. Behind us came a throng of our own deck-passengers, who seemed to recognize the proper shrines by a sort of devotional instinct, and were soon wholly absorbed in their prayers and prostrations. It is very evident to me that the Russian race still requires the formulas of the Eastern Church; a fondness for symbolic ceremonies and observances is far more natural to its character than to the nations of Latin or Saxon blood. In Southern Europe the peasant will exchange merry salutations while dipping his fingers in the holy water, or turn in the midst of his devotions to inspect a stranger; but the Russian, at such times, appears lost to the world. With his serious eyes fixed on the shrine or picture, or, maybe, the spire of a distant church, his face suddenly becomes rapt and solemn, and no lurking interest in neighboring things interferes with its expression.

One of the monks, who spoke a little French, took us into his cell. He was a tall, frail man of thirty-five, with a wasted face, and brown hair flowing over his shoulders, like most of his brethren of the same age. In those sharp, earnest features, one could see that the battle was not yet over. The tendency to corpulence does not appear until after the rebellious passions have been either subdued, or pacified by compromise. The cell was small, but neat and cheerful, on the ground-floor, with a window opening on the court, and a hard, narrow pallet against the wall. There was also a little table, with books, sacred pictures, and a bunch of lilacs in water. The walls were whitewashed, and the floor cleanly swept. The chamber was austere, certainly, but in no wise repulsive.

It was now growing late, and only the faint edges of the twilight glimmered overhead, through the fog. It was not night, but a sort of eclipsed day, hardly darker than our winter days under an overcast sky. We returned to the tower, where an old monk took us in charge. Beside the monastery is a special building for guests, a room in which was offered to us. It was so clean and pleasant, and the three broad sofa-couches with leather cushions looked so inviting, that we decided to sleep there, in preference to the crowded cabin. Our supply of shawls, moreover, enabled us to enjoy the luxury of undressing. Before saying good-night, the old monk placed his hand upon R.'s head. "We have matins at three o'clock," said he; "when you hear the bell, get up, and come to the church: it will bring blessing to you." We were soon buried in a slumber which lacked darkness to make it profound. At two o'clock the sky was so bright that I thought it six, and fell asleep again, determined to make three hours before I stopped. But presently the big bell began to swing: stroke after stroke, it first aroused, but was fast lulling me, when the chimes struck in and sang all manner of incoherent and undevout lines. The brain at last grew weary of this, when, close to our door, a little, petulant, impatient bell commenced barking for dear life. R. muttered and twisted in his sleep, and brushed away the sound several times from his upper ear, while I covered mine — but to no purpose. The sharp, fretful jangle went through shawls and cushions, and the fear of hearing it more distinctly prevented me from rising for matins. Our youth, also, missed his promised blessing, and so we slept until the sun was near five hours high — that is, seven o'clock.

The captain promised to leave for Kexholm at eight, which allowed us only an hour for a visit to the *Konkamen*, or Horse Rock, distant a mile, in the woods. P. engaged as guide a long-haired acolyte, who informed us that he had formerly been a lithographer in St. Petersburg. We did not ascertain the cause of his retirement from the world: his features were too commonplace to suggest a romance. Through the mist, which still hung heavy on the lake, we plunged into the fir-wood, and hurried on over its uneven carpet of moss and dwarf whortleberries. Small gray boulders then began to crop out, and gradually became so thick that the trees thrust them aside as they grew. All at once the wood opened on a rye-field belonging to the monks, and a short turn to the right brought us to a huge rock, of irregular shape, about forty feet in diameter by twenty in height. The crest overhung the base on all sides except one, up which a wooden staircase led to a small square chapel perched upon the summit.

The legends attached to this rock are various, but the most authentic seems to be, that in the ages when the Carelians were still heathen, they were accustomed to place their cattle upon this island in summer, as a protection against the wolves, first sacrificing a horse upon the rock. Whether their deity was the Perun of the ancient Russians or the Jumala of the Finns is not stated; the inhabitants at the present day say, of course, the Devil. The name of the rock may also be translated "Petrified Horse," and some have endeavored to make out a resemblance to that animal, in its form. Our acolyte, for instance, insisted thereupon, and argued very logically — "Why, if you omit the head and legs, you must see that it is exactly like a horse." The peasants say that the devil had his residence in the stone, and point to a hole which he made, on being forced by the exorcisms of Saint Arsenius to take his departure. A reference to the legend is also indicated in the name of the island, Konewitz, which our friend, the officer, gave to me in French as *Chevalisé*, or, in literal English, *The Horsefied*.

The stones and bushes were dripping from the visitation of the mist, and the mosquitoes were busy with my face and hands while I made a rapid drawing of the place. The quick chimes of the monastery, through which we fancied we could hear the warning boat-bell, suddenly pierced through the forest, recalling us. The Valamo had her steam up, when we arrived, and was only waiting for her rival, the Letuchie (Flyer), to get out of our way. As we moved from the shore, a puff of wind blew away the fog, and the stately white monastery, crowned with its bunch of green domes, stood for a moment clear and bright in the morning sun. Our pilgrims bent, bareheaded, in devotional farewell; the golden crosses sparkled an answer, and the fog rushed down again like a falling curtain.

We steered nearly due north, making for Kexholm, formerly a frontier Swedish town, at the mouth of the River Wuoxen. For four hours it was a tantalizing struggle between mist and sunshine — a fair blue sky overhead, and a dense cloud sticking to the surface of the lake. The western shore, though near at hand, was not visible; but our captain, with his usual skill, came within a quarter of a mile of the channel leading to the landing-place. The fog seemed to consolidate into the outline of trees; hard land was gradually formed, as we approached; and as the two river-shores finally inclosed us, the air cleared, and long, wooded hills arose in the distance. Before us lay a single wharf, with three wooden buildings leaning against a hill of sand.

"But where is Kexholm?"

"A verst inland," says the captain; "and I will give you just half an hour to see it."

There were a score of peasants, with clumsy two-wheeled carts and shaggy ponies at the landing. Into one of these we clambered, gave the word of command, and were whirled off at a gallop. There may have been some elasticity in the horse, but there certainly was none in the cart. It was a perfect conductor, and the shock with which it passed over stones and leaped ruts was instantly communicated to the *os sacrum*, passing thence along the vertebræ, to discharge itself in the teeth. Our driver was a sunburnt Finn, who was bent upon performing his share of the contract, in order that he might afterwards, with a better face, demand a ruble. On receiving just the half, however, he put it into his pocket, without a word of remonstrance.

"*Suomi?*" I asked, calling up a Finnish word with an effort.

"*Suomi-laïnen,*" he answered, proudly enough, though the exact meaning is, "I am a Swamplander."

Kexholm, which was founded in 1295, has attained since then a population of several hundreds. Grass grows between the cobble-stones of its broad streets, but the houses are altogether so bright, so clean, so substantially comfortable, and the geraniums and roses peeping out between snowy curtains in almost every window suggested such cozy interiors, that I found myself quite attracted towards the plain little town. "Here," said I to P., "is a nook which is really out of the world. No need of a monastery, where you have such perfect seclusion, and the indispensable solace of natural society to make it endurable." Pleasant faces occasionally looked out, curiously, at the impetuous strangers: had they known our nationality, I fancy the whole population would have run together. Reaching the last house, nestled among twinkling birch-trees on a bend of the river beyond, we turned about and made for the fortress — another conquest of the Great Peter. Its low ramparts had a shabby, neglected look; an old draw-bridge spanned the moat, and there was no sentinel to challenge us as we galloped across. In and out again, and down the long, quiet street, and over the jolting level to the top of the sand hill — we had seen Kexholm in half an hour.

At the mouth of the river still lay the fog, waiting for us, now and then stretching a ghostly arm over the woods and then withdrawing it, like a spirit of the lake, longing and yet timid to embrace the land. With the Wuoxen came down the waters of the Saima, that great, irregular lake, which, with its innumerable arms, extends for a hundred and fifty miles into the heart of Finland, clasping the forests and mountains of Savolax, where the altar-stones of Jumala still stand in the shade of sacred oaks, and the song of the Kalewala is sung by the descendants of Wainamöinen. I registered a vow to visit those Finnish solitudes, as we shot out upon the muffled lake, heading for the holy isles of Valaam. This was the great point of interest in our cruise, the shrine of our pilgrim-passengers. We had heard so little of these islands before leaving St. Petersburg, and so much since, that our curiosity was keenly excited; and thus, though too well seasoned by experience to worry unnecessarily, the continuance of the fog began to disgust us. We shall creep along as yesterday, said we, and have nothing of Valaam but the sound of its bells. The air was intensely raw; the sun had disappeared, and the bearded peasants again slept, with open mouths, on the deck.

Saints Sergius and Herrmann, however, were not indifferent either to them or to us. About the middle of the afternoon we suddenly and unexpectedly sailed out of the fog, passing, in the distance of a ship's length, into a clear atmosphere, with a far, sharp horizon! The nuisance of the lake lay behind us, a steep, opaque, white wall. Before us, rising in bold cliffs from the water and dark with pines, were the islands of Valaam. Off went hats and caps, and the crowd on deck bent reverently towards the consecrated shores. As we drew near, the granite fronts of the separate isles detached themselves from the plane in which they were blended, and thrust boldly out between the dividing inlets of blue water; the lighter green of birches and maples mingled with the sombre woods of coniferæ; but the picture, with all its varied features, was silent and lonely. No sail shone over the lake, no boat was hauled up between the tumbled masses of rock, no fisher's hut sat in the sheltered coves — only, at the highest point of the cliff, a huge wooden cross gleamed white against the trees.

As we drew around to the northern shore, point came out behind point, all equally bold with rock, dark with pines, and destitute of any sign of habitation. We were looking forward, over the nearest headland, when, all at once, a sharp glitter through the tops of the pines struck our eyes. A few more turns of the paddles, and a bulging dome of gold flashed splendidly in the sun! Our voyage, thus far, had been one of surprises, and this was not the least. Crowning a slender, pointed roof, its connection with the latter was not immediately visible: it seemed to spring into the air and hang there, like a marvelous meteor shot from the sun. Presently, however, the whole building appeared, — an hexagonal church, of pale-red brick, the architecture of which was an admirable reproduction of the older Byzantine forms. It stood upon a rocky islet, on either side of which a narrow channel communicated with a deep cove, cleft between walls of rock.

Turning in towards the first of these channels, we presently saw the inlet of darkest-blue water, pushing its way into the heart of the island. Crowning its eastern bank, and about half a mile distant, stood an immense mass of buildings, from the centre of which tall white towers and green cupolas shot up against the sky. This was the monastery of Valaam. Here, in the midst of this lonely lake, on the borders of the Arctic Zone, in the solitude of unhewn forests, was one of those palaces which religion is so fond of rearing, to show her humility. In the warm afternoon sunshine, and with the singular luxuriance of vegetation which clothed the terraces of rock on either hand, we forgot the high latitude, and, but for the pines in the rear, could have fancied ourselves approaching some cove of Athos or Eubœa. The steamer ran so near the rocky walls that the trailing branches of the birch almost swept her deck; every ledge traversing their gray, even masonry, was crowded with wild red pinks, geranium, saxifrage, and golden-flowered purslane; and the air, wonderfully pure and sweet in itself, was flavored with delicate woodland odors. On the other side, under the monastery, was an orchard of large apple-trees in full bloom, on a shelf near the water; above them grew huge oaks and maples, heavy with their wealth of foliage; and over the tops of these the level coping of the precipice, with a balustrade upon which hundreds of pilgrims, who had arrived before us, were leaning and looking down.

Beyond this point, the inlet widened into a basin where the steamer had room to turn around. Here we found some forty or fifty boats moored to the bank, while the passengers they had brought (principally from the eastern shore of the lake, and the district lying between it and Onega) were scattered over the heights. The captain pointed out to us a stately, two-story brick edifice, some three hundred feet long, flanking the monastery, as the house for guests. Another of less dimensions, on the hill in front of the landing-place, appeared to be appropriated especially to the use of the peasants. A rich succession of musical chimes pealed down to us from the belfry, as if in welcome, and our deck load of pilgrims crossed themselves in reverent congratulation as they stepped upon the sacred soil.

We had determined to go on with our boat to Serdopol, at the head of the lake, returning the next morning in season for the solemnities of the anniversary. Postponing, therefore, a visit to the church and monastery, we climbed to the summit of the bluff, and beheld the inlet in all its length and depth, from the open, sunny expanse of the lake to the dark strait below us, where the overhanging trees of the opposite cliffs almost touched above the water. The honeyed bitter of lilac and apple blossoms in the garden below steeped the air; and as I inhaled the scent, and beheld the rich green crowns of the oaks which grew at the base of the rocks, I appreciated the wisdom of Sergius and Herrmann that led them to pick out this bit of privileged summer, which seems to have wandered into the North from a region ten degrees nearer the sun. It is not strange if the people attribute miraculous powers to them, naturally mistaking the cause of their settlement on Valaam for its effect.

The deck was comparatively deserted, as we once more entered the lake. There were two or three new passengers, however, one of whom inspired me with a mild interest. He was a St. Petersburger, who according to his own account, had devoted himself to Art, and, probably for that reason, felt constrained to speak in the language of sentiment. "I enjoy above all things," said he to me, "communion with Nature. My soul is uplifted, when I find myself removed from the haunts of men. I live an ideal life, and the world grows more beautiful to me every year." Now there was nothing objectionable in this, except the manner of his saying it. Those are only shallow emotions which one imparts to every stranger at the slightest provocation. Your true lover of Nature is as careful of betraying his passion as the young man who carries a first love in his heart. But my companion evidently delighted in talking of his feelings on this point. His voice was soft and silvery, his eyes gentle, and his air languishing; so that, in spite of a heavy beard, the impression he made was remarkably smooth and unmasculine. I involuntarily turned to one of the young Finnish sailors, with his handsome, tanned face, quick, decided movements, and clean, elastic limbs, and felt, instinctively, that what we most value in every man, above even culture or genius, is the stamp of sex — the asserting, self-reliant, conquering air which marks the male animal.

After some fifteen or twenty miles from the island, we approached the rocky archipelago in which the lake terminates at its northern end — a gradual transition from water to land. Masses of gray granite, wooded wherever the hardy northern firs could strike root, rose on all sides, divided by deep and narrow channels. "This is the *scheer*," said our captain, using a word which recalled to my mind, at once, the Swedish *skär*, and the English *skerry*, used alike to denote a coast-group of rocky islets. The rock encroached more and more as we advanced; and finally, as if sure of its victory over the lake, gave place, here and there, to levels of turf, gardens, and cottages. Then followed a calm, land-locked basin, surrounded with harvest-fields, and the spire of Serdopol arose before us.

Of this town I may report that it is called, in Finnish, *Sordovala*, and was founded about the year 1640. Its history has no doubt been very important to its inhabitants, but I do not presume that it would be interesting to the world, and therefore spare myself a great deal of laborious research. Small as it is, and so secluded that Ladoga seems a world's highway in comparison with its quiet harbor, it nevertheless holds three races and three languages in its modest bounds. The government and its tongue are Russian; the people are mostly Finnish, with a very thin upper-crust of Swedish tradition, whence the latter language is cultivated as a sign of aristocracy.

We landed on a broad wooden pier, and entered the town through a crowd which was composed of all these elements. There was to be a fair on the morrow, and from the northern shore of the lake, as well as the wild inland region towards the Saïma, the people had collected for trade, gossip, and festivity. Children in ragged garments of hemp, bleached upon their bodies, impudently begged for pocket-money; women in scarlet kerchiefs curiously scrutinized us; peasants carried bundles of freshly mown grass to the horses which were exposed for sale; ladies with Hungarian hats, crushed their crinolines into queer old cabriolets; gentlemen with business faces and an aspect of wealth smoked paper cigars; and numbers of hucksters offered baskets of biscuit and cakes, of a disagreeable yellow color and great apparent toughness. It was a repetition, with slight variations, of a village fair anywhere else, or an election day in America.

Passing through the roughly paved and somewhat dirty streets, past shops full of primitive hardware, groceries which emitted powerful whiffs of salt fish or new leather, bakeries with crisp padlocks of bread in the windows, drinking-houses plentifully supplied with *qvass* and *vodki*, and, finally, the one watch-maker, and the vender of paper, pens, and Finnish almanacs, we reached a broad suburban street, whose substantial houses, with their courts and gardens, hinted at the aristocracy of Serdopol. The inn, with its Swedish sign, was large and comfortable, and a peep into the open windows disclosed as pleasant quarters as a traveller could wish. A little farther the town ceased, and we found ourselves upon a rough, sloping common, at the top of which stood the church with its neighboring belfry. It was unmistakably Lutheran in appearance, — very plain and massive and sober in color, with a steep roof for shedding snow. The only attempt at ornament was a fanciful shingle-mosaic, but in pattern only, not in color. Across the common ran a double row of small booths, which had just been erected for the coming fair; and sturdy young fellows from the country, with their rough carts and shaggy ponies, were gathering along the highway, to skirmish a little in advance of their bargains.

The road enticed us onwards into the country. On our left, a long slope descended to an upper arm of the harbor, the head of which we saw to be near at hand. The opposite shore was fairly laid out in grain-fields, through which cropped out here and there, long walls of granite, rising higher and higher towards the west, until they culminated in the round, hard forehead of a lofty hill. There was no other point within easy reach which promised much of a view; so, rounding the head of the bay, we addressed ourselves to climbing the rocks, somewhat to the surprise of the herd-boys, as they drove their cows into the town to be milked.

Once off the cultivated land, we found the hill a very garden of wild blooms. Every step and shelf of the rocks was cushioned with tricolored violets, white anemones, and a succulent, moss-like plant with a golden flower. Higher up there were sheets of fire-red pinks, and on the summit an unbroken carpet of the dwarf whortleberry, with its waxen bells. Light exhalations seemed to rise from the damp hollows, and drift towards us; but they resolved themselves into swarms of mosquitoes, and would have made the hill-top untenable, had they not been dispersed by a sudden breeze. We sat down upon a rock and contemplated the wide-spread panorama. It was nine o'clock, and the sun, near his setting, cast long gleams of pale light through the clouds, softening the green of the fields and forests where they fell, and turning the moist evening haze into lustrous pearl. Inlets of the lake here and there crept in between the rocky hills; broad stretches of gently undulating grain-land were dotted with the houses, barns, and clustered stables of the Finnish farmers; in the distance arose the smokes of two villages; and beyond all, as we looked inland, ran the sombre ridges of the fir-clad hills. Below us, on the right, the yellow houses of the town shone in the subdued light, — the only bright spot in the landscape, which elsewhere seemed to be overlaid with a tint of dark, transparent gray. It was wonderfully silent. Not a bird twittered; no bleat of sheep or low of cattle was heard from the grassy fields; no shout of children, or evening hail from the returning boats of the fishers. Over all the land brooded an atmosphere of sleep, of serene, perpetual peace. To sit and look upon it was in itself a refreshment like that of healthy slumber. The restless devil which lurks in the human brain was quieted for the time, and we dreamed — knowing all the while the vanity of the dream — of a pastoral life in some such spot, among as ignorant and simple-hearted a people, ourselves as untroubled by the agitations of the world.

We had scarce inhaled — or, rather, *insuded*, to coin a word for a sensation which seems to enter at every pore — the profound quiet and its suggestive fancies for the space of half an hour, when the wind fell at the going down of the sun, and the humming mist of mosquitoes arose again. Returning to the town, we halted at the top of the common to watch the farmers of the neighborhood at their horse-dealing. Very hard, keen, weather-browned faces had they, eyes tight-set for the main chance, mouths worn thin by biting farthings, and hands whose hard fingers crooked with holding fast what they had earned. Faces almost of the Yankee type, many of them, and relieved by the twinkling of a humorous faculty or the wild gleam of imagination. The shaggy little horses, of a dun or dull tan-color, seemed to understand that their best performance was required, and rushed up and down the road with an amazing exhibition of mettle. I could understand nothing of the Finnish tongue except its music; but it was easy to perceive that the remarks of the crowd were shrewd, intelligent, and racy. One young fellow, less observant, accosted us in the hope that we might be purchasers. The boys, suspecting that we were as green as we were evidently foreign, held out their hands for alms, with a very unsuccessful air of distress, but readily succumbed to the Russian interjection "*proch!*" (be off!) the repetition of which, they understood, was a reproach.

That night we slept on the velvet couches of the cabin, having the spacious apartment to ourselves. The bright young officer had left for the copper mines, the pilgrims were at Valaam, and our stout, benignant captain looked upon us as his only faithful passengers. The stewards, indeed, carried their kindness beyond reasonable anticipations. They brought us real pillows and other conveniences, bolted the doors against nightly intruders, and in the morning conducted us into the pantry, to wash our faces in the basin sacred to dishes. After I had completed my ablutions, I turned dumbly, with dripping face and extended hands, for a towel. My steward understood the silent appeal, and, taking a napkin from a plate of bread, presented it with alacrity. I made use of it, I confess, but hastened out of the pantry, lest I should happen to see it restored to its former place. *How not to observe* is a faculty as necessary to the traveller as its reverse. I was reminded of this truth at dinner, when I saw the same steward take a napkin (probably my towel!) from under his arm, to wipe both his face and a plate which he carried. To speak mildly, these people on Lake Ladoga are not sensitive in regard to the contact of individualities. But the main point is to avoid seeing what you don't like.

We got off at an early hour, and hastened back to Valaam over glassy water and under a superb sky. This time the lake was not so deserted, for the white wings of pilgrim-boats drew in towards the dark island, making for the golden sparkle of the chapel dome, which shone afar like a light-house of the day-time. As we rounded to in the land-locked inlet, we saw that the crowds on the hills had doubled since yesterday, and, although the chimes were pealing for some religious service, it seemed prudent first to make sure of our quarters for the night. Accordingly we set out for the imposing house of guests beside the monastery, arriving in company with the visitors we had brought with us from Serdopol. The entrance-hall led into a long, stone-paved corridor, in which a monk, bewildered by many applications, appeared to be seeking relief by promises of speedy hospitality. We put in our plea, and also received a promise. On either side of the corridor were numbered rooms, already occupied, the fortunate guests passing in and out with a provoking air of comfort and unconcern. We ascended to the second story, which was similarly arranged, and caught hold of another benevolent monk, willing, but evidently powerless to help us. Dinner was just about to be served; the brother in authority was not there; we must be good enough to wait a little while; — would we not visit the shrines, in the mean time?

The advice was sensible, as well as friendly, and we followed it. Entering the great quadrangle of the monastery, we found it divided, gridiron-fashion, into long, narrow court-yards by inner lines of buildings. The central court, however, was broad and spacious, the church occupying a rise of ground on the eastern side. Hundreds of men and women — Carelian peasants — thronged around the entrance, crossing themselves in unison with the congregation. The church, we found, was packed, and the most zealous wedging among the blue *caftans* and shining flaxen heads brought us no farther than the inner door.

Thence we looked over a tufted level of heads that seemed to touch — intermingled tints of gold, tawny, *silver*-blond, and the various shades of brown, touched with dim glosses through the incense-smoke, and occasionally bending in concert, with an undulating movement, like grain before the wind. Over these heads rose the vaulted nave, dazzling with gold and colors, and blocked up, beyond the intersection of the transept, by the *ikonostast*, or screen before the Holy of Holies, gorgeous with pictures of saints overlaid with silver. In front of the screen the tapers burned, the incense rose thick and strong, and the chant of the monks gave a peculiar solemnity to their old Sclavonic litany. The only portion of it which I could understand was the recurring response, as in the English Church, of " Lord, have mercy upon us ! "

Extricating ourselves with some difficulty, we entered a chapel-crypt, which contains the bodies of Sergius and Herrmann. They lie together, in a huge coffin of silver, covered with cloth of gold. Tapers of immense size burned at the head and foot, and the pilgrims knelt around, bending their foreheads to the pavement at the close of their prayers. Among others, a man had brought his insane daughter, and it was touching to see the tender care with which he led her to the coffin and directed her devotions. So much of habit still remained, that it seemed, for the time being, to restore her reason. The quietness and regularity with which she went through the forms of prayer, brought a light of hope to the father's face. The other peasants looked on with an expression of pity and sympathy. The girl, we learned, had but recently lost her reason, and without any apparent cause. She was betrothed to a young man who was sincerely attached to her, and the pilgrimage was undertaken in the hope that a miracle might be wrought in her favor. The presence of the shrine, indeed, struck its accustomed awe through her wandering senses, but the effect was only momentary.

I approached the coffin, and deposited a piece of money on the offering-plate, for the purpose of getting a glimpse of the pictured faces of the saints, in their silver setting. Their features were hard and regular, flatly painted, as if by some forerunner of Cimabue, but sufficiently modern to make the likeness doubtful. I have not been able to obtain the exact date of their settlement on the island, but I believe it is referred to the early part of the fifteenth century. The common people believe that the island was first visited by Andrew, the Apostle of Christ, who, according to the Russian patriarch Nestor, made his way to Kiev and Novgorod. The latter place is known to have been an important commercial city as early as the fourth century, and had a regular intercourse with Asia. The name of Valaam does not come from Balaam, as one might suppose, but seems to be derived from the Finnish *varamo*, which signifies "herring-ground." The more I attempted to unravel the history of the island, the more it became involved in obscurity, and this fact, I must confess, only heightened my interest in it. I found myself ready to accept the tradition of Andrew's visit, and I accepted without a doubt the grave of King Magnus of Sweden.

On issuing from the crypt, we encountered a young monk who had evidently been sent in search of us. The mass was over, and the court-yard was nearly emptied of its crowd. In the farther court, however, we found the people more dense than ever, pressing forward towards a small door. The monk made way for us with some difficulty — for, though the poor fellows did their best to fall back, the pressure from the outside was tremendous. Having at last run the gauntlet, we found ourselves in the refectory of the monastery, inhaling a thick steam of fish and cabbage. Three long tables were filled with monks and pilgrims, while the attendants brought in the fish on large wooden trenchers. The plates were of common white ware, but the spoons were of wood. Officers in gay uniforms were scattered among the dark anchorites, who occupied one end of the table, while the *bourgeoisie*, with here and there a blue-caftaned peasant wedged among them, filled the other end. They were eating with great zeal, while an old priest, standing, read from a Sclavonic Bible. All eyes were turned upon us as we entered, and there was not a vacant chair in which we could hide our intrusion. It was rather embarrassing, especially as the young monk insisted that we should remain, and the curious eyes of the eaters as constantly asked, "Who are these, and what do they want?" We preferred returning through the hungry crowd, and made our way to the guests' house.

Here a similar process was going on. The corridors were thronged with peasants of all ages and both sexes, and the good fathers, more than ever distracted, were incapable of helping us. Seeing a great crowd piled up against a rear basement-door, we descended the stairs, and groped our way through manifold steams and noises to a huge succession of kitchens, where cauldrons of cabbage were bubbling, and shoals of fish went in raw and came out cooked. In another room some hundreds of peasants were eating with all the energy of a primitive appetite. Soup leaked out of the bowls as if they had been sieves; fishes gave a whisk of the tail and vanished; great round boulders of bread went off, layer after layer, and still the empty plates were held up for more. It was *grand* eating, — pure appetite, craving only food in a general sense: no picking out of tidbits, no spying here and there for a favorite dish, but, like a huge fire, devouring everything that came in its way. The stomach was here a patient, unquestioning serf, not a master full of whims, requiring to be petted and conciliated. So, I thought, people must have eaten in the Golden Age: so Adam and Eve must have dined, before the fall made them epicurean and dyspeptic.

We — degenerate through culture — found the steams of the strong, coarse dishes rather unpleasant, and retreated by a back way, which brought us to a spiral staircase. We ascended for a long time, and finally emerged into the garret of the building, hot, close, and strawy as a barn-loft. It was divided into rooms, in which, on the floors covered deep with straw, the happy pilgrims who had finished their dinner were lying on their bellies, lazily talking themselves to sleep. The grassy slope in front of the house, and all the neighboring heights, were soon covered in like manner. Men, women, and children threw themselves down, drawing off their heavy boots, and dipping their legs, knee-deep, into the sun and air. An atmosphere of utter peace and satisfaction settled over them.

Being the only foreign and heterodox persons present, we began to feel ourselves deserted, when the favor of Sergius and Herrmann was again manifested. P. was suddenly greeted by an acquaintance, an officer connected with the Imperial Court, who had come to Valaam for a week of devotion. He immediately interested himself in our behalf, procured us a room with a lovely prospect, transferred his bouquet of lilacs and peonies to our table, and produced his bottle of lemon-syrup to flavor our tea. The rules of the monastery are very strict, and no visitor is exempt from their observance. Not a fish can be caught, not a bird or beast shot, no wine or liquor of any kind, nor tobacco in any form, used on the island. Rigid as the organization seems, it bears equally on every member of the brotherhood: the equality upon which such associations were originally based is here preserved. The monks are only in an ecclesiastical sense subordinate to the abbot. Otherwise, the fraternity seems to be about as complete as in the early days of Christianity.

The Valamo, and her rival, the Letuchie, had advertised a trip to the Holy Island, the easternmost of the Valaam group, some six miles from the monastery, and the weather was so fair that both boats were crowded, many of the monks accompanying us. Our new-found friend was also of the party, and I made the acquaintance of a Finnish student from the Lyceum at Kuopio, who gave me descriptions of the Saïma Lake and the wilds of Savolax. Running eastward along the headlands, we passed Chernoi Noss (Black-Nose), the name of which again recalled a term common in the Orkneys and Shetlands — *noss*, there, signifying a headland. The Holy Island rose before us, a circular pile of rock, crowned with wood, like a huge, unfinished tower of Cyclopean masonry, built up out of the deep water. Far beyond it, over the rim of the lake, glimmered the blue eastern shore. As we drew near, we found that the tumbled fragments of rock had been arranged, with great labor, to form a capacious foot-path around the base of the island. The steamers drew up against this narrow quay, upon which we landed, under a granite wall which rose perpendicularly to the height of seventy or eighty feet. The firs on the summit grew out to the very edge and stretched their dark arms over us. Every cranny of the rock was filled with tufts of white and pink flowers, and the moisture, trickling from above, betrayed itself in long lines of moss and fern.

I followed the pilgrims around to the sunny side of the island, and found a wooden staircase at a point where the wall was somewhat broken away. Reaching the top of the first ascent, the sweet breath of a spring woodland breathed around me. I looked under the broken roofage of the boughs upon a blossoming jungle of shrubs and plants which seemed to have been called into life by a more potent sun. The lily of the valley, in thick beds, poured out the delicious sweetness of its little cups; spikes of a pale-green orchis emitted a rich cinnamon odor; anemones, geraniums, sigillarias, and a feathery flower, white, freckled with purple, grew in profusion. The top of the island, five or six acres in extent, was a slanting plane, looking to the south, whence it received the direct rays of the sun. It was an enchanting picture of woodland bloom, lighted with sprinkled sunshine, in the cold blue setting of the lake, which was visible on all sides, between the boles of the trees. I hailed it as an idyl of the North — a poetic secret, which the earth, even where she is most cruelly material and cold, still tenderly hides and cherishes.

A peasant, whose scarlet shirt flashed through the bushes like a sudden fire, seeing me looking at the flowers, gathered a handful of lilies, which he offered to me, saying, "*Prekrasnie*" (beautiful). Without waiting for thanks, he climbed a second flight of steps and suddenly disappeared from view. I followed, and found myself in front of a narrow aperture in a rude wall, which had been built up under an overhanging mass of rocks. A lamp was twinkling within, and presently several persons crawled out, crossing themselves and muttering prayers.

"What is this?" asked a person who had just arrived.

"The cave of Alexander Svirski," was the answer.

Alexander of the Svir — a river flowing from the Onega Lake into Ladoga — was a hermit who lived for twenty years on the Holy Island, inhabiting the hole before us through the long, dark, terrible winters, in a solitude broken only when the monks of Valaam came over the ice to replenish his stock of provisions. Verily, the hermits of the Thebaïd were Sybarites, compared to this man! There are still two or three hermits who have charge of outlying chapels on the islands, and live wholly secluded from their brethren. They wear dresses covered with crosses and other symbols, and are considered as dead to the world. The ceremony which consecrates them for this service is that for the burial of the dead.

I managed, with some difficulty, to creep into Alexander Svirski's den. I saw nothing, however, but the old, smoky, and sacred picture before which the lamp burned. The rocky roof was so low that I could not stand upright, and all the walls I could find were the bodies of pilgrims who had squeezed in before me. A confused whisper surrounded me in the darkness, and the air was intolerably close. I therefore made my escape and mounted to the chapel, on the highest part of the island. A little below it, an open pavilion, with seats, has been built over the sacred spring from which the hermit drank, and thither the pilgrims thronged. The water was served in a large wooden bowl, and each one made the sign of the cross before drinking. By waiting for my turn I ascertained that the spring was icy-cold, and very pure and sweet.

I found myself lured to the highest cliff, whence I could look out, through the trees, on the far, smooth disk of the lake. Smooth and fair as the Ægean it lay before me, and the trees were silent as olives at noonday on the shores of Cos. But how different in color, in sentiment! Here, perfect sunshine can never dust the water with the purple bloom of the South, can never mellow its hard, cold tint of greenish-blue. The distant hills, whether dark or light, are equally cold, and are seen too nakedly through the crystal air to admit of any illusion. Bracing as is this atmosphere, the gods could never breathe it. It would revenge on the ivory limbs of Apollo his treatment of Marsyas. No foam-born Aphrodite could rise warm from yonder wave; not even the cold, sleek Nereids could breast its keen edge. We could only imagine it disturbed, temporarily, by the bath-plunge of hardy Vikings, who must have come out from it red and tingling from head to heel.

"Come!" cried P., "the steamer is about to leave!"

We all wandered down the steps, I with my lilies in my hand. Even the rough peasants seemed reluctant to leave the spot, and not wholly for the sake of Alexander Svirski. We were all safely embarked and carried back to Valaam, leaving the island to its solitude. Alexis (as I shall call our Russian friend) put us in charge of a native artist who knew every hidden beauty of Valaam, and suggested an exploration of the inlet, while he went back to his devotions. We borrowed a boat from the monks, and impressed a hardy fisherman into our service. I supposed we had already seen the extent of the inlet, but on reaching its head a narrow side-channel disclosed itself, passing away under a quaint bridge and opening upon an inner lake of astonishing beauty. The rocks were disposed in every variety of grouping — sometimes rising in even terraces, step above step, sometimes thrusting out a sheer wall from the summit, or lying slantwise in masses split off by the wedges of the ice. The fairy birches, in their thin foliage, stood on the edge of the water like Dryads undressing for a bath, while the shaggy male firs elbowed each other on the heights for a look at them. Other channels opened in the distance, with glimpses of other and as beautiful harbors in the heart of the islands. "You may sail for seventy-five versts," said the painter, "without seeing them all."

The fearlessness of all wild creatures showed that the rules of the good monks had been carefully obeyed. The wild ducks swam around our boat, or brooded, in conscious security, on their nests along the shore. Three great herons, fishing in a shallow, rose slowly into the air and flew across the water, breaking the silence with their hoarse trumpet note. Further in the woods there are herds of wild reindeer, which are said to have become gradually tame. This familiarity of the animals took away from the islands all that was repellent in their solitude. It half restored the broken link between man and the subject forms of life.

The sunset light was on the trees when we started, but here in the North it is no fleeting glow. It lingers for hours even, fading so imperceptibly that you scarcely know when it has ceased. Thus, when we returned after a long pull, craving the Lenten fare of the monastery, the same soft gold tinted its clustering domes. We were not called upon to visit the refectory, but a table was prepared in our room. The first dish had the appearance of a salad, with the accompaniment of black bread. On carefully tasting, I discovered the ingredients to be raw salt fish chopped fine, cucumbers, and — beer. The taste of the first spoonful was peculiar, of the second tolerable, of the third decidedly palatable. Beyond this I did not go, for we had fresh fish, boiled in enough water to make a soup. Then the same, fried in its own fat, and, as salt and pepper were allowed, we did not scorn our supper.

The next day was the festival of Peter and Paul, and Alexis had advised us to make an excursion to a place called Jelesniki. In the morning, however, we learned that the monastery and its grounds were to be consecrated in solemn procession. The chimes pealed out quick and joyously, and soon a burst of banners and a cloud of incense issued from the great gate. All the pilgrims — nearly two thousand in number — thronged around the double line of chanting monks, and it was found necessary to inclose the latter in a hollow square, formed by a linked chain of hands. As the morning sun shone on the bareheaded multitude, the beauty of their unshorn hair struck me like a new revelation. Some of the heads, of lustrous, flossy gold, actually shone by their own light. It was marvelous that skin so hard and coarse in texture should produce such beautiful hair. The beards of the men, also, were strikingly soft and rich. They never shave, and thus avoid bristles, the down of adolescence thickening into a natural beard.

As the procession approached, Alexis, who was walking behind the monks, inside the protecting guard, beckoned to us to join him. The peasants respectfully made way, two hands unlinked to admit us, and we became, unexpectedly, participants in the ceremonies. From the south side the procession moved around to the east, where a litany was again chanted. The fine voices of the monks lost but little of their volume in the open air; there was no wind, and the tapers burned and the incense diffused itself, as in the church. A sacred picture, which two monks carried on a sort of litter, was regarded with particular reverence by the pilgrims, numbers of whom crept under the line of guards to snatch a moment's devotion before it. At every pause in the proceedings there was a rush from all sides, and the poor fellows who formed the lines held each other's hands with all their strength. Yet, flushed, sweating, and exhausted as they were, the responsibility of their position made them perfectly proud and happy. They were the guardians of cross and shrine, of the holy books, the monks, and the abbot himself.

From the east side we proceeded to the north, where the dead monks sleep in their cemetery, high over the watery gorge. In one corner of this inclosure, under a group of giant maples, is the grave of King Magnus of Sweden, who is said to have perished by shipwreck on the island. Here, in the deep shade, a solemn mass for the dead was chanted. Nothing could have added to the impressiveness of the scene. The tapers burning under the thick-leaved boughs, the light smoke curling up in the shade, the grave voices of the monks, the bending heads of the beautiful-haired crowd, and the dashes of white, pink, scarlet, blue, and gold in their dresses, made a picture the solemnity of which was only heightened by its pomp of color. I can do no more than give the features; the reader must recombine them in his own mind.

The painter accompanied us to the place called Jelesniki, which, after a walk of four miles through the forests, we found to be a deserted village, with a chapel on a rocky headland. There was a fine bridge across the dividing strait, and the place may have been as picturesque as it was represented. On that side of the islands, however, there was a dense fog, and we could get no view beyond a hundred yards. We had hoped to see reindeer in the woods, and an eagle's nest, and various other curiosities; but where there was no fog there were mosquitoes, and the search became discouraging.

On returning to the monastery, a register was brought to us, in which, on looking back for several years, we could find but one foreign visitor — a Frenchman. We judged, therefore, that the abbot would possibly expect us to call upon him, and, indeed, the hospitality we had received exacted it. We found him receiving visitors in a plain but comfortable room, in a distant part of the building. He was a man of fifty-five, frank and self-possessed in his manners, and of an evident force and individuality of character. His reception of the visitors, among whom was a lady, was at once courteous and kindly. A younger monk brought us glasses of tea. Incidentally learning that I had visited the Holy Places in Syria, the abbot sent for some pictures of the monastery and its chosen saints, which he asked me to keep as a souvenir of Valaam. He also presented each of us with a cake of unleavened bread, stamped with the cross, and with a triangular piece cut out of the top, to indicate the Trinity. On parting, he gave his hand, which the orthodox visitors devoutly kissed. Before the steamer sailed, we received fresh evidence of his kindness, in the present of three large loaves of consecrated bread, and a bunch of lilacs from the garden of the monastery.

Through some misunderstanding, we failed to dine in the refectory, as the monks desired, and their hospitable regret on this account was the only shade on our enjoyment of the visit. Alexis remained, in order to complete his devotions by partaking of the Communion on the following Sabbath; but as the anniversary solemnities closed at noon, the crowd of pilgrims prepared to return home. The Valamo, too, sounded her warning bell, so we left the monastery as friends where we had arrived as strangers, and went on board. Boat after boat, gunwale-deep with the gay Carelians, rowed down the inlet, and in the space of half an hour but a few stragglers were left of all the multitude. Some of the monks came down to say another good-bye, and the under-abbot, blessing R., made the sign of the cross upon his brow and breast.

When we reached the golden dome of St. Nicholas, at the outlet of the harbor, the boats had set their sails, and the lake was no longer lonely. Scores of white wings gleamed in the sun, as they scattered away in radii from the central and sacred point, some north, some east, and some veering south around Holy Island. Sergius and Herrmann gave them smooth seas, and light, favorable airs; for the least roughness would have carried them, overladen as they were, to the bottom. Once more the bells of Valaam chimed farewell, and we turned the point to the westward, steering back to Kexholm.

Late that night we reached our old moorage at Konewitz, and on Saturday, at the appointed hour, landed in St. Petersburg. We carried the white cross at the fore as we descended the Neva, and the bells of the churches along the banks welcomed our return. And now, as I recall those five days among the islands of the Northern Lake, I see that it is good to go on a pilgrimage, even if one is not a pilgrim.

BETWEEN EUROPE AND ASIA.

"Pushed off from one shore, and not yet landed on the other."
Russian Proverb.

THE railroad from Moscow to Nijni-Novgorod had been opened but a fortnight before. It was scarcely finished, indeed; for, in order to facilitate travel during the continuance of the Great Fair at the latter place, the gaps in the line, left by unbuilt bridges, were filled up with temporary trestle-work. The one daily express-train was so thronged that it required much exertion, and the freest use of the Envoy's prestige, to secure a private carriage for our party. The sun was sinking over the low, hazy ridge of the Sparrow Hills as we left Moscow: and we enjoyed one more glimpse of the inexhaustible splendor of the city's thousand golden domes and pinnacles, softened by luminous smoke and transfigured dust, before the dark woods of fir intervened, and the twilight sank down on cold and lonely landscapes.

Thence, until darkness, there was nothing more to claim attention. Whoever has seen one landscape of Central Russia is familiar with three fourths of the whole region. Nowhere else — not even on the levels of Illinois — are the same features so constantly reproduced. One long, low swell of earth succeeds to another; it is rare that any other woods than birch and fir are seen; the cleared land presents a continuous succession of pasture, rye, wheat, potatoes, and cabbages; and the villages are as like as peas, in their huts of unpainted logs, clustering around a white church with five green domes. It is a monotony which nothing but the richest culture can prevent from becoming tiresome. Culture is to Nature what good manners are to man, rendering poverty of character endurable.

Stationing a servant at the door to prevent intrusion at

the way-stations, we let down the curtains before our windows, and secured a comfortable privacy for the night, whence we issued only once, during a halt for supper. I entered the refreshment-room with very slender expectations, but was immediately served with plump partridges, tender cutlets, and green peas. The Russians made a rush for the great *samovar* (tea-urn) of brass, which shone from one end of the long table; and presently each had his tumbler of scalding tea, with a slice of lemon floating on the top. These people drink beverages of a temperature which would take the skin off Anglo-Saxon mouths. My tongue was more than once blistered, on beginning to drink after they had emptied their glasses. There is no station without its steaming samovar; and some persons, I verily believe, take their thirty-three hot teas between Moscow and St. Petersburg.

There is not much choice of dishes in the interior of Russia; but what one does get is sure to be tolerably good. Even on the Beresina and the Dnieper I have always fared better than at most of the places in our country where "Ten minutes for refreshments!" is announced day by day and year by year. Better a single beef-steak, where tenderness is, than a stalled ox, all gristle and grease. But then our cooking (for the public at least) is notoriously the worst in the civilized world; and I can safely pronounce the Russian better, without commending it very highly.

Some time in the night we passed the large town of Vladimir, and with the rising sun were well on our way to the Volga. I pushed aside the curtains, and looked out, to see what changes a night's travel had wrought in the scenery. It was a pleasant surprise. On the right stood a large, stately residence, embowered in gardens and orchards; while beyond it, stretching away to the southeast, opened a broad, shallow valley. The sweeping hills on either side were dotted with shocks of rye; and their thousands of acres of stubble shone like gold in the level rays. Herds of cattle were pasturing in the meadows, and the peasants (serfs no longer) were straggling out of the villages to their labor in the fields. The crosses and polished domes of churches sparkled on the horizon. Here the patches of primitive forest were of larger growth, the trunks cleaner and straighter, than we had yet seen. Nature was half conquered, in spite of the climate, and, for the first time since leaving St. Petersburg, wore a habitable aspect. I recognized some of the features of Russian country-life which Puschkin describes so charmingly in his poem of "Eugene Onägin."

The agricultural development of Russia has been greatly retarded by the indifference of the nobility, whose vast estates comprise the best land of the empire, in those provinces where improvements might be most easily introduced. Although a large portion of the noble families pass their summers in the country, they use the season as a period of physical and pecuniary recuperation from the dissipations of the past, and preparation for those of the coming winter. Their possessions are so large (those of Count Scheremetieff, for instance, contain one hundred and thirty thousand inhabitants) that they push each other too far apart for social intercourse; and they consequently live *en déshabille*, careless of the great national interests in their hands. There is a class of our Southern planters which seems to have adopted a very similar mode of life — families which shabbily starve for ten months, in order to make a lordly show at "the Springs" for the other two. A most accomplished Russian lady, the Princess D——, said to me, — "The want of an active, intelligent country society is our greatest misfortune. Our estates thus become a sort of exile. The few, here and there, who try to improve the condition of the people, through the improvement of the soil, are not supported by their neighbors, and lose heart. The more we gain in the life of the capital, the more we are oppressed by the solitude and stagnation of the life of the country."

This open, cheerful region continued through the morning. The railroad was still a novelty; and the peasants everywhere dropped their scythes and shovels to see the train pass. Some bowed with the profoundest gravity. They were a fine, healthy, strapping race of men, only of medium height, but admirably developed in chest and limbs, and with shrewd, intelligent faces. Content, not stupidity, is the cause of their stationary condition. They are not yet a people, but the germ of one, and, as such, present a grand field for anthropological studies.

Towards noon the road began to descend, by easy grades, from the fair, rolling uplands into a lower and wilder region. When the train stopped, women and children whose swarthy skin and black eyes betrayed a mixture of Tartar blood, made their appearance, with wooden bowls of cherries and huckleberries for sale. These bowls were neatly carved and painted. They were evidently held in high value; for I had great difficulty in purchasing one. We moved slowly, on account of the many skeleton bridges; but presently a long, blue ridge, which for an hour past had followed us in the southeast, began to curve around to our front. I now knew that it must mark the course of the Oka River, and that we were approaching Nijni-Novgorod.

We soon saw the river itself; then houses and gardens scattered along the slope of the hill; then clusters of sparkling domes on the summit; then a stately, white-walled citadel; and the end of the blue ridge slanted down in an even line to the Volga. We were three hundred miles from Moscow, on the direct road to Siberia.

The city being on the farther side of the Oka, the railroad terminates at the Fair, which is a separate city, occupying the triangular level between the two rivers. Our approach to it was first announced by heaps of cotton-bales, bound in striped camel's-hair cloth, which had found their way hither from the distant valleys of Turkestan and the warm plains of Bukharia. Nearly fifty thousand camels are employed in the transportation of this staple across the deserts of the Aral to Orenburg, a distance of a thousand miles. The increase of price had doubled the production since the previous year, and the amount which now reaches the factories of Russia through this channel cannot be less than seventy-five thousand bales. The advance of modern civilization has so intertwined the interests of all zones and races, that a civil war in the United States affects the industry of Central Asia!

Next to these cotton-bales which, to us, silently proclaimed the downfall of that arrogant monopoly which has caused all our present woe, came the representatives of those who produced them. Groups of picturesque Asians — Bashkirs, Persians, Bukharians, and Uzbeks — appeared on either side, staring impassively at the wonderful apparition. Though there was sand under their feet, they seemed out of place in the sharp north-wind and among the hills of fir and pine.

The train stopped: we had reached the station. As I stepped upon the platform, I saw, over the level lines of copper roofs, the dragon-like pinnacles of Chinese buildings, and the white minaret of a mosque. Here was the certainty of a picturesque interest to balance the uncertainty of our situation. We had been unable to engage quarters in advance: there were two hundred thousand strangers before us, in a city the normal population of which is barely forty thousand; and four of our party were ladies. The Envoy, indeed, might claim the Governor's hospitality; but our visit was to be so brief that we had no time to expend on ceremonies, and preferred rambling at will through the teeming bazaars to being led about under the charge of an official escort.

A friend at Moscow, however, had considerately telegraphed in our behalf to a French resident of Nijni, and the latter gentleman met us at the station. He could give but slight hope of quarters for the night, but generously offered us his services. Droshkies were engaged to convey us to the old city, on the hill beyond the Oka; and, crowded two by two into the shabby little vehicles, we set forth. The sand was knee-deep, and the first thing that happened was the stoppage of our procession by the tumbling down of the several horses. They were righted with the help of some obliging spectators; and with infinite labor we worked through this strip of desert into a region of mud, with a hard, stony bottom somewhere between us and the earth's centre. The street we entered, though on the outskirts of the Fair, resembled Broadway on a sensation-day. It was choked with a crowd, composed of the sweepings of Europe and Asia. Our horses thrust their heads between the shoulders of Christians, Jews, Moslems, and Pagans, slowly shoving their way towards the floating bridge, which was a jam of vehicles from end to end. At the corners of the streets, the wiry Don Cossacks, in their dashing blue uniforms and caps of black lamb's-wool, regulated, as best they could, the movements of the multitude. It was curious to notice how they, and their small, well-knit horses, — the equine counterparts of themselves, — controlled the fierce, fiery life which flashed from every limb and feature, and did their duty with wonderful patience and gentleness. They seemed so many spirits of Disorder tamed to the service of Order.

It was nearly half an hour before we reached the other end of the bridge, and struck the superb inclined highway which leads to the top of the hill. We were unwashed and hungry; and neither the tumult of the lower town, nor the view of the Volga, crowded with vessels of all descriptions, had power to detain us. Our brave little horses bent themselves to the task; for task it really was, — the road rising between three and four hundred feet in less than half a mile. Advantage has been taken of a slight natural ravine, formed by a short, curving spur of the hill, which encloses a *pocket* of the greenest and richest foliage — a bit of unsuspected beauty, quite invisible from the other side of the river. Then, in order to reach the level of the Kremlin, the road is led through an artificial gap, a hundred feet in depth, to the open square in the centre of the city.

Here, all was silent and deserted. There were broad, well-paved streets, substantial houses, the square towers and crenelated walls of the Old Kremlin, and the glittering cupolas of twenty-six churches before us, and a lack of population which contrasted amazingly with the whirlpool of life below. Monsieur D., our new, but most faithful friend, took us to the hotel, every corner and cranny of which was occupied. There was a possibility of breakfast only, and water was obtained with great exertion. While we were lazily enjoying a tolerable meal, Monsieur D. was bestirring himself in all quarters, and came back to us radiant with luck. He had found four rooms in a neighboring street; and truly, if one were to believe De Custine or Dumas, such rooms are impossible in Russia. Charmingly clean, elegantly furnished, with sofas of green leather and beds of purest linen, they would have satisfied the severe eye of an English housekeeper. We thanked both our good friend and St. Macarius (who presides over the Fair) for this fortune, took possession, and then hired fresh droshkies to descend the hill.

On emerging from the ravine, we obtained a bird's-eye view of the whole scene. The waters of both rivers, near at hand, were scarcely visible through the shipping which covered them. Vessels from the Neva, the Caspian, and the rivers of the Ural, were here congregated; and they alone represented a floating population of between thirty and forty thousand souls. The Fair, from this point, resembled an immense flat city, — the streets of booths being of a uniform height, — out of which rose the great Greek church, the Tartar mosque, and the curious Chinese roofs. It was a vast, dark, humming plain, vanishing towards the west and northwest in clouds of sand. By this time there was a lull in the business, and we made our way to the central bazaar with less trouble than we had anticipated. It is useless to attempt an enumeration of the wares exposed for sale: they embraced everything grown, trapped, dug, or manufactured between Ireland and Japan. We sought, of course, the Asiatic elements, which first met us in the shape of melons from Astrakhan, and grapes from the southern slopes of the Caucasus. Then came wondrous stuffs from the looms of Turkestan and Cashmere, turquoises from the Upper Oxus, and glittering strings of Siberian topaz and amethyst, side by side with Nuremberg toys, Lyons silks, and Sheffield cutlery. About one third of the population of the Fair was of Asiatic blood, embracing representatives from almost every tribe north and west of the Himalayas.

This temporary city, which exists during only two months of the year, contained two hundred thousand inhabitants at the time of our visit. During the remaining ten months it is utterly depopulated, the bazaars are closed, and chains are drawn across the streets to prevent the passage of vehicles. A single statement will give an idea of its extent: the combined length of the streets is twenty-five miles. The Great Bazaar is substantially built of stone, after the manner of those in Constantinople, except that it incloses an open court, where a Government band performs every afternoon. Here the finer wares are displayed, and the shadowed air under the vaulted roofs is a very kaleidoscope for shifting color and sparkle. Tea, cotton, leather, wool, and the other heavier and coarser commodities, have their separate streets and quarters. The several nationalities are similarly divided, to some extent; but the stranger, of course, prefers to see them jostling together in the streets, — a Babel not only of tongues, but of feature, character, and costume.

Our ladies were eager to inspect the stock of jewelry

especially those heaps of exquisite color with which the Mohammedans very logically load the trees of Paradise; for they resemble fruit in a glorified state of existence. One can imagine virtuous grapes promoted to amethysts, blueberries to turquoises, cherries to rubies, and greengages to aqua-marine. These, the secondary jewels (with the exception of the ruby), are brought in great quantities from Siberia, but most of them are marred by slight flaws or other imperfections, so that their cheapness is more apparent than real. An amethyst an inch long, throwing the most delicious purple light from its hundreds of facets, quite takes you captive, and you put your hand in your pocket for the fifteen dollars which shall make you its possessor; but a closer inspection is sure to show you either a broad transverse flaw, or a spot where the color fades into transparency. The white topaz, known as the "Siberian diamond," is generally flawless, and the purest specimens are scarcely to be distinguished from the genuine brilliant. A necklace of these, varying from a half to a quarter of an inch in diameter, may be had for about twenty-five dollars. There were also golden and smoky topaz and beryl, in great profusion.

A princely Bashkir drew us to his booth, first by his beauty and then by his noble manners. He was the very incarnation of Boker's "Prince Adeb."

> "The girls of Damar paused to see me pass,
> I walking in my rags, yet beautiful.
> One maiden said, 'He has a prince's air!'
> I am a prince; the air was all my own."

This Bashkir, however, was not in rags, he was elegantly attired. His silken vest was bound with a girdle of gold thread studded with jewels, and over it he wore a caftan, with wide sleeves, of the finest dark-blue cloth. The round cap of black lamb's-wool became his handsome head. His complexion was pale olive, through which the red of his cheeks shone, in the words of some oriental poem, "like a rose-leaf through oil;" and his eyes, in their dark fire were more lustrous than smoky topaz. His voice was mellow and musical, and his every movement and gesture a new exhibition of human grace. Among thousands, yea, tens of thousands, of handsome men, he stood preëminent.

As our acquaintance ripened, he drew a pocket-book from his bosom, and showed us his choicest treasures: turquoises, bits of wonderful blue heavenly forget-me-nots; a jacinth, burning like a live coal, in scarlet light; and lastly, a perfect ruby, which no sum less than twenty-five hundred dollars could purchase. From him we learned the curious fluctuations of fashion in regard to jewels. Turquoises were just then in the ascendant; and one of the proper tint, the size of a parsnip-seed, could not be had for a hundred dollars, the full value of a diamond of equal size. Amethysts of a deep plum-color, though less beautiful than the next paler shade, command very high prices; while jacinth, beryl, and aqua-marine — stones of exquisite hue and lustre — are cheap. But then, in this department, as in all others, Fashion and Beauty are not convertible terms.

In the next booth there were two Persians, who unfolded before our eyes some of their marvelous shawls, where you forget the barbaric pattern in the exquisite fineness of the material and the triumphant harmony of the colors. Scarlet with palm-leaf border, — blue clasped by golden bronze, picked out with red, — browns, greens, and crimsons struggling for the mastery in a war of tints, — how should we choose between them? Alas! we were not able to choose; they were a thousand dollars apiece! But the Persians still went on unfolding, taking our admiration in pay for their trouble, and seeming even, by their pleasant smiles, to consider themselves well paid. When we came to the booths of European merchants, we were swiftly impressed with the fact that civilization, in following the sun westward, loses its grace in proportion as it advances. The gentle dignity, the serene patience, the soft, fraternal, affectionate demeanor of our Asiatic brethren vanished utterly when we encountered French and German salesmen; and yet these latter would have seemed gracious and courteous, had there been a few Yankee dealers beyond them. The fourth or fifth century, which still exists in Central Asia, was undoubtedly, in this particular, superior to the nineteenth. No gentleman, since his time, I suspect, has equaled Adam.

Among these Asiatics Mr. Buckle would have some difficulty in maintaining his favorite postulate, that tolerance is the result of progressive intelligence. It is also the result of courtesy, as we may occasionally see in wellbred persons of limited intellect. Such, undoubtedly, is the basis of that tolerance which no one who has had much personal intercourse with the Semitic races can have failed to experience. The days of the sword and fagot are past; but it was reserved for Christians to employ them in the name of religion alone. Local or political jealousies are at the bottom of those troubles which still occur from time to time in Turkey; the traveller hears no insulting epithet, and the green-turbaned Imâm will receive him as kindly and courteously as the skeptical Bey educated in Paris. I have never been so aggressively assailed, on religious grounds, as at home, — never so coarsely and insultingly treated, on account of a presumed difference of opinion, as by those who claim descent from the Cavaliers. The bitter fierceness of some of our leading reformers is overlooked by their followers, because it springs from "earnest conviction"; but in the Orient intensest faith coexists with the most gracious and gentle manners.

Be not impatient, beloved reader; for this digression brings me naturally to the next thing we saw at Novgorod. As we issued from the bazaar, the sunlit minaret greeted us through whirling dust and rising vapor, and I fancied I could hear the muezzin's musical cry. It was about time for the *asser* prayer. Droshkies were found, and we rode slowly through the long, low warehouses of "caravan tea" and Mongolian wool to the mound near the Tartar encampment. The mosque was a plain, white, octagonal building, conspicuous only through its position. The turbaned faithful were already gathering; and we entered, and walked up the steps among them, without encountering an unfriendly glance. At the door stood two Cossack soldiers, specially placed there to prevent the worshippers from being insulted by curious Christians. (Those who have witnessed the wanton profanation of mosques in India by the English officers will please notice this fact.) If we had not put off our shoes before entering the hall of worship, the Cossacks would have performed that operation for us.

I am happy to say that none of our party lacked a proper reverence for devotion, though it was offered through the channels of an alien creed. The ladies left their gaiters beside our boots, and we all stood in our stockings on the matting, a little in the rear of the kneeling crowd. The priest occupied a low daïs in front, but he simply led the prayer, which was uttered by all. The windows were open, and the sun poured a golden flood into the room. Yonder gleamed the Kremlin of Novgorod, yonder rolled the Volga, all around were the dark forests of the North, — yet their faces were turned, and their thoughts went southward, to where Mecca sits among the burning hills, in the feathery shade of her palm-trees. And the tongue of Mecca came from their lips, "*Allah!*" "*Allah akhbar!*" as the knee bent and the forehead touched the floor.

At the second repetition of the prayers we quietly withdrew; and good Monsieur D., forgetful of nothing, suggested that preparations had been made for a dinner in the great cosmopolitan restaurant. So we drove back again through the Chinese street, with its red horned houses, the roofs terminating in gilded dragons' tails, and, after pressing through an immense multitude enveloped in tobacco-smoke and the steam of tea-urns, found ourselves at last in a low room with a shaky floor and muslin ceiling. It was an exact copy of the dining-room of a California hotel. If we looked blank a moment, Monsieur D.'s smile reassured us. He had given all the necessary orders, he said, and would step out and secure a box in the theatre before the *zakouski* was served. During his absence, we looked out of the window on either side upon surging, whirling, humming pictures of the Great Fair, all vanishing in perspectives of dust and mist.

In half an hour our friend returned, and with him entered the zakouski. I cannot remember half the appetizing ingredients of which it was composed: anchovies, sardines, herrings, capers, cheese, caviare, *paté de foie*, pickles, cherries, oranges, and olives, were among them. Instead of being a prelude to dinner, it was almost a dinner in itself. Then, after a Russian soup, which always contains as much solid nutriment as meat-biscuit or Arctic pemmican, came the glory of the repast, a mighty *sterlet*, which was swimming in Volga water when we took our seats at the table. This fish, the exclusive property of Russia, is, in times of scarcity, worth its weight in silver. Its unapproachable flavor is supposed to be as evanescent as the hues of a dying dolphin. Frequently, at grand dinner-parties, it is carried around the table in a little tank, and exhibited, *alive*, to the guests, when their soup is served, that its freshness, ten minutes afterwards, may be put beyond suspicion. The fish has the appearance of a small, lean sturgeon; but its flesh resembles the melting pulp of a fruit rather than the fibre of its watery brethren. It sinks into juice upon the tongue, like a perfectly ripe peach. In this quality no other fish in the world can approach it; yet I do not think the flavor quite so fine as that of a brook-trout. Our sterlet was nearly two feet long, and may have cost twenty or thirty dollars.

With it appeared an astonishing salad, composed of watermelons, cantaloupes, pickled cherries, cucumbers, and certain spicy herbs. Its color and odor were enticing, and we had all applied the test of taste most satisfactorily before we detected the curious mixture of ingredients. After the second course, — a ragout of beef, accompanied with a rich, elaborate sauce, — three heavy tankards of chased silver, holding two quarts apiece, were placed upon the table. The first of these contained *kvass*, the second *kislischi*, and the third hydromel. Each one of these national drinks, when properly brewed, is very palatable and refreshing. I found the kislischi nearly identical with the ancient Scandinavian mead: no doubt it dates from the Varangian rule in Russia. The old custom of passing the tankards around the table, from mouth to mouth, is still observed, and will not be found objectionable, even in these days of excessive delicacy, when ladies and gentlemen are seated alternately at the banquet.

The Russian element of the dinner here terminated. Cutlets and roast fowls made their appearance, with bottles of Rüdesheimer and Lafitte, followed by a dessert of superb Persian melons, from the southern shore of the Caspian Sea.

By this time night had fallen, and Monsieur D. suggested an immediate adjournment to the theatre. What should be the entertainment? Dances of *almehs*, songs of gypsies, or Chinese jugglers? One of the Ivans brought a programme. It was not difficult to decipher the word "МАКБЕТЪ" and to recognize, further, in the name of "Ira Aldridge" a distinguished mulatto tragedian, to whom Maryland has given birth (if I am rightly informed) and Europe fame. We had often heard of him, yea, seen his portrait in Germany, decorated with the orders conferred by half a dozen sovereigns; and his presence here, between Europe and Asia, was not the least characteristic feature of the Fair. A mulatto Macbeth, in a Russian theatre, with a Persian and Tartar audience!

On arriving, we were ushered into two whitewashed boxes, which had been reserved for our party. The manager, having been informed of the Envoy's presence in Nijni-Novgorod, had delayed the performance half an hour, but the audience bore this infliction patiently. The building was deep and narrow, with space for about eight hundred persons, and was filled from top to bottom. The first act was drawing to a close as we entered. King Duncan, with two or three shabby attendants, stood in the court-yard of the castle, — the latter represented by a handsome French door on the left, with a bit of Tartar wall beyond, — and made his observations on the "pleasant seat" of Macbeth's mansion. He spoke Russian, of course. Lady Macbeth now appeared, in a silk dress of the latest fashion, expanded by the amplest of crinolines. She was passably handsome, and nothing could be gentler than her face and voice. She received the royal party like a well-bred lady, and they all entered the French door together.

There was no change of scene. With slow step and folded arms, Ira Macbeth entered and commenced the soliloquy, "If it were done," etc., to our astonishment, in English! He was a dark, strongly built mulatto, of about fifty, in a fancy tunic, and light stockings over Forrestian calves. His voice was deep and powerful; and it was very evident that Edmund Kean, once his master, was also the model which he carefully followed in the part. There were the same deliberate, over-distinct enunciation, the same prolonged pauses and gradually performed gestures, as I remember in imitations of Kean's manner. Except that the copy was a little too apparent, Mr. Aldridge's acting was really very fine. The Russians were enthusiastic in their applause, though very few of them, probably, understood the language of the part. The Oriental auditors were perfectly impassive, and it was impossible to guess how they regarded the performance.

The second act was in some respects the most amusing

thing I ever saw upon the stage. In the dagger-scene, Ira was, to my mind, quite equal to Forrest; it was impossible to deny him unusual dramatic talent; but his complexion, continually suggesting Othello, quite confounded me. The amiable Russian Lady Macbeth was much better adapted to the part of Desdemona: all softness and gentleness, she smiled as she lifted her languishing eyes, and murmured in the tenderest accents, "Infirm of purpose! give me the dagger!" At least, I took for granted that these were her words, for Macbeth had just said, "Look on't again I dare not." Afterwards, six Russian soldiers, in tan-colored shirts, loose trousers, and high boots, filed in, followed by Macduff and Malcolm, in the costume of Wallenstein's troopers. The dialogue — one voice English, and all the others Russian — proceeded smoothly enough, but the effect was like nothing which our stage can produce. Nevertheless, the audience was delighted, and when the curtain fell there were vociferous cries of *"Aïra! Aïra! Aldreetch! Aldreetch!"* until the swarthy hero made his appearance before the foot-lights.

Monsieur D. conducted our friend P. into the greenroom, where he was received by Macbeth in costume. He found the latter to be a dignified, imposing personage, who carried his tragic chest-tones into ordinary conversation. On being informed by P. that the American minister was present, he asked, —

"Of what persuasion?"

P. hastened to set him right, and Ira then remarked, in his gravest tone, — "I shall have the honor of waiting upon him to-morrow morning;" which, however, he failed to do.

This son of the South, no doubt, came legitimately (or, at least, naturally) by his dignity. His career, for a man of his blood and antecedents, has been wonderfully successful, and is justly due, I am convinced, since I have seen him, to his histrionic talents. Both black and yellow skins are sufficiently rare in Europe to excite a particular interest in those who wear them; and I had surmised, up to this time, that much of his popularity might be owing to his color. But he certainly deserves an honorable place among tragedians of the second rank.

We left the theatre at the close of the third act, and crossed the river to our quarters on the hill. A chill mist hung over the Fair, but the lamps still burned, the streets were thronged, and the Don Cossacks kept patient guard at every corner. The night went by like one unconscious minute, in beds unmolested by bug or flea; and when I arose, thoroughly refreshed, I involuntarily called to mind a frightful chapter in De Custine's "Russia," describing the prevalence of an insect which he calls the *persica*, on the banks of the Volga. He was obliged to sleep on a table, the legs whereof were placed in basins of water, to escape their attacks. I made many inquiries about these terrible *persicas*, and finally discovered that they were neither more nor less than — cockroaches! — called *Prossaki* (Prussians) by the Russians, as they are sometimes called *Schwaben* (Suabians) by the Germans. Possibly they may be found in the huts of the serfs, but they are rare in decent houses.

We devoted the first sunny hours of the morning to a visit to the citadel and a walk around the crest of the hill. On the highest point, just over the junction of the two rivers, there is a commemorative column to Minim, the patriotic butcher of Novgorod, but for whose eloquence, in the year 1610, the Russian might possibly now be the Polish Empire. Vladislas, son of Sigismund of Poland, had been called to the throne by the boyards, and already reigned in Moscow, when Minim appealed to the national spirit, persuaded General Pojarski to head an anti-Polish movement, which was successful, and thus cleared the way for the election of Michael Romanoff, the first sovereign of the present dynasty. Minim is therefore one of the historic names of Russia.

When I stood beside his monument, and the finest landscape of European Russia was suddenly unrolled before my eyes, I could believe the tradition of his eloquence, for here was its inspiration. Thirty or forty miles away stretched the rolling swells of forest and grain-land, fading into dimmest blue to the westward and northward, dotted with villages and sparkling domes, and divided by shining reaches of the Volga. It was truly a superb and imposing view, changing with each spur of the hill as we made the circuit of the citadel. Eastward, the country rose into dark, wooded hills, between which the river forced its way in a narrower and swifter channel, until it disappeared behind a purple headland, hastening southward to find a warmer home in the unfrozen Caspian. By embarking on the steamers anchored below us, we might have reached Perm, among the Ural Mountains, or Astrakhan, in less than a week; while a trip of ten days would have taken us past the Caucasus, even to the base of Ararat or Demavend. Such are the splendid possibilities of travel in these days.

The Envoy, who visited Europe for the first time, declared that this panorama from the hill of Novgorod was one of the finest things he had seen. There could, truly, be no better preparation to enjoy it than fifteen hundred miles of nearly unbroken level, after leaving the Russian frontier; but I think it would be a noted landscape anywhere. Why it is not more widely celebrated I cannot guess. The only person in Russia whom I heard speak of it with genuine enthusiasm was Alexander II.

Two hours upon the breezy parapet, beside the old Tartar walls, were all too little; but the droshkies waited in the river-street a quarter of a mile below us; our return to Moscow was ordered for the afternoon; there were amethysts and Persian silks yet to be bought, and so we sighed farewell to an enjoyment rare in Russia, and descended the steep foot-path.

P. and I left the rest of the party at the booth of the

handsome Bashkir, and set out upon a special mission to the Tartar camp. I had ascertained that the national beverage of Central Asia might be found there, — the genuine *koumiss* or fermented milk of the mares of the Uralian steppes. Having drunk palm-wine in India, *samshoo* in China, *saki* in Japan, *pulque* in Mexico, *bouza* in Egypt, mead in Scandinavia, ale in England, *bock-bier* in Germany, *mastic* in Greece, *calabogus* in Newfoundland, and — soda-water in the United States, I desired to complete the bibulous cosmos, in which *koumiss* was still lacking. My friend did not share my curiosity, but was ready for an adventure, which our search for mare's milk seemed to promise.

Beyond the mosques we found the Uzbeks and Kirghiz, — some in tents, some in rough shanties of boards. But they were without koumiss: they had had it, and showed us some empty kegs, in evidence of the fact. I fancied a gleam of diversion stole over their grave, swarthy faces, as they listened to our eager inquiries in broken Russian. Finally we came into an extemporized village, where some women, unveiled and ugly, advised us to apply to the traders in the khan, or caravanserai. This was a great barn-like building, two stories high, with broken staircases and creaking floors. A corridor ran the whole length of the second floor, with some twenty or thirty doors opening into it from the separate rooms of the traders. We accosted the first Tartar whom we met, and he promised, with great readiness, to procure us what we wanted. He ushered us into his room, cleared away a pile of bags, saddles, camel-trappings, and other tokens of a nomadic life, and revealed a low divan covered with a ragged carpet. On a sack of barley sat his father, a blind graybeard, nearly eighty years old. On our way through the camp I had noticed that the Tartars saluted each other with the Arabic, " *Salaam aleikoom!* " and I therefore greeted the old man with the familiar words. He lifted his head: his face brightened, and he immediately answered, "*Aleikoom salaam*, my son!"

"Do you speak Arabic?" I asked.

"A little; I have forgotten it," said he. "But thine is a new voice. Of what tribe art thou?"

"A tribe far away, beyond Bagdad and Syria," I answered.

"It is the tribe of Damascus. I know it now, my son. I have heard the voice, many, many years ago."

The withered old face looked so bright, as some pleasant memory shone through it, that I did not undeceive the man. His son came in with a glass, pulled a keg from under a pile of coarse caftans, and drew out the wooden peg. A gray liquid, with an odor at once sour and pungent, spirted into the glass, which he presently handed to me, filled to the brim. In such cases no hesitation is permitted. I thought of home and family, set the glass to my lips, and emptied it before the flavor made itself clearly manifest to my palate.

"Well, what is it like?" asked my friend, who curiously awaited the result of the experiment.

"Peculiar," I answered, with preternatural calmness,— "peculiar, but not unpleasant."

The glass was filled a second time; and P., not to be behindhand, emptied it at a draught. Then he turned to me with tears (not of delight) in his eyes, swallowed very hard two or three times, suppressed a convulsive shudder, and finally remarked, with the air of a martyr, "Very curious, indeed!"

"Will your Excellencies have some more?" said the friendly Tartar.

"Not before breakfast, if you please," I answered; "your koumiss is excellent, however, and we will take a bottle with us," — which we did, in order to satisfy the possible curiosity of the ladies. I may here declare that the bottle was never emptied.

The taste was that of aged buttermilk mixed with ammonia. We could detect no flavor of alcohol, yet were consci*ous* of a light exhilaration from the small quantity we drank. The beverage is said, indeed, to be very intoxicating. Some German physician has established a "koumiss-cure" at Piatigorsk, at the northern base of the Caucasus, and invites invalids of certain kinds to come and be healed by its agency. I do not expect to be one of the number.

There still remained a peculiar feature of the Fair, which I had not yet seen. This is the subterranean network of sewerage, which reproduces, in massive masonry, the streets on the surface. Without it, the annual city of two months would become uninhabitable. The peninsula between the two rivers being low and marshy, — frequently overflowed during the spring freshets, — pestilence would soon be bred from the immense concourse of people: hence a system of *cloacæ*, almost rivaling those of ancient Rome. At each street-corner there are wells containing spiral staircases, by which one can descend to the spacious subterranean passages, and there walk for miles under arches of hewn stone, lighted and aired by shafts at regular intervals. In St. Petersburg you are told that more than half the cost of the city is under the surface of the earth; at Nijni-Novgorod the statement is certainly true. Peter the Great at one time designed establishing his capital here. Could he have foreseen the existence of railroads, he would certainly have done so. Nijni-Novgorod is now nearer to Berlin than the Russian frontier was fifty years ago. St. Petersburg is an accidental city; Nature and the destiny of the empire are both opposed to its existence; and a time will come when its long lines of palaces shall be deserted for some new capital, in a locality at once more southern and more central.

Another walk through the streets of the Fair enabled me to analyze the first confused impression, and separate the motley throng of life into its several elements. I shall not attempt, however, to catch and paint its ever-changing.

fluctuating character. Our limited visit allowed us to see only the more central and crowded streets. Outside of these, for miles, extend suburbs of iron, of furs, wool, and other coarser products, brought together from the Ural, from the forests towards the Polar Ocean, and from the vast extent of Siberia. Here, from morning till night, the beloved *kvass* flows in rivers, the strong stream of *shchee* (cabbage-soup) sends up its perpetual incense, and the samovar of cheap tea is never empty. Here, although important interests are represented, the intercourse between buyers and sellers is less grave and methodical than in the bazaar. There are jokes, laughter, songs, and a constant play of that repartee in which even the serfs are masters. Here, too, jugglers and mountebanks of all sorts ply their trade; gypsies sing, dance, and tell fortunes; and other vocations, less respectable than these, flourish vigorously. For, whether the visitor be an Ostiak from the Polar Circle, an Uzbek from the Upper Oxus, a Crim-Tartar or Nogaï, a Georgian from Tiflis, a Mongolian from the Land of Grass, a Persian from Ispahan, a Jew from Hamburg, a Frenchman from Lyons, a Tyrolese, Swiss, Bohemian, or an Anglo-Saxon from either side of the Atlantic, he meets his fellow-visitors to the Great Fair on the common ground, not of human brotherhood, but of human appetite; and all the manifold nationalities succumb to the same allurements. If the various forms of indulgence could be so used as to propagate ideas, the world would speedily be regenerated; but as things go, "cakes and ale" have more force than the loftiest ideas, the noblest theories of improvement; and the impartial observer will make this discovery as readily at Nijni-Novgorod as anywhere else.

Before taking leave of the Fair, let me give a word to the important subject of tea. It is a much-disputed question with the connoisseurs of that beverage which neither cheers nor inebriates (though, I confess, it is more agreeable than koumiss), whether the Russian " caravan tea " is really superior to that which is imported by sea. After much patient observation, combined with serious reflection, I incline to the opinion that the flavor of tea depends, not upon the method of transportation, but upon the price paid for the article. I have tasted bad caravan tea in Russia, and delicious tea in New York. In St. Petersburg you cannot procure a good article for less than three roubles ($2.25, *gold*) per pound; while the finer kinds bring twelve and even sixteen roubles. Whoever is willing to import at that price can no doubt procure tea of equal excellence. The fact is, that this land-transportation is slow, laborious, and expensive; hence the finer kinds of tea are always selected, a pound thereof costing no more for carriage than a pound of inferior quality; whence the superior flavor of caravan tea. There is, however, one variety to be obtained in Russia which I have found nowhere else, not even in the Chinese sea-ports. It is called "imperial tea," and comes in elegant boxes of yellow silk emblazoned with the dragon of the Hang dynasty, at the rate of from six to twenty dollars a pound. It is yellow, and the decoction from it is almost colorless. A small pinch of it, added to ordinary black tea, gives an indescribably delicious flavor — the very aroma of the tea-blossom; but one cup of it, unmixed, is said to deprive the drinker of sleep for three nights.

Monsieur D. brought our last delightful stroll through the glittering streets to an untimely end. The train for Moscow was to leave at three o'clock; and he had ordered an early dinner at the restaurant. By the time this was concluded, it was necessary to drive at once to the station, in order to secure places. We were almost too late; the train, long as it was, was crammed to overflowing; and although both station-master and conductor assisted us, the eager passengers disregarded their authority. With great difficulty, one compartment was cleared for the ladies; in the adjoining one four merchants, in long caftans, with sacks of watermelons as provision for the journey, took their places, and would not be ejected. A scene of confusion ensued, in which station-master, conductor, Monsieur D., my friend P., and the Russian merchants were curiously mixed; but when we saw the sacks of watermelons rolling out of the door, we knew the day was ours. In two minutes more we were in full possession; the doors were locked, and the struggling throngs beat against them in vain.

With a grateful farewell to our kind guide, whose rather severe duties for our sake were now over, we moved away from the station, past heaps of cotton-bales, past hills of drifting sand, and impassive groups of Persians, Tartars, and Bukharians, and slowly mounted the long grade to the level of the upland, leaving the Fair to hum and whirl in the hollow between the rivers, and the white walls and golden domes of Novgorod to grow dim on the crest of the receding hill.

The next morning, at sunrise, we were again in Moscow.

WINTER-LIFE IN ST. PETERSBURG.

As September drew to an end, with only here and there a suggestion of autumn in chrome-colored leaves on the ends of birch-branches, we were told that any day might suddenly bring forth winter. I remembered that five years before, in precisely the same season, I had travelled from Upsala to Stockholm in a violent snow-storm, and therefore accepted the announcement as a part of the regular programme of the year. But the days came and went; fashionable equipages forsook their summer ground of the Islands, and crowded the Nevskoi Prospekt; the nights were cold and raw; the sun's lessening declination was visible from day to day, and still Winter delayed to make his appearance.

The Island drive was our favorite resort of an afternoon; and we continued to haunt it long after every summer guest had disappeared, and when the *datchas* and palaces showed plank and matting in place of balcony and window. In the very heart of St. Petersburg the one full stream of the Neva splits into three main arms, which afterwards subdivide, each seeking the Gulf of Finland at its own swift, wild will. The nearest of these islands, Vassili Ostrow, is a part of the solid city: on Kammenoi and Aptekarskoi you reach the commencement of gardens and groves; and beyond these the rapid waters mirror only palace, park, and summer theatre. The widening streams continually disclose the horizon-line of the Gulf; and at the farthest point of the drive, where the road turns sharply back again from the freedom of the shore into mixed woods of birch and pine, the shipping at Cronstadt — and sometimes the phantoms of fortresses — detach themselves from the watery haze, and the hill of Pargola, in Finland, rises to break the dreary level of the Ingrian marshes.

During the sunny evenings and the never-ending twilights of midsummer, all St. Petersburg pours itself upon these islands. A league-long wall of dust rises from the carriages and droshkies in the main highway; and the branching Neva-arms are crowded with skiffs and diminutive steamers bound for pleasure-gardens where gypsies sing and Tyrolese *yodel* and jugglers toss their knives and balls, and private rooms may be had for gambling and other cryptic diversions. Although with shortened days and cool evenings the tide suddenly took a reflux and the Nevskoi became a suggestion of Broadway (which, of all individual streets, it most nearly resembles), we found an indescribable charm in the solitude of the fading groves and the waves whose lamenting murmur foretold their speedy imprisonment. We had the whole superb drive to ourselves. It is true that Ivan, upon the box, lifted his brows in amazement, and sighed that his jaunty cap of green velvet should be wasted upon the desert air, whenever I said, "*Na Ostrowa*," but he was too genuine a Russian to utter a word of remonstrance.

Thus, day by day, unfashionable, but highly satisfied, we repeated the lonely drive, until the last day came, as it always will. I don't think I shall ever forget it. It was the first day of November. For a fortnight the temperature had been a little below the freezing-point, and the leaves of the alder-thickets, frozen suddenly and preserved as in a great out-door refrigerator, maintained their green. A pale blue mist rose from the Gulf and hung over the islands, the low sun showing an orange disk, which touched the shores with the loveliest color, but gave no warmth to the windless air. The parks and gardens were wholly deserted, and came and went, on either side, phantom-like in their soft, gray, faded tints. Under every bridge flashed and foamed the clear, beryl-green waters. And nobody in St. Petersburg, except ourselves, saw this last and sunniest flicker of the dying season!

The very next day was cold and dark, and so the weather remained, with brief interruptions, for months. On the evening of the 6th, as we drove over the Nikolai Bridge to dine with a friend on Vassili Ostrow, we noticed fragments of ice floating down the Neva. Looking up the stream, we were struck by the fact that the remaining bridges had been detached from the St. Petersburg side, floated over, and anchored along the opposite shore. This seemed a needless precaution, for the pieces of drift-ice were hardly large enough to have crushed a skiff. How surprised were we, then, on returning home, four hours later, to find the noble river gone, not a green wave to be seen, and, as far as the eye could reach, a solid floor of ice, over which people were already crossing to and fro!

Winter, having thus suddenly taken possession of the world, lost no time in setting up the signs of his rule. The leaves, whether green or brown, disappeared at one swoop; snow-gusts obscured the little remaining sunshine; the inhabitants came forth in furs and bulky wrappings; oysters and French pears became unreasonably dear; and sledges of frozen fish and game crowded down from the northern forests. In a few days the physiognomy of the capital was completely changed. All its life and stir withdrew from the extremities and gathered into a few central thoroughfares, as if huddling together for mutual warmth and encouragement in the cold air and under the gloomy sky.

For darkness, rather than cold, is the characteristic of the St. Petersburg winter. The temperature, which at Montreal or St. Paul would not be thought remarkably low, seems to be more severely felt here, owing to the absence of pure daylight. Although both Lake Ladoga and the Gulf of Finland are frozen, the air always retains a damp, raw, penetrating quality, and the snow is more frequently sticky and clammy than dry and crystalline. Few, indeed, are the days which are not cheerless and depressing. In December, when the sky is overcast for weeks together, the sun, rising after nine o'clock, and sliding along just above the horizon, enables you to dispense with lamplight somewhere between ten and eleven; but by two in the afternoon you must call for lights again. Even when a clear day comes, the yellow, level sunshine is a combination of sunrise and sunset, and neither tempers the air nor mitigates the general expression of gloom, almost of despair, upon the face of Nature.

The preparations for the season, of course, have been made long before. In most houses the double windows are allowed to remain through the summer, but they must be carefully examined, the layer of cotton between them, at the bottom, replenished, a small vessel of salt added to absorb the moisture and prevent it from freezing on the panes, and strips of paper pasted over every possible crack. The outer doors are covered with wadded leather, overlapping the frames on all sides. The habitations being thus almost hermetically sealed, they are easily warmed by the huge porcelain stoves, which retain warmth so tenaciously that one fire per day is sufficient for the most sensitive constitutions. In my own room, I found that one armful of birch-wood, reduced to coal, every alternate morning, created a steady temperature of 64°. Although the rooms are always spacious, and arranged in suites of from three to a dozen, according to the extent and splendor of the residence, the atmosphere soon becomes close and characterized by an unpleasant odor, suggesting its diminished vitality; for which reason pastilles are burned, or *eau de Cologne* reduced to vapor in a heated censer, whenever visits are anticipated. It was a question with me, whether or not the advantage of a thoroughly equable temperature was counterbalanced by the lack of circulation. The physical depression we all felt seemed to result chiefly from the absence of daylight.

One winter picture remains clearly outlined upon my memory. In the beginning of December we happened once to drive across the Admiralty Square in the early evening twilight,—three o'clock in the afternoon. The temperature was about 10° below zero, the sky a low roof of moveless clouds, which seemed to be frozen in their places. The pillars of St. Isaac's Cathedral—splendid monoliths of granite, sixty feet high—had precipitated the moisture of the air, and stood silvered with rime from base to capital. The Column of Alexander, the bronze statue of Peter, with his horse poised in air on the edge of the rock, and the trees on the long esplanade in front of the Admiralty, were all similarly coated, every twig rising as rigid as iron in the dark air. Only the huge golden hemisphere of the Cathedral dome, and the tall, pointed golden spire of the Admiralty, rose above the gloom, and half shone with a muffled, sullen glare. A few people, swaddled from head to foot, passed rapidly to and fro, or a droshky, drawn by a frosted horse, sped away to the entrance of the Nevskoi Prospekt. Even these appeared rather like wintry phantoms than creatures filled with warm blood and breathing the breath of life. The vast spaces of the capital, the magnitude of its principal edifices, and the display of gold and colors, strengthened the general aspect of unreality, by introducing so many inharmonious elements into the picture. A bleak moor, with the light of a single cottage-window shining across it, would have been less cold, dead, and desolate.

The temperature, I may here mention, was never very severe. There were three days when the mercury fluctuated between 15° and 20° below zero, five days when it reached 10° below, and perhaps twenty when it fell to zero, or a degree or two on either side. The mean of the five winter months was certainly not lower than $+12°$. Quite as much rain fell as snow. After two or three days of sharp cold, there was almost invariably **a day of rain or** fog, and for many weeks walking was so difficult that we were obliged to give up all out-door exercise except skating or sliding. The streets were either coated with glassy ice or they were a foot deep in slush. There is more and better sleighing in the vicinity of Boston almost any winter than in St. Petersburg during the winter of 1862-3. In our trips to the Observatory of Pulkova, twelve miles distant, we were frequently obliged to leave the highway and put our sled-runners upon the frosted grass of the meadows. The rapid and continual changes of temperature were more trying than any amount of steady cold. *Grippe* became prevalent, and therefore fashionable, and all the endemic diseases of St. Petersburg showed themselves in force. The city, it is well known, is built upon piles, and most of the inhabitants suffer from them. Children look pale and wilted, in the absence of the sun, and special care must be taken of those under five years of age. Some little relatives of mine, living in the country, had their daily tumble in the snow, and thus kept ruddy; but in the city this is not possible, and we had many anxious days before the long darkness was over.

As soon as snow had fallen and freezing weather set in, the rough, broken ice of the Neva was flooded in various places for skating-ponds, and the work of erecting ice-hills commenced. There were speedily a number of the latter in full play, in the various suburbs, — a space of level ground, at least a furlong in length, being necessary. They are supported by subscription, and I had paid ten rubles for permission to use a very fine one on the farther island, when an obliging card of admission came for the gardens of the Taurida Palace, where the younger members of the Imperial family skate and slide. My initiation, however, took place at the first-named locality, whither we were conducted by an old American resident of St. Petersburg.

The construction of these ice-hills is very simple. They are rude towers of timber, twenty to thirty feet in height, the summit of which is reached by a staircase at the back, while in front descends a steep concave of planking upon which water is poured until it is covered with a six-inch coating of solid ice. Raised planks at the side keep the sled in its place until it reaches the foot, where it enters upon an icy plain two to four hundred yards in length (in proportion to the height of the hill), at the extremity of which rises a similar hill, facing towards the first, but a little on one side, so that the sleds from the opposite ends may pass without collision.

The first experience of this diversion is fearful to a person of delicate nerves. The pitch of the descent is so sheer, the height so great (apparently), the motion of the sled so swift, and its course so easily changed, — even the lifting of a hand is sufficient, — that the novice is almost sure to make immediate shipwreck. The sleds are small and low, with smooth iron runners, and a plush cushion, upon which the navigator sits bolt upright with his legs close together, projecting over the front. The runners must be exactly parallel to the lines of the course at starting, and the least tendency to sway to either side must be instantly corrected by the slightest motion of the hand.

I engaged one of the *mujiks* in attendance to pilot me on my first voyage. The man having taken his position well forward on the little sled, I knelt upon the rear end, where there was barely space enough for my knees, placed my hands upon his shoulders, and awaited the result. He shoved the sled with his hands, very gently and carefully, to the brink of the icy steep: then there was a moment's adjustment: then a poise: then — sinking of the heart, cessation of breath, giddy roaring and whistling of the air, and I found myself scudding along the level with the speed of an express train. I never happened to fall out of a fourth-story window, but I immediately understood the sensations of the unfortunate persons who do. It was so frightful that I shuddered when we reached the end of the course and the man coolly began ascending the steps of the opposite hill, with the sled under his arm. But my companions were waiting to see me return, so I mounted after him, knelt again, and held my breath. This time, knowing what was coming, I caught a glimpse of our descent, and found that only the first plunge from the brink was threatening. The lower part of the curve, which is nearly a parabolic line, is more gradual, and the seeming headlong fall does not last more than the tenth part of a second. The sensation, nevertheless, is very powerful, having all the attraction, without the reality, of danger.

The ice-hills in the Taurida Gardens were not so high, and the descent was less abrupt: the course was the smooth floor of an intervening lake, which was kept clear for skating. Here I borrowed a sled, and was so elated at performing the feat successfully, on the first attempt, that I offered my services as charioteer to a lady rash enough to accept them. The increased weight gave so much additional impetus to the sled, and thus rendered its guidance a more delicate matter. Finding that it began to turn even before reaching the bottom, I put down my hand suddenly upon the ice. The effect was like an explosion; we struck the edge of a snow-bank, and were thrown entirely over it and deeply buried on the opposite side. The attendants picked us up without relaxing a muscle of their grave, respectful faces, and quietly swept the ice for another trial. But after that I preferred descending alone.

Good skaters will go up and down these ice-hills on their skates. The feat has a hazardous look, but I have seen it performed by boys of twelve. The young Grand Dukes who visited the Gardens generally contented themselves with skating around the lake at not too violent a speed. Some ladies of the court circle also timidly ventured to try the amusement, but its introduction was too recent for them to show much proficiency. On the Neva, in fact, the English were the best skaters. During the winter, one of them crossed the Gulf to Cronstadt, a distance of twenty-two miles, in about two hours.

Before Christmas, the Lapps came down from the North with their reindeer, and pitched their tents on the river, in front of the Winter Palace. Instead of the canoe-shaped *pulk*, drawn by a single deer, they hitched four abreast to an ordinary sled, and took half a dozen passengers at a time, on a course of a mile, for a small fee. I tried it once, for a child's sake, but found that the romance of reindeer travel was lost without the pulk. The Russian sleighs are very similar to our own for driving about the city: in very cold weather, or for trips into the country, the *kibitka*, a heavy closed carriage on runners, is used. To my eye, the most dashing team in the world is the *troika*, or three-span, the thill-horse being trained to trot rapidly, while the other two, very lightly and loosely harnessed, canter on either side of him. From the ends of the thills springs a wooden arch, called the *duga*, rising eighteen inches above the horse's shoulder, and usually emblazoned with gilding and brilliant colors. There was one magnificent troika on the Nevskoi Prospekt, the horses of which were full-blooded, jet-black matches, and their harness formed of overlapping silver scales. The Russians being the best coachmen in the world, these teams dash past each other at furious speed, often escaping collision by the breadth of a hair, but never coming in violent contact.

With the approach of winter the nobility returned from their estates, the diplomatists from their long summer vacation, the Imperial Court from Moscow, and the previous social desolation of the capital came speedily to an end. There were dinners and routs in abundance, but the season of balls was not fairly inaugurated until invitations had been issued for the first at the Winter Palace. This is usually a grand affair, the guests numbering from fifteen hundred to two thousand. We were agreeably surprised at finding half-past nine fixed as the hour of arrival, and took pains to be punctual; but there were already a hundred yards of carriages in advance. The toilet, of course, must be fully completed at home, and the huge pelisses of fur so adjusted as not to disarrange head-dresses, lace, crinoline, or uniform: the footmen must be prompt, on reaching the covered portal, to promote speedy alighting and unwrapping, which being accomplished, each sits guard for the night over his own special pile of pelisses and furred boots.

When the dresses are shaken out and the gloves smoothed, at the foot of the grand staircase, an usher, in a short, bedizened red tunic and white knee-breeches, with a cap surmounted by three colossal white plumes, steps before you and leads the way onward through the spacious halls, ablaze with light from thousands of wax candles. I always admired the silent gravity of these ushers, and their slow, majestic, almost mysterious march — until one morning at home, when I was visited by four common-looking Russians, in blue caftans, who bowed nearly to the floor and muttered congratulations. It was a deputation of the Imperial ushers, making their rounds for New Year's gifts!

Although the streets of St. Petersburg are lighted with gas, the palaces and private residences are still illuminated only with wax candles. Gas is considered plebeian, but it has probably also been found to be disagreeable in the close air of the hermetically sealed apartments. Candles are used in such profusion that I am told thirty thousand are required to light up an Imperial ball. The quadruple rows of columns which support the Hall of St. George are spirally entwined with garlands of wax-lights, and immense chandeliers are suspended from the ceiling. The wicks of each column are connected with threads dipped in some inflammable mixture, and each thread, being kindled at the bottom at the same instant, the light is carried in a few seconds to every candle in the hall. This instantaneous kindling of so many thousand wicks has a magical effect

At the door of the great hall the usher steps aside, bows gravely, and returns, and one of the deputy masters of ceremonies receives you. These gentlemen are chosen from among the most distinguished families of Russia, and are, without exception, so remarkable for tact, kindness, and discretion, that the multitude falls, almost unconsciously, into the necessary observances; and the perfection of ceremony, which hides its own external indications, is attained. Violations of etiquette are most rare, yet no court in the world appears more simple and unconstrained in its forms.

In less than fifteen minutes after the appointed time the hall is filled, and a blast from the orchestra announces the entrance of the Imperial family. The ministers and chief personages of the court are already in their proper places, and the representatives of foreign nations stand on one side of the door-way in their established order of precedence (determined by length of residence near the court), with the ladies of their body on the opposite side.

Alexander II. was much brighter and more cheerful than during the preceding summer. His care-worn, preoccupied air was gone; the dangers which then encompassed him had subsided; the nobility, although still chafing fiercely against the decree of emancipation, were slowly coming to the conclusion that its consummation is inevitable; and the Emperor began to feel that his great work will be safely accomplished. His dark-green uniform well becomes his stately figure and clearly chiseled, symmetrical head. He is Nicholas recast in a softer mould, wherein tenacity of purpose is substituted for rigid, inflexible will, and the development of the nation at home supplants the ambition for predominant political influence abroad. This difference is expressed, despite the strong personal resemblance to his father, in the more frank and gentle eye, the fuller and more sensitive mouth, and the rounder lines of jaw and forehead. A free, natural directness of manner and speech is his principal characteristic. He wears easily, almost playfully, the yoke of court ceremonial, temporarily casting it aside when troublesome. In two respects he differs from most of the other European rulers whom I have seen: he looks the sovereign, and he unbends as gracefully and unostentatiously as a man risen from the ranks of the people. There is evidently better stuff than kings are generally made of in the Románoff line.

Grace and refinement, rather than beauty, distinguish the Empress, though her eyes and hair deserve the latter epithet. She is an invalid, and appears pale and somewhat worn; but there is no finer group of children in Europe than those to whom she has given birth. Six sons and one daughter are her jewels; and of these, the third son, Vladimir, is almost ideally handsome. Her dress was at once simple and superb — a cloud of snowy *tulle*, with a scarf of pale-blue velvet, twisted with a chain of the largest diamonds and tied with a knot and tassel of pearls, resting half-way down the skirt, as if it had slipped from her waist. On another occasion, I remember her wearing a crown of five stars, the centres of which were single enormous rubies and the rays of diamonds, so set on invisible wires that they burned in the air over her head. The splendor which was a part of her *rôle* was always made subordinate to rigid taste, and herein prominently distinguished her from many of the Russian ladies, who carried great fortunes upon their heads, necks, and bosoms. I had several opportunities of conversing with her, generally upon Art and Literature, and was glad to find that she had both read and thought, as well as seen. The honored author of " Evangeline" numbers her among his appreciative readers.

After their Majesties have made the circle of the diplomatic corps, the *Polonaise*, which always opens a Court ball, commences. The Grand Dukes Nicholas and Michael (brothers of the Emperor), and the younger members of the Imperial family, take part in it, the latter evidently impatient for the succeeding quadrilles and waltzes. When this is finished, all palpable, obtrusive ceremony is at an end. Dancing, conversation, cards, strolls through the sumptuous halls, fill the hours. The Emperor wanders freely through the crowd, saluting here and there a friend, exchanging badinage with the wittiest ladies (which they all seem at liberty to give back, without the least embarrassment), or seeking out the scarred and gray-haired officers who have come hither from all parts of the vast empire. He does not scrutinize whether or not your back is turned towards him as he passes. Once, on entering a door rather hastily, I came within an ace of a personal collision; whereupon he laughed good-humoredly, caught me by the hands, and saying, "It would have been a shock, *n'est-ce pas?*" hurried on.

To me the most delightful part of the Winter Palace was the garden. It forms one of the suite of thirty halls, some of them three hundred feet long, on the second story. In this garden, which is perhaps a hundred feet square by forty in height, rise clumps of Italian cypress and laurel from beds of emerald turf and blooming hyacinths. In the centre, a fountain showers over fern-covered rocks, and the gravel-walks around the border are shaded by tall camellia-trees in white and crimson bloom. Lamps of frosted glass, hang among the foliage, and diffuse a mellow golden moonlight over the enchanted ground. The corridor adjoining the garden resembles a bosky alley, so completely are the walls hidden by flowering shrubbery.

Leaving the Imperial family, and the kindred houses of Leuchtenberg, Oldenburg, and Mecklenburg, all of which are represented, let us devote a little attention to the ladies, and the crowd of distinguished, though unroyal personages. The former are all *décolletées*, of course, — even the Countess ——, who, I am positively assured, is ninety-five years old; but I do not notice much uniformity of taste, except in the matter of head-dresses. *Chignons* have not yet made their appearance, but there are huge coils and sweeps of hair — a mane-like munificence, so disposed as to reveal the art and conceal the artifice. The ornaments are chiefly flowers, though here and there I see jewels, coral, mossy sticks, dead leaves, birds, and birds'-nests. From the blonde locks of yonder princess hang bunches of green brook-grass, and a fringe of the same trails from her bosom and skirt: she resembles a fished-up and restored Ophelia. Here passes a maiden with a picket-fence of rose coral as a *berthe*, and she seems to have another around the bottom of her dress; but, as the mist of tulle is brushed aside in passing, we can detect that the latter is a clever *chenille* imitation. There is another with small moss-covered twigs arranged in the same way; and yet another with fifty black-lace butterflies, of all sizes, clinging to her yellow satin skirt. All this swimming and intermingling mass of color is dotted over with sparkles of jewel-light; and even the grand hall, with its gilded columns and thousands of tapers, seems but a sober frame for so gorgeous a picture.

I can only pick out a few of the notable men present, because there is no space to give biographies as well as portraits. That man of sixty, in rich civil uniform, who entered with the Emperor, and who at once reminds an American of Edward Everett both in face and in the polished grace and suavity of his manner, is one of the first statesmen of Europe — Prince Alexander Gortchakoff. Of medium height and robust frame, with a keen, alert eye, a broad, thoughtful forehead, and a wonderfully sagacious mouth, the upper lip slightly covering the under one at the corners, he immediately arrests your attention, and your eye unconsciously follows him as he makes his way through the crowd, with a friendly word for this man and an elegant rapier-thrust for that. His predominant mood, however, is a cheerful good nature; his wit and irony belong rather to the diplomatist than to the man. There is no sounder or more prudent head in Russia.

But who is this son of Anak, approaching from the corridor? Towering a full head above the throng, a figure of superb strength and perfect symmetry, we give him that hearty admiration which is due to a man who illustrates and embellishes manhood. In this case we can give it freely; for that finely balanced head holds a clear, vigorous brain; those large blue eyes look from the depths of a frank, noble nature; and in that broad breast beats a heart warm with love for his country, and good-will for his fellow-men, whether high or low. It is Prince Suvóroff, the Military Governor of St. Petersburg. If I were to spell his name "Suwarrow," you would know who his grandfather was, and what place in Russian history he fills. In a double sense the present Prince is cast in an heroic mould. It speaks well for Russia that his qualities are so truly appreciated. He is beloved by the people, and trusted by the Imperial Government: for, while firm in his administration of affairs, he is humane, — while cautious, energetic, — and while shrewd and skillful, frank and honest. A noble man, whose like I wish were oftener to be found in the world.

Here are two officers, engaged in earnest conversation. The little old man, with white hair, and thin, weather-beaten, wrinkled face, is Admiral Baron Wrangel, whose Arctic explorations on the northern coast of Siberia are known to all geographers. Having read of them as a boy, and then as things of the past, I was greatly delighted at finding the brave old Admiral still alive, and at the privilege of taking his hand and hearing him talk in English as fluent as my own. The young officer, with rosy face, brown moustache, and profile strikingly like that of General McClellan, has already made his mark. He is General Ignatieff, the most prominent young man of the empire. Although scarcely thirty-five, he has already filled special missions to Bukharia and Peking, and took a leading part in the Treaty of Tien-tsin. At the time of which I write, he was Deputy Minister of Foreign Affairs and Chief of the Asiatic Department.

I might mention Count Bludoff, the venerable President of the Academy of Sciences; General Todleben; Admiral Lüttke; and the distinguished members of the Galitzin, Narischkin, Apraxin, Dolgorouky, and Scheremetieff families, who are present, — but by this time the interminable mazourka is drawing to a close, and a master of ceremonies suggests that we shall step into an adjoining hall to await the signal for supper. The refreshments previously furnished consisted simply of tea, orgeat, and cooling drinks made of cranberries, Arctic raspberries, and other fruits; it is two hours past midnight, and we may frankly confess hunger.

While certain other guests are being gathered together, I will mention another decoration of the halls, peculiar to St. Petersburg. On either side of all the doors of communication in the long range of halls, stands a negro in rich oriental costume, reminding one of the mute palace-guards in the Arabian tales. Happening to meet one of these men in the Summer Garden, I addressed him in Arabic; but he knew only enough of the language to inform me that he was born in Dar-Fur. I presume, therefore, they were obtained in Constantinople. In the large halls, which are illustrated with paintings of battles, in all the Russian campaigns from Pultowa to Sebastopol, are posted companies of soldiers at the farther end — a different regiment to each hall. For six hours these men and their officers stand motionless as statues. Not a movement, except now and then of the eyelid, can be detected; even their respiration seems to be suspended. There is something weird and uncanny in such a preternatural silence and apparent death-in-life. I became impressed with the idea that some form of catalepsy had seized and bound them in strong trance. The eyeballs were fixed: they stared at me and saw me not: their hands were glued to the weapons, and their feet to the floor. I suspect there must have been some stolen relief when no guest happened to be present, yet, come when I might, I found them unchanged. When I reflected that the men were undoubtedly very proud of the distinction they enjoyed, and that their case demanded no sympathy, I could inspect and admire them with an easy mind.

The Grand Chamberlain now advances, followed by the Imperial family, behind which, in a certain order of precedence, the guests fall into place, and we presently reach a supper-hall, gleaming with silver and crystal. There are five others, I am told, and each of the two thousand guests has his chair and plate. In the centre stands the Imperial table, on a low platform: between wonderful *épergnes* of gold spreads a bed of hyacinths and crocuses. Hundreds of other *épergnes*, of massive silver, flash from the tables around. The forks and spoons are gold, the decanters of frosted crystal, covered with silver vine-leaves; even the salt-cellars are works of art. It is quite proper that the supper should be substantial; and as one such entertainment is a pattern for all that succeed, I may be allowed to mention the principal dishes: *crème de l'orge, paté de foie gras*, cutlets of fowl, game, asparagus, and salad, followed by fruits, ices, and bon-bons, and moistened with claret, Sauterne, and Champagne. I confess, however, that the superb silver chasing, and the balmy hyacinths which almost leaved over my plate, feasted my senses quite as much as the delicate viands.

After supper, the company returns to the Hall of St. George, a quadrille or two is danced to promote digestion, and the members of the Imperial family, bowing first to the diplomatic corps, and then to the other guests, retire to the private apartments of the palace. Now we are at liberty to leave, — not sooner, — and rapidly, yet not with undignified haste, seek the main staircase. Cloaking and booting (Ivan being on hand, with eyes like a lynx) are performed without regard to head-dress or uniform, and we wait while the carriages are being called, until the proper *pozlannik* turns up. If we envied those who got off sooner, we are now envied by those who still must wait, bulky in black satin or cloth, in sable or raccoon skin. It is half past three when we reach home, and there are still six hours until sunrise.

The succeeding balls, whether given by the Grand Dukes, the principal members of the Russian nobility, or the heads of foreign legations, were conducted on the same plan, except that, in the latter instances, the guests were not so punctual in arriving. The pleasantest of the season was one given by the Emperor in the Hermitage Palace. The guests, only two hundred in number, were bidden to come in ordinary evening-dress, and their Imperial Majesties moved about among them as simply and unostentatiously as any well-bred American host and hostess. On a staircase at one side of the Moorish Hall sat a distinguished Hungarian artist, sketching the scene, with its principal figures, for a picture.

I was surprised to find how much true social culture exists in St. Petersburg. Aristocratic manners, in their perfection, are simply democratic; but this is a truth which is scarcely recognized by the nobility of Germany, and only partially by that of England. The habits of refined society are very much the same everywhere. The man or woman of real culture recognizes certain forms as necessary, that social intercourse may be *ordered* instead of being arbitrary and chaotic; but these forms must not be allowed to limit the free, expansive contact of mind with mind and character with character which is the charm and blessing of society. Those who meet within the same walls meet upon an equal footing, and all accidental distinctions cease for the time. I found these principles acted upon to quite as full an extent as (perhaps even more so than) they are at home. One of the members of the Imperial family, even, expressed to me the intense weariness occasioned by the observance of the necessary forms of court life, and the wish that they might be made as simple as possible.

I was interested in extending my acquaintance among the Russian nobility, as they, to a certain extent, represent the national culture. So far as my observations reached, I found that the women were better read, and had more general knowledge of art, literature, and even politics, than the men. My most instructive intercourse was with the former. It seemed that most men (here I am not speaking of the members of the Imperial Government) had each his specialty, beyond which he showed but a limited interest. There was one distinguished circle, however, where the intellectual level of the conversation was as high as I have ever found it anywhere, and where the only title to admission prescribed by the noble host was the capacity to take part in it. In that circle I heard not only the Polish Question discussed, but the Unity or Diversity of Races, Modern and Classic Art, Strauss, Emerson, and Victor Hugo, the ladies contributing their share. At a *soirée* given by the Princess Lvoff, I met Richard Wagner, the composer, Rubinstein, the pianist, and a number of artists and literary men.

A society, the head of which is a court, and where externals, of necessity, must be first considered, is not the place to seek for true and lasting intimacies; but one may find what is next best, in a social sense — cheerful and cordial intercourse. The circle of agreeable and friendly acquaintance continually enlarged; and I learned to know *one* friend (and perhaps one should hardly expect more than that in any year) whom I shall not forget, nor he me, though we never meet again. The Russians have been unjustly accused of a lack of that steady, tender, faithful depth of character upon which friendship must rest. Let us not forget that one of Washington Irving's dearest friends was Prince Dolgorouki.

Nevertheless, the constant succession of entertainments, agreeable as they were, became in the end fatiguing to quiet persons like ourselves. The routs and *soirées*, it is true, were more informal and unceremonious: one was not obliged to spend more than an hour at each, but then one was not expected to arrive before eleven o'clock. We fell, perforce, into the habits of the place, — of sleeping two or three hours after dinner, then rising, and after a cup of strong tea, dressing for the evening. After Carnival, the balls ceased; but there were still frequent routs, until Easter week closed the season.

I was indebted to Admiral Lüttke, President of the Imperial Geographical Society, for an invitation to attend its sessions, some of which were of the most interesting character. My great regret was, that a very imperfect knowledge of the language prevented me from understanding much of the proceedings. On one occasion, while a paper on the survey of the Caspian Sea was being read, a tall, stately gentleman, sitting at the table beside me, obligingly translated all the principal facts into French, as they were stated. I afterwards found that he was Count Panin, Minister of Justice. In the transactions of the various literary and scientific societies, the Russian language has now entirely supplanted the French, although the latter keeps its place in the *salons*, chiefly on account of the foreign element. The Empress has weekly *conversazioni*, at which only Russian is spoken, and to which no foreigners are admitted. It is becoming fashionable to have visiting-cards in both languages.

Of all the ceremonies which occurred during the winter, that of New Year's Day (January 13th, N. S.) was most interesting. After the members of the different legations had called in a body to pay their respects to the Emperor and Empress, the latter received the ladies of the Court, who, on this occasion, wore the national costume, in the grand hall. We were permitted to witness the spectacle, which is unique of its kind and wonderfully beautiful. The Empress, having taken her place alone near one end of the hall, with the Emperor and his family at a little distance on her right, the doors at the other end — three hundred feet distant — were thrown open, and a gorgeous procession approached, sweeping past the gilded columns, and growing with every step in color and splendor. The ladies walked in single file, about eight feet apart, each holding the train of the one preceding her. The costume consists of a high, crescent-shaped head-dress of velvet covered with jewels; a short, embroidered corsage of silk or velvet, with open sleeves; a full skirt and sweeping train of velvet or satin or *moiré*, with a deep border of point-lace. As the first lady approached the Empress, her successor dropped the train, spreading it, by a dexterous movement, to its full breadth on the polished floor. The lady, thus released, bent her knee, and took the Empress's hand to kiss it, which the latter prevented by gracefully lifting her and saluting her on the forehead. After a few words of congratulation, she passed across the hall, making a profound obeisance to the Emperor on the way.

This was the most trying part of the ceremony. She was alone and unsupported, with all eyes upon her, and it required no slight amount of skill and self-possession to cross the hall, bow, and carry her superb train to the opposite side, without turning her back on the Imperial presence. At the end of an hour the dazzling group gathered on the right equaled in numbers the long line marching up on the left — and still they came. It was a luxury of color, scarcely to be described, — all flowery and dewy tints, in a setting of white and gold. There were crimson, maroon, blue, lilac, salmon, peach-blossom, mauve, magenta, silver-gray, pearl-rose, daffodil, pale orange, purple, pea-green, sea-green, scarlet, violet, drab, and pink, — and, whether by accident or design, the succession of colors never shocked by too violent contrast. This was the perfection of scenic effect; and we lingered, enjoying it exquisitely, until the last of several hundred ladies closed the radiant spectacle.

The festival of Epiphany is celebrated by the blessing of the waters of the Neva, followed by a grand military review on the Admiralty Square. We were invited to witness both ceremonies from the windows of the Winter Palace, where, through the kindness of Prince Dolgorouki, we obtained favorable points of view. As the ceremonies last two or three hours, an elegant breakfast was served to the guests in the Moorish Hall. The blessing of the Neva is a religious festival, with the accompaniment of tapers, incense, and chanting choirs, and we could only see that the Emperor performed his part uncloaked and bareheaded in the freezing air, finishing by descending the steps of an improvised chapel and well (the building answered both purposes), and drinking the water from a hole in the ice. Far and wide over the frozen surface similar holes were cut, where, during the remainder of the day, priests officiated, and thousands of the common people were baptized by immersion. As they generally came out covered with ice, warm booths were provided for them on the banks, where they thawed themselves out, rejoicing that they would now escape sickness or misfortune for a year to come.

The review requires a practiced military pen to do it justice, and I fear I must give up the attempt. It was a "small review," only about twenty-five thousand troops being under arms. In the uniformity of size and build of the men, exactness of equipment, and precision of movement, it would be difficult to imagine anything more perfect. All sense of the individual soldier was lost in the grand sweep and wheel and march of the columns. The Circassian chiefs, in their steel skull-caps and shirts of chain mail seemed to have ridden into their places direct from the Crusades. The Cossacks of the Don, the Ukraine, and the Ural, managed their little brown or black horses (each regiment having its own color) so wonderfully, that, as we looked down upon them, each line resembled a giant caterpillar, moving sidewise with its thousand legs creeping as one. These novel and picturesque elements constituted the principal charm of the spectacle.

The passing away of winter was signalized by an increase of daylight rather than a decrease of cold. The rivers were still locked, the ice-hills frequented, the landscape dull and dead; but by the beginning of February we could detect signs of the returning sun. When the sky was clear (a thing of rarest occurrence), there was *white* light at noonday, instead of the mournful yellow or orange gloom of the previous two months. After the change had fairly set in, it proceeded more and more rapidly, until our sunshine was increased at the rate of seven or eight minutes per day. When the vernal equinox came, and we could sit down to dinner at sunset, the spell of death seemed to be at last broken. The fashionable drive, of an afternoon, changed from the Nevskoi Prospekt to the Palace Quay on the Neva; the Summer Garden was cleared of snow, and its statues one by one unboxed; in fine days we could walk there, and there coax back the faded color to a child's face. There, too, walked Alexander II., one of the crowd, leading his little daughter by the hand; and thither, in a plain little *calèche*, drove the Empress, with her youngest baby on her lap.

But when the first ten days of April had passed and there was still no sign of spring, we began to grow impatient. How often I watched the hedges around the Michaïloffsky Palace, knowing that the buds would there first swell! How we longed for a shimmer of green under the brown grass, an alder tassel, a flush of yellow on the willow wands, a sight of rushing green water! One day, a week or so later, we were engaged to dine on Vassili Ostrow. I had been busily occupied until late in the afternoon, and when we drove out upon the square, I glanced, as usual, towards Peter the Great. Lo! behind him flashed and glittered the free, the rejoicing Neva! Here and there floated a cake of sullen ice, but the great river had bared his breast to the sun, which welcomed him after six months of absence. The upper pontoon-bridges were already spanned and crowded with travel, but the lower one, carried away before it could be secured, had been borne down by the stream and jammed against and under the solid granite and iron of the Nikolaï Bridge. There was a terrible crowd and confusion at the latter place; all travel was stopped, and we could get neither forward nor backward. Presently, however, the Emperor appeared upon the scene; order was the instant result; the slow officials worked with a will; and we finally reached our host's residence half an hour behind the time. As we returned, at night, there was twilight along the northern sky, and the stars sparkled on the crystal bosom of the river.

This was the snapping of winter's toughest fetter, but it was not yet spring. Before I could detect any sign of returning life in Nature, May had come. Then, little by little, the twigs in the marshy thickets began to show yellow and purple and brown, the lilac-buds to swell, and some blades of fresh grass to peep forth in sheltered places. This, although we had sixteen hours of sunshine, with an evening twilight which shifted into dusky dawn under the North Star! I think it was on the 13th of May that I first realized that the season had changed, and for the last time saw the noble-hearted ruler who is the central figure of these memories. The People's Festival — a sort of Russian May-day — took place at Catharinenhof, a park and palace of the famous Empress, near the shore of the Finnish Gulf. The festival, that year, had an unusual significance. On the 3d of March the edict of Emancipation was finally consummated, and twenty-two millions of serfs became forever free: the Polish troubles and the menace of the Western powers had consolidated the restless nobles, the patient people, and the plotting revolutionists, the orthodox and dissenting sects, into one great national party, resolved to support the Emperor and maintain the integrity of the Russian territory: and thus the nation was marvelously strengthened by the very blow intended to cripple it.

At least a hundred thousand of the common people (possibly, twice that number) were gathered together in the park of Catharinenhof. There were booths, shows, flying-horses, refreshment saloons, jugglers, circuses, balloons, and exhibitions of all kinds: the sky was fair, the turf green and elastic, and the swelling birch-buds scented the air. I wandered about for hours, watching the lazy, contented people, as they leaped and ran, rolled on the grass, pulled off their big boots and aired their naked legs, or laughed and sang in jolly chorus. About three in the afternoon there was a movement in the main avenue of the park. Hundreds of young *mujiks* appeared, running at full speed, shouting out, tossing their caps high in the air, and giving their long, blonde locks to the wind. Instantly the crowd collected on each side, many springing like cats into the trees; booths and shows were deserted, and an immense multitude hedged the avenue. Behind the leaping, shouting, cap-tossing *avant-garde* came the Emperor, with three sons and a dozen generals, on horseback, cantering lightly. One cheer went up from scores of thousands; hats darkened the air; eyes blazing with filial veneration followed the stately figure of the monarch, as he passed by, gratefully smiling and greeting on either hand. I stood among the people and watched their faces. I saw the phlegmatic Slavonic features transformed with a sudden and powerful expression of love, of devotion, of gratitude, and then I knew that the throne of Alexander II. rested on a better basis than tradition or force. I saw therein another side of this shrewd, cunning, patient, and childlike race, whom no other European race yet understands and appreciates — a race yet in the germ, but with qualities out of which a people, in the best sense of the word, may be developed.

The month of May was dark, rainy, and cold; and when I left St. Petersburg, at its close, everybody said that a few days would bring the summer. The leaves were opening, almost visibly from hour to hour. Winter was really over, and summer was just at the door; but I found, upon reflection, that I had not had the slightest experience of spring.

THE LITTLE LAND OF APPENZELL.

The traveller who first reaches the Lake of Constance at Lindau, or crosses that sheet of pale green water to one of the ports on the opposite Swiss shore, cannot fail to notice the bold heights to the southward which thrust themselves between the opening of the Rhine Valley and the long, undulating ridges of the Canton Thurgau. These heights, broken by many a dimly hinted valley and ravine, appear to be the front of an Alpine table-land. Houses and villages, scattered over the steep ascending plane, present themselves distinctly to the eye; the various green of forest and pasture land is rarely interrupted by the gray of rocky walls; and the afternoon sun touches the topmost edge of each successive elevation with a sharp outline of golden light, through the rich gloom of the shaded slopes. Behind and over this region rise the serrated peaks of the Sentis Alp, standing in advance of the farther ice-fields of Glarus, like an outer fortress, garrisoned in summer by the merest forlorn hope of snow.

The green fronts nearest the lake, and the lower lands falling away to the right and left, belong to the Canton of St. Gall; but all aloft, beyond that frontier marked by the sinking sun, lies the *Appenzeller Ländli*, as it is called in the endearing diminutive of the Swiss German tongue, — the Little Land of Appenzell.

If, leaving the Lake of Constance by the Rhine Valley, you ascend to Ragatz and the Baths of Pfeffers, thence turn westward to the Lake of Wallenstatt, cross into the valley of the Toggenburg, and so make your way northward and eastward around the base of the mountains back to the starting point, you will have passed only through the territory of St. Gall. Appenzell is an Alpine island, wholly surrounded by the former canton. From whatever side you approach, you must climb in order to get into it. It is a nearly circular tract, falling from the south towards the north, but lifted, at almost every point, over the adjoining lands. This altitude and isolation is an historical as well as a physical peculiarity. When the Abbots of St. Gall, after having reduced the entire population of what is now two cantons to serfdom, became more oppressive as their power increased, it was the mountain shepherds who, in the year 1403, struck the first blow for liberty. Once free, they kept their freedom, and established a rude democracy on the heights, similar in form and spirit to the league which the Forest Cantons had founded nearly a century before. An echo from the meadow of Grütli reached the wild valleys around the Sentis, and Appenzell, by the middle of the fifteenth century, became one of the original states out of which Switzerland has grown.

I find something very touching and admirable in this fragment of hardly noticed history. The people isolated themselves by their own act, held together, organized a simple yet sufficient government, and maintained their sturdy independence, while their brethren on every side, in the richer lands below them, were fast bound in the gyves of a priestly despotism. Individual liberty seems to be a condition inseparable from mountain life; that once attained, all other influences are conservative in their character. The cantons of Unterwalden, Schwytz, Glarus, and Appenzell retain to-day the simple, primitive forms of democracy which had their origin in the spirit of the people nearly six hundred years ago.

Twice had I looked up to the little mountain republic from the lower lands to the northward, with the desire and the determination to climb one day the green buttresses which support it on every side; so, when I left St. Gall on a misty morning, in a little open carriage, bound for Trogen, it was with the pleasant knowledge that a land almost unknown to tourists lay before me. The only summer visitors are invalids, mostly from Eastern Switzerland and Germany, who go up to drink the whey of goats' milk; and, although the fabrics woven by the people are known to the world of fashion in all countries, few indeed are the travellers who turn aside from the near highways. The landlord in St. Gall told me that his guests were almost wholly commercial travellers, and my subsequent experience among an unspoiled people convinced me that I was almost a pioneer in the paths I traversed.

It was the last Saturday in April, and at least a month too soon for the proper enjoyment of the journey; but on the following day the *Landsgemeinde*, or Assembly of the People, was to be held at Hundwyl, in the manner and with the ceremonies which have been annually observed for the last three or four hundred years. This circumstance determined the time of my visit. I wished to study the character of an Alpine democracy, so pure that it has not yet adopted even the representative principle, — to be with and among a portion of the Swiss people at a time when they are most truly themselves, rather than look at them through the medium of conventional guides, on lines of travel which have now lost everything of Switzerland except the scenery.

There was bad weather behind, and, I feared, bad weather before me. "The sun will soon drive away these mists," said the postilion, "and when we get up yonder, you will see what a prospect there will be." In the rich valley of St. Gall, out of which we mounted, the scattered houses and cloud-like belts of blossoming cherry-trees almost hid the green; but it sloped up and down, on either side of the rising road, glittering with flowers and dew, in the flying gleams of sunshine. Over us hung masses of gray cloud, which stretched across the valley, hooded the opposite hills, and sank into a dense mass over the Lake of Constance. As we passed through this belt, and rejoiced in the growing clearness of the upper sky, I saw that my only prospect would be in cloud-land. After many windings, along which the blossoms and buds of the fruit-trees indicated the altitude as exactly as any barometer, we finally reached the crest of the topmost height, the frontier of Appenzell and the battle-field of Vöglisegg, where the herdsman first measured his strength with the soldier and the monk, and was victorious.

"Whereabouts was the battle fought?" I asked the postilion.

"Up and down, and all around here," said he, stopping the carriage at the summit.

I stood up and looked to the north. Seen from above, the mist had gathered into dense, rounded clouds, touched with silver on their upper edges. They hung over the lake, rolling into every bay and spreading from shore to shore, so that not a gleam of water was visible; but over their heaving and tossing silence rose, far away, the mountains of the four German states beyond the lake. An Alp in Vorarlberg made a shining island in the sky. The postilion was loud in his regrets, yet I thought the picture best as it was. On the right lay the land of Appenzell — not a table-land, but a region of mountain ridge and summit, of valley and deep, dark gorge, green as emerald up to the line of snow, and so thickly studded with dwellings, grouped or isolated, that there seemed to be one scattered village as far as the eye could reach. To the south, over forests of fir, the Sentis lifted his huge towers of rock, crowned with white, wintry pyramids.

"Here, where we are," said the postilion, "was the first battle; but there was another, two years afterwards, over there, the other side of Trogen, where the road goes down to the Rhine. Stoss is the place, and there's a chapel built on the very spot. Duke Frederick of Austria came to help the Abbot Kuno, and the Appenzellers were only one to ten against them. It was a great fight, they say, and the women helped — not with pikes and guns, but in this way: they put on white shirts, and came out of the woods, above where the fighting was going on. Now, when the Austrians and the Abbot's people saw them, they thought there were spirits helping the Appenzellers (the women were all white, you see, and too far off to show plainly), and so they gave up the fight after losing nine hundred knights and troopers. After that, it was ordered that the women should go first to the sacrament, so that no man might forget the help they gave in that battle. And the people go every year to the chapel, on the same day when it took place."

I looked, involuntarily, to find some difference in the population after passing the frontier. But I had not counted upon the leveling influence which the same kind of labor exercises, whether upon mountain or in valley. So long as Appenzell was a land of herdsmen, many peculiarities of costume, features, and manners must have remained. For a long time, however, Outer-Rhoden, as this part of the Canton is called, has shared with that part of St. Gall which lies below it the manufacture of fine muslins and embroideries. There are looms in almost every house, and this fact explains the density of population and the signs of wealth on every hand, which would otherwise puzzle the stranger. The houses are not only so near together that almost every man can call to his neighbors and be heard, but they are large, stately, and even luxurious, in contrast to the dwellings of other country people in Europe. The average population of Outer-Rhoden amounts to four hundred and seventy-five persons to the square mile, being nearly double that of the most thickly settled portions of Holland.

If one could only transport a few of these houses to the United States! Our country architecture is not only hideous, but frequently unpractical, being at worst shanties, and at best city residences set in the fields. An Appenzell farmer lives in a house from forty to sixty feet square, and rarely less than four stories in height. The two upper stories, however, are narrowed by the high, steep roof, so that the true front of the house is one of the gables. The roof projects at least four feet on all sides, giving shelter to balconies of carved wood, which cross the front under each row of windows. The outer walls are covered with upright, overlapping shingles, not more than two or three inches broad, and rounded at the ends, suggesting the scale armor of ancient times. This covering secures the greatest warmth; and when the shingles have aquired from age that rich burnt-sienna tint which no paint could exactly imitate, the effect is exceedingly beautiful. The lowest story is generally of stone, plastered and whitewashed. The stories are low (seven to eight feet), but the windows are placed side by side, and each room is thoroughly lighted. Such a house is very warm, very durable, and, without any apparent expenditure of ornament, is externally so picturesque that no ornament could improve it.

Many of the dwellings, I was told, could not be built with the present means of the population, at the present prices of labor and material. They date from the palmy days of Appenzell industry, before machinery had reduced the cost of the finer fabrics. Then, one successful manufacturer competed with another in the erection of showy houses, and fifty thousand francs (a large sum for the times) were frequently expended on a single dwelling. The view of a broad Alpine landscape, dotted all over with such beautiful homes, from the little shelf of green hanging on the sides of a rocky gorge and the strips of sunny pasture between the ascending forests, to the very summits of the lower heights and the saddles between them, was something quite new in my experience.

Turning around the point of Vöglisegg, we made for Trogen, one of the two capitals of Outer-Rhoden, which lay before us, across the head of the deep and wild St.

Martin's Tobel. (*Tobel* is an Appenzell word, corresponding precisely to the *gulch* of California.) My postilion mounted, and the breathed horse trotted merrily along the winding level. One stately house after another, with a clump of fruit-trees on the sheltered side, and a row of blooming hyacinths and wall-flowers on the balcony, passed by on either side. The people we met were sunburnt and ugly, but there was a rough air of self-reliance about them, and they gave me a hearty "God greet you!" one and all. Just before reaching Trogen, the postilion pointed to an old, black, tottering platform of masonry, rising out of a green slope of turf on the right. The grass around it seemed ranker than elsewhere.

This was the place of execution, where capital criminals are still beheaded with the sword, in the sight of the people. The postilion gave me an account, with all the horrible details, of the last execution, only three years ago, — how the murderer would not confess until he was brought out of prison to hear the bells tolling for his victim's funeral, — how thereupon he was sentenced, and — but I will not relate further. I have always considered the death penalty a matter of policy rather than principle; but the sight of that blood-stained platform, the blood-fed weeds around it, and the vision of the headsman, in his red mantle, looking down upon the bared neck stretched upon the block, gave me more horror of the custom than all the books and speeches which have been said and written against it.

At Trogen I stopped at the principal inn, two centuries old, the quaint front painted in fresco, the interior neat and fresh as a new toy — a very gem of a house! The floor upon which I entered from the street was paved with flat stones. A solid wooden staircase, dark with age, led to the guests' room in the second story. One side of this room was given up to the windows, and there was a charming hexagonal oriel in the corner. The low ceiling was of wood, in panels, the stove a massive tower, faced with porcelain tiles, the floor polished nearly into whiteness, and all the doors, cup-boards, and tables, made of brown nut-wood, gave an air of warmth and elegance to the apartment. All other parts of the house were equally neat and orderly. The hostess greeted me with, "Be you welcome!" and set about preparing dinner, as it was now nearly noon. In the pauses of her work she came into the room to talk, and was very ready to give information concerning the country and people.

There were already a little table and three plates in the oriel, and while I was occupied with my own dinner I did not particularly notice the three persons who sat down to theirs. The coarseness and harshness of their dialect, however, presently struck my ear. It was pure Appenzell, a German made up of singular and puzzling elisions, and with a very strong guttural k and g, in addition to the ch. Some knowledge of the Alemannic dialect of the Black Forest enabled me to understand the subject of conversation, which, to my surprise, was — the study of the classics! It was like hearing an Irishman talk of Shelley's "Witch of Atlas" in the broadest Tipperary brogue. I turned and looked at the persons. They were well dressed young men, evidently the best class of Appenzellers — possibly tutors in the schools of Trogen. Their speech in no wise differed from that of the common herdsmen, except that they were now and then obliged to use words which, being unknown to the people, had escaped mutilation. I entered into conversation, to ascertain whether true German was not possible to them, since they must needs read and write the language; but, although they understood me, they could only partly, and with evident difficulty, lay aside their own patois. I found this to be the case everywhere throughout the Canton. It is a circumstance so unusual, that, in spite of myself, associating a rude dialect with ignorance, I was always astonished when those who spoke it showed culture and knowledge of the world.

The hostess provided me with a guide and pack-bearer, and I set out on foot across the country towards Hundwyl. This guide, Jakob by name, made me imagine that I had come among a singular people. He was so short that he could easily walk under my arm; his gait was something between a roll and a limp, although he stoutly disclaimed lameness; he laughed whenever I spoke to him, and answered in a voice which seemed the cuneiform character put into sound. First, there was an explosion of gutturals, and then came a loud trumpet-tone, something like the *Honk! honk!* of wild geese. Yet, when he placed his squat figure behind a tavern table, and looked at me quietly with his mouth shut, he was both handsome and distinguished in appearance. We walked two miles together before I guessed how to unravel his speech. It is almost as difficult to learn a dialect as a new language, and but for the key which the Alemannic gave me, I should have been utterly at sea. Who, for instance, could ever guess that *a'Ma' g'si*, pronounced "ama*x*i" (the *x* representing a desperate guttural), really stands for *einen Mann gewesen*?

The road was lively with country people, many of whom were travelling in our own direction. Those we met invariably addressed us with "God. greet you!" or "*Guät ti!*" which it was easy to translate into "Good-day!" Some of the men were brilliant in scarlet jackets, with double rows of square silver buttons, and carried swords under their arms; they were bound for the *Landsgemeinde*, whither the law of the Middle Ages still obliges them to go armed. When I asked Jakob if he would accompany me as far as Hundwyl, he answered, "I can't; I daren't go there without a black dress, and my sword, and a cylinder hat."

The wild *Tobels*, opening downward to the Lake of Constance, which now shimmered afar through the gaps, were left behind us, and we passed westward along a broken, irregular valley. The vivid turf was sown with all the flowers of spring, — primrose, violet, buttercup, anemone, and veronica, — faint, but sweetest-odored, and the heralds of spring in all lands. So I gave little heed to the weird lines of cloud, twisting through and between the severed pyramids of the Sentis, as if weaving the woof of storms. The scenery was entirely lovely, and so novel in its population and the labor which, in the long course of time, had effaced its own hard traces, turning the mountains into lifted lawns and parks of human delight, that my own slow feet carried me through it too rapidly. We must have passed a slight water-shed somewhere, though I observed none; for the road gradually fell towards another region of deeply cloven *Tobels*, with snowy mountains beyond. The green of the landscape was so brilliant and uniform, under the cold gray sky, that it almost destroyed the perspective, which rather depended on the houses and the scattered woods of fir.

On a ridge, overlooking all this region, was the large village of Teufen, nearly as grand as Trogen in its architecture. Here Jakob, whose service went no further, conducted me to the "Pike" inn, and begged the landlady to furnish me with "*a' Ma'*" in his place. We had refreshments together, and took leave with many shakings of the hand and mutual wishes of good luck. The successor was an old fellow of seventy, who had been a soldier in Holland, and who with proper exertion could make his speech intelligible. The people nowhere inquired after my business or nationality. When the guide made the latter known, they almost invariably said, "But, of course, you were born in Appenzell?" The idea of a traveller coming among them, at least during this season of the year, did not enter their heads. In Teufen, the large and handsome houses, the church and schools, led me, foolishly, to hope for a less barbarous dialect; but no, it was the same thing everywhere.

The men in black, with swords under their arms, increased in number as we left the village. They were probably from the furthest parts of the Canton, and were thus abridging the morrow's journey. The most of them, however turned aside from the road, and made their way to one farm-house or another. I was tempted to follow their example, as I feared that the little village of Hundwyl would be crowded. But there was still time to claim private hospitality, even if this should be the case, so we marched steadily down the valley. The Sitter, a stream fed by the Sentis, now roared below us, between high, rocky walls, which are spanned by an iron bridge, two hundred feet above the water. The roads of Outer-Rhoden, built and kept in order by the people, are most admirable. This little population of forty-eight thousand souls has within the last fifteen years expended seven hundred thousand dollars on means of communication. Since the people govern themselves, and regulate their expenses, and consequently their taxation, their willingness to bear such a burden is a lesson to other lands.

After crossing the airy bridge, our road climbed along the opposite side of the *Tobel*, to a village on a ridge thrust out from the foot of the Hundwyl Alp, beyond which we lost sight of Teufen and the beautiful valley of the Sitter. We were now in the valley of the Urnäsch, and a walk of two miles more brought us to the village of Hundwyl. I was encouraged, on approaching the little place, by seeing none except the usual signs of occupation. There was a great new tank before the fountain, and two or three fellows in scarlet vests were filling their portable tubs for the evening's supply; a few children came to the doors to stare at me, but there was no sign that any other stranger had arrived.

"I'll take you to the Crown," said the guide; "all the Landamänner will be there in the morning, and the music; and you'll see what our Appenzell government is." The landlady gave me a welcome, and the promise of a lodging, whereupon I sat down in peace, received the greetings of all the members of the family, as they came and went, and made myself familiar with their habits. There was only one other guest in the house, — a man of dignified face and intellectual head, who carried a sword tied up with an umbrella, and must be, I supposed, one of the chief officials. He had so much the air of a reformer or a philosopher that the members of a certain small faction at home might have taken him for their beloved W. P.; others might have detected in him a resemblance to that true philanthropist and gentleman W. L. G.; and the believers in the divinity of slavery would have accepted him as Bishop ———. As no introductions are required in Appenzell, I addressed myself to him, hoping to open a profitable acquaintance; but it was worse than Coleridge's experience with the lover of dumplings. His sentiments may have been elevated and refined, for aught I knew, but what were they? My trumpeter Jakob was more intelligible than he; his upper teeth were gone, and the mutilated words were mashed out of all remaining shape against his gums. Then he had the singular habit of ejaculating the word *Ja!* (Yes!) in three different ways, after answering each of my questions. First, a decided, confirmatory *Ja!* then a pause, followed by a slow, interrogative *Ja?* as if it were the echo of some mental doubt; and finally, after a much longer pause, a profoundly melancholy, desponding, conclusive *Ja-a-a!* sighed forth from the very bottom of his lungs. Even when I only said, "Good-morning!" the next day, these ejaculations followed, in the same order of succession.

One may find a counterpart to this habit in the *Wa'al* of the Yankee, except that the latter never is, nor could it well be, so depressing to hear as the *Ja* of Appenzell.

In the evening a dozen persons gathered around one of the long tables, and drank a pale, weak cider, made of apples and pears, and called "Most." I gave to one, with whom I found I could converse most easily, a glass of red wine, whereupon he said, "It is very impudent in me to take it."

Upon asking the same person how it was that I could understand him so much more readily than the others, he answered, "O, I can talk the written language when I try, but these others can't."

"Here," said I, pointing to the philosopher, "is one who is quite incomprehensible."

"So he is to me."

They were all anxious to know whether our American troubles were nearly over; whether the President had the power to do further harm (he had too much power, they all thought); and whether our Congress could carry out its plan of reconstruction. Lincoln they said, was the best man we ever had; when the play of "Lincoln's Death" was performed in the theatre at St. Gall, a great many Appenzellers hired omnibuses and went down from the mountains to see it.

I was aroused at daybreak by the chiming of bells, and soon afterwards muskets began to crack, near and far. Then there were noises all over the house, and presently what seemed to be a procession of horses or elephants began to thunder up and down the wooden stairs. In vain I tried to snatch the last and best morning nap; there was no end to the racket. So I arose, dressed, and went forth to observe. The inn was already transformed, from top to bottom, into a vast booth for meat and drink. Bedding and all other furniture had disappeared; every room, and even the open hall on each story, was filled with tables, benches, and chairs. My friend of the previous evening, who was going about with a white apron on and sleeves rolled up, said to me: "I am to be one of the waiters to-day. We have already made places for six hundred."

There were at least a dozen other amateur waiters on hand and busy. The landlord wore a leathern apron, and went from room to room, blowing into the hole of a wooden tap which he carried in his hand, as if thereby to collect his ideas. A barrel of red and a barrel of white wine stood on trestles in the guests' room, and they were already filling the schoppins by hundreds and ranging them on shelves, — honestly filling, not as lager-bier is filled in New York, one third foam, but waiting until the froth subsided, and then pouring to the very brim. In the kitchen there were three fires blazing, stacks of *Bratwurst* on the tables, great kettles for the sour-krout and potatoes; and eggs, lettuce, and other finer viands, for the dignitaries, on the shelves. "Good morning," said the landlady, as I looked into this sanctuary, "you see we are ready for them."

While I was taking my coffee, the landlord called the waiters together, gave each a bag of small money for change, and then delivered a short, practical address concerning their duties for the day, — who were to be trusted and who not, how to keep order and prevent impatience, and, above all, how to preserve a proper circulation, in order that the greatest possible number of persons might be entertained. He closed with: "Once again, take notice and don't forget, every one of you, — *Most* 10 rappen (2 cents), bread 10, *Wurst* 15, tongue 10, wine 25 and 40," etc.

In the village there were signs of preparation, but not a dozen strangers had arrived. Wooden booths had been built against some of the houses, and the owners thereof were arranging their stores of gingerbread and coarse confectionery; on the open, grassy square, in front of the parsonage, stood a large platform, with a handsome railing around it, but the green slope of the hill in front was as deserted as an Alpine pasture. Looking westward over the valley, however, I could already see dark figures moving along the distant paths. The morning was overcast, but the Hundwyl Alp, streaked with snow, stood clear, and there was a prospect of good weather for the important day. As I loitered about the village, talking with the people, who, busy as they were, always found time for a friendly word, the movement in the landscape increased. Out of firwoods, and over the ridges and out of the foldings of the hills, came the Appenzellers, growing into groups, and then into lines, until steady processions began to enter Hundwyl by every road. Every man was dressed in black, with a rusty stove-pipe hat on his head, and a sword and umbrella in his hand or under his arm.

From time to time the church bells chimed; a brass band played the old melodies of the Canton; on each side of the governing Landamman's place on the platform stood a huge two-handed sword, centuries old, and the temper of the gathering crowd became earnest and solemn. Six old men, armed with pikes, walked about with an air of importance: their duty was to preserve order, but they had nothing to do. Policeman other than these, or soldier, was not to be seen; each man was a part of the government, and felt his responsibility. Carriages, light carts, and hay wagons, the latter filled with patriotic singers, now began to arrive, and I took my way to the "Crown," in order to witness the arrival of the members of the Council.

In order to make the proceedings of the day more intelligible, I must first briefly sketch certain features of this little democracy, which it possesses in common with three other mountain cantons — the primitive forms which the republican principle assumed in Switzerland. In the first place the government is only representative so far as is required for its permanent, practical operation. The highest power in the land is the *Landsgemeinde*, or General Assembly of the People, by whom the members of the Executive Council are elected, and who alone can change, adopt, or abolish any law. All citizens above the age of eighteen, and all other Swiss citizens after a year's residence in the Canton, are not only allowed, but required, to attend the *Landsgemeinde*. There is a penalty for non-attendance. Outer-Rhoden contains forty-eight thousand inhabitants, of whom eleven thousand are under obligations to be present and vote, from beginning to end of the deliberations.

In Glarus and Unterwalden, where the population is smaller, the right of discussion is still retained by these assemblies, but in Appenzell it has been found expedient to abolish it. Any change in the law, however, is first discussed in public meetings in the several communities, then put into form by the Council, published, read from all the pulpits for a month previous to the coming together of the *Landsgemeinde*, and then voted upon. But if the Council refuses to act upon the suggestion of any citizen whomsoever, and he honestly considers the matter one of importance, he is allowed to propose it directly to the people, provided he do so briefly and in an orderly manner. The Council, which may be called the executive power, consists of the governing Landamman and six associates, one of whom has the functions of treasurer, another of military commander, — in fact, a ministry on a small scale. The service of the persons elected to the Council is obligatory, and they receive no salaries. There is, it is true, a secondary Council, composed of the first, and representatives of the communities, one for every thousand inhabitants, in order to administer more intelligently the various departments of education, religion, justice, roads, the militia system, the poor, etc.; but the Assembly of the People can at any time reject or reverse its action. All citizens are not only equal before the law, but are assured liberty of conscience, of speech, and of labor. The right of support only belongs to those who are born citizens of the Canton. The old restriction of the *Heimathsrecht*, — the claim to be supported at the expense of the community in case of need, — narrow and illiberal as it seems to us, prevails all over Switzerland. In Appenzell a stranger can only acquire the right, which is really the right of citizenship, by paying twelve hundred francs into the cantonal treasury.

The governing Landamman is elected for two years, but the other members of the Council may be reëlected from year to year, as often as the people see fit. The obligation to serve, therefore, may sometimes seriously incommode the person chosen; he cannot resign, and his only chance of escape lies in leaving the Canton temporarily, and publishing his intention of quitting it altogether in case the people refuse to release him from office! This year, it happened that two members of the Council had already taken this step, while three others had appealed to the people not to reëlect them. The *Landsgemeinde* at Hundwyl was to decide upon all these applications, and therefore promised to be of more than usual interest. The people had had time to consider the matter, and it was supposed had generally made up their minds; yet I found no one willing to give me a hint of their action in advance.

The two remaining members presently made their appearance, accompanied by the Chancellor, to whom I was recommended. The latter kindly offered to accompany me to the parsonage, the windows of which, directly in the rear of the platform, would enable me to hear, as well as see the proceedings. The clergyman, who was preparing for the service which precedes the opening of the *Landsgemeinde*, showed me the nail upon which hung the key of the study, and gave me liberty to take possession at any time. The clock now struck nine, and a solemn peal of bells announced the time of service. A little procession formed in front of the inn; first the music, then the clergyman and the few members of the government, bareheaded, and followed by the two *Weibels* (apparitors), who wore long mantles, the right half white and the left half black. The old pikemen walked on either side. The people uncovered as the dignitaries took their way around the church to the chancel door; then as many as could be accommodated entered at the front.

I entered with them, taking my place on the men's side,

— the sexes being divided, as is usual in Germany. After the hymn, in which boy's voices were charmingly heard, and the prayer, the clergyman took a text from Corinthians, and proceeded to preach a good, sound political sermon, which, nevertheless, did not in the least shock the honest piety of his hearers. I noticed with surprise that most of the men put on their hats at the close of the prayer. Only once did they remove them afterwards, — when the clergyman, after describing the duties before them, and the evils and difficulties which beset every good work, suddenly said, "Let us pray to God to help and direct us!" and interpolated a short prayer in the midst of his sermon. The effect was all the more impressive, because, though so unexpected, it was entirely simple and natural. These democrats of Appenzell have not yet made the American discovery that pulpits are profaned by any utterance of national sentiment, or any application of Christian doctrine to politics. They even hold their municipal elections in the churches, and consider that the act of voting is thereby solemnized, not that the holy building is desecrated! But then, you will say, this is the democracy of the Middle Ages.

When the service was over, I could scarcely make my way through the throng which had meanwhile collected. The sun had come out hot above the Hundwyl Alp, and turned the sides of the valley into slopes of dazzling sheen. Already every table in the inns was filled, every window crowded with heads, the square a dark mass of voters of all ages and classes, lawyers and clergymen being packed together with grooms and brown Alpine herdsmen; and, after the government had been solemnly escorted to its private chamber, four musicians in antique costume announced, with drum and fife, the speedy opening of the Assembly. But first came the singing societies of Herisau, and forced their way into the centre of the throng, where they sang, simply yet grandly, the songs of Appenzell. The people listened with silent satisfaction; not a man seemed to think of applauding.

I took my place in the pastor's study, and inspected the crowd. On the steep slope of the village square and the rising field beyond, more than ten thousand men were gathered, packed as closely as they could stand. The law requires them to appear armed and "respectably dressed." The short swords, very much like our marine cutlasses, which they carried, were intended for show rather than service. Very few wore them: sometimes they were tied up with umbrellas, but generally carried loose in the hand or under the arm. The rich manufacturers of Trogen and Herisau and Teufen had belts and silver-mounted dress-swords. With scarce an exception, every man was habited in black, and wore a stove-pipe hat, but the latter was in most cases brown and battered. Both circumstances were thus explained to me: as the people vote with the uplifted hand, the hat must be of a dark color, as a background, to bring out the hands more distinctly; then, since rain would spoil a good hat (and it rains much at this season), they generally take an old one. I could now understand the advertisements of "second hand cylinder hats for sale," which I had noticed, the day before, in the newspapers of the Canton. The slope of the hill was such that the hats of the lower ranks concealed the faces of those immediately behind, and the assembly was the darkest and densest I ever beheld. Here and there the top of a scarlet waistcoat flashed out of the cloud with astonishing brilliancy.

With solemn music, and attended by the apparitors, in their two colored mantles, and the ancient pikemen, the few officials ascended the platform. The chief of the two Landammänner present took his station in front, between the two-handed swords, and began to address the assembly. Suddenly a dark cloud seemed to roll away from the faces of the people; commencing in front of the platform, and spreading rapidly to the edges of the compact throng, the hats disappeared, and the ten thousand faces, in the full light of the sun, blended into a ruddy mass. But no; each head retained its separate character, and the most surprising circumstance of the scene was the distinctness with which each human being held fast to his individuality in the multitude. Nature has drawn no object with so firm a hand, nor painted it with such tenacious clearness of color, as the face of man. The inverted crescent of sharp light had a different curve on each individual brow before me; the little illuminated dot on the end of the nose under it hinted at the form of the nostrils in shadow. As the hats had before concealed the faces, so now each face was relieved against the breast of the man beyond, and in front of me were thousands of heads to be seen, touching each other like so many ovals drawn on a dark plane.

The address was neither so brief nor so practical as it might have been. Earnest, well meant, and apparently well received, there was nevertheless much in it which the plain, semi-educated weavers and Alpadores in the assembly could not possibly have comprehended; as, for instance, " May a garland of confidence be twined around your deliberations!" At the close, the speaker said, "Let us pray!" and for a few moments there were bowed heads and utter silence. The first business was the financial report for the year, which had been printed and distributed among the people weeks before. They were now asked whether they would appoint a commission to test its accuracy, but they unanimously declined to do so. The question was put by one of the apparitors, who first removed his cocked hat, and cried, in a tremendous voice, "Faithful and beloved fellow-citizens, and brethren of the Union!"

Now came the question of releasing the tired Landammänner of the previous year from office. The first application in order was that of the governing Landamman, Dr. Zürcher. The people voted directly thereupon; there was a strong division of sentiment, but the majority allowed him to resign. His place was therefore to be filled at once. The names of candidates were called out by the crowd. There were six in all; and as both the members of the Council were among them, the latter summoned six well-known citizens upon the platform, to decide the election. The first vote reduced the number of candidates to two, and the voting was then repeated until one of these received an undoubted majority. Dr. Roth, of Teufen, was the fortunate man. As soon as the decision was announced, several swords were held up in the crowd to indicate where the new governor was to be found. The musicians and pikemen made a lane to him through the multitude, and he was conducted to the platform with the sound of fife and drum. He at once took his place between the swords, and made a brief address, which the people heard with uncovered heads. He did not yet, however, assume the black silk mantle which belongs to his office. He was a man of good presence, prompt, and self-possessed in manner, and conducted the business of the day very successfully.

The election of the remaining members occupied much more time. All the five applicants were released from service, and with scarcely a dissenting hand: wherein, I thought, the people showed very good sense. The case of one of these officials, Herr Euler, was rather hard. He was the *Landessäckelmeister* (Treasurer), and the law makes him personally responsible for every farthing which passes through his hands. Having, with the consent of the Council, invested thirty thousand francs in a banking-house at Rheineck, the failure of the house obliged him to pay this sum out of his own pocket. He did so, and then made preparations to leave the Canton in case his resignation was not accepted.

For most of the places from ten to fourteen candidates were named, and when these were reduced to two, nearly equally balanced in popular favor, the voting became very spirited. The apparitor, who was chosen on account of his strength of voice (the candidates for the office must be tested in this respect), had hard work that day. The same formula must be repeated before every vote, in this wise: "Herr Landamman, gentlemen, faithful and beloved fellow-citizens and brethren of the Union, if it seems good to you to choose so-and-so, as your treasurer for the coming year, so lift up your hands!" Then, all over the dark mass, thousands of hands flew into the sunshine, rested a moment, and gradually sank with a fluttering motion, which made me think of leaves flying from a hill-side forest in the autumn winds. As each election was decided, and the choice was announced, swords were lifted to show the location of the new official in the crowd, and he was then brought upon the platform with fife and drum. Nearly two hours elapsed before the gaps were filled, and the government was again complete.

Then followed the election of judges for the judicial districts, who, in most cases, were almost unanimously re-elected. These are repeated from year to year, so long as the people are satisfied. Nearly all the citizens of Outer-Rhoden were before me; I could distinctly see three fourths of their faces, and I detected no expression except that of a grave, conscientious interest in the proceedings. Their patience was remarkable. Closely packed, man against man, in the hot, still sunshine, they stood quietly for nearly three hours, and voted upwards of two hundred and seven times before the business of the day was completed. A few old men on the edges of the crowd slipped away for a quarter of an hour, in order, as one of them told me, "to keep their stomachs from giving way entirely," and some of the younger fellows took a schoppin of *Most* for the same purpose; but they generally returned and resumed their places as soon as refreshed.

The close of the *Landsgemeinde* was one of the most impressive spectacles I ever witnessed. When the elections were over and no further duty remained, the Pastor Etter of Hundwyl ascended the platform. The governing Landamman assumed his black mantle of office, and, after a brief prayer, took the oath of inauguration from the clergyman. He swore to further the prosperity and honor of the land, to ward off misfortune from it, to uphold the Constitution and laws, to protect the widows and orphans, and to secure the equal rights of all, nor through favor, hostility, gifts, or promises to be turned aside from doing the same. The clergyman repeated the oath sentence by sentence, both holding up the oath-fingers of the right hand, the people looking on silent and uncovered.

The governing Landamman now turned to the assembly, and read them their oath, that they likewise should further the honor and prosperity of the land, preserve its freedom and its equal rights, obey the laws, protect the Council and the judges, take no gift or favor from any prince or potentate, and that each one should accept and perform, to the best of his ability, any service to which he might be chosen. After this had been read, the Landamman lifted his right hand, with the oath-fingers extended; his colleagues on the platform, and every men of the ten or eleven thousand present did the same. The silence was so profound that the chirp of a bird on the hillside took entire possession of the air. Then the Landamman slowly and solemnly spoke these words: "I have well understood that — which has been read to me; — I will always and exactly observe it, — faithfully and without reservation, — so truly as I wish and pray — that God help me!" At each pause, the same words were repeated by every man, in a low, subdued tone. The hush was else so complete, the words were spoken with such measured firmness, that I caught each as it came, not as from the lips of men, but from a vast supernatural murmur in the air. The effect was indescribable. Far off on the horizon was the white vision of an Alp, but all the hidden majesty of those supreme mountains was nothing to the scene before me. When the last words had been spoken, the hands sank slowly, and the crowd stood a moment locked together, with grave faces and gleaming eyes, until the spirit that had descended upon them passed. Then they dissolved; the *Landsgemeinde* was over.

In my inn, I should think more than the expected six hundred had found place. From garret to cellar, every corner was occupied; bread, wine, and steamy dishes passed in a steady whirl from kitchen and tap-room into all the roaring chambers. In the other inns it was the same, and many took their drink and provender in the open air. I met my philosopher of the previous evening, who said, "Now, what do you think of our *Landsgemeinde?*" and followed my answer with his three *Ja's*, the last a more desponding sigh than ever. Since the business was over, I judged that the people would be less reserved — which, indeed, was the case. Nearly all with whom I spoke expressed their satisfaction with the day's work. I walked through the crowds in all directions, vainly seeking for personal beauty. There were few women present, but a handsome man is only less beautiful than a beautiful woman, and I like to look at the former when the latter is absent. I was surprised at the great proportion of undersized men; only weaving, in close rooms, for several generations, could have produced so many squat bodies and short legs. The Appenzellers are neither a handsome nor a picturesque race, and their language harmonizes with their features; but I learned, during that day at Hundwyl, to like and to respect them.

Pastor Etter insisted on my dining with him; two younger clergymen were also guests, and my friend the Chancellor Engwiller came to make further kind offers of service. The people of each parish, I learned, elect their own pastor, and pay him his salary. In municipal matters the same democratic system prevails as in the cantonal government. Education is well provided for, and the morals of the community are watched and guarded by a committee consisting of the pastor and two officials elected by the people. Outer-Rhoden is almost exclusively Protestant, while Inner-Rhoden — the mountain region around the Sentis — is Catholic. Although thus geographically and politically connected, there was formerly little intercourse between the inhabitants of the two parts of the Canton, owing to their religious differences; but now they come together in a friendly way, and are beginning to intermarry.

After dinner, the officials departed in carriages, to the sound of trumpets, and thousands of the people followed. Again the roads and paths leading away over the green hills were dark with lines of pedestrians; but a number of those whose homes lay nearest to Hundwyl lingered to drink and gossip out the day. A group of herdsmen, over whose brown faces the high stove-pipe hat looked doubly absurd, gathered in a ring, and while one of them *yodelled* the *Ranz des Vaches* of Appenzell, the others made an accompaniment with their voices, imitating the sound of cowbells. They were lusty, jolly fellows, and their songs hardly came to an end. I saw one man who might be considered as positively drunk, but no other who was more than affectionately and socially excited. Towards sunset they all dropped off, and when the twilight settled down heavy, and threatening rain, there was no stranger but myself in the little village. "I have done tolerably well," said the landlord, " but I can't count my gains until day after to-morrow, when the scores run up to-day must be paid off." Considering that in my own bill lodging was set down at six, and breakfast at twelve cents, even the fifteen hundred guests whom he entertained during the day could not have given him a very splendid profit.

Taking a weaver of the place as guide, I set off early the next morning for the village of Appenzell, the capital of Inner-Rhoden. The way led me back into the valley of the Sitter, thence up towards the Sentis Alp, winding around and over a multitude of hills. The same smooth, even, velvety carpet of grass was spread upon the landscape, covering every undulation of the surface, except where the rocks had frayed themselves through. There is no greener land upon the earth. The grass, from centuries of cultivation, has become so rich and nutritious, that the inhabitants can no longer spare even a little patch of ground for a vegetable garden, for the reason that the same space produces more profit in hay. The green comes up to their very doors, and they grudge even the foot-paths which connect them with their neighbors. Their vegetables are brought up from the lower valleys of Thurgau. The first mowing had commenced at the time of my visit, and the farmers were employing irrigation and manure to bring on the second crop. By this means they are enabled to mow the same fields every five or six weeks. The process gives the whole region a smoothness, a mellow splendor of color, such as I never saw elsewhere, not even in England.

A walk of two hours through such scenery brought me out of the Sitter Tobel, and in sight of the little Alpine basin in which lies Appenzell. It was raining slowly and dismally, and the broken, snow-crowned peaks of the Kamor and the Hohe Kasten stood like livid spectres of mountains against the stormy sky. I made haste to reach the compact, picturesque little town, and shelter myself in an inn, where a landlady with rippled golden hair and features like one of Dante Rossetti's women, offered me trout for dinner. Out of the back window I looked for the shattered summits of the Sentis, which rise five thousand feet above the valley, but they were invisible. The vertical walls of the Ebenalp, in which are the grotto and chapel of Wildkirchli, towered over the nearer hills, and I saw with regret that they were still above the snow line. It was impossible to penetrate much further without better weather; but I decided, while enjoying my trout, to make another trial — to take the road to Urnäsch, and thence pass westward into the renowned valley of the Toggenburg.

The people of Inner-Rhoden are the most picturesque of the Appenzellers. The men wear a round skull-cap of leather, sometimes brilliantly embroidered, a jacket of coarse drilling, drawn on over the head, and occasionally knee-breeches. Early in May the herdsmen leave their winter homes in the valleys and go with their cattle to the *Matten*, or lofty mountain pastures. The most intelligent cows, selected as leaders for the herd, march, in advance, with enormous bells, sometimes a foot in diameter, suspended to their necks by bands of embroidered leather; then follow the others, and the bull, who, singularly enough carries the milking-pail garlanded with flowers, between his horns, brings up the rear. The Alpadores are in their finest Sunday costume, and the sound of yodel-songs — the very voice of Alpine landscapes — echoes from every hill. Such a picture as this, under the cloudless blue of a fortunate May day, makes the heart of the Appenzeller light. He goes joyously up to his summer labor, and makes his herb-cheese on the heights, while his wife weaves and embroiders muslin in the valley until his return.

In the afternoon I set out for Urnäsch, with a bright boy as guide. Hot gleams of sunshine now and then struck like fire across the green mountains, and the Sentis partly unveiled his stubborn forehead of rock. Behind him, however, lowered inky thunder-clouds, and long before the afternoon's journey was made it was raining below and snowing aloft. The scenery grew more broken and abrupt the further I penetrated into the country, but it was everywhere as thickly peopled and as wonderfully cultivated. At Gonten, there is a large building for the whey-cure of overfed people of the world. A great many such, I was told, come to Appenzell for the summer. Many of the persons we met not only said, "God greet you!" but immediately added, "Adieu!"—like the *Salve et vale!* of classical times.

Beyond Gonten the road dropped into a wild ravine, the continual windings of which rendered it very attractive. I found enough to admire in every farm-house by the wayside, with its warm wood-color, its quaint projecting balconies, and coat of shingle mail. When the ravine opened, and the deep valley of Urnäsch, before me, appeared between cloven heights of snow, disclosing six or eight square miles of perfect emerald, over which the village is scattered, I was fully repaid for having pressed farther into the heart of the land. There were still two hours until night, and I might have gone on to the Rossfall,—a cascade three or four miles higher up the valley,—but the clouds were threatening, and the distant mountain-sides already dim under the rain.

At the village inn I found several herdsmen and mechanics, each with a bottle of Rheinthaler wine before him. They were ready and willing to give me all the information I needed. In order to reach the Toggenburg, they said, I must go over the Krätzernwald. It was sometimes a dangerous journey; the snow was many cubits deep, and at this time of the year it was frequently so soft, that a man would sink to his hips. To-day, however, there had been thunder, and after thunder the snow is always hard-packed, so that you can walk on it; but to cross the Krätzernwald without a guide,—never! For two hours you were in a wild forest, not a house, nor even a *Sennhütt'* (herdsman's cabin) to be seen, and no proper path, but a clambering hither and thither, in snow and mud; with this weather,— yes, one *could* get into Toggenburg that way, they said, but not alone, and only because there had been thunder on the mountains.

But all night the rain beat against my chamber window, and in the morning the lower slopes on the mountains were gray with new snow, which no thunder had packed. Indigo-colored clouds lay heavily on all the Alpine peaks; the air was raw and chilly, and the roads slippery. In such weather the scenery is not only shrouded, but the people are shut up in their homes, — wherefore further travel would not have been repaid. I had already seen the greater part of the little land, and so gave up my thwarted plans the more cheerfully. When the post-omnibus for Herisau came to the inn door, I took my seat therein, saying, like Schiller's "Sennbub'," "*Ihr Matten, lebt wohl! ihr sonnige Weiden!*"

The country became softer and lovelier as the road gradually fell towards Herisau, which is the richest and stateliest town of the Canton. I saw little of it except the hospitable home of my friend the Chancellor, for we had brought the Alpine weather with us. The architecture of the place, nevertheless, is charming, the town being composed of country-houses, balconied and shingled, and set down together in the most irregular way, every street shooting off at a different angle. A mile beyond, I reached the edge of the mountain region, and again looked down upon the prosperous valley of St. Gall. Below me was the railway, and as I sped towards Zurich that afternoon, the top of the Sentis, piercing through a mass of dark rain-clouds, was my last glimpse of the Little Land of Appenzell.

FROM PERPIGNAN TO MONTSERRAT.

"Out of France and into Spain," says the old nursery rhyme; but at the eastern base of the Pyrenees one seems to have entered Spain before leaving France. The rich vine-plains of Roussillon once belonged to the former country; they retain quite as distinct traces of the earlier Moorish occupancy, and their people speak a dialect almost identical with that of Catalonia. I do not remember the old boundaries of the province, but I noticed the change immediately after leaving Narbonne. Vine-green, with the grays of olive and rock, were the only colors of the landscape. The towns, massive and perched upon elevations, spoke of assault and defense; the laborers in the fields were brown, dark-haired, and grave, and the semi-African silence of Spain seemed already to brood over the land.

I entered Perpignan under a heavy Moorish gateway, and made my way to a hostel through narrow, tortuous streets, between houses with projecting balconies, and windows few and small, as in the Orient. The hostel, though ambitiously calling itself a hotel, was filled with that Mediterranean atmosphere and odor which you breathe everywhere in Italy and the Levant, — a single characteristic flavor, in which, nevertheless, you fancy you detect the exhalations of garlic, oranges, horses, cheese, and oil. A mild whiff of it stimulates the imagination, and is no detriment to physical comfort. When, at breakfast, red mullet came upon the table, and oranges fresh from the tree, I straightway took off my Northern nature as a garment, folded it and packed it neatly away in my knapsack, and took, out in its stead, the light, beribboned, and bespangled Southern nature, which I had not worn for some eight or nine years. It was like a dressing-gown after a dress-coat, and I went about with a delightfully free play of the mental and moral joints.

There were four hours before the departure of the diligence for Spain, and I presume I might have seen various historical or architectural sights of Perpignan; but I was really too comfortable for anything else than a lazy meandering about the city, feeding my eyes on quaint houses groups of people full of noise and gesture, the scarlet blossoms of the pomegranate, and the glitter of citron-leaves in the gardens. A one-legged fellow, seven feet high, who called himself a *commissionaire*, insisted on accompanying me, and I finally accepted him, for two reasons; — first, he knew nothing whatever about the city; and secondly, tourists are so rare that he must have been very poor. His wooden leg, moreover, easily kept pace with my loitering steps, and though, as a matter of conscience, he sometimes volunteered a little information, he took my silence meekly and without offense. In this wise, I gained some pleasant pictures of the place; and the pictures which come with least effort are those which remain freshest in memory.

There was one point, however, where my limping giant made a stand, and set his will against expostulation or entreaty. I *must* see the avenue of sycamores, he said; there was plenty of time; France, the world, had no such avenue; it was near at hand; every stranger went to see it and was amazed; — and therewith he set off, without waiting for my answer. I followed, for I saw that otherwise he would not have considered his fee earned. The avenue of sycamores was indeed all that he had promised. I had seen larger trees in Syria and Negropont, but here was a triple avenue, nearly half a mile in length, so trained and sculptured that they rivaled the regularity of masonry. Each trunk, at the height of ten or twelve feet, divided into two arms, which then leaned outwards at the same angle, and mingled their smaller boughs, fifty feet overhead The aisles between them thus took the form of very slender pyramids, truncated near the top. If the elm gives the Gothic, this was assuredly the Cyclopean arch. In the beginning, the effect must have been artificially produced, but the trees were now so old, and had so accustomed themselves to the forms imposed, that no impression of force or restraint remained. Through the roof of this superb green minster not a beam of sunshine found its way. On the hard gravel floor groups of peasants, soldiers, nurses, and children strolled up and down, all with the careless and leisurely air of a region where time has no particular value.

We passed a dark-haired and rather handsome gentleman and lady. "They are opera-singers, Italians," said my companion, "and they are going with you in the diligence." I looked at my watch and found that the hour of departure had nearly arrived, and I should have barely time to procure a little Spanish money. When I reached the office, the gentleman and lady were already installed in the two corners of the *coupé*. My place, apparently, was between them. The agent was politely handing me up the steps, when the gentleman began to remonstrate; but in France the regulations are rigid, and he presently saw that the intrusion could not be prevented. With a sigh and a groan he gave up his comfortable corner to me, and took the middle seat, for which I was booked! "Will you have your place?" whispered the agent. I shook my head. "You get the best seat, don't you see?" he resumed, "because"— But the rest of the sentence was a wink and a laugh. I am sure there is the least possible of a Don Juan in my appearance; yet this agent never lost an opportunity to wink at me whenever he came near the diligence, and I fancied I heard him humming to himself, as we drove away,—

"Ma — nella Spagna — mille e tre!"

I endeavored to be reasonably courteous, without familiarity, towards the opera-singers, but the effect of the malicious winks and smiles made the lady appear to me timid and oppressed, and the gentleman an unexploded mine of jealousy. My remarks were civilly if briefly answered, and then they turned towards each other and began conversing in a language which was not Italian, although melodious, nor French, although nasal. I pricked up my ears and listened more sharply than good manners allowed — but only until I had recognized the Portuguese tongue. Whomsoever I may meet in wandering over the world, it rarely happens that I cannot discover some common or "mutual" friend, and in this instance I determined to try the experiment. After preliminaries, which gently led the conversation to Portugal, I asked, —

"Do you happen to know Count M———?"

"Only by name."

"Or Senhor O———, a young man and an astronomer?"

"Very well!" was the reply. "He is one of the most distinguished young men of science in Portugal."

The ice was thereupon broken, and the gentleman became communicative and agreeable. I saw, very soon, that the pair were no more opera-singers than they were Italians; that the lady was not timid, nor her husband jealous; but he had simply preferred, as any respectable husband would, to give up his comfortable seat rather than have a stranger thrust between himself and his wife.

Once out of Perpignan, the Pyrenees lay clear before us. Over bare red hills, near at hand, rose a gray mountain rampart, neither lofty nor formidable; but westward, between the valleys of the Tech and the Tet, towered the solitary pyramid of the Canigou, streaked with snow-filled ravines. The landscapes would have appeared bleak and melancholy, but for the riotous growth of vines which cover the plain and climb the hillsides wherever there is room for a terrace of earth. These vines produce the dark, rich wine of Roussillon, the best vintage of Southern France. Hedges of aloes, clumps of Southern cypress, poplars by the dry beds of winter streams, with brown tints in the houses and red in the soil, increased the resemblance to Spain. Rough fellows, in rusty velvet, who now and then dug their dangling heels into the sides of the mules or asses they rode, were enough like *arrieros* or *contrabandistas* to be the real article. Our stout and friendly coachman, even, was hailed by the name of Moreno, and spoke French with a foreign accent.

At the post-station of Le Boulou, we left the plain of Roussillon behind us. At this end of the Pyrenean chain there are no such trumpet-names as Roncesvalles, Fontarabia, and Bidassoa. Hannibal, Cæsar, Charlemagne, and the Saracens have marched through these defiles, and left no grand historic footprint, but they will always keep the interest which belongs to those natural barriers and division walls whereby races and histories were once separated. It was enough for me that here were the Pyrenees, and I looked forward, perhaps, with a keener curiosity, to the character and forms of their scenery, than to the sentiment which any historic association could produce. A broad and perfect highway led us through shallow valleys, whose rocky sides were hung with rows of olive-trees, into wilder and more abrupt dells, where vegetation engaged in a struggle with stone, and without man's help would have been driven from the field. Over us the mountains lifted themselves in bold bastions and parapets, disforested now, if those gray upper plateaus ever bore forests, and of a uniform slaty gray in tone except where reddish patches of oxidation showed like the rust of age.

But, like "all waste and solitary places," the scenery had its own peculiar charm. Poussin and Salvator Rosa would have seated themselves afresh at every twist of the glen, and sketched the new picture which it unfolded. The huge rocks, fallen from above, or shattered in the original upheaval of the chain, presented a thousand sharp, forcible outlines and ragged facets of shadow, and the two native growths of the Pyrenees — box and cork-oak — fringed them as thickets or overhung them as trees, in the wildest and most picturesque combinations. Indeed, during this portion of the journey, I saw scores of sketches waiting for the selected artist who has not yet come for them, — sketches full of strength and beauty, and with a harmony of color as simple as the chord of triple tones in music. When to their dark grays and greens came the scarlet Phrygian cap of the Catalonian, it was brighter than sunshine.

The French fortress of Bellegarde, crowning a drum-shaped mass of rock, which blocked up the narrow valley in front, announced our approach to the Spanish frontier. The road wound back and forth as it climbed through a stony wilderness to the mouth of a gorge under the fortress, and I saw, before we entered this last gateway into Spain, the peak of the Canigou touched with sunset, and the sweep of plain beyond it black under the shadow of storm-clouds. On either side were some heaps of stone, left from forts and chapels of the Middle Ages, indicating that we had already reached the summit of the pass, which is less than a thousand feet above the sea-level. In ten minutes the gorge opened, and we found ourselves suddenly rattling along the one street of the gay French village of Perthus. Officers from Bellegarde sat at the table in front of the smart *café*, and drank absinthe; soldiers in red trousers chatted with the lively women who sold tobacco and groceries; there were trees, little gardens, arbors of vine, and the valley opened southwards, descending and broadening towards a cloudless evening sky.

At the end of the village I saw a granite pyramid, with the single word " Gallia " engraved upon it; a few paces farther, two marble posts bore the half-obliterated arms of Spain. Here the diligence paused a moment, and an officer of customs took his seat beside the coachman. The telegraph pole behind us was of barked pine, the next one in front was painted gray; the *vente de tabac* became *estanco nacional*, and the only overlapping of the two nationalities which I observed — all things else being suddenly and sharply divided — was that some awkward and dusty Spanish soldiers were walking up the street of Perthus, and some trim, jaunty French soldiers were walking down the road, towards the first Spanish wine-shop. We also went down, and swiftly, in the falling twilight, through which, erelong, gardens and fields began to glimmer, and in half an hour drew up in the little Spanish town of La Junquera, the ancient "place of rushes." Here there was a rapid and courteous examination of baggage, a call for passports, which were opened and then handed back to us without *visé* or fee being demanded, and we were declared free to journey in Spain. Verily the world is becoming civilized, when Spain, the moral satrapy of Rome, begins to pull down her barriers and let the stranger in!

I inspected our "insides," as they issued forth, and found, in addition to a priest and three or four commercial individuals with a contraband air, a young French naval officer, and an old German who was too practical for a professor and too stubborn in his views to be anything else. He had made fifteen journeys to Switzerland, he informed me, knew Scotland from the Cheviots to John o' Groat's, and now proposed the conquest of Spain. Here Moreno summoned us to our places, and the diligence rolled onward. Past groups of Catalans, in sandals and scarlet bonnets, returning from the harvest fields; past stacks of dusky grain and shadowy olive-orchards; past open houses, where a single lamp sometimes flashed upon a woman's head; past a bonfire, turning the cork-trees into transparent bronze, and past the sound of water, plunging under the idle mill-wheel, in the cool, delicious summer air, — we journeyed on. The stars were beginning to gather in the sky, when square towers and masses of cubic houses rose against them, and the steady roll of our wheels on the smooth highway became a dreadful clatter on the rough cobble-stones of Figueras.

The Pyrenees were already behind us; the town overlooks a wide, marshy plain. But the mountains make their vicinity felt in a peculiar manner. The north-wind, gathered into the low pass of Bellegarde and drawn to a focus of strength, blows down the opening valley with a force which sometimes lays an embargo on travel. Diligences are overturned, postilions blown out of their saddles, and pedestrians carried off their feet. The people then pray to their saints that the *tramontana* may cease; but, on the other hand, as it is a very healthy wind, sweeping away the feverish exhalations from the marshy soil, they get up a grand annual procession to some mountain-shrine of the Virgin, and pray that it may blow. So, when the Virgin takes them at their word, the saints are invoked on the other side, and the wonder is that both parties don't get out of patience with the people of Figueras.

The diligence drew up at the door of a *fonda*, and Moreno announced that we were to take supper and wait until midnight. This was welcome news to all; but the old German drew me aside as we entered the house, and whispered, "Now our stomachs are going to be tried." "Not at all," I answered, "we shall find very good provender." "But the guide-book says it is very bad," he persisted. And he looked despondent, even with a clean table-cloth and a crisp roll of bread before him, until the soup steamed under his nose. His face brightened at the odor, grew radiant at the flavor, and long before we reached the roast pullet and salad, he expressed his satisfaction with Spanish cookery. With the dessert came a *vino rancio*, full of summer fire, and the tongues of the company were loosened. From the weather and the Paris Exposition we leaped boldly into politics, and, being on Spanish soil, discussed France and the Mexican business. The French officer was silent and annoyed; he was a pleasant fellow, and I, for one, had a little sympathy with his annoyance, but I could not help saying that all Americans (except the

Rev. ——) considered the action of France as an outrage and an impertinence, and were satisfied with her miserable failure. The Spanish passengers nodded and smiled.

I should not have spoken, had I foreseen one consequence of my words. The German snatched the reins of conversation out of our hands, and dashed off at full speed, trampling France and her ruler under his feet. At the first pause, I said to him, in German: "Pray don't be so violent in your expressions, — the gentleman beside me is a naval officer." But he answered: "I don't care, I must speak my mind, which I could not do in Paris. France has been the curse of Spain, as well as of all Europe, and there will be no peace until we put a stop to her pretensions!" Thereupon he said the same thing to the company; but the Spaniards were too politic to acquiesce openly. The officer replied, "France has not injured Spain, but, on the contrary, has protected her!" and he evidently had not the slightest suspicion that there was anything offensive in his words. The Spaniards still remained silent, but another expression came into their eyes. It was time to change the subject; so the principle of non-intervention, in its fullest, most literal sense, was proposed and accepted. A grave Majorcan gentleman distributed cigars; his daughter, with her soft, melodious voice, was oil to the troubled waters, and before midnight we were all equally courteous and cosmopolitan.

Of the four ensuing hours I can give no account. Neither asleep nor awake, hearing with closed eyes or seewith half-closed senses, one can never afterwards distinguish between what is seen and what is dreamed. This is a state in which the body may possibly obtain some rest, but the mind becomes inexpressibly fatigued. One's memory of it is a blurred sketch, a faded daguerreotype. I welcomed that hour when —

> "The wind blows cold
> While the morning doth unfold."

for it blew away this film, which usurped the place of the blessed mantle of sleep. Chill, even here in African Spain, where the pale pearl of the dawn foretold a burning noon, and where, in May, the harvests were already reaped, the morning brightened; but we were near the end of the journey. At sunrise, the towers of Girona stood fast and firm over the misty level of the shimmering olive-groves; then the huge dull mass of the cathedral, the walls and bastions of the hill-forts, which resisted a siege of seven months during the Peninsular War, and finally the monotonous streets of the lower town, through which we drove.

The industrious Catalans were already awake and stirring. Smokes from domestic hearths warmed the cool morning air; cheerful noises of men, animals, and fowls broke the silence; doors were open as we entered the town, and the women were combing and twisting their black hair in the shadows within. At the post some brown grooms lounged about the door. A priest passed, — a genuine Don Basilio, in inky gown and shovel hat; and these graceless grooms looked after him, thrust their tongues into their cheeks, and made an irreverent grimace. The agent at Perpignan came into my mind; I winked at the fellows, without any clear idea wherefore, but it must have expressed something, for they burst into a laugh and repeated the grimace.

The lower town seemed to be of immense length. Once out of it, a superb avenue of plane trees received us, at the end of which was the railway station. In another hour the train would leave for Barcelona. Our trunks must be again examined. When I asked the reason why this annoying regulation, obsolete elsewhere in Europe, is here retained, the Spaniards gravely informed me that, if it were abolished, a great many people would be thrown out of employment. Not that they get much pay for the examination, — but they are constantly bribed not to examine! There was a *café* attached to the station, and I advised my fellow-passengers to take a cup of the delicious ropy chocolate of Spain, after which one accepts the inevitable more patiently.

I found the landscapes from Girona to Barcelona very bright and beautiful. Our locomotive had fallen into the national habit: it was stately and deliberate, it could not be hurried, its very whistle was subdued and dignified. We went forward at an easy pace, making about fifteen miles an hour, which enabled me to notice the patient industry of the people, as manifested on every plain and hillside. The Catalans are called rough and ungraceful; beside the sprightly Andalusians they seem cold and repellent; they have less of that blue blood which makes the beggar as proud as the grandee, but they possess the virtue of labor, which, however our artistic tastes may undervalue it, is the basis from which all good must spring. When I saw how the red and rocky hills were turned into garden-terraces, how the olive-trees were pruned into health and productiveness, how the wheat stood so thick that it rolled but stiffly under the breeze, I forgot the jaunty *majos* of Seville, and gave my hearty admiration to the strong-backed reapers in the fields of Catalonia.

The passengers we took up on the way, though belonging to the better class, and speaking Spanish whenever it was necessary, all seemed to prefer the popular dialect. Proprietors of estates and elegant young ladies conversed together in the rough patois of the peasants, which to me was especially tantalizing, because it sounded so familiar, and yet was so unintelligible. It is in reality the old *langue limousine* of France, kindred to the Provençal, and differs very slightly from the dialect spoken on the other side of the Pyrenees. It is terse, forcible, and expressive, and I must confess that the lisping Spanish, beside it, seems to gain in melody at the expense of strength.

We approached Barcelona across the wide plain of the Llobregat, where orange gardens and factory chimneys, fountains "i' the midst of roses," and machine-shops full of grimy workmen, succeed each other in a curious tangle of poetry and greasy fact. The Mediterranean gleams in a blue line on the left, the citadel of Monjuich crowns a bluff in front; but the level city hides itself behind the foliage of the plain, and is not seen. At the station you wait half an hour, until the baggage is again deposited on the dissecting-tables of the custom officers; and here, if, instead of joining the crowd of unhappy murmurers in the anteroom, you take your station in the doorway, looking down upon porters, peddlers, idlers, and policemen, you are sure to be diverted by a little comedy acted in pantomime. An outside porter has in some way interfered with the rights of a station-porter; a policeman steps between the two, the latter of whom, lifting both hands to heaven in a wild appeal, brings them down swiftly and thrusts them out before him, as if descending to earthly justice. The outsider goes through the same gestures, and then both, with flashing eyes and open mouths, teeth glittering under the drawn lips, await the decision. The policeman first makes a sabre-cut with his right arm, then with his left; then also lifts his hands to heaven, shakes them there a moment, and, turning as he brings them down, faces the outside porter. The latter utters a passionate cry, and his arms begin to rise; but he is seized by the shoulder and turned aside; the crowd closes in, and the comedy is over.

We have a faint interest in Barcelona for the sake of Columbus; but, apart from this one association, we set it down beside Manchester, Lowell, and other manufacturing cities. It was so crowded within its former walls, that little space was left for architectural display. In many of the streets I doubt whether four persons could walk abreast. Only in the Rambla, a broad central boulevard, is there any chance for air and sunshine, and all the leisure and pleasure of the city is poured into this one avenue. Since the useless walls have been removed, an ambitious modern suburb is springing up on the west, and there will, in time, be a new city better than the old.

This region appears to be the head-quarters of political discontent in Spain, — probably because the people get to be more sensible of the misrule under which they languish, in proportion as they become more active and industrious. Nothing could have been more peaceable upon the surface than the aspect of things; the local newspapers never reported any disturbance, yet intelligence of trouble in Catalonia was circulating through the rest of Europe, and *something* — I could not ascertain precisely what it was — took place during my brief visit. The telegraph-wires were cut, and some hundreds of soldiers were sent into the country; but the matter was never mentioned, unless two persons whom I saw whispering together in the darkest corner of a *café* were discussing it. I believe, if a battle had been fought within hearing of the cannon, the Barcelonese would have gone about the streets with the same placid, unconcerned faces. Whether this was cunning, phlegm, or the ascendency of solid material interests over the fiery, impulsive nature of the Spaniard, was not clear to a passing observer. In either case it was a prudent course.

If, in the darkened streets — or rather lanes — of Barcelona, I saw some suggestive pictures; if the court-yard of the cathedral, with its fountains and orange-trees, seemed a thousand miles removed from the trade and manufacture of the city; if the issuing into sunshine on the mole was like a blow in the eyes, to which the sapphire bloom of the Mediterranean became a healing balm; and if the Rambla, towards evening, changed into a shifting diorama of color and cheerful life, — none of these things inclined me to remain longer than the preparation for my further journey required. Before reaching the city, I had caught a glimpse, far up the valley of the Llobregat, of a high, curiously serrated mountain, and that old book of the "Wonders of the World" (now, alas! driven from the library of childhood) opened its pages and showed its rough woodcuts, in memory, to tell me what the mountain was. How many times has that wonderful book been the chief charm of my travels, causing me to forget Sulpicius on the Ægean Sea, Byron in Italy, and Humboldt in Mexico!

To those who live in Barcelona, Montserrat has become a common-place, the resort of Sunday excursions and picnics, one fourth devotional, and three fourths epicurean. Wild, mysterious, almost inaccessible as it stands in one's fancy, it sinks at this distance into the very material atmosphere of railroad and omnibus; but, for all that, we are not going to give it up, though another "Wonder of the World" should go by the board. Take the Tarragona train then with me, on a cloudless afternoon. In a few minutes the scattered suburban blocks are left behind, and we enter the belt of villas, with their fountained terraces and tropical gardens. More and more the dark red earth shows through the thin foliage of the olives, as the hills draw nearer, and it finally gives color to the landscapes. The vines covering the levels and lower slopes are wonderfully luxuriant; but we can see how carefully they are cultivated. Hedges of aloe and cactus divide them; here and there some underground cavern has tumbled in, letting down irregular tracts of soil, and the vines still flourish at the bottom of the pits thus made. As the plain shrinks to a valley, the hills on either side ascend into rounded summits, which begin to be dark with pine forests; villages with square, brown church-towers perch on the lower heights; cotton-mills draw into their service the scanty waters of the river, and the appearance of cheerful, thrifty labor increases as the country becomes rougher.

All this time the serrated mountain is drawing nearer, and breaking into a wilder confusion of pinnacles. It stands alone, planted across the base of a triangular tract of open country, — a strange, solitary, exiled peak, drifted away in the beginning of things from its brethren of the Pyrenees, and stranded in a different geological period. This circumstance must have long ago impressed the inhabitants of the region — even in the ante-historic ages. When Christianity rendered a new set of traditions necessary, the story arose that the mountain was thus split and shattered at the moment when Christ breathed his last on the cross of Calvary. This is still the popular belief; but the singular formation of Montserrat, independent of it, was sufficient to fix the anchoretic tastes of the early Christians. It is set apart by Nature, not only towering above all the surrounding heights, but drawing itself haughtily away from contact with them, as if conscious of its earlier origin.

At the station of Martorel I left the train, and took a coach which was in waiting for the village of Collbató, at the southern base of the mountain. My companion in the *coupé* was a young cotton-manufacturer, who assured me that in Spain the sky and soil were good, but the *entresol* (namely, the human race) was bad. The interior was crowded with country-women, each of whom seemed to have four large baskets. I watched the driver for half an hour attempting to light a broken cigar, and then rewarded his astonishing patience with a fresh one, whereby we became good friends. Such a peaceful light lay upon the landscape, the people were so cheerful, the laborers worked so quietly in the vineyards, that the thought of a political disturbance the day before seemed very absurd. The olive-trees, which clothed the hills wherever their bony roots could find the least lodgment of soil, were of remarkably healthy and vigorous growth, and the regular cubic form into which they were pruned marked the climbing terraces with long lines of gray light, as the sun slanted across them.

"You see," said the Spaniard, as I noticed this peculiarity, " the *entresol* is a little better in this neighborhood than elsewhere in Spain. The people cut the trees into this shape in order that they may become more compact and produce better; besides which, the fruit is more easily gathered. In all those orchards you will not find a decayed or an unhealthy tree; such are dug up and burned, and young ones planted in their place."

At the village of Esparaguerra the other passengers left, and I went on towards Collbató alone. But I had Montserrat for company, towering more grandly, more brokenly, from minute to minute. Every change in the foreground gave me a new picture. Now it was a clump of olives with twisted trunks; now an aloe, lifting its giant candelabrum of blossoms from the edge of a rock; now a bank of dull vermilion earth, upon which goats were hanging. The upper spires of the mountain disappeared behind its basal buttresses of gray rock, a thousand feet in perpendicular height, and the sinking sun, as it crept westward, edged these with sharp lines of light. Up, under the tremendous cliffs, and already in shadow, lay Collbató, and I was presently set down at the gate of the *posada*.

Don Pedro, the host, came forward to meet and welcome me, and his pretty daughter, sitting on the steps, rose up and dropped a salute. In the entrance hall I read, painted in large letters on the wall, the words of St. Augustine: "*In necessariis unitas; in dubiis libertas; in omnibus, caritas.*" Verily, thought I, Don Pedro must be a character. I had no sooner comfortably seated myself in the doorway to contemplate the exquisite evening landscape, which the Mediterranean bounded in the distance, and await my supper, than Don Pedro ordered his daughter to bring the guests' book, and then betook himself to the task of running down a lean chicken. In the record of ten years I found that Germans were the most frequent visitors; Americans appeared but thrice. One party of the latter registered themselves as "gentlemen," and stated that they had seen the "promanent points," — which gave occasion to a later Englishman to comment upon the intelligence of American gentlemen. The host's daughter, Pepita, was the theme of praise in prose and raptures in poetry.

"Are you Pepita?" I asked, turning to the girl, who sat on the steps before me, gazing into the evening sky with an expression of the most indolent happiness. I noticed for the first time, and admired, her firm, regular, almost Roman profile and the dark masses of *real* hair on her head. Her attitude, also, was very graceful, and she would have been, to impressible eyes, a phantom of delight, but for the ungraceful fact that she inveterately scratched herself whenever and wherever a flea happened to bite.

"No, señor," she answered; "I am Carmen. Pepita was married first, and then Mariquita. Angelita and myself are the only ones at home."

"I see there is also a poem to Angelita," I remarked, turning over the last leaves.

"O, that was a poet!" said she, — "a funny man! Everybody knows him: he writes for the theatre, and all that is about some eggs which Angelita fried for him. We can't understand it all, but we think it's good-natured."

Here the mother came, not as duenna, but as companion, with her distaff and spindle, and talked and span until I could no longer distinguish the thread against her gray dress. When the lean chicken was set before me, Don Pedro announced that a mule and guide would be in readiness at sunrise, and I could, if I chose, mount to the topmost peak of San Geronimo. In the base of the mountain, near Collbató, there are spacious caverns, which most travellers feel bound to visit; but I think that six or seven caves, one coal mine, and one gold mine are enough for a life-time, and have renounced any further subterranean researches. Why delve into those dark, moist, oppressive crypts, when the blessed sunshine of years shows one so little of the earth and of human life? Let any one that chooses come and explore the caverns of Montserrat, and then tell me (as people have a passion for doing), "You missed the best!" The best is that with which one is satisfied.

Instead of five o'clock, when I should have been called, I awoke naturally at six, and found that Don Pedro had set out for San Geronimo four hours before, while neither guide nor mule was forthcoming. The old woman pointed to some specks far up in the shadow of the cliffs, which she assured me were travellers, and would arrive with mules in fifteen minutes. But I applied the words *in dubiis libertas*, and insisted on an immediate animal and guide, both of which, somewhat to my surprise, were produced. The black mule was strong, and the lank old Catalan shouldered my heavy valise and walked off without a murmur. The sun was already hot; but once risen above the last painfully constructed terrace of olives, and climbing the stony steep, we dipped into the cool shadow of the mountain. The path was difficult but not dangerous, winding upward through rocks fringed with dwarf ilex, box, and mastic, which made the air fragrant. Thyme, wild flax, and aconite blossomed in the crevices. The botany of the mountain is as exceptional as its geology; it includes five hundred different species.

The box-tree, which my Catalan guide called *bösch* in his dialect, is a reminiscence, wherever one sees it, of Italy and Greece — of ancient culture and art. Its odor, as Holmes admirably says, suggests eternity. If it was not the first plant that sprang up on the cooling planet, it ought to have been. Its glossy mounds, and rude, statuesque clumps, which often seem struggling to mould themselves into human shape, cover with beauty the terrible rocks of Montserrat. M. Delavigne had warned me of the dangers of the path I was pursuing, — walls on one side, and chasms a thousand feet deep on the other, — but the box everywhere shaped itself into protecting figures, and whispered as I went by, "Never fear; if you slip, I will hold you!"

The mountain is an irregular cone, about thirty-five hundred feet in height, and cleft down the middle by a torrent which breaks through its walls on the northeastern side. It presents a perpendicular face, which seems inaccessible, for the shelves between the successive elevations, when seen from below, appear as narrow fringes of vegetation, growing out of one unbroken wall. They furnish, indeed, but scanty room for the bridle-path, which at various points is both excavated and supported by arches of masonry. After nearly an hour, I found myself over Collbató, upon the roofs of which, it seemed, I might fling a stone. At the next angle of the mountain, the crest was attained, and I stood between the torn and scarred upper wilderness of Montserrat on the one hand, and the broad, airy sweep of landscape, bounded by the sea, on the other. To the northward a similar cape thrust out its sheer walls against the dim, dissolving distances, and it was necessary to climb along the sides of the intervening gulf, which sank under me into depths of shadow. Every step of the way was inspiring, for there was the constant threat, without the reality, of danger. My mule paced securely along the giddy brinks; and through the path seemed to terminate fifty paces ahead, I was always sure to find a loop-hole or coigne of vantage which the box and mastic had hidden from sight. So in another hour the opposite foreland was attained, and from its crest I saw, all along the northern horizon, the snowy wall of the Pyrenees.

Here a path branched off to the peak of San Geronimo, — a two hours' clamber through an absolute desert of rock. My guide, although panting and sweating with his load, proposed the ascent; but in the film of heat which overspread the land I should have only had a wider panorama in which all distinct forms were lost, — vast, no doubt, but as blurred and intangible as a metaphysical treatise. I judged it better to follow the example of a pious peasant and his wife whom we had overtaken, and who, setting their faces toward the renowned monastery, murmured an *Ave* from time to time. Erelong, on emerging from the thickets, we burst suddenly upon one of the wildest and most wonderful pictures I ever beheld. A tremendous wall of rock arose in front, crowned by colossal turrets, pyramids, clubs, pillars, and ten-pin shaped masses, which were drawn singly, or in groups of incredible distortion, against the deep blue of the sky. At the foot of the rock, the buildings of the monastery, huge and massive, the church, the houses for pilgrims, and the narrow gardens, completely filled and almost overhung a horizontal shelf of the mountain, under which it again fell sheer away, down, down into misty depths, the bottom of which was hidden from sight. I dropped from the mule, sat down upon the grass, and, under pretense of sketching, studied this picture for an hour. In all the galleries of memory I could find nothing resembling it.

The descriptions of Montserrat must have made a powerful impression upon Goethe's mind, since he deliberately appropriated the scenery for the fifth act of the Second Part of Faust. Goethe was in the steadfast habit of choosing a local and actual habitation for the creations of his imagination; his landscapes were always either painted from nature, or copied from the sketch-books of others. The marvelous choruses of the fifth act floated through my mind as I drew; the "Pater Ecstaticus" hovered in the sunny air, the anchorites chanted from their caves, and the mystic voices of the undeveloped child-spirits came between, like the breathing of an Æolian harp. I suspect that the sanctity of the mountain really depends as much upon its extraordinary forms, as upon the traditions which have been gradually attached to it. These latter, however, are so strange and grotesque, that they could only be accepted here.

The monastery owes its foundation to a miraculous statue of the Virgin, sculptured by St. Luke, and brought to Spain by no less a personage than St. Peter. In the year 880, some shepherds who had climbed the mountain in search of stray goats heard celestial harmonies among the rocks. This phenomenon coming to the ears of Bishop Gondemar, he climbed to the spot, and was led by the music to the mouth of a cave, which exhaled a delicious perfume. There, enshrined in light, lay the sacred statue. Gondemar and his priests, chanting as they went, set out for Manresa, the seat of the diocese, carrying it with them; but on reaching a certain spot, they found it impossible to move farther. The statue obstinately refused to accompany them — which was taken as a sign that there, and nowhere else, the shrine should be built. Just below the monastery there still stands a cross, with the inscription, "Here the Holy Image declared itself immovable, 880."

The chapel when built was intrusted to the pious care of Fray Juan Garin, whose hermitage is pointed out to you, on a peak which seems accessible only to the eagle. The Devil, however, interfered, as he always does in such cases. He first entered into Riquilda, the daughter of the Count of Barcelona, and then declared through her mouth that he would not quit her body except by the order of Juan Garin, the hermit of Montserrat. Riquilda was therefore sent to the mountain and given into the hermit's charge. A temptation similar to that of St. Anthony followed, but with exactly the opposite result. In order to conceal his sin, Juan Garin cut off Riquilda's head, buried her, and fled. Overtaken by remorse, he made his way to Rome, confessed himself to the Pope, and prayed for a punishment proportioned to his crime. He was ordered to become a beast, never lifting his face towards heaven, until the hour when God Himself should signify his pardon.

Juan Garin went forth from the Papal presence on his hands and knees, crawled back to Montserrat, and there lived seven years as a wild animal, eating grass and bark, and never lifting his face towards heaven. At the end of this time his body was entirely covered with hair, and it so happened that the hunters of the count snared him as a strange beast, put a chain around his neck, and took him to Barcelona. In the mansion of the Count there was an infant only five months old, in its nurse's arms. No sooner had the child beheld the supposed animal, than it gave a loud cry and exclaimed: "Rise up, Juan Garin; God has pardoned thee!" Then, to the astonishment of all, the beast arose and spoke in a human tongue. He told his story, and the Count set out at once with him to the spot where Riquilda was buried. They opened the grave and the maiden rose up alive, with only a rosy mark, like a thread, around her neck. In commemoration of so many miracles, the Count founded the monastery.

At present, the monks retain but a fragment of their former wealth and power. Their number is reduced to nineteen, which is barely enough to guard the shrine, perform their offices, and prepare and bless the rosaries and other articles of devotional traffic. I visited the church, courts, and corridors, but took no pains to get sight of the miraculous statue. I have already seen both the painting and the sculpture of St. Luke, and think him one of the worst artists that ever existed. Moreover, the place is fast assuming a secular, not to say profane air. There is a modern restaurant, with bill of fare and wine list, inside the gate, ticket-office for travellers, and a daily omnibus to the nearest railway station. Ladies in black mantillas lounge about the court-yards, gentlemen smoke on the balconies, and only the brown-faced peasant pilgrims, arriving with weary feet, enter the church with an expression of awe and of unquestioning faith. The enormous wealth which the monastery once possessed — the offering of kings — has disappeared in the vicissitudes of Spanish history, the French, in 1811, being the last pillagers. Since then, the treasures of gold and jewels have not returned; for the crowns offered to the Virgin by the city of Barcelona and by a rich American are of gilded silver, set with diamonds of paste!

I loitered for hours on the narrow terraces around the monastery, constantly finding some new and strange combination of forms in the architecture of the mountain. The bright silver-gray of the rock contrasted finely with the dark masses of eternal box, and there was an endless play of light and shade as the sun burst suddenly through some unsuspected gap, or hid himself behind one of the giant ten-pins of the summit. The world below swam in dim red undulations, for the color of the soil showed everywhere through its thin clothing of olive-trees. In hue as in form, Montserrat had no fellowship with the surrounding region.

The descent on the northern side is far less picturesque, inasmuch as you are perched upon the front seat of an omnibus, and have an excellent road — a work of great cost and labor — the whole way. But, on the other hand, you skirt the base of a number of the detached pillars and pyramids into which the mountain separates, and gain fresh pictures of its remarkable structure. There is one isolated shaft, visible at a great distance, which I should judge to be three hundred feet in height by forty or fifty in diameter. At the western end, the outline is less precipitous, and here the fields of vine and olive climb much higher than elsewhere. In an hour from the time of leaving the monastery, we were below the last rampart, rolling through dust in the hot valley of the Llobregat, and tracing the course of the invisible road across the walls of Montserrat, with a feeling of incredulity that we had really descended from such a point.

At the village of Montrisol, on the river, there is a large cotton factory. The doors opened as we approached, and the workmen came forth, their day's labor done. Men and women, boys and girls, in red caps and sandals, or bareheaded and barefooted, they streamed merrily along the road, teeth and eyes flashing as they chatted and sang. They were no pale, melancholy factory slaves, but joyous and light-hearted children of labor, and, it seemed to me, the proper successors of the useless idlers in the monastery of Montserrat. Up there, on the mountain, a system, all-powerful in the past, was swiftly dying; here, in the valley, was the first life of the only system that can give a future to Spain.

BALEARIC DAYS.

I.

As the steamer Mallorca slowly moved out of the harbor of Barcelona, I made a rapid inspection of the passengers gathered on deck, and found that I was the only foreigner among them. Almost without exception they were native Majorcans, returning from trips of business or pleasure to the Continent. They spoke no language except Spanish and Catalan, and held fast to all the little habits and fashions of their insular life. If anything more had been needed to show me that I was entering upon untrodden territory, it was supplied by the joyous surprise of the steward when I gave him a fee. This fact reconciled me to my isolation on board, and its attendant awkwardness.

I knew not why I should have chosen to visit the Balearic Islands, unless for the simple reason that they lie so much aside from the highways of travel, and are not represented in the journals and sketch-books of tourists. If any one had asked me what I expected to see, I should have been obliged to confess my ignorance; for the few dry geographical details which I possessed were like the chemical analysis of a liquor wherefrom no one can reconstruct the taste. The *flavor* of a land is a thing quite apart from its statistics. There is no special guide-book for the islands, and the slight notices in the works on Spain only betray the haste of the authors to get over a field with which they are unacquainted. But this very circumstance, for me, had grown into a fascination. One gets tired of studying the bill of fare in advance of the repast. When the sun and the Spanish coast had set together behind the placid sea, I went to my berth with the delightful certainty that the sun of the morrow, and of many days thereafter, would rise upon scenes and adventures which could not be anticipated.

The distance from Barcelona to Palma is about a hundred and forty miles; so the morning found us skirting the southwestern extremity of Majorca — a barren coast, thrusting low headlands of gray rock into the sea, and hills covered with parched and stunted chaparral in the rear. The twelfth century, in the shape of a crumbling Moorish watch-tower, alone greeted us. As we advanced eastward into the Bay of Palma, however, the wild shrubbery melted into plantations of olive, solitary houses of fishermen nestled in the coves, and finally a village, of those soft ochre-tints which are a little brighter than the soil, appeared on the slope of a hill. In front, through the pale morning mist which still lay upon the sea, I saw the cathedral of Palma, looming grand and large beside the towers of other churches, and presently, gliding past a mile or two of country villas and gardens, we entered the crowded harbor.

Inside the mole there was a multitude of the light craft of the Mediterranean, — xebecs, feluccas, speronaras, or however they may be termed, — with here and there a brigantine which had come from beyond the Pillars of Hercules. Our steamer drew into her berth beside the quay, and after a very deliberate review by the port physician we were allowed to land. I found a porter, Arab in everything but costume, and followed him through the water-gate into the half-awake city. My destination was the Inn of the "Four Nations," where I was cordially received, and afterwards roundly swindled, by a French host. My first demand was for a native attendant, not so much from any need of guide as simply to become more familiar with the people through him; but I was told that no such serviceable spirit was to be had in the place. Strangers are so rare that a class of people who live upon them has not yet been created.

"But how shall I find the Palace of the Government, or the monastery of San Domingo, or anything else?" I asked.

"O, we will give you directions, so that you cannot miss them," said the host; but he laid before me such a confusion of right turnings and left turnings, ups and downs, that I became speedily bewildered, and set forth, determined to let the spirit in my feet guide me. A labyrinthine place is Palma, and my first walks through the city were so many games of chance. The streets are very narrow, changing their direction, it seemed to me, at every tenth step; and whatever landmark one may select at the start is soon shut from view by the high, dark houses. At first, I was quite astray, but little by little I regained the lost points of the compass.

After having had the Phœnicians, Greeks, Carthaginians, Romans, Vandals, and Saracens as masters, Majorca was first made Spanish by King Jaime of Aragon, the Conquistador, in the year 1235. For a century after the conquest it was an independent kingdom, and one of its kings was slain by the English bowmen at the battle of Crecy. The Spanish element has absorbed, but not yet entirely obliterated, the characteristics of the earlier races who inhabited the island. Were ethnology a more positively developed science, we might divide and classify this confused inheritance of character; as it is, we vaguely feel the presence of something quaint, antique, and unusual, in walking the streets of Palma, and mingling with the inhabitants. The traces of Moorish occupation are still noticeable everywhere. Although the Saracenic architecture no longer exists in its original forms, its details may be detected in portals, court-yards, and balconies, in almost every street. The conquerors endeavored to remodel the city, but in doing so they preserved the very spirit which they sought to destroy.

My wanderings, after all, were not wholly undirected.

I found an intelligent guide, who was at the same time an old acquaintance. The whirligig of time brings about, not merely its revenges, but also its compensations and coincidences. Twenty-two years ago, when I was studying German as a boy in the old city of Frankfort, guests from the south of France came to visit the amiable family with whom I was residing. They were M. Laurens, a painter and a musical enthusiast, his wife, and Mademoiselle Rosalba, a daughter as fair as her name. Never shall I forget the curious letter which the artist wrote to the manager of the theatre, requesting that Beethoven's *Fidelio* might be given (and it was!) for his own especial benefit, nor the triumphant air with which he came to us one day, saying, "I have something of most precious," and brought forth, out of a dozen protecting envelopes, a single gray hair from Beethoven's head. Nor shall I forget how Madame Laurens taught us French plays, and how the fair Rosalba declaimed André Chénier to redeem her pawns; but I might have forgotten all these things, had it not been for an old volume [1] which turned up at need, and which gave me information, at once clear, precise, and attractive, concerning the streets and edifices of Palma. The round, solid head, earnest eyes, and abstracted air of the painter came forth distinct from the limbo of things overlaid but never lost, and went with me through the checkered blaze and gloom of the city.

The monastery of San Domingo, which was the headquarters of the Inquisition, was spared by the progressive government of Mendizabal, but destroyed by the people. Its ruins must have been the most picturesque sight of Palma; but since the visit of M. Laurens they have been removed, and their broken vaults and revealed torture-chambers are no longer to be seen. There are, however,

---

[1] *Souvenirs d'un Voyage d'Art à l'Isle de Majorque.* Par J. B. Laurens.

two or three buildings of more than ordinary interest. The *Casa Consistorial*, or City Hall, is a massive Palladian pile of the sixteenth century, resembling the old palaces of Pisa and Florence, except in the circumstance that its roof projects at least ten feet beyond the front, resting on a massive cornice of carved wood with curious horizontal caryatides in the place of brackets. The rich burnt-sienna tint of the carvings contrasts finely with the golden-brown of the massive marble walls — a combination which is shown in no other building of the Middle Ages. The sunken rosettes, surrounded by raised arabesque borders, between the caryatides, are sculptured with such a careful reference to the distance at which they must be seen, that they appear as firm and delicate as if near the spectator's eye.

The Cathedral, founded by the Conquistador, and built upon, at intervals, for more than three centuries, is not yet finished. It stands upon a natural platform of rock, overhanging the sea, where its grand dimensions produce the greatest possible effect. In every view of Palma, it towers solidly above the houses and bastioned walls, and insists upon having the sky as a background for the light Gothic pinnacles of its flying buttresses. The government has recently undertaken its restoration, and a new front of very admirable and harmonious design is about half completed. The soft amber-colored marble of Majorca is enriched in tint by exposure to the air, and even when built in large, unrelieved masses retains a bright and cheerful character. The new portion of the cathedral, like the old, has but little sculpture, except in the portals; but that little is so elegant that a greater profusion of ornament would seem out of place.

Passing from the clear, dazzling day into the interior, one finds himself, at first, in total darkness; and the dimensions of the nave — nearly three hundred feet in length by one hundred and forty in height — are amplified by the gloom. The wind, I was told, came through the windows on the sea side with such force as to overturn the chalices, and blow out the tapers on the altar, whereupon every opening was walled up, except a rose at the end of the chancel, and a few slits in the nave, above the side-aisles. A sombre twilight, like that of a stormy day, fills the edifice. Here the rustling of stoles and the muttering of prayers suggest incantation rather than worship; the organ has a hollow, sepulchral sound of lamentation; and there is a spirit of mystery and terror in the stale, clammy air. The place resembles an ante-chamber of Purgatory much more than of Heaven. The mummy of Don Jaime II., son of the Conquistador and first king of Majorca, is preserved in a sarcophagus of black marble. This is the only historic monument in the Cathedral, unless the stranger chooses to study the heraldry of the island families from their shields suspended in the chapels.

When I returned to the "Four Nations" for breakfast, I found at the table a gentleman of Palma, who invited me to sit down and partake of his meal. For the first time this Spanish custom, which really seems picturesque and fraternal when coming from shepherds or muleteers in a mountain inn, struck me as the hollowest of forms. The gentleman knew that I would not accept his invitation, nor he mine; he knew, moreover, that I knew he did not wish me to accept it. The phrase, under such conditions, becomes a cheat which offends the sacred spirit of hospitality. How far the mere form may go was experienced by George Sand, who having accepted the use of a carriage most earnestly offered to her by a Majorcan count, found the equipage at her door, it is true, but with it a letter expressing so much vexation, that she was forced to withdraw her acceptance of the favor at once, and to apologize for it! I have always found much hospitality among the common people of Spain, and I doubt not that the spirit exists in all classes; but it requires some practice to distinguish between empty phrase and the courtesy which comes from the heart. A people who boast of some special virtue generally do not possess it.

My own slight intercourse with the Majorcans was very pleasant. On the day of my arrival, I endeavored to procure a map of the island, but none of the bookstores possessed the article. It could be found in one house in a remote street, and one of the shopmen finally sent a boy with me to the very door. When I offered money for the service, my guide smiled, shook his head, and ran away. The map was more than fifty years old, and drawn in the style of two centuries ago, with groups of houses for the villages, and long files of conical peaks for the mountains. The woman brought it down, yellow and dusty, from a dark garret over the shop, and seemed as delighted with the sale as if she had received money for useless stock. In the streets, the people inspected me curiously, as a stranger, but were always ready to go out of their way to guide me. The ground-floor being always open, all the features of domestic life and of mechanical labor are exposed to the public. The housewives, the masters and apprentices, busy as they seem, manage to keep one eye disengaged, and no one passes before them without notice. Cooking, washing, sewing, tailoring, shoemaking, coopering, rope and basket making, succeed each other, as one passes through the narrow streets. In the afternoon, the mechanics frequently come forth and set up their business in the open air, where they can now and then greet a country acquaintance, or a city friend, or sweetheart.

When I found that the ruins of San Domingo had been removed, and a statue of Isabella II. erected on the Alameda, I began to suspect that the reign of old things was over in Majorca. A little observation of the people made this fact more evident. The island costume is no longer worn by the young men, even in the country; they have passed into a very comical transition state. Old men, mounted on lean asses or mules, still enter the gates of Palma, with handkerchiefs tied over their shaven crowns, and long gray locks falling on their shoulders, — with short, loose jackets, shawls around the waist, and wide Turkish trousers gathered at the knee. Their gaunt brown legs are bare, and their feet protected by rude sandals. Tall, large-boned, and stern of face, they hint both of Vandal and of Moslem blood. The younger men are of inferior stature, and nearly all bow-legged. They have turned the flowing trousers into modern pantaloons, the legs of which are cut like the old-fashioned *gigot* sleeve, very big and baggy at the top, and tied with a drawing-string around the waist. My first impression was, that the men had got up in a great hurry, and put on their trousers hinder end foremost. It would be difficult to invent a costume more awkward and ungraceful than this.

In the city the young girls wear a large triangular piece of white or black lace, which covers the hair, and tightly incloses the face, being fastened under the chin and the ends brought down to a point on the breast. Their almond-shaped eyes are large and fine, but there is very little positive beauty among them. Most of the old country-women are veritable hags, and their appearance is not improved by the broad-brimmed stove-pipe hats which they wear. Seated astride on their donkeys, between panniers of produce, they come in daily from the plains and mountains, and you encounter them on all the roads leading out of Palma. Few of the people speak any other language than the *Mallorquin*, a variety of the Catalan, which, from the frequency of the terminations in *ch* and *tz*, constantly suggests the old Provençal literature. The word *vitch* (son) is both Celtic and Slavonic. Some Arabic terms are also retained, though fewer, I think, than in Andalusia.

In the afternoon I walked out into the country. The wall, on the land side, which is very high and massive, is pierced by five guarded gates. The dry moat, both wide and deep, is spanned by wooden bridges, after crossing which one has the choice of a dozen highways, all scantily shaded with rows of ragged mulberry-trees, glaring white in the sun and deep in impalpable dry dust. But the sea-breeze blows freshening across the parched land; shadows of light clouds cool the arid mountains in the distance; the olives roll into silvery undulations; a palm in full, rejoicing plumage rustles over your head; and the huge spatulate leaves of a banana in the nearest garden twist and split into fringes. There is no languor in the air, no sleep in the deluge of sunshine; the landscape is active with signs of work and travel. Wheat, wine, olives, almonds, and oranges are produced, not only side by side, but from the same fields, and the painfully thorough system of cultivation leaves not a rood of the soil unused.

I had chosen, at random, a road which led me west toward the nearest mountains, and in the course of an hour I found myself at the entrance of a valley. Solitary farmhouses, each as massive as the tower of a fortress and of the color of sunburnt gold, studded the heights, overlooking the long slopes of almond orchards. I looked about for water, in order to make a sketch of the scene; but the bed of the brook was as dry as the highway. The nearest house toward the plain had a splendid sentinel palm beside its door, — a dream of Egypt, which beckoned and drew me towards it with a glamour I could not resist. Over the wall of the garden the orange-trees lifted their mounds of impenetrable foliage; and the blossoms of the pomegranates, sprinkled against such a background, were like coals of fire. The fig-bearing cactus grew about the house in clumps twenty feet high, covered with pale-yellow flowers. The building was large and roomy, with a court-yard, around which ran a shaded gallery. The farmer who was issuing therefrom as I approached wore the shawl and Turkish trousers of the old generation, while his two sons, reaping in the adjoining wheat-fields, were hideous in the modern *gigots*. Although I was manifestly an intruder, the old man greeted me respectfully, and passed on to his work. Three boys tended a drove of black hogs in the stubble, and some women were so industriously weeding and hoeing in the field beyond, that they scarcely stopped to cast a glance upon the stranger. There was a grateful air of peace, order, and contentment about the place; no one seemed to be suspicious, or even surprised, when I seated myself upon a low wall, and watched the laborers.

The knoll upon which the farm-house stood sloped down gently into the broad, rich plain of Palma, extending many a league to the eastward. Its endless orchards made a dim horizon-line, over which rose the solitary double-headed mountain of Felaniche, and the tops of some peaks near Arta. The city wall was visible on my right, and beyond it a bright arc of the Mediterranean. The features of the landscape, in fact, were so simple, that I fear I cannot make its charm evident to the reader. Looking over the nearer fields, I observed two peculiarities of Majorca, upon which depends much of the prosperity of the island. The wheat is certainly, as it is claimed to be, the finest of any Mediterranean land. Its large, perfect grains furnish a flour of such fine quality that the whole produce of the island is sent to Spain for the pastry and confectionery of the cities, while the Majorcans import a cheap, inferior kind in its place. Their fortune depends on their abstinence from the good things which Providence has given them. Their pork is greatly superior to that of Spain, and it leaves them in like manner; their best wines are now bought up by speculators and exported for the fabrication of sherry; and their oil, which might be the finest in the world, is so injured by imperfect methods of preservation that it might pass for the worst. These things, however, give them no annoyance. Southern races are sometimes indolent, but rarely Epicurean in their habits; it is the Northern man who sighs for his flesh-pots.

I walked forward between the fields towards another road, and came upon a tract which had just been ploughed and planted for a new crop. The soil was ridged in a labyrinthine pattern, which appeared to have been drawn with square and rule. But more remarkable than this was the difference of level, so slight that the eye could not possibly detect it, by which the slender irrigating streams were conducted to every square foot of the field, without a drop being needlessly wasted. The system is an inheritance from the Moors, who were the best natural engineers the world has ever known. Water is scarce in Majorca, and thus every stream, spring, rainfall — even the dew of heaven — is utilized. Channels of masonry, often covered to prevent evaporation, descend from the mountains, branch into narrow veins, and visit every farm on the plain, whatever may be its level. Where these are not sufficient, the rains are added to the reservoir, or a string of buckets, turned by a mule, lifts the water from a well. But it is in the economy of distributing water to the fields that the most marvelous skill is exhibited. The grade of the surface must not only be preserved, but the subtle, tricksy spirit of water so delicately understood and humored that the streams shall traverse the greatest amount of soil with the least waste or wear. In this respect, the most skillful application of science could not surpass the achievements of the Majorcan farmers.

Working my way homeward through the tangled streets, I was struck with the universal sound of wailing which filled the city. All the tailors, shoemakers, and basket-makers, at work in the open air, were singing, rarely in measured strains, but with wild, irregular, lamentable cries, exactly in the manner of the Arabs. Sometimes the song was antiphonal, flung back and forth from the furthest visible corners of a street; and then it became a contest of lungs, kept up for an hour at a time. While breakfasting, I had heard, as I supposed, a *miserere* chanted by some procession of monks, and wondered when the doleful strains would cease. I now saw that they came from the mouths of some cheerful coopers, who were heading barrels a little further down the street. The Majorcans still have their troubadours, who are hired by languishing lovers to improvise strains of longing or reproach under the windows of the fair, and perhaps the latter may listen with delight; but I know of no place where the Enraged Musician would so soon become insane. The isle is full of noises, and a Caliban might say that they hurt not; for me they murdered sleep, both at midnight and at dawn.

I had decided to devote my second day to an excursion to the mountain paradise of Valldemosa, and sallied forth early, to seek the means of conveyance. Up to this time I had been worried — tortured, I may say, without exaggeration — by desperate efforts to recover the Spanish tongue, which I had not spoken for fourteen years. I still had the sense of possessing it, but in some old drawer of memory, the lock of which had rusted and would not obey the key. Like Mrs. Dombey with her pain, I felt as if there were Spanish words somewhere in the room, but I could not positively say that I had them — a sensation which, as everybody knows, is far worse than absolute ignorance. I had taken a carriage for Valldemosa, after a long talk with the proprietor, a most agreeable fellow, when I suddenly stopped, and exclaimed to myself, "You are talking Spanish, did you know it?" It was even so: as much of the language as I ever knew was suddenly and unaccountably restored to me. On my return to the "Four Nations," I was still further surprised to find myself repeating songs, without the failure of a line or word, which I had learned from a Mexican as a school-boy, and had not thought of for twenty years. The unused drawer had somehow been unlocked or broken open while I slept.

Valldemosa is about twelve miles north of Palma, in the heart of the only mountain-chain of the island, which forms its western, or rather northwestern coast. The average altitude of these mountains will not exceed three thousand feet; but the broken, abrupt character of their outlines, and the naked glare of their immense precipitous walls, give them that intrinsic grandeur which does not depend on measurement. In their geological formation they resemble the Pyrenees; the rocks are of that *palombino*, or dove-colored limestone, so common in Sicily and the Grecian islands — pale bluish gray, taking a soft orange tint on the faces most exposed to the weather. Rising directly from the sea on the west, they cease almost as suddenly on the land side, leaving all the central portion of the island a plain, slightly inclined toward the southeast, where occasional peaks or irregular groups of hills interrupt its monotony.

In due time my team made its appearance — an omnibus of basket-work, with a canvas cover, drawn by two horses. It had space enough for twelve persons, yet was the smallest vehicle I could discover. There appears to be nothing between it and the two-wheeled cart of the peasant, which, on a pinch, carries six or eight. For an hour and a half we traversèd the teeming plain, between stacks of wheat worthy to be laid on the altar at Eleusis, carob trees with their dark, varnished foliage, almond-orchards bending under the weight of their green nuts, and the country houses with their garden clumps of orange, cactus, and palm. As we drew near the base of the mountains, olive-trees of great size and luxuriance covered the earth with a fine sprinkle of shade. Their gnarled and knotted trunks, a thousand years old, were frequently split into three or four distinct and separate trees, which in the process assumed forms so marvelously human in their distortion, that I could scarcely believe them to be accidental. Doré never drew anything so weird and grotesque. Here were two club-headed individuals fighting, with interlocked knees, convulsed shoulders, and fists full of each other's hair; yonder a bully was threatening attack, and three cowards appeared to be running away from him with such speed that they were tumbling over one another's heels. In one place a horrible dragon was devouring a squirming, shapeless animal; in another, a drunken man, with whirling arms and tangled feet, was pitching forward upon his face. The living wood in Dante was tame beside these astonishing trees.

We now entered a wild ravine, where, nevertheless, the mountain-sides, sheer and savage as they were, had succumbed to the rule of man, and nourished an olive or a carob tree on every corner of earth between the rocks. The road was built along the edge of the deep, dry bed of a winter stream, so narrow that a single arch carried it from side to side, as the windings of the glen compelled. After climbing thus for a mile in the shadows of threatening masses of rock, an amphitheatre of gardens, enframed by the spurs of two grand, arid mountains, opened before us. The bed of the valley was filled with vines and orchards, beyond which rose long terraces, dark with orange and citron trees, obelisks of cypress and magnificent groups of palm, with the long white front and shaded balconies of a hacienda between. Far up, on a higher plateau between the peaks I saw the church-tower of Valldemosa. The sides of the mountains were terraced with almost incredible labor, walls massive as the rock itself being raised to a height of thirty feet, to gain a shelf of soil two or three yards in breadth. Where the olive and the carob ceased, box and ilex took possession of the inaccessible points, carrying up the long waves of vegetation until their foam-sprinkles of silver-gray faded out among the highest clefts. The natural channels of the rock were straightened and made to converge at the base, so that not a wandering cloud could bathe the wild growths of the summit without being caught and hurried into some tank below. The wilderness was forced, by pure toil, to become a Paradise;

and each stubborn feature, which toil could not subdue, now takes its place as a contrast and an ornament in the picture. Verily, there is nothing in all Italy so beautiful as Valldemosa!

Lest I should be thought extravagant in my delight, let me give you some words of George Sand, which I have since read. "I have never seen," she says, "anything so bright, and at the same time so melancholy, as these perspectives where the ilex, the carob, pine, olive, poplar, and cypress mingle their various hues in the hollows of the mountain — abysses of verdure, where the torrent precipitates its course under mounds of sumptous richness and an inimitable grace. . . . . While you hear the sound of the sea on the northern coast, you perceive it only as a faint shining line beyond the sinking mountains and the great plain which is unrolled to the southward — a sublime picture, framed in the foreground by dark rocks covered with pines; in the middle distance by mountains of boldest outline, fringed with superb trees; and beyond these by rounded hills which the setting sun gilds with burning colors, where the eye distinguishes, a league away, the microscopic profile of trees, fine as the antennæ of butterflies, black and clear as pen-drawings of India ink on a ground of sparkling gold. It is one of those landscapes which oppress you because they leave nothing to be desired, nothing to be imagined. Nature has here created that which the poet and the painter behold in their dreams. An immense *ensemble*, infinite details, inexhaustible variety, blended forms, sharp contours, dim, vanishing depths — all are present, and art can suggest nothing further. Majorca is one of the most beautiful countries of the world for the painter, and one of the least known. It is a green Helvetia under the sky of Calabria, with the solemnity and silence of the Orient."

The village of Valldemosa is a picturesque, rambling place, brown with age, and buried in the foliage of fig and orange trees. The highest part of the narrow plateau where it stands is crowned by the church and monastery of the Trappists (*Cartusa*), now deserted. My coachman drove under the open roof of a venta, and began to unharness his horses. The family, who were dining at a table so low that they appeared to be sitting on the floor, gave me the customary invitation to join them, and when I asked for a glass of wine brought me one which held nearly a quart. I could not long turn my back on the bright, wonderful landscape without; so, taking books and colors, I entered the lonely cloisters of the monastery. Followed first by one small boy, I had a retinue of at least fifteen children before I had completed the tour of the church, court-yard, and the long drawn, shady corridors of the silent monks; and when I took my seat on the stones at the foot of the tower, with the very scene described by George Sand before my eyes, a number of older persons added themselves to the group. A woman brought me a chair, and the children then planted themselves in a dense row before me, while I attempted to sketch under such difficulties as I had never known before. Precisely because I am no artist, it makes me nervous to be watched while drawing; and the remarks of the young men on this occasion were not calculated to give me courage.

When I had roughly mapped out the sky with its few floating clouds, some one exclaimed, "He has finished the mountains, there they are!" and they all crowded around me, saying, "Yes, there are the mountains!" While I was really engaged upon the mountains, there was a violent discussion as to what they might be; and I don't know how long it would have lasted, had I not turned to some cypresses nearer the foreground. Then a young man cried out: "O, that's a cypress! I wonder if he will make them all, — how many are there? One, two, three, four, five, — yes, he makes five!" There was an immediate rush, shutting out earth and heaven from my sight, and they all cried in chorus, "One, two, three, four, five — yes, he has made five!"

"Cavaliers and ladies," I said, with solemn politeness, "have the goodness not to stand before me."

"To be sure! Santa Maria! How do you think he can see?" yelled an old woman, and the children were hustled away. But I thereby won the ill-will of those garlic-breathing and scratching imps, for very soon a shower of water-drops fell upon my paper. Next a stick, thrown from an upper window, dropped on my head, and more than once my elbow was intentionally jogged from behind. The older people scolded and threatened, but young Majorca was evidently against me. I therefore made haste to finish my impotent mimicry of air and light, and get away from the curious crowd.

Behind the village there is a gleam of the sea, near, yet at an unknown depth. As I threaded the walled lanes seeking some point of view, a number of lusty young fellows, mounted on unsaddled mules, passed me with a courteous greeting. On one side rose a grand pile of rock, covered with ilex-trees — a bit of scenery so admirable, that I fell into a new temptation. I climbed a little knoll and looked around me. Far and near no children were to be seen; the portico of an unfinished house offered both shade and seclusion. I concealed myself behind a pillar, and went to work. For half an hour I was happy; then a round black head popped up over a garden wall, a small brown form crept towards me, beckoned, and presently a new multitude had assembled. The noise they made provoked a sound of cursing from the interior of a stable adjoining the house. They only made a louder tumult in answer; the voice became more threatening, and at the end of five minutes the door burst open. An old man, with wrath flashing from his eyes, came forth. The children took to their heels; I greeted the new-comer politely, but he hardly returned the salutation. He was a very fountain of curses, and now hurled stones with them after the fugitives. When they had all disappeared behind the walls, he went back to his den, grumbling and muttering. It was not five minutes, however, before the children were back again, as noisy as before; so, at the first thunder from the stable, I shut up my book, and returned to the inn.

While the horses were being harnessed, I tried to talk with an old native, who wore the island costume, and was as grim and grizzly as Ossawatomie Brown. A party of country people from the plains, who seemed to have come up to Valldemosa on a pleasure trip, clambered into a two-wheeled cart drawn by one mule, and drove away. My old friend gave me the distances of various places, the state of the roads, and the quality of the wine; but he seemed to have no conception of the world outside of the island. Indeed, to a native of the village, whose fortune has simply placed him beyond the reach of want, what is the rest of the world? Around and before him spreads one of its loveliest pictures; he breathes its purest air; and he may enjoy its best luxuries, if he heeds or knows how to use them.

Up to this day the proper spice and flavor had been wanting. Palma had only interested me, but in Valldemosa I found the inspiration, the heat and play of vivid, keen sensation, which one (often somewhat unreasonably) expects from a new land. As my carriage descended, winding around the sides of the magnificent mountain amphitheatre, in the alternate shadows of palm and ilex, pine and olive, I looked back, clinging to every marvelous picture, and saying to myself, over again, "I have not come hither in vain." When the last shattered gate of rock closed behind me, and the wood of insane olive-trunks was passed, with what other eyes I looked upon the rich orchard-plain! It had now become a part of one superb whole; as the background of my mountain view, it had caught a new glory, and still wore the bloom of the invisible sea.

In the evening I reached the "Four Nations," where I was needlessly invited to dinner by certain strangers, and dined alone, on meats cooked in rancid oil. When the cook had dished the last course, he came into a room adjoining the dining apartment, sat down to a piano in his white cap, and played loud, long, and badly. The landlord had papered this room with illustrations from all the periodicals of Europe: dancing-girls pointed their toes under cardinals' hats, and bulls were baited before the shrines of saints. Mixed with the wood-cuts were the landlord's own artistic productions, wonderful to behold. All the house was proud of this room, and with reason; for there is assuredly no other room like it in the world. A notice in four languages, written with extraordinary flourishes, announced in the English division that travellers will find "confortation and modest prices." The former advantage, I discovered, consisted in the art of the landlord, the music and oil of the cook, and the attendance of a servant so distant that it was easier to serve myself than seek him; the latter may have been "modest" for Palma, but in any other place they would have been considered brazenly impertinent. I should therefore advise travellers to try the "Three Pigeons," in the same street, rather than the "Four Nations."

The next day, under the guidance of my old friend, M. Laurens, I wandered for several hours through the streets, peeping into court-yards, looking over garden-walls, or idling under the trees of the Alameda. There are no pleasant suburban places of resort, such as are to be found in all other Spanish cities; the country commences on the other side of the moat. Three small cafés exist, but cannot be said to flourish, for I never saw more than one table occupied. A theatre has been built, but is only open during the winter, of course. Some placards on the walls, however, announced that the national (that is, Majorcan) diversion of baiting bulls with dogs would be given in a few days.

The noblesse appear to be even haughtier than in Spain, perhaps on account of their greater poverty; and much more of the feudal spirit lingers among them, and gives character to society, than on the main-land. Each family has still a crowd of retainers, who perform a certain amount of service on the estates, and are thenceforth entitled to support. This custom is the reverse of profitable; but it keeps up an air of lordship, and is therefore retained. Late in the afternoon, when the new portion of the Alameda is in shadow, and swept by a delicious breeze from the sea, it begins to be frequented by the people; but I noticed that very few of the upper class made their appearance. So grave and sombre are these latter, that one would fancy them descended from the conquered Moors, rather than the Spanish conquerors.

M. Laurens is of the opinion that the architecture of Palma cannot be ascribed to an earlier period than the beginning of the sixteenth century. I am satisfied, however, either that many fragments of Moorish sculpture must have been used in the erection of the older buildings, or that certain peculiarities of Moorish art have been closely imitated. For instance, that Moorish combination of vast, heavy masses of masonry with the lightest and airiest style of ornament, which the Gothic sometimes attempts, but never with the same success, is here found at every step. I will borrow M. Laurens' words, descriptive of the superior class of edifices, both because I can find no better of my own, and because this very characteristic has been noticed by him. "Above the ground-floor," he says, "there is only one story and a low garret. The entrance is a semi-circular portal without ornament; but the number and dimensions of the stones, disposed in long radii, give it a stately aspect. The grand halls of the main story are lighted by windows divided by excessively slender columns, which are entirely Arabic in appearance. This character is so pronounced, that I was obliged to examine more than twenty houses constructed in the same manner, and to study all the details of their construction, in order to assure myself that the windows had not really been taken from those fairy Moresque palaces, of which the Alhambra is the only remaining specimen. Except in Majorca, I have nowhere seen columns which, with a height of six feet, have a diameter of only three inches. The fine grain of the marble of which they are made, as well as the delicacy of the capitals, led me to suppose them to be of Saracenic origin."

I was more impressed by the *Lonja*, or Exchange, than any other building in Palma. It dates from the first half of the fifteenth century, when the kings of the island had built up a flourishing commerce, and expected to rival Genoa and Venice. Its walls, once crowded with merchants and seamen, are now only opened for the Carnival balls and other festivals sanctioned by religion. It is a square edifice, with light Gothic towers at the corners, displaying little ornamental sculpture, but nevertheless a taste and symmetry, in all its details, which are very rare in Spanish architecture. The interior is a single vast hall, with a groined roof, resting on six pillars of exquisite beauty. They are sixty feet high, and fluted spirally from top to bottom, like a twisted cord, with a diameter of not more than two feet and a half. It is astonishing how the airy lightness and grace of these pillars relieve the immense mass of masonry, spare the bare walls the necessity of ornament, and make the ponderous roof light as a tent. There is here the trace of a law of which our modern architects seem to be ignorant. Large masses of masonry are always oppressive in their effect; they suggest pain and labor, and the Saracens, even more than the Greeks, seem to have discovered the necessity of introducing a sportive, fanciful element, which shall express the delight of the workman in his work.

In the afternoon, I sallied forth from the western coast-gate, and found there, sloping to the shore, a village inhabited apparently by sailors and fishermen. The houses were of one story, flat-roofed, and brilliantly whitewashed. Against the blue background of the sea, with here and there the huge fronds of a palm rising from among them, they made a truly African picture. On the brown ridge above the village were fourteen huge windmills, nearly all in motion. I found a road leading along the brink of the overhanging cliffs, toward the castle of Belver, whose brown mediæval turrets rose against a gathering thunder-cloud. This fortress, built as a palace for the kings of Majorca immediately after the expulsion of the Moors, is now a prison. It has a superb situation, on the summit of a conical hill, covered with umbrella-pines. In one of its round, massive towers, Arago was imprisoned for two months in 1808. He was at the time employed in measuring an arc of the meridian, when news of Napoleon's violent measures in Spain reached Majorca. The ignorant populace immediately suspected the astronomer of being a spy and political agent, and would have lynched him at once. Warned by a friend, he disguised himself as a sailor, escaped on board a boat in the harbor, and was then placed in Belver by the authorities, in order to save his life. He afterwards succeeded in reaching Algiers, where he was seized by order of the Bey, and made to work as a slave. Few men of science have known so much of the romance of life.

I had a long walk to Belver, but I was rewarded by a grand view of the Bay of Palma, the city and all the southern extremity of the island. I endeavored to get into the fields, to seek other points of view; but they were surrounded by such lofty walls that I fancied the owners of the soil could only get at them by scaling-ladders. The grain and trees on either side of the road were hoary with dust, and the soil, of the hue of burnt chalk, seemed never to have known moisture. But while I loitered on the cliffs the cloud in the west had risen and spread; a cold wind blew over the hills, and the high gray peaks behind Valldemosa disappeared, one by one, in a veil of rain. A rough *tartana*, which performed the service of an omnibus, passed me returning to the city, and the driver, having no passengers, invited me to ride. "What is your fare?" I asked. "Whatever people choose to give," said he, — which was reasonable enough; and I thus reached the "Four Nations" in time to avoid a deluge.

The Majorcans are fond of claiming their island as the birthplace of Hannibal. There are some remains supposed to be Carthaginian near the town of Alcudia, but, singularly enough, not a fragment to tell of the Roman domination, although their *Balearis Major* must have been then, as now, a rich and important possession. The Saracens, rather than the Vandals, have been the spoilers of ancient art. Their religious detestation of sculpture was at the bottom of this destruction. The Christians could consecrate the old temple to a new service, and give the names of saints to the statues of the gods; but to the Moslem every representation of the human form was worse than blasphemy. For this reason, the symbols of the most ancient faith, massive and unintelligible, have outlived the monuments of those which followed.

In a forest of ancient oaks near the village of Arta, there still exist a number of Cyclopean constructions, the character of which is as uncertain as the date of their erection. They are cones of huge, irregular blocks, the jambs and lintels of the entrances being of single stones. In a few the opening is at the top, with rude projections resembling a staircase to aid in the descent. Cinerary urns have been found in some of them, yet they do not appear to have been originally constructed as tombs. The Romans may have afterwards turned them to that service. In the vicinity there are the remains of a Druid circle, of large upright monoliths. These singular structures were formerly much more numerous, the people (who call them "the altars of the Gentiles") having destroyed a great many in building the village and the neighboring farm-houses.

I heard a great deal about a cavern on the eastern coast of the island, beyond Arta. It is called the Hermit's Cave, and the people of Palma consider it the principal thing to be seen in all Majorca. Their descriptions of the place, however, did not inspire me with any very lively desire to undertake a two days' journey for the purpose of crawling on the belly through a long hole, and then descending a shaky rope-ladder for a hundred feet or more. When one has performed these feats, they said, he finds himself in an immense hall, supported by stalactitic pillars, the marvels of which cannot be described. Had the scenery of the eastern part of the island been more attractive, I should have gone as far as Arta; but I wished to meet the steamer Minorca at Alcudia, and there were but two days remaining.

BALEARIC DAYS.

II.

The same spacious omnibus and span of dun-colored ponies which had taken me to Valldemosa came to carry me across the island. As there is an excellent highway, and the distance to Alcudia is not more than ten leagues, I could easily have made the journey in a day; but I purposely divided it, in order to secure a quiet, unhurried enjoyment of the scenery of the interior. It had rained violently all night, and the morning of my departure from Palma was cold and overcast. The coachman informed me that four months had elapsed since a drop of rain had fallen, and that for two years past the island had suffered from drought. I therefore wrapped myself in my cloak, contented with the raw air and threatening sky, since the dry *acequias* would now flow with new streams, and the empty tanks of the farmers be filled.

It was like a rainy day in the tropics. There was a gray veil all over the sky, deepening into blackness where the mountains drew down the showers. The soil, yesterday as dry as a cinder, already looked soggy and drenched, and in place of white, impalpable dust, puddles of water covered the road. For the first two leagues we drove over a dead level, seeing nothing but fig, olive, and almond trees, with an occasional palm or cactus, fading out of sight in the rain. Majorca is in reality the orchard of the Mediteranean. All its accessible surface is not only covered with fruit-trees, but the fruit is of the most exquisite quality. The apricots are not dry and insipid, but full of juice, and with a flavor as perfect as that of a peach. The oranges and figs seemed to me the finest I had ever tasted; even the date-palm matures its fruit, and the banana grows in the same garden with the cherry and apple. The valley of Soller, the only port on the western side of the mountains, was described to me as one unbroken orchard of superb orange-trees, a league or two in length. The difficulty of transportation has hitherto robbed the people of the profits of their production, and a new prosperity has come with the recent improvement of their roads. Within a league of Palma an entire village has been built within the last five years; and most of the older towns are in rapid process of enlargement.

After the second league, the country became undulating, the trees were loftier and more luxuriant, and woods of picturesque Italian pine covered the rocky crests of the hills. The mountains on the left assumed very bold and violent forms, rising through the dim atmosphere like so many detached towers and fortresses. There were two dominant peaks, which in the sheer escarpment of their summits resembled the crags of Königstein and Lilienstein in Saxony. They were the Torrella and the Puig (Peak) Major — grand, naked, almost inaccessible mountains, which shed the rain like a roof. The water-courses which came down from them were no longer dry hollows, but filled to the brim with swift, roaring, turbid floods. These peaks appeared to be detached nearly to the base, and between their steep abutments the mouths of dim, folding gorges gave promise of rare and original scenery within their recesses.

We passed Santa Maria, a beautiful little village of two streets, at the intersection of which rises a fine square belfry, connected with the buildings of a defunct monastery. The picture was so pleasant that I brought its outlines away with me. In spite of the rain, the people were at work in the fields, turning the red soil about the roots of the olive-trees. The flowing trousers were no longer to be seen; even the old men here wore the *gigot*. Others, with the words *Peon caminero* on their caps, were breaking stones by the roadside. I received a friendly *Bŏn di'!* from each and all. Both robbery and beggary are unknown in Majorca; they have no place in a land of so much material order and cheerful industry.

Beyond Santa Maria the road again became quite level, and the courses of the streams pointed to the northern shore. The fruit-trees temporarily gave place to vineyards so luxuriant that the shoots, unsupported by stake or trellis, threw their tendrils around each other, and hid the soil under a deluge of green. The wine of Benisalem (Arabic *beni-salaam,* "the children of peace") is considered the best on the island. It is a fiery, golden-brown vintage, resembling ripe old Malaga in flavor.

We were within a league of Inca, — my destination, — when the rain, which had already blotted out the mountains, began to drive over the plain. A fine spray beat through the canvas cover of the omnibus, condemning me to a blind, silent, and cheerless half-hour of travel. Then, between garden-walls, over which the lemon-trees hung great boughs breaking with fruit, and under clumps of rustling and dripping palms, I entered Inca. My equipage drew up before the door of a new *fonda* in a narrow old street. There were billiards and coffee on the groundfloor; over them a long hall, out of which all the doors and staircases issued, served as a dining-room. The floors were tiled, the walls white-washed and decorated with the lithographed histories of Mazeppa and Hernan Cortez, and the heavy pine joists of the ceiling were fresh and unpainted. There was an inconsiderate waste of space in the disposition of the rooms and passages which was pleasant to behold. Contrary to the usual habit of travellers, I ventured into the kitchen, and found it — as it ought to be — the most cheerful and attractive part of the house. The landlord brought a glass of the wine of Benisalem to stay my hunger; but I was not obliged to wait overlong for the excellent meal of eggs, kid with pepper-sauce, and an exquisite dish of lobster stewed with leeks and tomatoes, which I tasted for the first time.

Towards evening the rain subsided, and I went forth to view the place, finding a picture at every turn. First, a group of boys burning shavings before a church-door; then a gable embowered with one enormous grape-vine, and touched with sunshine, while beneath, in the gloom of a large arch, the family ate their supper; then a guitar-player in the door of a barber's shop, with a group around him, or a company of women, filling their jars at a fountain. The town is built upon an irregular hill, overlooking the finest orchards of Majorca. The clusters of palm-trees which spring from its topmost gardens are far more beautiful than its church-towers. Nothing can be more picturesque than the narrow valleys on either side, which slope sufficiently to bring out in sumptuous contrast the foliage of the terraced gardens. The people looked at me curiously, but with no unfriendly air, as I followed the winding streets into the country, or loitered through some country lane back into the town. Only two persons spoke to me — the letter-carrier, and a boy who was trying to knock down swallows with a long pole. The latter made a remark which I did not understand, but it was evidently witty, for we both laughed. The workmen at their avocations sang with all their force, and very dismally. It was difficult to say which were the more insignificant — the melodies or the words of their songs. One specimen of the latter will suffice to give an idea of both: —

> " On Sundays the young girls you may view,
> (Since they nothing better have then to do),
> Watering their pots of carnations sweet:
> Saying, Drink, my dears, for you cannot eat! "

When I returned to the fonda, the landlord took me into a part of his house which was built like a tower above the level of the city roofs. A thunderous mass of clouds still hung over the Puig Major, but between its rifts the low sun cast long lines of brassy radiance over the wide landscape. Westward rose the torn and shattered mountains; eastward the great orchard-plain stretched away into purple dimness, only broken by the chapel-crowned peak of Santa Maddalena, near at hand, and the signal mountain of Felaniche in the distance. Inca, under my feet, resounded with wailing noises, which, nevertheless, expressed the cheerfulness and content of the inhabitants. Through the lanes dividing the rich vegetation, the laborers were flocking homeward from their fields; rude *tartanas* rattled along the broad white highway; and the chimes of vesper presently floated over the scene in slow, soothing vibrations. "You see how beautiful the country is!" said the landlord; "I suppose there is nothing finer in the world. You will think so too, when you have been to the cemetery, and have seen the new monument. It is wonderful! A basket full of flowers, and if they were not all white, you would take them to be real. They say it cost an immense amount of money."

When I asked for *juevos* (eggs) for my supper, the landlady shook her head, until somebody suggested *joãos!* with a sound like the whistling of wind through a keyhole. They were then speedily forthcoming, with another dish of the lobster and leeks, and a bottle of excellent wine. I was kept awake for a long time, that night, by the thrumming of guitars and the click of billiard balls in the café below; and when sleep finally came, it was suddenly broken by the bursting open of the doors and windows of my room. The house seemed to rock under the stress of the hurricane; the lightning played through the torrents of rain in rapid flashes of transparent silver, accompanied with peals like the crashing down of all the *Puigs* in the mountain-chain. But at sunrise, when I went upon the roof, I found the island sparkling under the purest of morning skies, every leaf washed, every outline of the landscape recut, and all its colors bright as if newly dyed. A bracing north wind blew over the fields, and there was an expression of joy in the very dance of the boughs and the waving of the vines.

When we set out for Alcudia, the coachman first drove to a fountain at the foot of the hill, and watered his horses. There was a throng about the place, — old women with huge earthen amphoræ, young girls with jars which they carried on the hip, donkeys laden with casks, and children carrying all sorts of smaller vessels. The water is brought from the mountains to this fountain, which never fails in its supply. It is shaded by grand old plane and carob trees, which throw a network of light and gloom over the great stone tanks and the picturesque moving crowds. Rising out of the glen where it stands, I saw the mountains bare in the morning sun, every crevice and jag of their rocky fronts painted with a pre-Raphaelite pencil. Past the foot of the solitary mountain of Santa Maddalena ran our road, and then northward over a second plain, even richer than that of Palma.

The olive and almond trees by the roadside had been washed clean of dust, but they hissed in the breeze as dryly as if they had never known rain. The very colors of the olive, ilex, and myrtle express aridity. Their dry leaves seem to repel moisture, even as the mellow, sappy green of the North seems to attract it. But their soft grays relieve the keen, strong tints of soil, sea, and sky, and we could ill spare them from these landcapes. As accessories to sun-browned houses, or masses of ruined architecture, they are invaluable. They belong naturally to an atmosphere of age and repose, while fresh turf and deciduous trees perpetually reproduce the youth of Nature. Something of Attica always comes to me with the olive, something of Tusculum and the Sabine Farm with the ilex. The box, I know not why, suggests the Euphrates; and the myrtle in bloom, the Garden of Eden.

While these thoughts were passing through my mind,

the road slowly fell to the northward; and I beheld in the distance fields of a green so dazzling that the hackneyed term "emerald" seems much too dull to express it. It positively *burned* in the sun, drawing into itself the lustre of the sky, the distant sea, and the leagues of glittering foliage. Over it rose, as a completer foil, the gray mountains of the peninsula dividing the bays of Pollenza and Alcudia. I was at a loss to guess what plant could give such an indescribable color; and not until we were within a stone's throw did I recognize the leaves of hemp. An open, marshy plain, entirely bare of trees, bordered the bay at this point. The splendid orchards ceased; the road crossed some low hills overgrown with ilex and pine, a turbid, roaring stream, with poplars on its banks; and then a glimmer of the sea on either hand showed that we had reached the peninsula. There were Moorish *atalayas*, or watch-towers, on the summits nearest the sea, and a large ruined fortress of the Middle Ages on a hill inland. Alcudia, with its yellow walls, its cypress and palm trees, now appeared at the foot of the barren heights, oriental in every feature. It was a picture from the Syrian coast, needing only the old Majorcan costume for the laborers in the fields to be perfect.

Contrasted with those parts of the island which I had seen, the country appeared singularly lonely and deserted. Few persons met us on the road, and we passed none on their way to the town. Grass grew on the huge walls of defense, the stones were slipping from the arch of the gateway, and we passed into a silent street without seeing a living thing. My coachman stopped before a mean-looking house, with no sign or other indication of its character, and informed me that it was the only fonda in the place. A woman who came to the door confirmed this statement, modestly adding, "We are not very fine, but we will give you what we have." A narrow room on the ground-floor was at once entrance-hall, dining-room, and kitchen; it contained one table, three chairs, much dirt, and very nimble insects. The inmates were two women, and a small dog with a bell on his neck, which, whenever he scratched his head with his hind foot, rang a peal of alarm through the house. Feeling the need of consolation, I summoned a boy from the street, and gave him some money to bring me cigars from the *estanco;* but the hostess, taking the coin, cried out in great excitement: "Don't send that! Holy Mother, don't send that! You'll lose a *'chavo* on it!" The coachman burst into a laugh, repeating, "Lose a *'chavo!*" — which is about the eighth part of a cent; but the woman was so horrified at the idea that I gave the boy another coin.

While the eggs and tough scraps of beef destined for my meal were simmering in pans of strong oil, the hostess conducted me into a room above, which contained a large and very ancient bed, five blue chests, and twenty-three pictures of saints. "There!" she exclaimed, with a wave of the arm and a look of triumph, "my own room, but you shall have it! We may not be very fine, but we give what we have." Whatever my thoughts may have been, it was quite impossible to avoid expressing my entire satisfaction.

I took my books, went outside the walls to a tower which I had noticed on the ridge, and there found the very view of the town, the mountains, and the bay, which a stranger would desire to take home with him. In the full noonday sunshine, there was scarcely shadow enough to relieve the clear golden tints of the landscape; but the place was entirely deserted, which was a better fortune than I enjoyed at Valldemosa. Three peasants were reaping wheat in a little field behind the tower; now and then a donkey and rider jogged slowly along the distant highway; but no one seemed to notice the mysterious stranger. I had an undisturbed dream of two hours, for the forms before me, half borrowed from my memories of Oriental life, half drawn from those landscapes which rise in our minds as we read the stories of the Middle Ages, satisfied both the eye and the fancy. Some scenes suggest the sound of a flute and Theocritan idyls; others, horns and trumpets, and fragments of epic poetry; but here the only accompaniment was cymbals, the only poems suggested were "Fatima" and "Rudel to the Lady of Tripoli."

In the afternoon I walked around the city walls, climbed upon them, visited the deserted monastery of San Diego, and wandered at will through its picturesque ruins. The place is surrounded by double walls of great strength, divided by a moat cut out of the solid rock. The caperplant, the ivy, and the wild fig-tree have taken possession of the parapet and the rifts between the stones, goats browse in the bottom of the moat, and children's faces peep forth from the watch-towers on the ramparts. Outside the principal gate, I came upon a Gothic cross, resting on an octagonal base, so very old and weather-beaten that it must certainly have been erected during the first years of the conquest. The walls of the city are said to be Saracenic; but the people are poor authority on this or any other historical point. It is certain, at least, that Alcudia was formerly much more important than now. Its bay was a naval station, whence expeditions were sent out to Africa or the Levant; and there were times when the kings of Spain built whole fleets from the forests of the island.

Of late, a little fresh life has begun to flow into the silent old town. On the shore of the bay, a few miles off, an English company has undertaken agricultural operations on a grand scale. Many square leagues of the former useless, pestiferous marshes have been drained, steam-engines erected to supply water for irrigation, and an attempt made to cultivate cotton. Concerning the success of the undertaking, I heard the most contradictory accounts. The people could only tell me of the immense sums expended, — sums which appeared almost fabulous to them. The agents, of course, claimed to be entirely successful, notwithstanding the cotton-plants, this year, will scarcely produce enough to pay for the seed. Last year (1866), I was informed, the yield was very fine : the staple being equal to that of our Sea-island cotton. The intention of the English capitalists was probably to produce a similar article, and it cannot be denied that they have shrewdly chosen the spot for the experiment.

When the afternoon shadow filled the street, I seated myself at the door of the fonda, and amused myself with the movements of some carpenters in an opposite shop. Two lusty apprentices were engaged in the slow labor of sawing beams into boards, while the master fitted together the parts of a door. The former used an upright saw, one standing on a frame overhead, and the other on the floor below; they were just an hour and a half in sawing five boards from a beam a foot wide and sixteen feet long. Whenever a neighbor dropped in to gossip with the master, the saw stopped, and the apprentices took an active part in the conversation. There was also a boy of twelve years old, who did no work except in the way of singing. With his head thrown back, and his mouth open to its fullest extent, he poured forth an endless succession of piercing cries, recommencing, at the end of each lamentable close of the measure, with a fury and frenzy which nearly drove me wild. The little dog in the fonda, from time to time, rang a suggestive peal upon his bell, and echoes from other streets, and distant bells from other tormented dogs, filled up the pauses of the performance.

At sunset the other inmates of the fonda began to collect. First, there arrived two French workmen, of mean aspect; then a Spanish cavalier, who was evidently a person of some importance, for he invited nobody to partake of his supper. He was a large, olive-colored man, with a loud voice and opaque gray eyes, in which, as he fixed them upon my face, I read the question, "Are you not going to salute me?" I returned the look, and my eyes answered, "Who art thou, that I should salute thee?" After these remarks, which both understood, we spoke no more. Several natives came, during the evening, to be paid for some service; but they received no money. The two Frenchmen supped with the hostess and her family, but the important Spaniard and myself had our meals apart. Finally the comedy became tiresome, and I went to bed.

Not to sleep, alas! The little dog's bell was silent through the night, but had there been one around my neck it would have chimed the quarter-hours without a single failure. The steamer for Minorca was expected in the bay at sunrise; so I arose with the first stir in the house, and found two gentlemen who had come from Palma during the night, and three man-of-war's men, waiting in the street for an omnibus which was to carry us to the mole. We all waited together an hour, took chocolate, and then, after another half-hour, were requested to climb into a two-wheeled cart, drawn by a single horse. The hostess said to me, "We are not very fine, and I don't know how much you ought to pay, but I will take what you think right," — which she did, with honest thanks, and then we clattered out of the gate.

A descent of two miles between fields of wheat and olives brought us to the mole, where we found only a few lazy boatmen lying upon heaps of iron castings, which were waiting, apparently, for the English engineers. Shoals of young sardines sprinkled the clear green deeps of the sea with a million points of light, and some dead flounders lay like lozenges of silver among the dark weeds of the bottom. A new fish-crate, floating beside the pier, was a mild evidence of enterprise. The passengers sat in the sun until it became too powerful, then in the shade, and so another hour and a half rolled away. With the first appearance of the steamer, we got into a boat, and slowly floated out between two crystal atmospheres (so transparent is the sea) into the roadstead.

The extent of the Bay of Alcudia cannot be less than fifteen miles, for our deliberate steamer was nearly two hours in getting its southern headland abeam. Once outside, the eastern coast of Majorca opened finely with a long, diminishing group of mountains, and the dim, nearly level outline of Minorca appeared in front. The sea was like a mirror, broken only at times by a floating turtle or the leap of a dolphin. I found the Mahonese on board to be a very different class of persons from the Majorcans in whose company I had left Barcelona. Port Mahon was for twenty years our Mediterranean naval station; and although for twenty years it has ceased to be so, there are still traces of intelligence, of sympathy, of language, and of blood, which our quasi-occupation has left behind. Two of the passengers had visited America, one had an American wife in Minorca, and all became friendly and communicative when my nationality was announced. They had faithfully followed the history of our navy through the war, and took especial pains to claim Admiral Farragut as a countryman. His father, they said, was a Minorcan, and the farm in the interior of the island upon which he once lived still bears the family name. I was brought back suddenly from the times of Tancred (which had faded out of sight with the walls of Alcudia) to our stormy politics and the new names they have given to history.

All the afternoon we skirted the southern coast of Minorca. The town of Ciudadela, at its western extremity, showed like a faint white mark in the distance; then some groups of hills interrupted the level table of the island, and, farther eastward, the solitary mountains of El Toro. The two gentlemen of Palma, neither of whom had ever before made a journey, went below and slept the sleep of indifference. Many of the Mahonese followed their example; and, the quarter-deck being left clear, I stretched myself out over the cabin skylight, and quietly watched the moving shore, as if it were some immense diorama unrolled for my eyes only.

The white cliffs along the sea, the tawny harvest-fields, the gray olives embosoming villages and country-houses, and the occasional shafts of cypress or palm, slowly photographed themselves upon my consciousness, and became enduring pictures. Had I climbed and hammered the cliffs as a geologist, scoured the fields as a botanist, analyzed the soil, or even measured its undulations, I could not have obtained a completer impression of Minorca.

El Toro was drifting astern, and the island of Ayre showed its light-house in front, when the sound of a guitar disturbed my comfortable process of absorption, and brought the sleepy passengers upon deck. The performer was a blind Spaniard, a coarse-featured, clumsy man, whose life and soul had gone into his instrument, separating light, beauty, and refinement from earthy darkness. When he played, the guitar really seemed to be the man, and his body a mere holder, or music-stand. The Mahonese, I was glad to see, not only appreciated the performance, but were very liberal in their contributions.

The island of Ayre lies off the southeastern extremity of Minorca. In the intervening strait, the sea was so wonderfully transparent that the alternations of bare limestone floor and fields of sea-weed far below our keel, changed the color of the water from a turquoise so dazzling that I can only call it blue fire to an emerald gloom pierced with golden lightnings. Even that southern temperament which cares so little for Nature, was aroused by the sight of these splendors. The passengers hung over the railing with cries of admiration, and the blind minstrel was left to soliloquize on his guitar. Against a headland in front, the smooth sea suddenly rose in a crest of foam, behind which a gleam of darker sapphire denoted the mouth of a harbor. In a few minutes more we were abreast of the entrance to Port Mahon, with a great ascending slope of new fortifications on the north. Hundreds of men are now employed on defenses which the new developments in naval warfare have rendered useless; and the officials conceal, with the most jealous fear, the plan of a system of forts and batteries which no other nation need care to know.

The lower ground, on the southern side of the entrance to the inner harbor, is entirely covered with the ruins of the immense fortress of San Felipe, built by the English during their occupation of Minorca from 1708 to 1802. The fate of Admiral Byng, executed for a naval victory over the French, gives a tragic interest to these ruins, which, in their extent, resemble those of a city. All governments (our own included) know how to make their individual servants the scapegoats for their blunders or their incapacity; but I know not, in all history, of a case so flagrant as that of Byng. The destruction of Fort San Felipe cost nearly half a million of dollars, and yet it appears to be only partial.

On passing the channel between the fort and Cape Mola, we found ourselves in the port, but only at its entrance; the city was not yet visible. A bright white town crowned the low cliffs of the southern shore — the former Georgetown of the English, the present Villa Carlos of the Spaniards. Opposite to it, the long quarantine island divided the intensely blue water; and my fellow-passengers claimed with pride that it was capable of accommodating a whole fleet. Beyond this island the harbor bends southward, shutting out of sight the sea entrance; it becomes a still lake, inclosed by bare, bright hills. The Isle of the King, with a splendid military hospital; the ship-yard, with a vessel of a thousand tons on the stocks, and various other public constructions, appeared successively on our right. The nearer southern shore, a wall of dark gray rock, broken by deep gashes in which houses were hidden and steep roads climbed to the summit, increased in height: as we approached the end of the harbor, quays along the water, and a fresh, many-colored, glittering town on the rocks, showed that we had reached Port Mahon. Nature has made this basin as picturesque as it is secure. The wild cliffs of the coast here pierce inland, but they are draped with splendid gardens; fields of wheat climb the hills, and orchards of olive clothe their feet; over the table-land of the island rises in the distance the purple peak of El Toro; and the city before you, raised on a pedestal a hundred feet in height, seems to be one of the most beautiful of the Mediterranean. "Did you ever see a place like that?" asked a Mahonese at my elbow. "Captain ——, of your navy, used to say that there were only three good harbors in the Mediterranean, — the months of July and August, and Port Mahon!" Captain ——, however, as my friend perhaps did not know, borrowed the remark from Admiral Andrea Doria, who made it centuries ago.

The "Fonda del Oriente" looked down upon me invitingly from the top of the rock, which was made accessible by a road carried up in steep, zigzag ramps. At the door of the hotel I was received by a stout old man with a cosmopolitan face, who, throwing his head on one shoulder, inspected me for a few moments with a remarkably knowing air. Then, with a nod of satisfaction at his own acuteness, he said, "Walk in, sir; how do you find yourself?" Ushering me into a chamber furnished with an old mahogany secretary, heavy arm-chairs, and antiquated prints, — the atmosphere of Portsmouth or Gravesend hanging over everything, — he continued, after another critical survey, "Mr. Alexander, I believe?"

"That is not my name," I said.

"Not Alexander! Then it must be Sykes; they are brothers-in-law, you know," persisted the stout old man.

I answered him with a scrutinizing stare, and the words, "Your name is Bunsby, I think?"

"O no!" he exclaimed; "I am Antonio. You can't be Mr. Sykes, either, or you'd know me."

"You are talking of Englishmen; I am not English."

"Not English?" he cried. "H'm, well, that's queer; but, to be sure, you must be American. I know all the

American officers that ever were here, and they know me. Ask Commodore —— and —— if they don't know Antonio! The greatest mistake I ever made was that I didn't move to Spezia with the squadron."

"Can you give me dinner?" I asked, cutting off the coming yarn.

"Stop!" he said; "don't tell me; I can guess what you want. A beefsteak rare, hey? and mixed pickles, hey? and potatoes with their jackets on, hey? But it's too late to make a pudding, and there's no Stilton cheese! Never mind! let me alone; nobody in Port Mahon can come nearer the real thing than I can."

In vain I declared my willingness to take the Minorcan dishes. Such a taste had probably never before been expressed in all Antonio's experience of English and Americans; and my meals then and thenceforth were a series of struggles to reproduce Portsmouth or Gravesend. But the hotel was large, airy, and perfectly clean; Antonio honestly endeavored to make me comfortable; he knew a great many of my naval friends, and I had no complaint to make with his reckoning at the close of my stay. He was, moreover, a man of progress; he corned beef, and cured hams, and introduced the making of butter (not very successfully), and taught the people how to cook potatoes. He even dispatched a cheese, as a present, to Marshal Serrano, before I left Port Mahon.

Refreshed by a long sleep, which was not disturbed by any little dog with a bell on his neck, or that which the sound of the latter suggested, I sallied forth in the morning without any objective point. The city must first be seen, because it lay between me and the country. I was delighted to find wide, well-paved streets as compared with those of Palma, clean, cheerful houses, and an irregularity sufficient for picturesque effect, without being bewildering to a stranger. Very few of the buildings appeared to be older than the last century; there was nothing characteristic in their architecture; but the city, from end to end, was gay, sunny, full of color, *riante*, and without a trace of the usual Spanish indolence and uncleanliness. It has somewhat fallen from its former estate. Grass grows in many of the streets, and there is less noise and movement than one would look for with the actual population — some fifteen thousand. Three or four small craft in the harbor did not indicate an active commerce, and I presume the place is kept alive mainly by the visits of foreign men-of-war. A great many of the common people speak a few words of English, and you may even read " Adams, Sastre," over the door of a native tailor!

The climate, although considered harsh by the Spaniards, seemed to me perfect. The sun of June shone in a cloudless sky, flooding the sharp, clear colors of the town with a deluge of light; yet a bracing wind blew from the north, and the people in the fields and gardens worked as steadily as Connecticut farmers. I saw no loafers upon the island; and I doubt whether there are enough of them to form a class among the native population. While there was evidently a great deal of poverty, I encountered no beggars. I felt, as in Majorca, that I was among a simple-minded, ignorant, but thoroughly honest and industrious people.

The street I had chosen gradually rose as I proceeded inland; walled gardens succeeded to the houses, and then fields of wheat or vines, separated by huge agglomerations of stones. I looked over an undulating table-land, covered with such lines and mounds of rocky *débris*, that they seemed to be the ruins of a city. Every patch of grain or fruit was inclosed by a cannon-proof fortification, and the higher ridges terminated in bald parapets, whereon the dark mounds of box and ilex held fast and flourished without any appearance of soil. At the foot of these wild growths the fig-tree grew with wonderful luxuriance, and very often the foliage of the untamable rock was mingled with that of the gardens. Here every foot of ground had been won by the rudest, the most patient toil. Even the fields conquered centuries ago are not yet completely manageable; hundreds of stony fangs still protrude from the surface, and the laborer is obliged to follow the plough with hoe and spade. Thus, in spite of the almost incredible triumphs of agriculture with which the island is covered, its general aspect is that of a barren, torn, hopeless wilderness. Without broad or grand features of landscape, it is crowded with startling contrasts and picturesque details.

I wandered southward between the high, loose walls, towards a mound which promised me a wider inland view; but on approaching it, the road entered an impenetrable shade, and passed beyond. There was no gate or entrance of any kind into the fields, so I took advantage of a jagged corner of the wall, and climbed to the top. On the other side there was a wheat-field, in which three men were reaping. I now saw that what I had taken for a mound was a circular tower, the top of which had been torn down, forming a slope around its base, which was covered with rank thickets of mastic and myrtle. I asked the men, who had stopped work, and were curiously regarding me, whether I might cross their field and visit the ruin. "Certainly, Señor," said the master; "come down and walk about where you please." He then called, in a loud voice, "Miguel!" and presently a small boy came to light from behind a pile of rocks. "Miguel," said he, "go with the Señor to the *atalaya*, and show him the steps."

I clambered down into the little field, which, sunken between enormous walls of stone, somewhat resembled a volcanic crater. Miguel piloted me silently across the stubble, between solid mounds of ilex, which seemed no less ancient and indestructible than the rocks upon which they grew, and by a gap in an outer wall into the bed of a dry moat around the tower. The latter, though only ten feet wide, stood thick with ripe wheat; but it was bridged in one place by a line of stones, and we thus crossed without trampling down the precious stalks. There were no steps to the tower, but a zigzag path had been trampled among the ruins, at the foot of which I dismissed Miguel, and then mounted to the summit. I first looked abroad upon the bright, busy, wild, savage, wonderfully cultivated fields and gardens, the white towers and tiled roofs of the city behind me, and a single blue fragment of the sea (like a piece chipped out of the edge of a bowl) in the east. The characteristics of Minorcan scenery, which I have already described, gave the view a character so novel and so remarkable, that I studied them for a long time before examining more closely the ruin upon which I stood.

The farmer had called it an *atalaya*, and the tower was clearly of Moorish construction. Its height must have been originally much greater, or it could not have answered its purpose of watching the sea. The hollow interior is entirely filled with the fragments, so that nothing of the structure remains except its circular form. Outside of the dry moat there is a massive pentangular wall, with a lozenge-shaped pile of solid masonry at each corner; the whole evidently designed for defense, and of later date than the tower itself. Such quantities of stones had been heaped upon the old foundations by the farmers, in clearing spaces for their crops, that very little of the masonry was to be seen. To be of service, however, the walls must have been at least twenty feet higher than at present. Many of the stones have no doubt been carried away for buildings, and there are still huge piles of them in the adjacent fields. Towering out of one of these piles I caught a glimpse of another relic of a still remoter past — an object so unexpected that I at first took it for an accidental disposition of the stones. I descended to the moat, clambered over the outer wall, and made my way to the spot.

It was a Celtic *tor*, or altar — a large upright block of gray limestone, supporting a horizontal block about ten feet in length. The pillar was so buried in fragments which had been piled about it, that I could not ascertain its height; but the character of the monument was too distinctly marked to admit of a question. After returning to Port Mahon, I found that its existence was well known. In fact, the first question asked me was, "Have you seen the Phœnician altar?" When and by whom these remarkable monuments — which are found in all the Mediterranean islands between Greece and Gibraltar — were erected, is a point which I will leave antiquarians to discuss. It pleased me, as I sat under a fig-tree which shot up through the stones, to fancy that the remains of three memorable phases in the history of man were before me, — of the Druids in the crumbling altar, of the Saracens in the watch-tower, and of the house of Aragon or Castile in the fortress enclosing it.

According to Strabo, the Balearic Islands were colonized by the Rhodians; but Strabo probably knew less about the matter than any respectable antiquarian of our own day. The people of Minorca firmly believe that Magon, the brother of Hannibal, founded Port Mahon, and they attribute the Druidic stones and the Cyclopean constructions (which are here found side by side) to the Phœnicians. The English occupation, which left at least a good map behind it, led to no historic investigations; and I cannot learn that any detailed account of the antiquities of the island has ever been published. Those remains which we call Druidic are very numerous; some of the upright monoliths are more than twenty feet in height, supporting horizontal stones of nearly equal dimensions. Nothing but the lack of archæological knowledge prevented me from making a journey through the interior for the purpose of examining the other monuments.

I made use of my brief visit, however, to test the truth of another story, which is among the permanent traditions of the American navy. Every one has read the account of a captain's son leaping from the main-truck of a frigate; and in the days when Morris was popular, his verses commencing —

"Old Ironsides at anchor lay
In the harbor of Mahon,"

went the rounds of all the country newspapers. There was a melodramatic air about the incident which made me suspicious. I suppose the lines recalled themselves to my mind from the fact that Port Mahon is nowhere else noted in song. The Consul, who kindly seconded my curiosity in a matter of so little importance, went to an old Mahonese, who has had the greatest experience of our vessels and officers, and questioned him, taking care not to suggest the story in advance. But the old man instantly said: "O yes! I remember all about it. Fifty years ago, or more, when the Constitution frigate was here, a boy climbed to the very top of the mainmast, and was obliged to jump into the harbor, as there was no other way of getting down. Not many persons saw the act, but it was much talked about, and nobody doubted that the boy had done it." Whether the captain forced his son to take the terrible leap by threatening to shoot him with a rifle, the old man could not tell.

The next morning the Consul accompanied me on another excursion into the country. We passed through the town, and descended to an alameda which skirts the harbor to its western end, where the highway to Ciudadela strikes off towards the centre of the island. The harbor once penetrated a mile deeper into the country than at present, so the people say; but it must have been a shallow, marshy basin, as the hills around could not possibly spare enough soil to fill up and make fruitful the valley which one now enters after leaving the harbor-wall. This valley is the largest tract of unbroken garden land which I saw in Minorca. Its productiveness is apparently unlimited. Maize, cabbages, sweet potatoes, hemp, vines, vegetables of all kinds, covered the surface; date-palms and orange-trees, so overwhelmed with fruit that scarcely a green-leaf showed through the dazzling gold, turned it into a garden of the tropics; while precipitous walls of limestone, resting on rough natural vaults and arches, shut out the rocky upper plateau from view. The laborers were planting new crops in the place of the old; so valuable is this rich basin that no part of its surface is allowed to lie fallow for a day.

On the left, the inclosing walls were broken by the mouth of a glen, the sides of which — regular terraces of rock, resting on arched foundations — seemed at first sight to be the work of art. Here, in the shade of a group of poplars and sycamores, stood the chapel of San Juan, white, cool, and solitary. A fountain, issuing from the base of the rocks near it, formed a little pool in which some women were washing clothes. The picture was Oriental in every feature, — so much so that I was surprised not to hear " Saba' el-kheyr! " when the women said to us, " Bōn di' tenga ! "

Entering the glen behind the chapel, a few paces brought us into a different world. Except upon some painfully constructed shelf of soil, built up or rescued in some way from the rocks, there was no cultivation. Our path was a natural pavement, torn by the occasional rains; bare cliffs of gray limestone, vaulted at the base, overhung us on either side, and the mounds of box on the summit sparkled against the sky. Every feature of the scenery bore the marks of convulsion. Enormous blocks had been hurled from above; the walls were split with deep, irregular crevices; and even the stubborn evergreen growths took fantastic shapes of horns, fluttering wings, tufts of hair, or torn garments. Now and then a dry-leaved ilex rustled and rattled in the breeze; and the glen, notwithstanding it brimmed over with intensest sunshine, would have seemed very drear and desolate but for the incessant songs of the nightingales. While I crept under a rock to sketch a singularly picturesque combination of those crag-forms, — every one of which was a study, — the joyous birds made the place ring with their pæans. The *day*-song of the nightingale is as cheerful as that of the lark; its passion and sorrow is kept for the night.

If I had been an artist, I should have spent a fortnight in the glen of San Juan; but as it was, having only another day in Minorca, I could not linger there beyond an hour. At the point where I sat it divides into two branches, which gradually rise, as they wind, to the level of the table-land; and the great stone-heaps commence immediately behind the topmost fringe of box. The island, in fact, is a single rock, upon the level portions of which a little soil has lodged. Wherever one may travel in the interior, it presents the same appearance. The distance from Port Mahon to the old town of Ciudadela, at the western extremity of Minorca, is about twenty-five miles; and the Consul informed me that I should find the same landscapes all the way. There is nothing remarkable in Ciudadela except a cathedral of the thirteenth century, and some Saracenic walls. On the way are the three other principal towns of the island — Alayor, Mercadal, and Ferrerias, — all of which are rudely built, and have an equal air of poverty. It was for a moment a question with me whether I should employ my little remaining time in a rapid journey to Ciudadela and back, or in strolling leisurely through the country around Port Mahon, and setting down my observations as typical of all Minorca. The reports of the Consul justified me in adopting the latter and easier course.

In the afternoon we walked to the village of San Luis, about four miles distant, and recently made accessible by a superb highway. The great drought which has prevailed in all the Balearic Islands during the past two years has seriously injured the crops, and there is much suffering in Minorca, which is so much less favored by nature than its larger sister island. I heard of families of five persons living for months on less than twenty-five cents a day. Agriculture is profitable in good seasons, on account of the excellent quality of the wheat, oil, and oranges; but the deposit of soil, as I have already explained, is very shallow, there is no sheltering range of mountains as in Majorca, no supply of water for irrigation, and the average production is therefore much less certain. The price of land is high, for the reason that the proprietors are satisfied if it yields them annually two per cent. of its value. Shoe-making is one of the principal branches of industry in Port Mahon; but of late the foreign market has been disturbed, and the profits are so slight — whether through slow and imperfect labor or the sharpness of contractors I did not ascertain — that any check in the trade brings immediate suffering. The people, nevertheless, are very patient; they invariably prefer work to mendicancy, and are cheerful and contented so long as they succeed in clothing and feeding themselves.

The Minorcans seemed to me even more independent and original in character than the Majorcans. There is still less of the Spaniard, but also less of the Moor, about them. I should guess their blood to be mostly Vandal, but I stand ready to be corrected by any ethnologist who knows better. They have a rugged, sturdy air, little grace and elegance, either of body or of manner, and a simplicity which does not exclude shrewdness or cunning. It is considered almost an insult if the stranger speaks of them as Spaniards. The Governor of the island said to Marshal Serrano, the other day, when the latter was in Port Mahon in temporary exile: "The Minorcans are a curious people. You probably find that they do not take off their hats to you in the street, as you are accustomed to be saluted in Madrid?" "Yes," answered the Marshal, "I have already learned that they care nothing whatever for either you or me." The older people look back on the

English occupation with regret; the younger generation would be exceedingly well satisfied if Spain would sell the island to the United States for a naval station. But all unite in calling themselves Minorcans, or Mahonese, and in drawing a very broad line between themselves and the Spaniards of the Peninsula.

The Consul confirmed my first impressions of the honesty of the people. "You may walk on any road in the island," said he, "at any hour of the day or night, with the most perfect security." He also gave them the highest praise for cleanliness and order in their domestic life, which are certainly not Spanish qualities. The young men and women who are betrothed save every penny of their earnings, and invest them in the articles of furniture necessary to the establishment of a household. Simple as are these latter, many years often elapse before they are all procured and the nuptials may be celebrated, the parties remaining steadfastly constant to each other during the long time of waiting. They are a people in whom almost any honest system of education, any possible sound ideas of progress, would take immediate root; but under the combined shadow of Spain and Rome, what progress *is* possible?

I have never seen Broek, in Holland, but I think San Luis must be the cleanest village in Europe. I attributed its amazing brightness, as we approached, to the keen, semi-African sun and the perfectly clear air; but I found that all the houses had been whitewashed that very afternoon, as they regularly are every Saturday. The street was swept so conscientiously that we might have seated ourselves and taken our dinner anywhere, without getting more than each man's inevitable proportion of dust in the dishes. In the open doors, as I passed, I saw floors of shining tiles, clean wooden furniture, women in threadbare but decent dresses, and children — no, the children *were* dirty, and I confess I should not have been pleased to see them otherwise. The sand and fig-stains on those little faces and hands were only health-marks, and they made the brightness of the little village endurable. It would else have seemed to be struck with an unusual disease. We went into a house where two old women — very, very poor they were, but uncomplaining — received us with simple, unaffected friendliness. I spoke in Spanish and they in Minorcan, so that the conversation was not very intelligible; but the visit gave me a fleeting impression of the sterling qualities of the people, inasmuch as it harmonized with all that I had previously seen and heard.

The Consul conducted me to a little *casino*, where refreshments, limited in character, were to be procured. The *maestro*, a stout fellow, with the air of a Bowery butcher, opened his heart on learning that we were Americans. He had served a year on board one of our men-of-war, and repeated, over and over again, "The way things were managed there satisfied me, — it corresponded with my own ideas!" He made me read, around a spiral pillar, the words, "Casino del Progreso," saying, "*That*'s what I go for!" There was a church nearly opposite, and from its architecture a man with half an eye could see that the Jesuits had had a hand in building it. This I sketched, and the progressive host, leaning over my shoulder, interpreted the drawing correctly. His extravagant admiration made me feel that I had done well, and we parted mutually satisfied. Indeed, this little village interested me even more than Port Mahon, because it was more purely Minorcan in character.

The quantities of the fig-bearing cactus about the country-houses surprised me, until I learned that the fleshy leaves are used during the dry season as food for the mules and asses. The fruit, which is said to be remarkably fine on the island, is eaten by the inhabitants, and must form, in times of want, an important article of their food; yet so much space would not be given to the plant, or rather tree, if the animals had not been taught to subsist upon it. I have never before heard, in any part of the world, of the cactus being made useful in this way. Its huge, grotesque masses are an inseparable part of every landscape on the island.

We walked back to Port Mahon in the face of a north wind which was almost cold, which blew away the rich color from the sunset sky, leaving it pale, clear, and melancholy in tone; yet thunder and violent rain followed in the night. I spent my last evening with the Consul and his agreeable family, and embarked on the steamer for Barcelona in the morning. As we passed out of the harbor, Antonio's daughter waved her handkerchief from the window high above, on the cliff. The salute was not intended for me, but for her husband, who was bound for Madrid, carrying with him the cheese for Marshal Serrano. Rocked on a rough sea, and with a keen wind blowing, we again coasted along the southern shore of Minorca, crossed the strait, touched at Alcudia, and then, passing the mouth of the Bay of Pollenza, reached the northern headland of Majorca at sunset. Here the mountain-chain falls off in perpendicular walls a thousand feet in height, the bases of which are worn into caverns and immense echoing vaults. The coast-forms are as grand and wonderful as those of Norway. Point after point, each more abrupt and distorted than the last, came into view as we cleared the headland — all growing luminous in the mist and the orange light of the setting sun.

Then the light faded; the wild mountain-forms were fused together in a cold gray mass above the sea; the stars came out, and my last Balearic day was at an end.

CATALONIAN BRIDLE-ROADS.

"And mule-bells tinkling down the mountain-paths of Spain."
Whittier.

I LEARNED something of the bridle-roads of Catalonia in defiance of advice and warning, and almost against my own inclination. My next point of interest, after leaving the Balearic Islands, was the forgotten Republic of Andorra, in the Pyrenees; and the voice of the persons whom I consulted in Barcelona — none of whom had made the journey, or knew any one who had — was unanimous that I should return to France, and seek an entrance from that side. Such a course would certainly have been more comfortable; but the direct route, from the very insecurity which was predicted, offered a prospect of adventure, the fascination of which, I regret to say, I have not yet entirely outgrown. "It is a country of smugglers and robbers," said the banker who replenished my purse; "and I seriously advise you not to enter it. Moreover, the roads are almost impassable, and there is nothing to be seen on the way."

These words, uttered with a grave face by a native Catalan, ought to have decided the matter, yet they did not. To be sure, I thanked the man for his warning, and left him to suppose that I would profit by it, rather than enter into any discussion; but when I quitted his office, with fresh funds in my pocket, and corresponding courage in my bosom, my course was already decided. Had I not heard the same warnings, in all parts of the world, and had not the picturesque danger always fled as I approached it? Nevertheless, there came later moments of doubt, the suggestions of that convenient life which we lead at home, and the power of which increases with our years. Fatigue and hardship do not become lighter from repetition, but the reverse; the remembrance of past aches and past hunger returns whenever the experience is renewed, and aggravates it.

So, when I had descended from Montserrat, and was waiting in the cool of the evening at the door of the rudest possible restaurant, at the railway station of Monistrol, a little imp whispered: "The first train is for Barcelona. Take it and you will be in France to-morrow night. This way is safe and speedy; you know not what the other may be." I watched the orange-light fade from the topmost pinnacles of Montserrat; a distant whistle sounded, and the other pilgrims hurried towards the ticket-office. I followed them as far as the door, paused a moment, and then said to myself: "No, if I back out now, I shall never be sure of myself again!" Then I returned to my seat beside the door, and saw the train go by, with the feeling of a man who has an appointment with a dentist.

In another hour came the upward train, which would carry me as far as the town of Manresa, where my doubtful journey commenced. It was already dusk, and deliciously cool after the fierce heat of the day. A full moon shone upon the opposite hills as I sped up the valley of the Llobregat, and silvered the tops of the olives; but I only saw them in glimpses of unconquerable sleep, and finally descended at the station of Manresa not fully awake.

A rough, ragged porter made a charge upon my valise, which I yielded to his hands. "Take it to the best hotel," I said. "Ah, that is the 'Chicken!'" he replied. Now, the driver of the omnibus from Montserrat had recommended the "San Domingo," which had altogether a better sound than the "Chicken;" but I did not think of resisting my fate. I was conscious of a wonderful moonlight picture,— of a town on a height, crowned by a grand cathedral; of a winding river below; of steep slopes of glimmering houses; of lofty hills, seamed with the shadows of glens; and of the sparkle of orange-leaves in the hanging gardens. This while we were crossing a suspension-bridge; at the end, we plunged into narrow, winding streets, full of gloom and disagreeable odors. A few oil-lamps burned far apart; there were lights in the upper windows of the houses, and the people were still gossiping with their neighbors. When we emerged into a plaza, it was more cheerful; the single *café* was crowded, the *estanco* for the sale of tobacco, and the barber's shop were still open. A little farther and we reached the "Chicken," which was an ancient and uninviting house, with a stable on the ground-floor. Here the porter took his fee with a grin, and saying, "You will want me in the morning!" wished me good night.

I mounted to a dining-room nearly fifty feet in length, in which a lonely gentleman sat, waiting for his supper. When the hostess had conducted me to a bedroom of equal dimensions, and proceeded to put clean sheets upon a bed large enough for four Michigan soldiers, I became entirely reconciled to my fate. After trying in vain to extract any intelligence from a Madrid newspaper, I went to bed and slept soundly; but the little imp was at my ear when I woke, saying: "Here you leave the railway; after this it will not be so easy to turn back." "Very well," I thought, "I will go back now." I opened the shutters, let the full morning sun blaze into the room, dipped my head into water, and then cried out: "Begone, tempter! I go forwards." But, alas! it was not so once. There is a difference between springing nimbly from one's rest with a "Hurrah! there's another rough day before me!" and a slow clinging to one's easy pillow, with the sigh, "Ah! must I go through another rough day?" However, that was my last moment of weakness, and physical only — being an outcry of the muscles against the coming aches and strains, like that of the pack-camel before he receives his load.

The first stage of my further journey, I learned, could be made by a diligence which left at eleven o'clock. In the mean time I wandered about the town, gathering an impression of its character quite distinct from that of the previous evening. It has no architectural monuments; for the cathedral, like all such edifices in Spain, is unfinished, internally dark, and well supplied with bad pictures. Its position, nevertheless, is superb, and the platform of rock upon which it stands looks over a broad, bright, busy landscape. The sound of water-wheels and the humming looms of factories fills the air; however primitive the other forms of labor may be, the people all seem to be busy. The high houses present an agreeable variety of color, although a rich brown is predominant; many of them have balconies, and the streets turn at such unexpected angles that light and shade assist in making pictures everywhere. Manresa has a purely Spanish aspect, and the groups on the plaza and in the shady alleys are as lively and glowing as any in Andalusia.

I read the history of the place, as given in the guide-books, but will not here repeat it. According to my English guide, it was sacked and its inhabitants butchered by the French, during the Peninsular War; according to the French guide, nothing of the kind ever took place. As I read the books alternately, I came to the conclusion that both sides must have been splendidly victorious in the battles which were fought in Spain. When the Englishman said: "Here our army, numbering only eighteen thousand men (of whom eight thousand were Spanish allies, of doubtful service), encountered thirty-seven thousand French, and completely routed them," the Frenchman had: "Here our army, numbering only fifteen thousand, including seven thousand Spaniards, put to flight thirty-three thousand English — one of the most brilliant actions of the war." At this rate of representation, it will be a disputed question, in the next century, whether Soult or Wellington was driven out of Spain.

My porter of the night before made his appearance, and as I had suspected him of interested motives in conducting me to the "Chicken," I tested his character by giving a smaller fee for an equal service; but he took it with the same thanks. Moreover, the diligence office was in the "San Domingo Hotel," and I satisfied myself that the "Chicken" was really better than the Saint. Two lumbering yellow coaches stood in the spacious stable, which was at the same time entrance-hall and laundry. On one side some lean mules were eating their barley; on another, a pump and stone trough supplied the house with water; a stone staircase led to the inhabited rooms, and three women were washing clothes at a tank in the rear. Dogs ran about scratching themselves; country passengers, with boxes and baskets, sat upon stone posts and did the same; and now and then a restless horse walked forth from the stalls, snuffing at one person after another, as if hoping to find one who might be eatable. Two *mayorals* or coachmen, followed by two grooms, bustled about with bits of harness in their hands, and the washerwomen made a great clatter with their wooden beetles; but the time passed, and nothing seemed to be accomplished on either side. The whole scene was so thoroughly Spanish that no one would have been surprised had the Don and Sancho ridden into the doorway. One of the women at the tank was certainly Maritornes.

At length, after a great deal of ceremony, one of the vehicles drove off. "It's going to Berga," said a man in faded velvet, in answer to my question; "and all I know is, that *that*'s the way to Puigcerda." The mules were now harnessed to our diligence and we took our places — my friend in velvet; two stout women, one of whom carried six dried codfish tied in a bundle; a shriveled old man, a mild brown soldier, and myself. It was an hour behind the appointed time, but no one seemed to notice the delay. We rolled out of the ammoniated shadows of the stable into a blaze which was doubled on the white highway, and thrown back to us from the red, scorched rocks beside it. The valley of the Cardoner, which we entered on leaving Manresa, quivered in the breathless heat: the stream was almost exhausted in its bed, and the thin gray foliage of the poplars and olives gave but a mockery of shadow. Everywhere the dry, red soil baked in the sunshine. The only refreshing thing I saw was a break in an irrigating canal, which let down a cascade over the rocks into the road. No water in the world ever seemed so cool, so fresh, so glittering; in the thirsty landscape it flashed like a symbol of generous, prodigal life. Who could fling gold around him with so beautiful a beneficence?

The features of the scenery, nevertheless, were too bold and picturesque to be overlooked. As we gained a longer vista, Montserrat lifted his blue horns over the nearer hills, and a dim streak of snow, far in the northwest, made signal for the Pyrenees. Abrupt as were the heights inclosing the valley, they were cultivated to the summit, and the brown country-houses, perched on projecting spurs, gave them a life which the heat and thirsty color of the soil could not take away. Our destination was Cardona, and after a smothering ride of two hours we reached the little village of Suria, half-way in distance, but by no means in time. Beyond it, the country became rougher, the road steep and toilsome; and our three mules plodded slowly on, with drooping heads and tails, while, inside, the passengers nodded one after the other, and became silent. We crossed the Cardoner, and ascended a long slope of the hills, where the view, restricted to the neighboring fields, became so monotonous that I nodded and dozed with the rest.

We were all aroused by the diligence stopping beside a large farm-house. There was a general cry for water, and the farmer's daughter presently came out with a stone pitcher, cool and dripping from the well. The glass was first given to me, as a stranger; and I was about setting it to my lips, when two or three of the passengers suddenly cried out, "Stop!" I paused, and looked around in surprise. The man in velvet had already dropped a piece of sugar into the water, and the old woman opposite took a bottle from her basket, saying, "This is better!" and added a spoonful of anise-seed brandy. "Now," exclaimed both at the same time, "you can drink with safety." The supply of sugar and anise-seed held out, and each passenger was regaled at the expense of the two Samaritans. After this, conversation brightened, and we all became talkative and friendly. The man in velvet, learning my destination, exclaimed: "O, you ought to have gone by way of Berga! It is a dreadful country about Solsona and the Rio Segre." But the old woman leaned over and whispered: "Don't mind what he says. *I* come from Solsona, and it's a good country — a very good country, indeed. Go on, and you will see!"

The valley of the Cardoner had become narrower, the mountains were higher, and there were frequent ruins of mediæval castles on the summits. When we had reached the top of the long ascent, the citadel of Cardona in front suddenly rose sharp and abrupt over the terraced slopes of vine. It appeared to be within a league, but our coachman was so slow and the native passengers so patient, that we did not arrive for two hours. Drawing nearer, the peculiar colors of the earth around the base of an isolated mountain announced to us the celebrated salt-mines of the place. Red, blue, purple, yellow, and gray, the bare cliffs glittered in the sun as if frosted over with innumerable crystals. This mass of native salt is a mile and a half in circumference, with a height of about two hundred and fifty feet. The action of the atmosphere seems to have little effect upon it, and the labor of centuries has no more than tapped its immense stores. As in Wieliczka, in Poland, the workmen in the mines manufacture cups, ornaments, pillars, and even chandeliers, from the pure saline crystal — objects which, although they remain perfect in the dry atmosphere of Spain, soon melt into thin air when carried to Northern lands.

The town of Cardona occupies the crest of a sharp hill,

rising above the mountain of salt. Between it and the river, on the north, stands the citadel, still more loftily perched, like a Greek acropolis. Our road passed entirely around the latter and mounted to the town on the opposite side, where the diligence set us down in front of a rude *fonda*. The old gate was broken down, the walls ruined, and the first houses we passed were uninhabited. There was no longer an *octroi;* in fact, the annoyances of travel in Spain diminish in proportion as one leaves the cities and chief thoroughfares. As I dismounted, the coachman took hold of my arm, saying, " Cavalier, here is a decent man who will get a horse for you, and travel with you to the Seo de Urgel. I know the man, and it is I who recommend him." The person thus introduced was a sturdy, broad-shouldered fellow, with short black hair, and hard, weather-beaten features. He touched his red Catalan cap, and then looked me steadily in the face while, in answer to my inquiries, he offered to be ready at four o'clock the next morning, and demanded six dollars for himself and horse, the journey requiring two days. There were two or three other *arrieros* present, but I plainly saw that none of them would enter into competition with a man recommended by the coachman. Moreover, as far as appearances went, he was the best of the lot, and so I engaged him at once.

While the fat hostess of the *fonda* was preparing my dinner, I strolled for an hour or two about the town. The church is renowned for having been founded in the year 820, immediately after the expulsion of the Moors from this part of Spain, and for containing the bodies of St. Celadonio and St. Emeterio — whoever those holy personages may have been. I confess I never heard of them before. What I admired in the church was the splendid mellow brown tint of its massive ancient front. Brown is the characteristic color of Spain, from the drapery of Murillo and the walls of cathedrals to the shadow of cypresses and the arid soil of the hills. Whether brightening into gold or ripening into purple, it always seems to give the key of color. In the streets of Cardona, it was the base upon which endless picturesque groups of people were painted, — women spinning flax, children cooling their bare bodies on the stones, blacksmiths and cobblers forging and stitching in the open air — all with a keen glance of curiosity, but also a respectful greeting for the stranger. The plaza, which was called, like all plazas in Catalonia, *de la Constitucion,* overhung the deep ravine at the foot of the salt mountain. From its parapet I lôoked upon the vineyard-terraces into which the hills have been fashioned, and found them as laboriously constructed as those of the Rheingau. A cliff of salt below sparkled like prismatic glass in the evening light, but all the nearer gardens lay in delicious shadow, and the laden asses began to jog homewards from the distant fields. There was a *café* on the plaza patronized only by two or three military idlers; the people still worked steadily while the daylight lasted, charming away their fatigue by the most melancholy songs.

The inn was not an attractive place. The kitchen was merely one corner of the public room, in which chairs lay overturned and garments tumbled about, as if the house had been sacked. The members of the family sat and chattered in this confusion, promising whatever I demanded, but taking their own time about getting it. I had very meagre expectations of dinner, and was therefore not a little surprised when excellent fresh fish, stewed rabbits, and a roasted fowl were set successively before me. The merry old landlady came and went, anxious to talk, but prevented by her ignorance of the pure Spanish tongue. However, she managed to make me feel quite at home, and well satisfied that I had ventured so far into the region of ill-repute.

What was going on in the town that night I cannot imagine; but it was a tumult of the most distracting kind. First, there were drums and — as it seemed to me — tin pans beaten for an hour or two in the street below; then a chorus of piercing, dreadfully inharmonious voices; then a succession of short cries or howls, like those of the oriental dervishes. Sometimes the noises moved away, and I settled myself to sleep, whereupon they came back worse than before. " O children of Satan!" I cried, " will ye never be still?" Some time after midnight the voices became hoarse: one by one dropped off, and the charivari gradually ceased, from the inability of the performers to keep it up longer. Then horses were led forth from the stable on the ground-floor, whips were violently cracked, and the voices of grooms began to be heard. At three o'clock Juan, my new guide, came into the room with a coarse bag, in which he began packing the contents of my valise, which could not otherwise be carried on horseback, and so my rest was over before it had commenced.

I found the diligence about starting on its return to Manresa, and my horse, already equipped, standing in the stable. The sack, valise, and other articles were so packed, before and behind the saddle, that only a narrow, deep cleft remained for me to sit in. The sun had not yet risen, and the morning air was so cool that I determined to walk down the hill and mount at the foot. Stepping over two grooms who were lying across the stable door on a piece of hide, sound asleep, we set forth on our journey.

The acropolis rose dark against the pearly sky, and the valley of the Cardoner lay cool and green in the lingering shadows. Early as was the hour, laborers were already on their way to the fields; and when we reached the ancient bridge of seven arches, I saw the two old ladies of Solsona in advance, mounted on mules, and carrying their baskets, boxes, and dried codfish with them. Although my French guide-book declared that the road before me was scarcely practicable, the sight of these ladies was a better authority to the contrary. I mounted at the bridge, and joined the cavalcade, which was winding across a level tract of land, between walled fields and along the banks of irrigating canals. Juan, however, found the mules too slow, and soon chose a side-path, which, in the course of a mile or two, brought us into the main track, some distance in advance of the old ladies. By this time the sun was up and blazing on all the hills; the wide, open country about Cardona came to an end, and we struck into a narrow glen, covered with forests of pine. Juan directed me to ford the river and follow the track on the opposite side, while he went on to a foot-bridge farther up. "In a few minutes," he said, "you will find a *carretera*," — a cart-road, which proved to be a superb macadamized highway, yet virgin of any wheel. Men were working upon it, smoothing the turf on either side, and leveling the gravel as carefully as if the Queen's mail-coach travelled that way; but the splendid piece of workmanship has neither beginning nor end, and will be utterly useless until it touches a finished road somewhere.

A short distance farther the glen expanded, and I recrossed the river by a lofty new bridge. The road was carried over the bottom-land on an embankment at least forty feet high, and then commenced ascending the hills on the northern bank. After passing a little village on the first height, we entered a forest of pine, which continued without interruption for four or five miles. The country became almost a wilderness, and wore a singular air of loneliness, contrasted with the busy region I had left behind. As I approached the summit, the view extended far and wide over a dark, wooded sweep of hills, rarely broken by a solitary farm-house and the few cleared fields around it. On the nearer slope below me there was now and then such a house; but the most of them were in ruins, and young pines were shooting up in the deserted vineyards. The Catalans are so laborious in their habits, so skilled in the art of turning waste into fruitful land, that there must have been some special reason for this desolation. My guide either could not or would not explain it.

When we reached the northern side of the mountain, cultivation again commenced, and I saw the process of clearing woodland and preparing the soil for crops. The trees are first removed, the stumps and roots dug up, and then all the small twigs, brambles, weeds, and dry sticks, — everything, in fact, which cannot be used for lumber and firewood, — are gathered into little heaps all over the ground, and covered with the top soil. A year, probably, must elapse, before these heaps are tolerably decomposed; then they are spread upon the surface and ploughed under. The virgin soil thus acquired is manured after every crop, and there is no such thing as an exhausted field.

The fine highway came to an end as suddenly as it had commenced, in the rough forest, with no village near. The country became broken and irregular, and the bridle-path descended continually through beautiful groves of oak, with an undergrowth of box and lavender, the odors from which filled the air. I was nearly famished, when, after a journey of five or six leagues, we emerged from the woods, and saw the rich valley-basin of Solsona before us, with the dark old town in its centre. Here, again, every available foot of soil was worked into terraces, drained or irrigated as the case might be, and made to produce its utmost. As I rode along the low walls, the ripe, heavy ears of wheat leaned over and brushed my head. Although there is no wheeled vehicle — not even a common cart — in this region, all the roads being the rudest bridle-paths, the town is approached by a magnificent bridge of a dozen arches, spanning a grassy hollow, at the bottom of which flows a mere thread of a brook.

At the farther end of the bridge, a deserted gateway ushers the traveller into Solsona. Few strangers, I suspect, ever enter the place; for labor ceased as I passed along the streets, and even Don Basilio, on his way home from morning mass, lifted his shovel hat, and bowed profoundly. Many of the houses were in ruins, and bore the marks of fire and balls. I rode into the ground-floor of a dark house which bore no sign or symbol over the door, but Juan assured me that it was an inn. A portly, dignified gentleman advanced out of the shadows, and addressed me in the purest Castilian; he was the landlord, and his daughter was cook and waiting-maid. The rooms above were gloomy and very ancient; there was scarcely a piece of furniture which did not appear to be two centuries old; yet everything was clean and orderly.

"Can we have breakfast?" I asked.

"Whatever we have is at your disposition," said the landlord. "What would you be pleased to command?"

"Eggs, meat, bread, and wine; but nothing that cannot be got ready in a few minutes."

The landlord bowed, and went into the kitchen. Presently he returned and asked, "Did I understand you to wish for *meat*, Cavalier?"

"Certainly, if you have it," I replied.

"Yes, we have it in the house," said he; "but I didn't know what your *custom* was."

I did not guess what he meant until a plate of capital mutton-chops was smoking under my nose. Then it flashed across my mind that the day was Friday, and I no better than a heathen in the eyes of my worthy host. According to the country custom of Spain, master and groom fare alike, and Juan took his seat beside me without waiting for an invitation. I ought to have invited the landlord, but I was too hungry to remember it. To my surprise — and relief also — Juan ate his share of the chops, and there was a radiant satisfaction on his countenance. I have no doubt he looked upon me as the responsible party, and did not even consider it worth while to confess afterwards.

"You have a beautiful country here," I remarked to the

landlord, knowing that such an expression is always accepted as a half-compliment.

"It is a country," he exclaimed with energy, "*que nada falta*, — which lacks nothing! There is everything you want; there is not a better country under the sun! No, it is not the *country* that we complain of."

"What then?" I asked.

For a moment he made no reply, then, apparently changing the subject, said, "Did you see the houses in ruins as you came into Solsona? That was done in the Carlist wars. We suffered terribly: nearly half the people of this region were slaughtered."

"What good comes of these wars?" I asked. "Is anything better than it was before? What have you to offset all that fire and murder?"

"That's it!" he cried; "that was what I meant."

He shook his head in a melancholy way, drank a glass of wine, and said, as if to prevent my continuing the subject: "You understand how to travel, or you would not come into such wild parts as these. But here, instead of having the rattling of cart-wheels in your ears all day, you have the songs of the nightingales. You don't have dust in your nose, but the smell of grain and flowers; you can start when you please, and ride as far as you like. That's *my* way to travel, and I wish there were more people of the same mind. We don't often see a foreign cavalier in Solsona, yet it's not a bad country, as you yourself say."

By this time Juan and I had consumed the chops and emptied the bottle; and, as there were still six leagues to be travelled that day, we prepared to leave Solsona. The town, of barely two thousand inhabitants, has an ancient church, a deserted palace of the former Dukes of Cardona, and a miraculous image of the Virgin — neither of which things is sufficiently remarkable in its way to be further described. The age of the place is apparent; a dark, cool, mournful atmosphere of the Past fills its streets, and the traces of recent war seem to have been left from mediæval times.

The sky was partly overcast, but there was an intense, breathless heat in the air. Our path led across the bounteous valley into a wild ravine, which was spanned by two ancient aqueducts. The pointed arch of one of them hinted of Moorish construction, as well as the platform and tank of a fountain in a rocky nook beyond. Here the water gushed out in a powerful stream, as in those fountains of the Anti-Lebanon in the country of Galilee. Large plane-trees shaded the spot, and the rocks overhung it on three sides, yet no one was there to enjoy the shade and coolness. The place was sad, because so beautiful and so lonely.

At the farther end of the ravine we entered a forest of pine, with an undergrowth of box, and commenced ascending the mountain-range dividing the Valley of Solsona from that of the Rio Salado. It might have been the Lesser Atlas, and the sky that of Africa, so fierce was the heat, so dry and torn the glens up the sides of which toiled my laboring horse. Birds and insects were alike silent: the lizard, scampering into his hole in the red bank of earth, was the only living thing. For an hour or more we slowly plodded upward; then, emerging from the pine wood upon a barren summit, I looked far and wide over a gray, forbidding, fiery land. Beyond the Salado Valley, which lay beneath me, rose a range of uninhabited mountains, half clothed with forest or thicket, and over them the outer Pyrenees, huge masses of bare rock, cut into sharp, irregular forms. A house or two, and some cultivated patches, were visible along the banks of the Salado; elsewhere, there was no sign of habitation.

The *bajada*, or descent to the river, was so steep and rough that I was forced to dismount and pick my way down the zigzags of burning sand and sliding gravel. At the bottom I forded the river, the water of which is saline, and then hastened to a mill upon the further bank, to procure a cup of water. The machinery was working in charge of a lusty girl, who shut off the water while she ran to a spring in the ravine behind, and filled an earthen jar. There was nothing of Spanish grace and beauty about her. She had gray eyes, a broad, flat nose, brown hair, broad shoulders, and the arms and legs of a butcher. But she was an honest, kind-hearted creature, and the joyous goodwill with which she served me was no less refreshing than the water.

The path now followed the course of the Rio Salado, under groves of venerable ilex, which fringed the foot of the mountain. Thickets of box and tamarisk overhung the stream, and the sight of the water rushing and murmuring through sun and shade, made the heat more endurable. Another league, however, brought me to the little hamlet of Ojern, where my road took to the hills again. Nature has given this little place a bay of rich soil between the river and the mountains, man has blackened it with fire and riddled it with shot; and between the two it has become a complete and surprising picture. Out of superb gardens of orange and fig trees, over hedges of roses and wild mounds of woodbine, rise the cracked and tottering walls — heaps of ruin, but still inhabited. Nothing could be finer than the contrast of the riotous vegetation, struggling to grow away from the restraining hand into its savage freedom, with the firm texture, the stubborn forms and the dark, mellow coloring of the masonry. Of course the place was dirty, and offended one sense as much as it delighted the other. It is a pity that neatness and comfort cannot be picturesque.

I knew that the Rio Segre could not be very distant, but I was far from guessing how much the way might be lengthened by heat and almost impracticable roads. This ascent was worse than the former, since there was no forest to throw an occasional shade. A scrubby chaparral covered the red and flinty slopes, upon which the sun beat until the air above them quivered. My horse was assailed with a large gad-fly, and kicked, stamped, and whirled his head as if insane. I soon had occasion to notice a physiological fact — that the bones of a horse's head are more massive than those of the human shin. When we reached the summit of the mountain, after a long, long pull, I was so bruised, shaken, and exhausted that Juan was obliged to help me out of the saddle, or rather, the crevice between two piles of baggage in which I was wedged. The little imp came back chuckling, and said, "I told you so!" In such cases, I always recall Cicero's consolatory remark, and go on my way with fresh courage.

Moreover, far below, at the base of the bare peaks of rock which rose against the western sky, I saw the glitter of the Rio Segre, and knew that my day's labor was nearly at an end. The descent was so rugged that I gave the reins to Juan, and went forward on foot. After getting down the first steep, the path fell into and followed the dry bed of a torrent, which dropped rapidly towards the river. In half an hour I issued from the fiery ravine, and was greeted by a breeze that had cooled its wings on the Pyrenean snow. Olive-trees again shimmered around me, and a valley-bed of fruitful fields expanded below. A mile further, around the crest of the lower hills, I found myself on a rocky point, just over the town of Oliana. It was the oldest and brownest place I had seen, up to this time; but there was shade in its narrow streets, and rest for me under one of its falling roofs. A bell in the tall, square tower of the church chimed three; and Juan, coming up with the horse, insisted that I should mount, and make my entrance as became a cavalier.

I preferred comfort to dignity; but when everybody can see that a man *has* a horse, he really loses nothing by walking. The first houses we passed appeared to be deserted; then came the main street, in which work, gossip, and recreation were going on in the open air. Here there was a swinging sign with the word "Hostal" over the inn door, and most welcome was that inn, with its unwashed floors, its fleas, and its odors of garlic. I was feverish with the absorption of so much extra heat, and the people gave me the place of comfort at an open window, with a view of green fields between the poplars. Below me there was a garden belonging to the priest, who, in cassock and shovel-hat, was inspecting his vegetables. Gathering up his sable skirts, he walked mincingly between the rows of lettuce and cauliflower, now and then pointing out a languishing plant, which an old woman in attendance then proceeded to refresh by flinging water upon it with a paddle, from a tank in a corner of the garden. Browning's "Soliloquy in a Spanish Cloister" came into my head, and I think I should have cried out, could the padre have understood the words: "O, that rose has prior claims!" I must say, however, that the garden was admirably kept, and the priest's table was all the better for his horticultural tastes.

There were three or four jolly fellows in the inn, who might have served in Sherman's army, they were so tall and brown and strong. My attention was drawn from the priest by their noise and laughter, and I found them gathered about a wild-looking man, dressed in rags. The latter talked so rapidly, in the Catalan dialect, that I could understand very little of what he said; but the landlady came up and whispered, "He's a *loco* (an idiot), but he does no harm." To me he seemed rather to be a genius, with a twist in his brain. He was very quick in retort, and often turned the laugh upon his questioner; while from his constant appeals to "Maria Santissima," a strong religious idea evidently underlay his madness. The landlord gave him a good meal, and he then went on his way, cheerful, perhaps happy, in his isolation.

I suppose Juan must have been well satisfied to eat

meat on a Friday without the sin being charged to his personal account, and must therefore have given a hint to the landlord; for, without my order, a chicken was set before me at dinner, and he took the drumsticks as of right. When the sun got behind the tall mountain opposite, I wandered about the town, seeing nothing that seems worthy of being recorded, yet every view was a separate delight which I cannot easily forget. There were no peculiarities of architecture or of costume; but the houses were so quaintly irregular, the effects of light and shade so bold and beautiful, the colors so balanced, that each street with its inhabitants might have been painted without change. There was a group before the shoemaker's door — the workman on his bench, a woman with a shoe, a young fellow in a scarlet cap, who had paused to say a word, and two or three children tumbling on the stones; another at the fountain — women filling jars, coming and going with the load on hip or head; another at the barber's, and all framed by houses brown as Murillo's color, with a background of shadow as rich as Rembrandt's. These are subjects almost too simple to paint with the pen; they require the pencil.

In the evening, the sultry vapors which had been all day floating in the air settled over the gorge, and presently thunder-echoes were buffeted back and forth between the rocky walls. The skirts of a delicious rain trailed over the valley, and Night breathed odor and coolness and healing balsam as she came down from the western peaks. Rough and dirty as was the guests' room of the "hostal," my bedroom was clean and pleasant. A floor of tiles, a simple iron washstand resembling an ancient tripod, one chair, and a bed, coarsely, but freshly spread — what more can a reasonable man desire? The linen (though it is a bull to say so) was of that roughly woven cotton which one finds only in southern Europe, Africa, and the Orient, which always seems cool and clean, and has nothing in common with the frouzy, flimsy stuff we find in cheap places at home. Whoever has slept in a small new town (I beg pardon, "city") on an Illinois prairie, knows the feeling of soft, insufficient sheets and flabby pillows, all hinting of frequent use, between which he thinks, ere sleep conquers his disgust, of the handkerchief which awaits him as towel in the morning. In the poorest inn in Spain I am better lodged than in the Jimplecute House in Roaring City.

Juan called me at three o'clock, for another severe day was before us. Our road followed the course of the Rio Segre, and there were no more burning mountains to climb; but both M. de Lavigne and Mr. Ford, in the little which they vouchsafed to say of this region, mentioned the frightful character of the gorges through which the river breaks his way downward to the Ebro; and their accounts, if the timid traveller believes them, may well deter him from making the journey. In the cool half-hour before sunrise, as I rode across the circular valley, or *conque*, of Oliana, towards the gloomy portals of rock out of which the river issues, my spirits rose in anticipation of the wild scenery beyond. The vineyards and orchards were wet and fresh, and the air full of sweet smells. Clouds rested on all the stony summits, rising or falling as the breeze shifted. The path mounted to the eastern side of the gorge, where, notched along the slanting rock, it became a mere thread to the eye, and finally disappeared.

As I advanced, however, I found that the passage was less dangerous than it seemed. The river roared far below, and could be reached by a single plunge; but there was a good, well-beaten mule-track — the same, and probably the only one, which has been used since the first human settlement. Soon after entering the gorge, it descended to within a hundred feet of the river, and then crossed to the opposite bank by a bold bridge of a single arch, barely wide enough for a horse to walk upon. The parapet on either side was not more than two feet high, and it was not a pleasant sensation to look down from the saddle upon the roaring and whirling flood. Yet the feeling was one which must be mastered; for many a mile of sheer precipice lay before me. The Segre flows through a mere cleft in the heart of the terrible mountains, and the path continuously overhangs the abyss. Bastions of naked rock, a thousand feet high, almost shut out the day; and the traveller, after winding for hours in the gloom of their shadows, feels as if buried from the world.

The sides of the gorge are nearly perpendicular, and the dark gray rock is unrelieved by foliage, except where soil enough has lodged to nourish a tuft of box; yet here and there, wherever a few yards of less abrupt descent occur, in spots not entirely inaccessible, the peasants have built a rude wall, smoothed the surface, and compelled a scanty tribute of grass or grain. Tall, wild-looking figures, in brown jackets and knee-breeches, with short, broad-bladed scythes flashing on their shoulders, met us; and as they leaned back in the hollows of the rock to let us pass, with the threatening implements held over their heads, a very slight effort of the imagination made them more dangerous than the gulf which yawned on the opposite side of the path. They were as rough and savage as the scenery in appearance; but in reality they were simple-hearted, honest persons. All that I saw of the inhabitants of this part of Catalonia assured me that I was perfectly safe among them. After the first day of my journey, I gave up the prospect of finding danger enough to make an adventure.

By and by the path, so lonely for the first hour after starting, began to be animated. The communication between the valleys of the Spanish Pyrenees and the lower Segre, as far as Lerida, is carried on through this defile, and pack-mules were met from time to time. Juan walked in advance, listening for the tinkling bells of the coming animals, and selecting places were the road was broad enough for us to pass without danger. Sometimes I waited, sometimes they — one leaning close against the rock, one pacing slowly along the brink, with the river below booming into caverns cut out of the interlocking bases of the mountains. As the path sank or rose, accommodating itself to the outline of the cliffs, and the bells of the unseen mules or horses chimed in front around some corner of the gorge, they chimed to my ears the words of another, who foresaw as well as remembered.

O, dear and distant Friend and Poet! henceforth I shall hear your voice in this music of Spain. All that day, in the wild and wonderful cañons of the Segre, you rode with me; and poetical justice demanded that I should have paid, like Uhland to his boatman, for the other spirit who sat upon my weary steed. I tried to look with your clear eyes, so quick to detect and interpret beauty; and I try now to write of the scenery, so that you may behold it through mine. As turn after turn of the winding gorge disclosed some grander conformation of the overhanging heights, some new pinnacle of rock piercing the air, or cavern opening its dark arch at the base of a precipice, I drew you from your quiet cottage by the Merrimack, and said, as we paused together in a myrtle-roofed niche in the rocks, "All this belongs to us, for we alone have seen it!"

But, alas! how much of subtle form, of delicate gradation of color, of fleeting moods of atmosphere, escapes us when we try to translate the experience of the eyes! I endeavor to paint the living and breathing body of Nature, and I see only a hard black silhouette, like those shadows of grandfathers which hang in old country homes. Only to minds that of themselves understand and can guess is the effort not lost. A landscape thus partly describes itself; and so, in this case, I must hope that something of the grand and lonely valley of the Rio Segre may have entered into my words.

Perhaps the best general impression of the scenery may be suggested by a single peculiarity. Two hours after entering the defile, I issued from it into the *conque* of Nargo — an open circular basin some three miles in breadth, beyond which the mountains again interlock. The term *conque* (shell?) is applied to these valleys, which occur regularly at intervals of from six to ten miles; and their arrangement is picturesquely described in French as as being *en chapelet,* for they are literally strung like beads on the thread of the river. No part of Europe is so old (to the eye) as these valleys. There seems to have been no change for a thousand years. If the air were not so dry, one could fancy that the villages would be gradually buried under a growth of moss and lichens. The brown rust on their masonry is almost black, the walls of the terraced fields are as secure in their places as the natural rock, and the scars left by wars are not to be distinguished from those of age. Whenever there is a surplus of population it must leave, for it cannot be subsisted. There may be mountain-paths leading inland from these valleys, but none are visible; each little community is inclosed by a circle of tremendous stony walls and pinnacles, which the river alone has been able to pierce.

At the further end of the *conque* of Nargo lay the village, perched upon a bold crag. Several sharp, isolated mountains, resembling the horns and needles of the Alps, rose abruptly out of the open space; and their lower faces of dark vermilion rock made a forcible contrast with the splendid green of the fields. We did not pause in the village, but descended its ladder of a street to the river-wall, and plunged at once into a second gorge, as grand and savage as the first, though no more than a league in extent. Juan again went ahead and warned the coming muleteers. In another hour I reached the *conque* of Organá, a rich and spacious tract of land, with the village of the same name on a rock, precisely like Nargo. A high, conical peak on the left appeared to be inaccessible, yet there was a white chapel on its very summit. "Look there!" said Juan, "*that* saint likes a cool place."

Fine old walnut-tree made their appearance in this valley; water was everywhere abundant, and the gardens through which I approached the village were filled with shade and the sound of streams. Indeed, the terraces of ancient vines and fruit-trees, mixed with cypresses and bosky alleys of flowering shrubs, might have belonged to the palaces of an extinct nobility; but the houses which followed were those of peasants, smoky with age, low, dark, and dirty. A pack of school-children, in the main street, hailed me with loud shouts, whereat the mechanics looked up from their work, and the housewives came to the doors. There was a dusky inn, with a meek, pinched landlady, who offered eggs and a *guisado* (stew) with tomatoes. While these were cooking, she placed upon the table a broad-bellied bottle with a spout, something like an old-fashioned oil-can in shape. I was not Catalan enough to drink without a glass; but Juan raising the bottle above his head, spirted a thin stream of wine into his open mouth, and drank long and luxuriously. When he was satisfied, a dexterous turn of the wrist cut off the stream, and not a drop was spilled. At the table, these bottles pass from hand to hand — one cannot say from mouth to mouth, for the lips never touch them. I learned to drink in the same fashion without much difficulty, and learned thereby that much of the flavor of the wine is lost. The custom seems to have been invented to disguise a bad vintage.

While we were breakfasting, a French peasant, whom I had seen at Oliana, arrived. He was on foot, and bound for Foix, by way of Andorra. This was also my route, and I accepted his offer of engaging another horse for me at Urgel, in the evening, and accompanying me over the Pyrenees. He was not a very agreeable person, but it was a satisfaction to find some one with whom I could speak. I left him at the table, with a company of Spanish muleteers, and never saw him afterwards.

Before leaving Organá, I was stopped in the street by a

man who demanded money, saying something about the "Pons," which I could not comprehend. It finally occurred to me that the defile through which I was about to pass is named *Los tres Pons* (The Three Bridges) on the old maps of Catalonia, and that the man was asking for toll — which proved to be the case. The three *cuartos* which I paid were the veriest trifle for the privilege of passing over such a road as followed. The mountains were here loftier, and therefore more deeply cloven; the former little attempts at cultivation ceased, for even Catalonian thrift shrank from wresting any profit out of walls so bare and bluff that scarcely a wild goat could cling to their ledges. Two hundred feet below, the river beat against the rocks with a sullen, mysterious sound, while, from one to two thousand feet above, the jagged coping of the precipices cut the sky. A cool, steady wind drew down the cleft, filling it with a singular humming sound. The path crossed to the eastern side by a tremulous wooden bridge laid flat upon natural abutments; then, a mile further, recrossed by a lofty stone arch, under which there was a more ancient one, still perfect. Several miles of the same wonderful scenery succeeded — scenery the like of which I know not where to find in Switzerland. The gorge of Gondo, on the Italian side of the Simplon, is similar in character, but less grand and majestic. Far up in the enormous cliffs, I saw here and there the openings of caverns, to which no man has ever climbed; cut into the heart of inaccessible walls were unexpected glens, green nests of foliage, safe from human intrusion, where the nightingales sang in conscious security; and there were points so utterly terrible in all their features that the existence of a travelled path was the greatest wonder of all.

In the preceding defiles, Nature had accidentally traced out the way, but here it had been forced by sheer labor and daring. Sometimes it was hewn into the face of the upright rock; sometimes it rested on arches built up from below, the worn masonry of which threatened to give way as I passed over. Now, fortunately, the tinkling of mule-bells was rare, for there were few points where travellers could safely meet. Convulsion was as evident in the structure of the mountains themselves as in their forcible separation. In some places the perpendicular strata were curiously bent, as if the top had cooled rapidly and begun to lean over upon the fluid ascending mass. The summits assumed the wildest and most fantastic forms, especially about the centre of the mountain range. When I had crossed the third bridge, which is more than a league above the second, the heights fell away, the glen gradually opened, and I saw before me the purple chain of the Pyrenees, mottled with dark patches of forest, and crested with snow.

The pass of The Three Bridges has its tragic episode of recent history, in addition to those which the centuries have forgotten. Here, forty years ago, the Count of Spain, who governed Catalonia in the name of Ferdinand VII., was betrayed by his own adjutant, by whom, and by a priest named Ferrer, he was murdered. The deed is supposed to have been committed at the instigation of Don Carlos. A stone was tied to the corpse, and it was flung from the rocks into the torrent of the Segre. The place breathes of vengeance and death; and one seems to inhale a new air when he emerges into the *conque* of Le Pla, after being inclosed for two hours within those terrible gates.

It was a double delight to me to come upon lush meadows, and smell the vernal sweetness of the flowering grass. Leaving the river on my left, I struck eastward along the sides of clayey hills, with slopes of vine above me, and the broad green meadows below. The vegetation had already a more northern character; clumps of walnut, poplar, and willow grew by the brooksides, and the fields of wheat were not yet ripe for harvest. I passed a picturesque, tumbling village called Arfa, crossed the Segre for the last time, and then rode onward into a valley several miles in diameter, the bed of which was broken by rounded hills. This was the Valley of Urgel, or "the See," — *el seú*, as it is called by the people in their dialect. The term recalls the days when the Bishop was a sovereign prince, and his see a temporal, as well as ecclesiastical government.

Juan pointed out a fortress in advance, which I supposed to be the town. Near it, on the slope of the hill, there was a mass of buildings, baking in the afternoon sun; and I know not which was most melancholy, the long lines of cracked, deserted ramparts on the hill, or the crumbling, uninhabited houses on the slope below. I did not see six persons in the place, which was not Urgel, but Castel Ciudad. The former city is a mile further, seated in the centre of the plain. I saw, on my left, the mouth of a glen of the Pyrenees, and guessed, before the groom said so, that within its depths lay the forgotten Republic of Andorra. The Valira, the one stream of the Republic, poured upon the plain its cold green waters, which I forded, in several channels, before reaching the gates of Urgel.

Juan had cheered me with the promise of a good inn. The exterior of the house was, if anything, a trifle meaner than that of the neighboring houses; the entrance was through a stable, and the kitchen and public room very dirty; yet, these once passed, I entered a clean, spacious, and even elegant bedroom. A door therefrom opened upon a paved terrace, with a roof of vine and a superb view of the Pyrenees; and hither, as I sat and rested my weary bones, came the landlord, and praised the country. There was inexhaustible coal in the mountains, he said; there was iron in the water; the climate was the best in Spain; people were healthy and lived long — and the only thing wanting was a road to some part of the world.

The towns through which I had passed seemed as old and lonely as any towns could well be; but they are tame beside the picturesque antiquity of Urgel. Nothing seems to have been changed here since the twelfth century. The streets are narrow and gloomy, but almost every house rests on massive arches, which form continuous arcades, where the mechanics sit and ply their avocations. The vistas of these arched passages are closed either with a single building of very primitive and ponderous architecture, or by the stones of a wall as old as the times of the Moors. The place is like a gallery of old sepia drawings. I attracted the usual wonder, as I loitered through the gloom of the arcades; work was suspended while I passed, and tongues were silent. When I entered the venerable cathedral, which was finished six hundred years ago, the solitary worshipper stopped in the midst of an *ave*, and stared at me with open mouth. The spacious Gothic nave, however, was less attractive than the pictures outside; so I passed from the interior to the exterior shadows — one about as dense as the other. Presently I came upon a massive house, with a magnificent flat-roofed arbor of grapes beside it, and was saying to myself that there was one fortunate person in the poverty-stricken capital, when the door opened and Don Basilio came forth with sweeping cassock and enormous hat. A little further, I found myself in a small plaza, one side of which was occupied by a building resembling a fortress. Over the door I read the inscription, " Princeps soberan del Valls de Andorra." This was the residence of the bishop, who claims the title of sovereign of the little republic; his powers, in fact, being scarcely more than nominal.

I was tempted to present myself to his Reverence, and state my intention of visiting Andorra; but my information with regard to the republic was so vague that I knew not how such a visit might be regarded. I might be creating difficulty where none existed. With this prudent reflection I returned to the inn, and engaged a fresh horse and guide for the morrow, sending Juan back to Cardona. It was but an hour's ride, the landlord said, to the frontier.

The region of ill-repute lay behind me; the difficult bridle-roads were passed, and all evil predictions had come to naught. By-ways are better than highways, and if an intelligent young American, who knows the Spanish language, will devote a year to the by-ways of Spain, living with the people and in their fashion, he will find that all the good books of observation and adventure have not yet been written.

THE REPUBLIC OF THE PYRENEES.

There are remote, forgotten corners of history, as there are of geography. When Halévy brought out his opera *Le Val d'Andorre*, the name meant no more to the most of those who heard it than the Valley of Rasselas to our ears, — a sound, locating a fiction. But the critic, who must seem to know everything, opened one of his lexicons, and discovered that Andorra was an actual valley, buried in the heart of the Pyrenees. Furthermore, he learned, for the first time, that its territory was an independent republic, preserved intact since the days of Charlemagne; that both France and Spain, incredible as the fact may appear, have always scrupulously respected the rights granted to its inhabitants more than a thousand years ago. While the existence of every other state has in turn been menaced, while hundreds of treaties have been made only to be broken, here is a place where, like the castle of the Sleeping Beauty, time has stood still, and History shut up her annals.

Napoleon, when a deputation from the little republic visited him in Paris, said: "I have heard of this Andorra, and have purposely abstained from touching it, because I thought it ought to be preserved as a political curiosity." Louis Philippe, thirty years later, exclaimed: "What! is it possible that I have a neighbor whose name I never heard before?" I suspect that the name of Andorra on the excellent German maps, which overlook nothing, was the first indication of the existence of the state to many of those who are now acquainted with it. It was so in my case. From noting its position, and seeing its contracted boundaries, so carefully marked out, I went further, and picked up what fragments of information could be found in French and German geographical works. These were sufficiently curious to inspire me with the design of visiting the valley.

On reaching Urgel, in the Spanish Pyrenees, I was within a league of the Andorran frontier. My way thither lay through the deep gorge out of which the river Valira issues, on its way to the Segre. The bald, snow-streaked summits in the north belonged to the territory of the republic, but whatever of life and labor it contained was buried out of sight in their breast. Nevertheless, the vague and sometimes threatening reports of the people which had reached me at a distance here vanished. Everybody knew Andorra, and spoke well of it. I had some difficulty in finding a horse, which the landlord declared was on account of the unpractical shape and weight of my valise; but, when I proposed going on foot, an animal was instantly produced. The arrieros could not let a good bargain slip out of their hands.

It was a wonderful morning in mid June. The shadow of the Pyrenees still lay cool upon the broad basin of Urgel; but the brown ramparts of Castel Ciudad on the rocks, and all the western heights, sparkled in sunshine. I found a nimble mountain pony waiting for me at the door of the inn, and Julian, my guide, a handsome fellow of twenty, in rusty velvet jacket and breeches, and scarlet Phrygian cap. A skin as brown as an Arab's; an eye full of inexpressible melancholy; a grave, silent, but not gloomy nature — all these had Julian; yet he was the very companion for such a journey. He strode from the gate of Urgel with a firm, elastic step, and I followed through the gray olive orchards across the plain. The lower terraces of the mountain were silvery with the olive; but when the path turned into the gorge of the Valira, the landscape instantly changed. On one side rose a rocky wall; on the other, meadows of blossoming grass, divided by thickets of alder and willow, slanted down to the rapid stream, the noise of which could scarcely be heard for the songs of the nightingales. Features like these, simple as they may seem, sometimes have a singular power to warm one's anticipations of what lies beyond. There is a *promise* in certain scenery; wherein it exists I cannot tell, but I have felt it frequently, and have never yet been disappointed.

After I had threaded the gorge for two miles, it expanded into a narrow valley, where the little Spanish village of Arcacel lay huddled among the meadows. Beyond it, the mountains closed together again, forming an almost impassable cañon, along the sides of which the path was laboriously notched. There were a great many people abroad, and Julian was obliged to go in advance, and select spots where my horse could pass their mules without one or the other being pushed into the abyss below. Some of those I met were probably Andorrans, but I found as yet no peculiarities of face or costume. This is the only road from Spain into the republic, and is very rarely, if ever, traversed by a foreign tourist. The few persons who have visted Andorra, made their way into the valley from the side of France.

As I rode forward, looking out from time to time, for some mark which would indicate the frontier, I recalled what little I had learned of the origin of the republic. There is not much which the most patient historian could establish as positive fact; but the traditions of the people and the few records which they have allowed to be published run nearly parallel, and are probably as exact as most of the history of the ninth century. On one point all the accounts agree — that the independence of the valley sprang indirectly from the struggle between the Franks and Saracens. When the latter possessed themselves of the Peninsula, in the beginning of the eighth century, a remnant of the Visigoths took refuge in this valley, whence, later, they sent to Charlemagne, imploring assistance. After Catalonia had been reconquered, the Emperor — so runs the popular tradition — gave them the valley as a reward for their bravery in battle. The more probable account is, that Charlemagne sent his son, Louis le Débonnaire, who followed the last remnants of the Saracen army up the gorge of the Valira, and defeated them on the spot where the town of Andorra now stands. After the victory, he gave the valley to certain of his soldiers, releasing them from all allegiance except to himself. This was in the year 805. What is called the " Charter of Charlemagne," by some of the French writers, is evidently this grant of his son.

Within the following century, however, certain difficulties arose, which disturbed the inhabitants of the little state less than their powerful neighbors. Charlemagne had previously given, it appears, the tithes of all the region to Possidonius, Bishop of Urgel, and the latter insisted on retaining his right. Moreover, Charles the Bald, in 843, presented to Siegfrid, Count of Urgel, the right of sovereignty over Andorra, which Louis le Débonnaire had reserved for himself and his successors. Thus the spiritual and temporal lords of Urgel came in direct conflict, and the question remained undecided for two centuries; the Andorrans, meanwhile, quietly attending to their own affairs, and consolidating the simple framework of their government. Finally, at the consecration of the Cathedral of Urgel, in the year 1040, the widowed Countess Constance publicly placed the sovereignty claimed by her house in the hands of Bishop *Heribald*. (How curious it seems to find the name of Garibaldi occurring in this obscure history!) But this gift of Constance was not respected by her successors, and the trouble broke out anew in the following century. We have but a meagre chain of detached incidents, yet what passion, what intrigue, what priestly thirst of power and jealous resistance on the part of the nobles are suggested, as we follow the scanty record! The Bishop of Urgel triumphs to this day, as he reads the inscription over his palace-door: "Princeps soberan del Valls de Andorra."

At the end of the twelfth century, Arnald, Count of Castelbo, purchased certain privileges in the valley from Ermengol, Count of Urgel. The sale was resisted by the bishop, and a war ensued, in which the latter was defeated. Raymond-Roger, Count of Foix, was then called to aid the episcopal cause — his promised reward being a share in the sovereignty of Andorra, the territory of which bordered his own. Notwithstanding he was victorious, having taken and sacked the city of Urgel, he seems to have considered his claim to the reward still insecure. In the year 1202 he married his son and successor, Roger-Bernard II., to the daughter and only child of the Count of Castelbo. Thus the Bishop of Urgel saw the assumption of sovereignty which he had resisted transferred to the powerful house of Foix. It is stated, however, that, in all the wars which followed, both parties refrained from touching the disputed territory, in order that the value of the revenue expected from it might not be diminished. The Andorrans themselves, though certainly not unconcerned, remained perfectly passive. The fastnesses of the Pyrenees on all sides of them resounded with the noise of war, while they, one generation after another, tended their flocks and cultivated their fields.

The quarrel (and it is almost the end of all history relating to Andorra) came to a close in the year 1278. Roger-Bernard III. of Foix, before the gates of Urgel, which must soon have yielded to him, accepted the proposal for an arbitration — Don Pedro of Aragon having offered his name as security for the fulfillment of the terms which might be agreed upon. Two priests and four knights were the arbitrators; and the *Pariatges* (Partitions) which they declared on the 7th of September of the year already mentioned settled the question of the sovereignty of Andorra from that day to this. Its principal features were that a slight tribute should be paid by the people, on alternate years, to the Counts of Foix and the Bishops of Urgel; and that certain officials of the Valley should, in like manner, be named alternately by the two parties. In all other respects, the people were left free. The neutrality of their territory, which had been so marvelously preserved for four centuries and a half, was reaffirmed; and it has never since been violated. During the wars of Napoleon, a French army appeared on the frontiers of the republic with the intention of marching through it into Spain; but on the judges and consuls representing to the commanding general the sacred neutrality of their valley, he turned about and chose another route.

The house of Foix became merged in that of Béarn, and the inheritance of the latter, in turn, passed into the hands of the Bourbons. Thus the crown of France succeeded to the right reserved by Louis le Débonnaire, and presented by Charles the Bald to Siegfrid, Count of Urgel. The Andorrans, who look upon their original charter as did the Hebrews on their Ark of the Covenant, consider that the *Pariatges* are equally sanctioned by time and the favor of God; and, so far from feeling that the tribute is a sign of subjection, they consider that it really secures their independence. They therefore do not allow the revolutions, the change of dynasties which France has undergone, to change their relation to the governing power. They were filled with dismay, when, in 1793, the representative of the French Republic in Foix refused to accept the tribute, on the ground that it was a relic of the feudal system. For six or seven years thereafter they feared that the end of things was at hand; but the establishment of the Empire, paradoxical as it may appear, secured to them their republic. They seem never to have considered that the refusal of the French authorities gave them a valid pretext to cease the further payment of the tribute.

This is the sum and substance of the history of Andorra.

No one can help feeling that a wholly exceptional fortune has followed this handful of people. All other rights given by Charlemagne and his successors became waste paper long since: the Counts of Urgel, the houses of Foix and Béarn, have disappeared, and the Bourbons have ceased to reign in France,— yet the government of the little republic preserves the same forms which were established in the ninth century, and the only relations which at present connect it with the outer world date from the year 1278. I endeavored to impress these facts upon my mind, as the gorge opened into a narrow green valley, blocked up in front by the Andorran mountains. I recalled that picturesque legend of the knight of the Middle Ages, who, penetrating into some remote nook of the Apennines, found a forgotten Roman city, where the people still kept their temples and laid their offerings on the altars of the gods. The day was exquisitely clear and sunny; the breezes of the Pyrenees blew away every speck of vapor from the mountains, but I saw everything softly through that veil which the imagination weaves for us.

Presently we came upon two or three low houses. At the door of the furthest two Spanish soldiers were standing, one of whom stepped forward when he saw me. A picture of delay, examination, bribery, rose in my mind. I assumed a condescending politeness, saluted the man gravely, and rode forward. To my great surprise no summons followed. I kept on my way without looking back, and in two minutes was out of Spain. Few travellers have ever left the kingdom so easily.

The features of the scenery remained the same — narrow, slanting shelves of grass and grain, the Valira foaming below, and the great mountains of gray rock towering into the sky. In another half-hour I saw the little town of San Julian de Loria, one of the six municipalities of Andorra. As old and brown as Urgel, or the villages along the Rio Segre, it was in no wise to be distinguished from them. The massive stone walls of the houses were nearly black; the roofs of huge leaves of slate were covered with a red rust; and there were no signs that anything had been added or taken away from the place for centuries. As my horse clattered over the dirty paving-stones, mounting the one narrow, twisted street, the people came to the doors, and looked upon me with a grave curiosity. I imagined at once that they were different from the Catalans, notwithstanding they spoke the same dialect, and wore very nearly the same costume. The expression of their faces was more open and fearless; a *cheerful* gravity marked their demeanor. I saw that they were both self-reliant and contented.

While Julian stopped to greet some of his friends, I rode into a very diminutive plaza, where some thirty or forty of the inhabitants were gossiping together. An old man, dressed in pale blue jacket and knee-breeches, with a red scarf around his waist, advanced to meet me, lifting his scarlet cap in salutation.

"This is no longer Spain?" I asked.

"It is neither France nor Spain," said he; "it is Andorra."

"The Republic of Andorra?"

"They call it so."

"I am also a citizen of a republic," I then said; but, although his interest was evidently excited, he asked me no questions. The Andorran reserve is proverbial throughout Catalonia; and as I had already heard of it, I voluntarily gave as much information respecting myself as was necessary. A number of men, young and old, had by this time collected, and listened attentively. Those who spoke Spanish mingled in the conversation, which, on my part, was purposely guarded. Some degree of confidence, however seemed to be already established. They told me that they were entirely satisfied with their form of government and their secluded life; that they were poor, but much wealth would be of no service to them, and, moreover (which was true), that they were free because they were poor. When Julian appeared, he looked with surprise upon the friendly circle around me, but said nothing. It was still two hours to *Andorra la Vella* (Old Andorra), the capital, which I had decided to make my first resting-place; so I said, "Adios!"—all the men responding, "Dios guarda!"

Beyond the village I entered upon green meadow-land, shaded by grand walnut-trees, mounds of the richest foliage. The torrent of Aviña came down through a wild glen on the left, to join the Valira, and all the air vibrated with the sound of waters and the incessant songs of the nightingales. People from the high, unseen mountain farms and pasture-grounds met me on their way to San Julian; and their greeting was always "God guard you!" — hinting of the days when travel was more insecure than now. When the mountains again contracted, and the path clung to the sides of upright mountain walls, Julian went in advance, and warned the coming muleteers. Vegetation ceased, except the stubborn clumps of box, which had fastened themselves in every crevice of the precipices; and the nightingales, if any had ventured into the gloomy gorge, were silent. For an hour I followed its windings, steadily mounting all the while; then the rocks began to lean away, the smell of flowering grass came back to the air, and I saw, by the breadth of blue sky opening ahead, that we were approaching the Valley of Andorra.

The first thing that met my eyes was a pretty pastoral picture. Some rills from the melting snows had been caught and turned into an irrigating canal, the banks of which were so overgrown with brambles and wild-flowers that it had become a natural stream. Under a gnarled, wide-armed ilex sat a father, with his two youngest children; two older ones gathered flowers in the sun; and the mother, with a basket in her hand, paused to look at me in the meadow below. The little ones laughed and shouted; the father watched them with bright, happy eyes, and over and around them the birds sang without fear. And this is the land of smugglers and robbers! I thought. Turning in the saddle, I watched the group as long as it was visible.

When I set my face forward again, it was with a sudden catch of the breath and a cry of delight. The promise of the morning was fulfilled; beautiful beyond anticipation was the landscape expanded before me. It was a valley six miles in length, completely walled in by immense mountains, the bases of which, withdrawn in the centre, left a level bed of meadows, nearly a mile broad, watered by the winding Valira. Terraces of grain, golden below, but still green above, climbed far up the slopes; then forest and rock succeeded; and finally the gray pinnacles, with snow in their crevices, stood mantled in their own shadows. Near the centre of the valley, on a singular rocky knoll, the old houses and square tower of Andorra were perched, as if watching over the scene. In front, where the river issued from a tremendous split between two interlocking mountains, I could barely distinguish the houses of Escaldas from the cliffs to which they clung. Nothing could be simpler and grander than the large outlines of the scene, nothing lovelier than its minuter features, — so wonderfully suggesting both the garden and the wilderness, the fresh green of the North and the hoary hues and antique forms of the South. Brimming with sunshine and steeped in delicious odors, the valley — after the long, dark gorge I had threaded — seemed to flash and sparkle with a light unknown to other lands.

Shall I ever forget the last three miles of my journey? Crystal waters rushed and murmured beside my path; great twisted ilex-trees sprang from the masses of rock; mounds of snowy eglantine or purple clematis crowned the cliffs or hung from them like folded curtains; and the dark shadows of walnut and poplar lay upon the lush fields of grass and flowers. The nightingale and thrush sang on the earth, and the lark in the air; and even the melancholy chant of the young farmer in his fields seemed to be only that soft undercurrent of sadness which was needed to make the brightness and joy of the landscape complete.

Climbing the rocks to the capital, I was pleasantly surprised to see the sign "Hostal" before I had made more than two turns of the winding street. The English guides, both for France and Spain, advise the adventurous tourist who wishes to visit Andorra to take his provender with him, since nothing can be had in the valley. A friendly host came to the door, and welcomed me. Dinner, he said, would be ready in an hour and a half; but the appearance of the cheerful kitchen into which I was ushered so provoked my already ravenous hunger that an omelette was made instantly, and Julian and I shared it between us. An upper room, containing a coarse but clean bed, which barely found room for itself in a wilderness of saddles and harness, was given to me, and I straightway found myself at home in Andorra. So much for guide-books!

I went forth to look at the little capital before dinner. Its population is less than one thousand; the houses are built of rudely broken stones of schist or granite, and roofed with large sheets of slate. The streets seem to have been originally located where the surface of the rock rendered them possible; but there are few of them, and what the place has to show may be speedily found. I felt at once the simple, friendly, hospitable character of the people: they saluted me as naturally and genially as if I had been an old acquaintance. Before I had rambled many minutes, I found myself before the *Casa del Valls*, the House of Government. It is an ancient, cracked building, but when erected I could not ascertain. The front is simple and massive, with three irregular windows, and a large arched entrance. A tower at one corner threatens to fall from want of repair. Over the door is the inscription: "Domus consilii, sedes justitiæ." There is also a marble shield, containing the arms of the Republic, and apparently inserted at a more recent date. The shield is quartered with the mitre and crosier of the Bishop of Urgel, the four crimson bars of Catalonia, the three bars on an azure field of Foix, and the cows of Béarn. Under the shield is sculptured the Latin verse: —

> "Suspice : sunt vallis neutrius stemmata ; sunt que
> Regna, quibus gaudent nobiliora tegi :
> Singula si populos alios, Andorra, beabunt,
> Quidni juncta ferent aurea secla tibi ! "

I suspect, although I have no authority for saying so, that this verse comes from Fiter, the only scholar Andorra ever produced, who flourished in the beginning of the last century. The ground-floor of the building consists of stables, where the members of the council lodge their horses when they meet officially. A tumbling staircase leads to the second story, which is the council-hall, containing a table and three chairs on a raised platform, a picture of Christ between the windows, and oaken benches around the walls. The great object of interest, however, is a massive chest, built into the wall, and closed with six strong iron locks, connected by a chain. This contains the archives of Andorra, including, as the people devoutly believe, the original charters of Charlemagne and Louis le Débonnaire. Each consul of the six parishes is intrusted with the keeping of one key, and the chest can only be opened when all six are present. It would be quite impossible for a stranger to get a sight of the contents. The archives are said to be written on sheets of lead, on palm-leaves, on parchment, or on paper, according to the age from which they date. The chest also contains the "Politar," or Annals of Andorra, with a digest of the laws, compiled by the scholar Fiter. The government did not allow the work to be published, but there is another manuscript copy in the possession of the Bishop of Urgel.

I climbed the huge mass of rock behind the building,

and sat down upon its crest to enjoy the grand, sunny picture of the valley. The mingled beauty and majesty of the landscape charmed me into a day-dream, in which the old, ever-recurring question was lazily pondered, whether or not this plain, secluded, ignorant life was the happiest lot of man. But the influences of the place were too sweet and soothing for earnest thought, and a clock striking noon recalled me to the fact that a meal was ready in the hostal. The host sat down to the table with Julian and myself, and the spout of the big-bellied Catalonian bottle overhung our mouths in succession. We had a rough but satisfactory dinner, during which I told the host who I was and why I came, thereby winning his confidence to such an extent that he presently brought me an old, dirty Spanish pamphlet, saying, "You may read this."

Seeing that it was a brief and curious account of Andorra, I asked, "Cannot I buy this or another copy?"

"No," he answered; "it is not to be bought. You can read it; but you must give it to me again."

I selected a dark corner of the kitchen, lit my cigar, and read, making rapid notes when I was not observed. The author was a nephew of one of the bishops of Urgel, and professed to have seen with his own eyes the charter of Louis le Débonnaire. That king, he stated, defeated the Saracens on the plain towards Escaldas, where the western branch of the Valira comes down from the Valley of Ordino. Before the battle, a passage from the Book of Kings came into his mind: "Endor, over against Mount Tabor, where the children of Israel, preparing for war against the heathen, pitched their camp"; and after the victory he gave the valley the name of Endor, whence Andorra. The resemblance, the author innocently remarks, is indeed wonderful. In both places there are high mountains; the same kinds of trees grow (!); a river flows through each; there are lions and leopards in Endor, and bears and wolves in Andorra! He then gives the following quotation from the charter, which was written in Latin; "The men who actually live in this country are Licindo, Laurentio, Obaronio, Antimirio, Guirinio, Suessonio, Barrulio, rustic laborers, and many others." Louis le Débonnaire returned to France by the present Porte de Fontargente, where, on the summit of the Pyrenees, he caused a chain to be stretched from rock to rock. The holes drilled for the staples of the rings are still to be seen, the people say.

When I had finished the book, I went out again, and in the shade of a willow in the meadow below, made a rough sketch of the town and the lofty Mont Anclar (*mons clarus*) behind it. As I returned, the lower part of the valley offered such lovely breadths of light and shade that I sought a place among the tangle of houses and rocks to make a second drawing. The women, with their children around them, sat at their doors, knitting and chatting. One cried out to another, as I took my seat on the ground, "Why don't you bring a chair for the cavalier?" The chair was brought immediately, and the children gathered around, watching my movements. The mothers kept them in good order, every now and then crying out, "Don't go too near, and don't stand in front!" Among themselves they talked freely about me; but, as they asked no questions, I finally said, "I understand you; if you will ask, I will answer," — whereupon they laughed and were silent.

I have already said that reserve is a marked characteristic of the Andorrans. No doubt it sprang originally from their consciousness of their weakness, and their fear to lose their inherited privileges by betraying too much about themselves. When one of them is questioned upon a point concerning which he thinks it best to be silent, he assumes a stupid expression of face, and appears not to understand. That afternoon a man came to me in the inn, produced a rich specimen of galena, and said, "Do you know what that is?" "Certainly," I answered; "it is the ore of lead. Where did you get it?" He put it in his pocket, looked up at the sky, and said, "What fine weather we have!" It is known that there is much lead in the mountains, yet the mines have never been worked. The people say, "We must keep poor, as our fathers have been. If we become rich, the French will want our lead and the Spaniards our silver, and then one or the other will rob us of our independence."

So well is this peculiarity of the inhabitants understood, that in Catalonia to assume ignorance is called "to play the Andorran." A student from the frontier, on entering a Spanish theological seminary, was called upon to translate the New Testament. When he came to the words, "Jesus autem tacebat," he rendered them, in perfect good faith, "Jesus played the Andorran." For the same reason, the hospitality of the people is of a passive rather than of an active character. The stranger may enter any house in the valley, take his seat at the family board, and sleep under the shelter of the roof; he is free to come and go; no questions are asked, although voluntary information is always gladly received. They would be scarcely human if it were not so.

The principal features of the system of government which these people have adopted may be easily described. They have no written code of laws, the *Politar* being only a collection of precedents in certain cases, accessible to the consuls and judges, and to them alone. When we come to examine the modes in which they are governed, — procedures which, based on long custom, have all the force of law, — we find a singular mixture of the elements of democracy, aristocracy, and monarchy. The sovereignty of France and the Bishop of Urgel is acknowledged in the appointment of the two *viguiers* (*vicarii*), who, it is true, are natives of the valley, and devoted to its interests. In all other respects the forms are democratic; but the circumstance that the officials are unpaid, that they must be married, and that they must be members of families in good repute, has gradually concentrated the government in the hands of a small number of families, by whom it is virtually inherited. Moreover, the law of primogeniture prevails to the fullest extent, still further lessening the number of qualified persons.

The Republic consists of six communes, or parishes, each of which elects two consuls and two councillors, whose term of service is four years; one official of each class being elected every two years. There is no restriction of the right of suffrage. The twenty-four officials form the deliberative body, or Grand Council, who alone have the power of electing the Syndic, the executive head of the government. He is chosen for life; he presides over the Council, and carries its decisions into effect, yet is responsible to it for his actions. Only half the Council being chosen at one time, the disadvantage of having an entirely new set of men suddenly placed in office is obviated. The arrangement, in fact, is the same which we have adopted in regard to the election of United States Senators.

The consuls, in addition, have their municipal duties. Each one names ten petty magistrates, called decurions, whose functions are not much more important than those of our constables. They simply preserve order, and assist in bringing offenses to light. All the persons of property, or who exercise some useful mechanical art, form what is called the Parish Council, whose business it is to raise the proportionate share of the tribute, to apportion the pastures, fix the amount of wood to be sold (part of the revenue of Andorra being derived from the forests), and to regulate all ordinary local matters. These councils, of course, are self-existing; every person who is not poor and insignificant taking his place naturally in them. No one can be chosen as consul who is under thirty years of age, who has not been married, who is blind, deaf, deformed, or epileptic, who is addicted to drink, or who has committed any offense against the laws.

The functions of the parish councils and the Grand Council of the Republic are carefully separated. The former have charge of inns, forges, bakeries, weaving, and the building of dwelling-houses; the latter has control of the forests, the ways of communication, the chase, the fisheries, the finances, and the building of all edifices of a public character. It has five sessions a year. Its members are not paid, but they are lodged and fed, during these sessions, at the public expense. Each parish owns two double-beds in the upper story of the *Casa del Valls* at Andorra; in each bed sleep two consuls or two councillors. There is a kitchen, with an enormous pot, in which their frugal meals are cooked, and a dining-room in which they are served. Formerly their sessions were held in the church-yard, among the tombs, as if to render them more solemnly impressive; but this practice has long been discontinued.

The expenses of the state, one will readily guess, must be very slight. The tribute paid to France is nineteen hundred and twenty francs; that to the Bishop of Urgel, eight hundred and forty-two francs — an average of two hundred and seventy-five dollars per annum. The direct tax is five cents annually for each person; but a moderate revenue is derived from the sale of wood and charcoal, and the rent of pastures on the northern slope of the Pyrenees. Import, export, and excise duties, licenses, and stamps are unknown, although, in civil cases, certain moderate fees are established. The right of tithes, given by Charlemagne to Possidonius, remains in force; but they are generally paid in kind; and in return the Bishop of Urgel, who appoints the priests, contributes to their support. The vicars, of whom there is one to each parish, are paid by the government. The inhabitants are, without exception, devout Catholics, yet it is probably ancient custom, rather than the influence of the priests, which makes them indifferent to education. The schools are so few that they hardly deserve to be mentioned. Only one man in a hundred, and one woman in five hundred, can read and write.

The two viguiers, one of whom is named by France and the other by the Bishop of Urgel, exercise the functions of judges. They are the representatives of the two sovereign powers, and their office is therefore surrounded with every mark of respect. Although nominally of equal authority, their activity is in reality very unequally divided. Usually some prominent official of the Département de l'Ariége is named on the part of France, and contents himself with an annual visit to the valley. The Bishop, on the other hand, always names a native Andorran, who resides among the people, and performs the duties of both viguiers. When a new viguier is appointed, he must be solemnly installed at the capital. The members of the Grand Council then appear in their official costume — a long surtout of black cloth, with crimson facings, a red shawl around the waist, gray knee-breeches, sky-blue stockings, and shoes with silver buckles. The Syndic of the Republic wears a crimson mantle; but the viguier is dressed in black, with a sword, cocked hat, and gold-headed staff. As the tribute paid to France is much larger than that paid to the Bishop, the people have voluntarily added to the latter a Christmas offering of the twelve best hams, the twelve richest cheeses, and the twelve fattest capons to be found in the six parishes.

The sovereign powers have two other representatives in addition to the viguiers. These are the *batlles* (*bailes*, bailiffs?) who are chosen from a list of six persons selected by the Grand Council. Their principal duty is to hear and decide, in the first instance, all civil and criminal cases, except those which the government specially reserves for its own judgment. The batlles, however, are called upon to prevent, rather than solve litigation. When a case occurs, they first endeavor to reconcile the parties, or substitute a private arbitration. If that fails, the case is considered; and, after the help of God is solemnly invoked, judgment is pronounced. Where the dispute involves a delicate or doubtful point, the batlle consults separately the three men of best character and most familiar with the laws who are to be found in the parish, and decides as the judgment of two of them may coincide. It rarely happens that any serious lawsuit occurs, or that any capital crime is committed. The morals of the people are guarded with equal care; any slip from chastity is quietly looked after by the priests and officials, and the parties, if possible, legally united.

The more important cases, or appeals from the decision of the batlles, come before the Supreme Tribunal of Justice, which is composed of the two viguiers, a judge of appeal (chosen to give the casting vote when there is a difference of opinion between the viguiers), a government prosecutor, and two *rahonadors* (pleaders) chosen for the defense by the Grand Council. This tribunal has the power to pronounce a capital sentence, which is then carried out by an executioner brought either from France or Spain.

The army, if it may be called such, consists of six hundred men, or one from each family. They are divided into six companies, according to the parishes, with a captain for each; the decurions acting as subaltern officers. The only special duty imposed upon them, beyond the occasional escort and guard of prisoners, is an annual review by the viguiers and the Grand Council, which takes place on the meadow below Andorra. The officials are seated in state around a large table, upon which a muster-roll of the army is laid. When the first name is read, the soldier to whom it belongs steps forward, discharges his musket in the air, then advances to the table and exhibits his ammunition, which must consist of a pound of powder, twenty-four balls, and as many caps. Each man is called in turn, until the whole six hundred have been thus reviewed.

Such is an outline of the mode of government and the forms of judicial procedure in this little republic. I have not thought it necessary to add the more minute details which grow naturally out of the peculiarities already described. Two things will strike the reader: first, the sufficiency of the system, quaint and singular as it may be in some respects, to the needs of the people; secondly, the skill with which they have reconciled the conditions imposed upon them by the Pariatges, in 1278, with the structure of government they had already erected. For a people so ignorant, so remote from the movement of the world, and so precariously situated, their course has been directed by a rare wisdom. No people value independence more; they have held it, with fear and trembling, as a precious gift; and for a thousand years they have taken no single step which did not tend to secure them in its possession.

According to the host's volume, the population of the towns is as follows: Andorra, 850 inhabitants; San Julian de Loria, 620; Encamp, 520; Canillo, 630; Ordino, 750; and Massana, 700. The population of the smaller hamlets, and the scattered houses of the farmers and herdsmen, will probably amount to about as many more, which would give eight thousand persons as the entire population of the state. I believe this estimate to be very nearly correct. It is a singular circumstance, that the number has not materially changed for centuries. Emigration from the valley has been rare until recent times; the climate is healthy; the people an active, vigorous race; and there must be some unusual cause for this lack of increase. A young man, a native of the parish of Ordino, with whom I had a long conversation in the evening, gave me some information upon this point. The life of families in Andorra is still regulated on the old patriarchal plan. The landed property descends to the oldest son or daughter, or, in default of direct issue, to the nearest relative. This, indeed, is not the law, which gives only a third to the chief inheritor, and divides the remainder equally among the other members of the family. But it has become a custom stronger than law — a custom which is now never violated — to preserve the old possessions intact. The *caps*, or heads of families, are held in such high estimation, that all other family and even personal rights are subordinate to theirs. They are rich and respected, while the younger brothers and sisters, who, by this arrangement, may be left too poor to marry, cheerfully accept a life of celibacy. "I am a younger son," said my informant; "but I have been able to marry, because I went down into Catalonia, entered into business, and made some money." When a daughter inherits, she is required to marry the nearest relative permitted by canonical law, who takes her family name and perpetuates it.

In the course of centuries, however, the principal families have become so inter-related that their interests frequently require marriages within the prohibited degrees. In this case the Andorran undertakes a journey to Rome, to procure a special dispensation from the Pope. He is generally the representative of other parties, similarly situated, who assist in defraying the expenses of the journey. After a collective dispensation has been issued, all the marriages must be celebrated by proxy — the Andorran and a Roman woman who is paid for the service representing, in turn, each bridal pair at home. The latter must afterwards perform public penance in church, kneeling apart from the other worshippers, with lighted tapers in their hands and ashes upon their heads.

Owing to the strictness of these domestic laws, the remarkable habit of self-control among the people, and the careful guard over their morals exercised by the officials, they have become naturally virtuous, and hence great freedom of social intercourse is permitted among the sexes. Their sports and pleasures are characterized by a pastoral simplicity and temperance. Excesses are very rare because all ages and classes of both sexes meet together, and the presence of the priests and *caps grossos* (chief men) acts as a check upon the young men. At the festival of some patron saint of the valley, mass in the chapel is followed by a festive meal in the open air, after which the priest himself gives the signal for the dances to commence. The lads and lasses then assemble on a smooth piece of turf, where the sounds of bagpipe and tambourine set their feet in motion. The old people are not always gossiping spectators, speculating on the couples that move before them in the rude, wild dances of the mountains; they often enter the lists, and hold their ground with the youngest.

Thus, in spite of acquired reserve and predetermined poverty, the life of the Andorrans has its poetical side. The republic has produced one historian (perhaps I should say compiler), but no author; and only Love, the source and soul of Art, keeps alive a habit of improvisation in the young which they appear to lose as they grow older. During Carnival, a number of young men in the villages assemble under the balcony of some chosen girl, and praise, in turn, in words improvised to a familiar melody, her charms of person and of character. When this trial of the Minnesingers begins to lag for want of words or ideas, the girl makes her appearance on the balcony, and with a cord lets down to her admirers a basket containing cakes of her own baking, bottles of wine, and sausages. Before Easter, the unmarried people make bets, which are won by whoever, on Easter morning, can first catch the other and cry out, "It is Easter, the eggs are mine!" Tricks, falsehoods, and deceptions of all kinds are permitted: the young man may even surprise the maiden in bed, if he can succeed in doing so. Afterwards they all assemble in public, relate their tricks, eat their Easter eggs, and finish the day with songs and dances.

Two ruling ideas have governed the Andorrans for centuries past, and seem to have existed independent of any special tradition. One is, that they must not become rich; the other, that no feature of their government must be changed. The former condition is certainly the more difficult of fulfillment, since they have had frequent opportunities of increasing their wealth. There is one family which, on account of the land that has fallen to it by inheritance, would be considered rich in any country; half a dozen others possessing from twenty to thirty thousand dollars; and a large number who are in comfortable circumstances simply because their needs are so few. I had heard that a party opposed to the old traditional ideas was growing up among the young men, but it was not so easy to obtain information on the subject. When I asked the gentleman from Ordino about it, he "acted the Andorran," — put on an expression of face almost idiotic, and talked of something else. He and two others with whom I conversed during the evening admitted, however, that a recent concession of the government (of which I shall presently speak) was the entering wedge by which change would probably come upon the hitherto changeless republic.

With the exception of this incommunicativeness, — in itself rather an interesting feature — no people could have been more kind and friendly. When I went to bed among the saddles and harness in the little room, I no longer felt that I was a stranger in the place. All that I had heard of the hospitality of the people seemed to be verified by their demeanor. I remembered how faithfully they had asserted the neutrality of their territory in behalf of political exiles from France and Spain. General Cabrera, Armand Carrel, and Ferdinand Flocon have at different times found a refuge among them. Although the government reserves the right to prohibit residence to any person whose presence may threaten the peace of the valley, I have not heard that the right was ever exercised. Andorra has been an ark of safety to strangers, as well as an inviolate home of freedom to its own inhabitants.

Julian called me at four o'clock, to resume our journey up the valley, and the host made a cup of chocolate while my horse was being saddled. Then I rode forth into the clear, cold air, which the sun of the Pyrenees had not yet warmed. The town is between three and four thousand feet above the sea, and the limit of the olive tree is found in one of its sheltered gardens. As I issued from the houses, and took a rugged path along the base of Mont Anclar, the village of Escaldas and the great gorge in front lay in a cold, broad mantle of shadow, while the valley was filled to its topmost brims with splendid sunshine. I looked between the stems of giant ilexes upon the battle-field of Louis le Débonnaire. Then came a yawning chasm, down which foamed the western branch of the Valira, coming from an upper valley in which lie the parishes of Ordino and Massana. The two valleys thus form a Y, giving the territory of Andorra a rough triangular shape, about forty miles in length — its base, some thirty miles in breadth, overlapping the Pyrenees, and its point nearly touching the Rio Segre, at Urgel.

A bridge of a single arch spanned the chasm, the bottom of which was filled with tumbling foam; while every ledge of rock, above and below, was draped with eglantine, wild fig, clematis, and ivy. Thence, onward towards Escaldas, my path lay between huge masses which had fallen from the steeps, and bowers completely snowed over with white roses, wherein the nightingales were just beginning to awaken. Then, one by one, the brown houses above me clung like nests to the rocks, with little gardens hanging on seemingly inaccessible shelves. I entered the enfolding shadows, and, following the roar of waters, soon found myself at Escaldas — a place as wonderfully picturesque as Ronda or Tivoli, directly under the tremendous perpendicular walls of the gorge; the arrowy Valira sweeping the foundations of the houses on one side, while the dark masses of rock crowded against and separated them on the other. From the edge of the river, and between the thick foliage of ilex and box behind the houses, rose thin columns of steam, marking the hot springs whence the place (*aguas caldas*) was named.

Crossing the river, I halted at the first of these springs, and took a drink. Some old people who collected informed me that there were ten in all, besides a number of cold mineral fountains, furnishing nine different kinds of water — all of which, they said, possessed wonderful healing properties. There were both iron and sulphur in that which I tasted. A little further, a rude fulling-mill was at work in the open air; and in a forge on the other side of the road three blacksmiths were working the native iron of the mountains. A second and third hot spring followed; then a fourth, in which a number of women were washing clothes. All this in the midst of a chaos of rock, water, and foliage.

These springs of Escaldas have led to the concession which the Andorrans described to me as opening a new, and, I fear, not very fortunate, phase of their history. The exploiters of the gambling interest of France, on the point of being driven from Wiesbaden, Homburg, and Baden-Baden, ransacked Europe for a point where they might at the same time ply their business and attract the fashionable world. They detected Andorra; and by the most consummate diplomacy they have succeeded in allaying the suspicions of the government, in neutralizing the power of its ancient policy, and in acquiring privileges which, harmless as they seem, may in time wholly subvert the old order of things. It is impossible that this result could have been accomplished unless a party of progress, the existence of which has been hinted, has really grown up among the people. The French speculators, I am told, undertake to build a carriage-road across the Pyrenees; to erect bathing-establishments and hotels on a magnificent scale at Escaldas, and to conduct the latter, under the direction of the authorities of Andorra, for a period of forty years, at the end of which time the latter shall be placed in possession of the roads, buildings, and all other improvements. The expense of the undertaking is estimated at ten millions of francs. A theatre and a bank (faro?) are among the features of the speculation. Meanwhile, until the carriage-road shall be built, temporary hotels and gaming-houses are to be erected in the valley of the Ariège, on the French side of the Pyrenees, but within the territory belonging to Andorra.

I do not consider it as by any means certain that the plan will be carried out; but if it should be, the first step towards the annexation of Andorra to France will have been taken. In any case, I am glad to have visited the republic while it is yet shut from the world.

Behind Escaldas an affluent of the Valira dashed down the mountain on the right, breaking the rich masses of foliage with silver gleams. I halted on the summit of the first rocky rampart, and turned to take a last view of the valley. What a picture! I stood in the deep shadow of the mountains, in the heart of a wilderness of rocks which towered out of evergreen verdure, and seemed to vibrate amidst the rush, the foam, and the thunder of streams. The houses of the village, clinging to and climbing the sides of the opening pass, made a dark frame, through which the green and gold of the splendid valley, drowned in sunshine, became, by the force of contrast, limpid and luminous as a picture of the air. The rocks and houses of Old Andorra and the tower of the House of Government made the central point of the view; dazzling meadows below and mountain terraces above basked in the faint prismatic lustre of the morning air. High up, in the rear of the crowning cliffs, I caught glimpses of Alpine pastures; and on the right, far away, streaks of snow. It was a vision never to be forgotten: it was one of the few perfect landscapes of the world.

As the path rose in rapid zigzags beside the split through

which the river pours, I came upon another busy village. In an open space among the rocks there were at least a hundred bee-hives, formed of segments of the hollowed trunks of trees. They stood in rows, eight or ten feet apart; and the swarms that continually came and went, seemed to have their separate paths marked out in the air. They moved softly and swiftly through each other without entanglement. After passing the gateway of the Valira, the path still mounted, and finally crept along the side of a deep trough, curving eastward. There were fields on both slopes, wherever it was possible to create them. Here I encountered a body of road-makers, whom the French speculators had set to work. They were engaged in widening the bridle-path, so that carts might pass to Escaldas from the upper valleys of Encamp and Canillo. The rock was blasted on the upper side; while, on the lower, workmen were basing the walls on projecting points of the precipice. In some places they hung over deep gulfs, adjusting the great masses of stone with equal skill and coolness.

In an hour the gorge opened upon the Valley of Encamp, which is smaller, but quite as wild and grand in its features as that of Andorra. Here the fields of rye and barley were only beginning to grow yellow, the flowers were those of an earlier season, and the ilex and box alone remained of the southern trees and shrubs. Great thickets of the latter fringed the crags. A high rock on the left served as a pedestal for a church, with a tall, square belfry, which leaned so much from the perpendicular that it was not pleasant to ride under it. The village of Encamp occupied a position similar to that of Escaldas, at the farther end of the valley, and in the opening of another gorge, the sides of which are so closely interfolded that the river appears to issue out of the very heart of the mountain. It is a queer, dirty, mouldy old place. Even the immemorial rocks of the Pyrenees look new and fresh beside the dark rust of its walls. The people had mostly gone away to their fields and pastures; only a few old men and women, and the youngest children, sunned themselves at the doors. The main street had been paved once, but the stones were now displaced, leaving pits of mud and filth. In one place the houses were built over it, forming dark, badly smelling arches, under which I was forced to ride.

The path beyond was terribly rough and difficult, climbing the precipices with many windings, until it reached a narrow ledge far above the bed of the gorge. There were frequent shrines along the way, at the most dangerous points; and Julian, who walked ahead, always lifted his cap and muttered a prayer as he passed them. After three or four miles of such travel, I reached the church of Merichel, on an artificial platform, cut out of the almost perpendicular side of the mountain. This is the shrine of most repute in Andorra, and the goal of many a summer pilgrimage. Here the mass, the rustic banquet, and the dance draw old and young together from all parts of the republic.

I climbed another height, following the eastern curve of the gorge, and finally saw the village of Canillo, the capital of one of the six parishes, lying below me, in the lap of a third valley. It had a brighter and fresher air than Encamp; the houses were larger and cleaner, and there were garden-plots about them. In this valley the grain was quite green; the ilex had disappeared, making way for the poplar and willow, but the stubborn box still held its ground. In every bush on the banks of Valira sat a nightingale; the little brown bird sings most lustily where the noise of water accompanies his song. I never saw him so fearless; I could have touched many of the minstrels with my hand as I passed.

At Canillo I crossed the Valira, and thenceforward the path followed its western bank. This valley was closed, like all the others, by a pass cloven through the mountains. Upon one of the natural bastions guarding it there is an ancient tower, which the people say was built by the Saracens before the Frank conquest. The passage of the gorge which followed was less rugged than the preceding ones,—an indication of my approach to the summit of the Pyrenees. In following the Rio Segre and the Valira, I had traversed *eight* of those tremendous defiles, varying from one to six miles in length; and the heart of the mountain region, where the signs of force and convulsion always diminish, was now attained. One picture on the way was so lovely that I stopped and drew it. In the centre of the valley, on a solitary rock, stood an ancient church and tower, golden-brown in the sun. On the right were mountains clothed with forests of pine and fir; in the distance, fields of snow. All the cleared slopes were crimson with the Alpine-rose, a dwarf variety of rhododendron. Perfect sunshine covered the scene, and the purest of breezes blew over it. Here and there a grain-field clung to the crags, or found a place among their tumbled fragments, but no living being was to be seen.

The landscapes were now wholly northern, except the sun and sky. Aspens appeared on the heights, shivering among the steady pines. After a time I came to a point where there were two valleys, two streams, and two paths. Julian took the left, piloting me over grassy meadows, where the perfume from beds of daffodil was almost too powerful to breathe. On one side, all the mountain was golden with broom-flowers; on the other, a mass of fiery crimson, from the Alpine-rose. The valley was dotted with scattered cottages of the herdsmen, as in Switzerland. In front there were two snowy peaks, with a "saddle" between — evidently one of the *portes* of the Pyrenees; yet I saw no indications of the hamlet of Soldeu, which we must pass. Julian shouted to a herdsman, who told us we had taken the wrong valley. The porte before us was that of Fontargente, across which Louis le Débonnaire stretched his chain on leaving Andorra.

We retraced our steps, and in half an hour reached Soldeu, in a high, bleak pasture-valley, where cultivation ceases. It is at least six thousand feet above the sea, and the vegetation is that of the high Alps. We were nearly famished, and, as there was no sign of a "hostal," entered the first house. The occupant, a woman, offered to give us what she had, but said that there was another family who made a business of entertaining travellers, and we would there be better served. We found the house, and truly, after waiting an hour, were refreshed by a surprising dinner of five courses. There was another guest, in the person of a French butcher from the little town of Hospitalet, in the valley of the Ariége. It was so cold that we all crowded about the kitchen fire. Two Andorrans came in, and sat down to the table with us. I have dined at stately entertainments where there was less grace and refinement among the company than the butcher and the two peasants exhibited. There was a dessert of roasted almonds and coffee (with a *chasse*); and after the meal we found the temperature of the air very mild and balmy.

Hospitalet being also my destination, I accepted the butcher's company, and at one o'clock we set forth for the passage of the Pyrenees. On leaving Soldeu I saw the last willow, in which sat and sang the last nightingale. The path rose rapidly along the steep slopes of grass, with an amphitheatre of the highest summits around us. The forests sank out of sight in the glens; snow-fields multiplied far and near, sparkling in the thin air, and the scenery assumed a bleak, monotonous grandeur. I traced the Valira, now a mere thread, to its source in seven icy lakes, fed by the snow: in those lakes, said the butcher, are the finest trout of the Pyrenees. The *Porte de Valira* was immediately above us, on the left; a last hard pull up the steep, between beds of snow, and we stood on the summit.

The elevation of the pass is nearly eight thousand feet above the sea. On either hand you descry nothing but the irregular lines of the French and Spanish Pyrenees, rising and falling in receding planes of distance. Rocks, grass, and snow make up the scenery, which, nevertheless, impresses by its very simplicity and severity.

The descent into France is toilsome, but not dangerous. A mile or two below the crest we saw the fountain of the Ariége, at the base of a grand escarpment of rock. Thence for two hours we followed the descending trough of the river through bleak, grassy solitudes, uncheered by a single tree, or any sign of human life except the well-worn path. Finally the cottage of a grazing-farm came into view, but it was tenantless — all the inhabitants having been overwhelmed by an avalanche three years ago. Then I discovered signs of a road high up on the opposite mountain, saw workmen scattered along it, and heard a volley of explosions. This was the new highway to Porte St. Louis and Puigcerdá. On a green meadow beside the river walked two gentlemen and two ladies in round hats and scarlet petticoats.

"They are picking out a spot to build their gaming-houses upon," said the butcher; "this is still Andorra."

A mile further there was a little bridge — the Pont de Cerda. A hut, serving as a guard-house, leaned against the rocks, but the *gens d'armes* were asleep or absent, and I rode unquestioned into France. It was already sunset in the valley, and the houses of Hospitalet, glimmering through the shadows, were a welcome sight. Here was the beginning of highways and mail-coaches, the movement of the living world again. I supped and slept (not very comfortably, I must confess) in the house of my friend the butcher, said good-by to Julian in the morning, and by noon was resting from my many fatigues in the best inn of Foix.

But henceforth the Valley of Andorra will be one of my enthusiasms.

THE GRANDE CHARTREUSE.

On my way from the Pyrenees to Germany, I turned aside from the Rhone highway of travel to make acquaintance with a place of which everybody has heard, yet which seems to have been partly dropped from the rapid itineraries which have come into fashion with railways. This is the celebrated monastery called the "Grande Chartreuse," situated in an Alpine wilderness known as the "Desert," on the borders of Savoy. During the last century, when Gray and Horace Walpole penetrated into those solitudes, it was a well-known point of interest in the "grand tour;" but it seems to have been neglected during and since the great upheaval of the French Revolution and the Napoleonic Empire. The name, however, is kept alive on the tongues of gourmands by a certain greenish, pungent, perfumed liquor, which comes upon their tables at the end of dinner.

The traveller from Lyons to Marseilles passes within a six-hours' journey of the Grande Chartreuse. If he leave the train at Valence, the branch road to Grenoble will take him up the Valley of the Isère, and he will soon exchange the rocky vine-slopes of the Rhone for Alpine scenery on a scale hardly surpassed in Switzerland. This was the route which I took, on my way northward. The valley of the Isère, at first broad, and showing on its flat, stony fields traces of frequent inundations, gradually contracted; the cultivation of silk gave place to that of grain and vines, and the meadows of deep grass, studded with huge walnut-trees, reproduced, but on a warmer and richer scale, the character of Swiss scenery. Night came on before I reached the Vale of Grésivaudan, which is considered the paradise of Dauphiné, and when the train halted at the station of Voreppe, it was pitch-dark under a gathering rain. There was a rustic omnibus in waiting, into which I crowded with a priest and two farmers, all of whom recommended the "Petit Paris" as the best inn, and thither, accordingly, I went when we reached the village.

It was a primitive, but picturesque and inviting place. I was ushered into a spacious kitchen, with a paved floor, and a huge stone range standing in the centre. The landlady stood before her pans and gave the finishing touch to some cutlets while she received my orders and those of the priest. The latter, when he came into the light, proved to be a young man, pale, thin, and melancholy, with a worn breviary under his arm. He asked to have a bed immediately. In an adjoining room, a company of peasants were drinking cider and thin wine, and discussing crops around a deal table. I listened awhile, but finding it impossible to understand their dialect, followed the example of the priest. The landlady gave me a clean bed in a clean room, and I speedily slept in spite of rain and thunder.

I had barely taken coffee in the morning before an omnibus drove up, on its way to St. Laurent du Pont, a village at the mouth of the ravine which descends from the Grande Chartreuse. There was a place inside, between two sharp-featured women and opposite another priest, who was middle-aged and wore an air of cheerful resignation. This place I occupied, and was presently climbing the long mountain road, with a glorious picture of the Vale of Grésivaudan deepening and widening below. Halfway up the mountains beyond the Isère floated shining belts of cloud, the shadows of which mottled the sunlit fields and gardens. Above us, huge walls of perpendicular rock, crowned with forests, shut out the morning sky, but the glens plunging down from their bases were filled with the most splendid vegetation. Our way upward was through the shadows of immense walnut-trees, beside the rushing of crystal brooks, and in the perfume of blossoming grass and millions of meadow flowers. It seemed incredible that we should be approaching a "Desert" through such scenery.

My fellow-travellers were inclined to be social. We lost the women at the first little hamlet above Voreppe, and there only remained the priest and a stout, swaggering person, who had the appearance and manners of a government contractor. The former told us that he had a parish on the high, windy table-lands of Champagne, and had never before seen such wonderful mountain landscapes. He was now on his way to Rome — one of the army of six thousand "migratory ravens" (as the Italians called them), who took part in the Festival of St. Peter. He was cheerful and tolerant, with more heart than intellect, and we got on very agreeably. The contractor informed us that the monks of the Chartreuse had an income of a million francs a year, a part of which they spend in building churches and schools. They have recently built a new church for the village of St. Laurent du Pont.

In an hour or more we had reached the highest point of the road, which now ran eastward along the base of a line of tremendous mountains. On the topmost heights, above the gray ramparts of rock, there were patches of a bright rosy color, which I at first took to be the Alpine rhododendron in blossom, but they proved to be forests of beech, which the recent severe frosts had scorched. The streams from the heights dropped into gulfs yawning at the base of the mountains, making cataracts of several hundred feet. Here the grain, already harvested in the valley of the Rhone, was still green, and the first crop of hay uncut.

St. Laurent du Pont is a little village directly in the mouth of the gorge. The omnibus drew up before the café, and my clerical friend got into a light basket wagon for the journey to the monastery, two leagues distant. I preferred to climb the gorge leisurely, on foot, and set about engaging a man as companion rather than guide. The sky was full of suspicious clouds, there were mutterings of thunder in the mountains, and the sun stung with an insupportable power; but after breakfast I set out with a middle-aged man, who had an eye to profit, followed the stream for a mile, and found myself in the heart of a terrific wilderness of rock and forest. In front the mountains closed, and only a thin line of shadow revealed the split through which we must pass. Before reaching it, there is an ancient forge on the left, and a massive building on the right, which the monks have recently erected for the manufacture of the *liqueur* which bears the name of their monastery.

Just beyond the forge are the remains of an ancient gate, which once closed the further passage. The road is hewn out of the solid rock, and the sides of the cleft are so near together that the masonry supporting the road is held firm by timbers crossing the abyss and morticed into the opposite rock. Formerly there was only a narrow and dangerous mule-path, and the passage must have had an exhilarating character of danger which the present security of the road destroys. It was so in Gray's time, inspiring him with these almost Horatian lines: —

> "Per invias rupes, fera per juga,
> Clivosque præruptos, sonantes
> Inter aquas, nemorumque noctem."

This closed throat of the mountains is short: it soon expands a little, allowing the splendid deciduous forests to descend to the water's brink. But above, on all sides, the rocks start out in sheer walls and towers, and only a narrow strip of sky is visible between their crests. After a mile of this scenery I reached a saw-mill, beside which there was some very fine timber. Still another mile, and the road was carried across the defile by a lofty stone bridge of a single arch. "This is the bridge of San

Bruno," said the guide, "and we are now just half-way to the monastery." In spite of the shadows of the forests, the air was almost stifling in its still heat, and I sat down on the parapet of the bridge to take breath. This was the "Desert," whither the Bishop of Grenoble directed San Bruno to fly from the temptations of the world. At that time it could have been accessible only with great labor and danger, and was much more secluded than the caves of the Thebaid. But the word conveys no idea of the character of the scenery. For the whole distance it is a deep cleft in the heart of lofty mountains, overhung with precipices a thousand feet high, yet clothed, wherever a root can take hold, by splendid forests. Ferns and wild flowers hang from every ledge, and the trees are full of singing birds.

Still climbing, we mounted high above the stream, and in twenty minutes reached a natural gateway, formed by a solitary pillar of rock, three hundred feet high, and not more than forty feet in diameter. Here, six weeks before, a wagon with six young peasants went over the brink, and fell into the terrible abyss. The driver, whose carelessness occasioned the accident, leaped from the wagon; the other five went down, and were dashed to pieces. Between the *aiguille* (needle), as it is called, and the mountain-wall, there was formerly a gate, beyond which no woman was allowed to pass. The sex is now permitted to visit the monastery, but not to enter its gates. This part of the road is almost equal to the famous Via Mala. A series of tunnels have been cut through the sheer, projecting crags, the intervening portions of the road being built up with great labor from below. One hangs in mid-air over the dark chasm, where the foam of the rushing waters shines like a phosphoric light.

Finally, the slope of the mountains becomes less abrupt, the shattered summits lean back, and the glen grows brighter under a broader field of sky. On the right the forests are interrupted by pasture grounds; the road is now safe, though very steep, and the buildings of the monastery presently come into view, a mass of quadrangular piles of masonry, towers, and pyramidal roofs, inclosed by a high wall which must be considerably more than a mile in circuit. The place, in fact, resembles a fortified city. The gateway was closed on the side by which I approached, but an old monk, with shaven head and flowing beard, who was driving an ox-cart (the first time I ever saw one of his class so usefully employed), directed me to go around to the eastern front. An isolated house, shaded by a group of old linden-trees, is set apart for the use of the female visitors, who are attended by an old woman, usually a sister of some conventual order.

My guide rang the bell at the entrance, and the door was immediately opened by a young monk in a long, brown gown. "Can I be admitted?" I asked. "Yes," said he in a whisper, "the guide will take you to the father who receives strangers." I was conducted across a grassy court-yard, in which there were two large stone fountains, to the main building. Several brethren in brown were passing swiftly to and fro in the cool, spacious corridors, but they took no notice of me. I found the father in a comfortable chamber, hung with maps. He was a bright, nimble man of sixty, with shaven head and face; but for his keen eyes, he would not have seemed more than half alive, his complexion and his shroud-like gown being nearly the same color. I told him who I was, why I came, and asked permission to stay until the next day. "Certainly," he whispered, "as long as you please. I will show you into the refectory, and order that you have a room."

I was somewhat unwell, and the heat and fatigue had made me weak, which the father probably noticed, for on reaching the refectory — a great, bare apartment, with an old-fashioned chimney-place for burning logs — he said: "You must have a glass of our *liqueur*, the green kind, which is the strongest." It was like an aromatic flame, but it really gave me a different view of life, in the space of fifteen minutes. The *garçon* was a sturdy fellow in a blue blouse, evidently a peasant hired for the season. His services were confined to the refectory. Another brother in brown, with a mild, ignorant countenance, conducted me to an upper chamber, or rather cell, containing a bed, a table, a chair, and bowl of water, with a large private altar and *prie-dieu*. Having taken possession and put the key in my pocket, I returned to the refectory, where the white father begged me to make myself at home, and likewise vanished. There are fixed hours when strangers are conducted through the buildings, and, as I had still some time to wait, I went forth from the monastery and set to work at a sketch of the place.

The monks of the Chartreuse now belong to the order of La Trappe. San Bruno first came hither in the year 1084, and the foundation of the monastery dates from 1137. The Trappist, or silent system, arose in the sixteenth century, but I am ignorant of the date when it was here introduced. It is probably the severest and most unnatural of all forms of monastic discipline. Isolation is cruel enough in itself, without the obligation of silence. The use of monasteries, as conservatories of learning, as sanctuaries of peace in the midst of normal war, has long since ceased: they are now an anachronism and they will soon become an offense. The grand pile of buildings before me was ravaged during the French Revolution, and the monks turned adrift. Although the government still keeps its hold on the greater part of the property then sequestrated, it has favored the monastery in every other possible way. France swarms with black robes, as it has not before for a hundred years. The Empress Eugenie is a petted daughter of the Church of Rome, and the willing instrument of its plans, so far as her influence extends. The monks of La Chartreuse, however, to judge from what I saw of their industry and business talent, are far less objectionable than those of their brethren who are not bound to solitude and silence.

At the appointed hour I was again admitted with a whisper, and joined three dark priests (also on their way to Rome) for a tour of the interior. The mild brother in brown was our guide. After calling our attention to a notice which requested that all visitors to the monastery would neither stand still nor speak above their breath, he unlocked a gate and ushered us into the inner corridors. We walked down the dim echoing vaults of solid masonry, and paused at a door, through which came the sound of a sepulchral chant. It was the church, wherein two ancient fathers were solemnly intoning a service which seemed like a *miserere*. The brother conducted us to an upper gallery, dipped his fingers into the font, and presented the holy water to me with a friendly smile. I am afraid he was cut to the heart when I shook my head, saying: "Thank you, I don't need it." There was an expression of stupefaction in his large, innocent eyes, and thenceforward he kept near me, always turning to me with a tender, melancholy interest, as if hoping and praying that there might, for me, be some escape from the hell of heretics.

There was nothing worthy of notice in the architecture of the church, or the various chapels. That for the dead was hung with skulls and cross-bones, on a ground of black; the grave-yard, in which the dead monks lie, like the Quakers, under unmarked mounds, was more cheerful. Here, at least, grass and wild-flowers are not prohibited, the sweetest mountain breezes find their way over the monastic walls, and the blue sky above is filled with a silence, in which there is nothing painful. The most interesting thing I saw was the Hall of the Order, filled with portraits of its generals, and with frescoes illustrating the life of San Bruno. A statue of the Saint represents him as a venerable man, of pure, noble, and benevolent aspect. The head, I suspect, is imaginary, but it is very fine. As works of art, the pictures have no merit; the three priests, however, looked upon them with awful reverence. So much depends on place, circumstance, and sentiment! The brush of Raphael could have added nothing to the impression which these men drew from the stiff workmanship of some unknown painter.

I was astonished at the extent of the buildings. There is a single corridor, Gothic, of solid stone, six hundred and sixty feet in length. Looking down it, the perspective dwindles almost to a point. Opening from it and from the other intersecting corridors are the cells of the monks, each with a Biblical sentence in Latin (generally of solemn import) painted on the doors. The furniture of these cells is very simple, but a human skull is always part of it. In the rear of each is a small garden, inclosed by a wall, where the fathers and brothers attend to their own flowers and vegetables. They *must* have, it seems, some innocent solace; the silence, the fasting, the company of the skull, and the rigid ceremonials, would else, I imagine, drive the most of them mad. Those whom we met in the corridor walked with an excited, flying step, as if trying to outrun their own thoughts. Their faces were pale and stern; they rarely looked at us, and, of course, never spoke. The gloom and silence, the hushed whispers of the priests and guide, and the prohibition put upon my own tongue, oppressed me painfully at last. I longed to startle the dead repose of the corridors by a shout full of freedom and rejoicing.

There are at present forty *patres* and twenty *fratres* in the monastery. The direction of external matters is intrusted to a few, who enjoy more contact with the world, and must be absolved from the obligation of silence. Moreover the rules in this respect are not so strenuously enforced as formerly. The monks are allowed to converse slightly on Sundays and saints' days, and once a week, when they walk in procession to the Chapel of St. Bruno, higher up the mountain. An experienced father has charge of the manufacture of the *liqueur*, which is made, I learned, from the young shoots of the mountain fir, mixed with certain aromatic herbs. Some parts of the process are kept secret. The *Chartreuse* is sold, even on the spot, at a high price, and is sent to all parts of the world.

When we returned to the refectory, I found several gentlemen from Chambéry in waiting. They, also, intended to stay all night, and to start at one in the morning for the ascent of the Grand Somme, the highest pinnacle of the mountain. I predicted rain, but they were not to be discouraged. The result was, as I learned next morning, that they rose at the appointed time, groped about in the forest in perfect darkness, and came back in half an hour drenched to the skin. The servitor informed me that two Englishmen had arrived, and were entertained in another part of the monastery. I learned for the first time that, the better to preserve quiet and order, the guests are separated according to their nationalities. This explained the meaning of " Salle de la France " on the door of the hall in which I found myself. Americans are rare visitors, and I presume they thought it safest to put me with the Frenchmen.

It is always Lent in the Grand Chartreuse. Nevertheless, the dinner of eggs, fish, fruits, cheese, and wine which was served to us was of excellent quality. The bed was coarse but clean, and after putting out my lamp to hide the reproachful eyes of the Virgin, I slept soundly. Breakfast, however, was a little too lean for my taste. Instead of coffee they gave me half-cooked cabbage soup and a lump of black bread. The bill was five francs. Herein, I think, the monks are right. They make a moderate charge for what they furnish, instead of expecting the traveller (as in other monasteries) to give five times the worth of it as a donation. Living in such a wilderness, at the height of 4,300 feet above the sea, it is a great labor to keep the requisite supplies on hand. Poor travellers are not only lodged and fed gratuitously, but sometimes receive a small addition to their funds.

Nevertheless, while I felt a positive respect for the industry, fortitude, and charity of the monks of the Chartreuse, I drew a long breath of relief as I issued from its whispering corridors. I believe I talked to my guide in a much louder voice than usual, as we returned down the gorge. The visit had been full of interest, yet I could not have guessed, in advance, how oppressive was the prohibition of speech. I shall never again admire the silent and solitary system of some of our penitentiaries.

At St. Laurent du Pont I took the omnibus, getting a front seat beside the coachman, which I kept, not only to Voreppe, but down the magnificent valley of Grèsivaudan to Grenoble. The mountains, on the side toward the Isère, appear to be absolutely inaccessible. No one would guess, on looking up at them from below, what a remarkable settlement has existed for centuries within their solitudes.

THE KYFFHÄUSER AND ITS LEGENDS.

THÜRINGIA, "The Heart of Germany," has for many a century ceased to be a political designation, yet it still lives in the mouths and the songs of the people as the well-beloved name for all that middle region lying between the Hartz on the north and the mountain-chain stretching from the Main to the Elbe on the south. A few points, such as Eisenach, Weimar, and Jena, are known to the tourist; the greater part, although the stage whereon many of the most important events in early and mediæval German history were enacted, has not yet felt the footstep of the curious stranger. From the overthrow of its native monarchy by the Franks, in the sixth century, to the close of the Thirty Years' War, in the seventeenth, the fortunes of this land symbolized, in a great measure, those of the Teutonic race. Behind battle and crime and knightly deed sprang up those flowers of legend whose mature seed is poetry. In no part of Europe do they blossom so thickly as here.

I had already stood in the hall of the Minnesingers on the Wartburg; had crept into the Cave of Venus, on the mountain of Tannhäuser; had walked through the Valley of Joy, where the two wives of the Count of Gleichen first met face to face; and had stood on the spot where Winfried, the English apostle, cut down the Druid oaks, and set up in their stead the first altar to Christ. But on the northern border of Thüringia, where its last mountains look across the Golden Mead towards the dark summits of the Hartz, there stands a castle, in whose ruins sleeps the favorite tradition of Germany, — a legend which, changing with the ages, became the embodiment of an idea, and now represents the national unity, strength, and freedom. This is the Kyffhäuser; and the Emperor Frederick Barbarossa sleeps under it, in a crypt of the mountain, waiting for the day when the whole land, from the Baltic to the Alps, shall be ready to receive a single ruler. Then he will come forth, and the lost Empire will be restored.

Many a time, looking towards the far-away Brocken from the heights of the Thüringian Forest, had I seen the tower of the Kyffhäuser like a speck on the horizon, and as often had resolved to cross the twenty intervening leagues. The day was appointed and postponed — for years, as it happened; but a desire which is never given up works out its own fulfillment in the course of time, and so it was with mine. It is not always best to track a legend too closely. The airy brow of Tannhäuser's Mountain proved to be very ugly rock and very tenacious clay, when I had climbed it; and I came forth from the narrow slit of a cavern torn, squeezed out of breath, and spotted with tallow. Something of the purple atmosphere of the mountain and the mystery of its beautiful story has vanished since then. But the day of my departure for the Kyffhäuser was meant for an excursion into dream-land. When the Summer, departing, stands with reluctant feet; when the Autumn looks upon the land, yet has not taken up her fixed abode; when the freshness of Spring is revived in every cloudless morning, and the afternoons melt slowly into smoke and golden vapor, — then comes, for a short space, the season of illusion, of credulity, of winsome superstition.

On such a day I went northward from Gotha into a boundless, undulating region of tawny harvest and stubble fields. The plain behind me, stretching to the foot of the Thüringian Forest, was covered with a silvery, shimmering atmosphere, on which the scattered villages, the orchards, and the poplar-bordered highways were dimly blotted, like the first timid sketch of a picture, which shall grow into clear, confident color. Far and wide, over the fields, the peasants worked silently and steadily among their flax, oats, and potatoes, — perhaps rejoicing in the bounty of the sunshine, but too much in earnest to think of singing. Only the harvest of the vine is gathered to music. The old swallows collected their flocks of young on the ploughed land, and drilled them for the homeward flight. The sheep, kept together in a dense gray mass, nibbled diligently among the stubble, guarded only by a restless dog. At a corner of the field the box-house of the shepherd rested on its wheels, and he was probably asleep within it. Wains, laden with sheaves, rumbled slowly along the road towards the village barns. Only the ravens wheeled and croaked uneasily, as if they had a great deal of work to do, and couldn't decide what to undertake first.

I stretched myself out luxuriously in the carriage, and basked in the tempered sunshine. I had nothing to do but to watch the mellow colors of the broadening landscape, as we climbed the long waves of earth, stretching eastward and westward out of sight. Those mixed, yet perfect moods, which come equally from the delight of the senses and the release of the imagination, seem to be the very essence of poetry, yet how rarely do they become poetry! The subtile spirit of song cannot often hang poised in thin air; it must needs rest on a basis, however slender, of feeling or reflection. Eichendorff is the only poet to whom completely belongs the narrow border-land of moods and sensations. Yet the key-note of the landscape around me was struck by Tennyson in a single fortunate word, —

"In looking on the *happy* Autumn-fields."

The earth had finished its summer work for man, and now breathed of rest and peace from tree, and bush, and shorn stubble, and reviving grass. It was still the repose of lusty life; the beginning of death, the sadness of the autumn was to come.

In crossing the last hill, before descending to the city of Langensalza, I saw one of the many reverse sides of this fair picture of life. A peasant girl, ragged, dusty, and tired, with a young child in her lap, sat on a stone seat by the wayside. She had no beauty; her face was brown and hard, her hair tangled, her figure rude and strong, and she held the child with a mechanical clasp, in which there was instinct, but not tenderness. Yet it needed but a single glance to read a story of poverty, and of shame and desertion ignorantly encountered and helplessly endured. Here was no acute sense of degradation; only a blind, brutish wretchedness. It seemed to me, as I saw her, looking stolidly into the sunny air, that she was repeating the questions, over and over, without hope of answer: "Why am I in the world? What is to become of me?"

At Langensalza I took a lighter carriage, drawn by a single horse, which was harnessed loosely on the left side of a long pole. Unfortunately I had a garrulous old driver who had seen something of last year's battle, and supposed that nothing could interest me more than to know precisely where certain Prussian regiments were posted. Before I had divined his intention, he left the highway, and carried me across the fields to the top of the Jews' Hill, which was occupied at the commencement of the battle by the Prussian artillery. The turf is still marked with the ragged holes of the cannon-balls. In the plain below, many trees are slowly dying from an overdose of lead. In the fields which the farmers were ploughing one sees here and there a headstone of granite or an iron crucifix; but all other traces of the struggle have disappeared. The little mill, which was the central point of the fight, has been well repaired; only some cannon-balls, grim souvenirs, are left sticking in the gable-wall. A mile further, across the Unstrut, at the commencement of the rising country, is the village of Merxleben, where the Hanoverians were posted. Its streets are as dull and sleepy as ever before. Looking at the places where the plaster has been knocked off the houses, one would not guess the instruments by which it was done.

Some distance further, at a safe height, my old man halted beside two poplars. "Here," he said, "the King of Hanover stood." Did he keep up the mimicry of sight, I wonder, while the tragedy was going on? This blind sovereign represents the spirit of monarchy in its purest essence. Though totally blind, from a boy, he pretends to see, because — the people must perceive no defect in a king. When he rides out, the adjutants on both sides are attached to his arms by fine threads; and he is thus guided, while appearing to guide himself. He visits picture-galleries, admires landscapes, and makes remarks upon the good or ill appearance of his courtiers. After the battle of Langensalza, which he pretended to direct, he sent his uniform to the museum at Hanover, with some straws and wheat-blades from the field where he stood sewed upon it in various places! Other monarchs of Europe have carried the tattered trappings of absolutism into a constitutional form of government, but none of them has been so exquisitely consistent as this man.

We plodded forward over vast tawny waves of landscape, as regular as the swells of the sea. All this territory, once so rich and populous, was reduced to a desert during the Thirty Years' War, and two centuries have barely sufficed to reclaim it. After that war, Germany possessed only twenty-five per cent. of the men, the cattle, and the dwellings which she owned when it began, and this was the least of the evil. The new generation had grown up in insecurity, in idleness, immorality, and crime; the spirit of the race was broken, its blood was tainted, and it has ever since then been obliged to struggle from decadence into new power. We must never lose sight of these facts when we speak of the Germany of the present day. Well for us that we have felt only the shock and struggle, the first awakening of the manly element, not the later poison of war!

After more than two hours on the silent, lonely heights,

— scarcely a man being here at work in the fields or abroad on the road, — I approached a little town called Ebeleben, in the principality of Schwarzburg-Sondershausen. The driver insisted on baiting his horse at the " municipal tavern," as it was called; and I remembered that in the place lived a gentleman whom I had met nine years before. Everybody knew the Amtsrath; he was at home; it was the large house beside the castle. Ebeleben was a former residence of the princess; but now its wonderful rococo gardens have run wild, the fountains and waterfalls are dry, the stone statues have lost their noses and arms, and the wooden sentries posted at all the gates have rotted to pieces. The remains are very funny. Not a particle of melancholy can be attached to the decayed grotesque.

I went into the court-yard of the house to which I had been directed. A huge parallelogram of stone and steep roofs inclosed it; there were thirteen ploughs in a row on one side, and three mountains of manure on the other. As no person was to be seen, I mounted the first flight of steps, and found myself in a vast, antiquated kitchen. A servant, thrusting her head from behind a door, told me to go forward. Pantries and store-rooms followed, passages filled with antique household gear, and many a queer nook and corner; but I at last reached the front part of the building, and found its owner. His memory was better than I had ventured to hope; I was made welcome so cordially, that only the sad news that the mistress of the house lay at the point of death made my visit brief. The Amtsrath, who farms a thousand acres, led me back to the tavern through his garden, saying, " We must try and bear all that comes to us," as I took leave.

A few years ago there was a wild, heathery moorland, the haunt of gypsies and vagabonds, beyond Ebeleben. Now it is all pasture and grain-field, of thin and barren aspect, but steadily growing better. The dark-blue line I had seen to the north, during the day, now took the shape of hills covered with forest, and the road passed between them into the head of a winding valley. The green of Thüringian meadows, the rich masses of beech and oak, again refreshed my eyes. The valley broadened as it fell, and the castle and spires of Sondershausen came into view. An equipage, drawn by four horses, came dashing up from a side-road. There were three persons in it; the short, plain-faced man in a felt hat was the reigning prince, Günther von Schwarzburg. There was not much of his illustrious namesake, the Emperor, in his appearance; but he had an honest, manly countenance, and I thought it no harm to exchange greetings.

I think Sondershausen must be the quietest capital in Europe. It is said to have six thousand inhabitants, about two hundred of whom I saw. Four were walking in a pleasant, willow-shaded path beside the mills; ten were wandering in the castle-park; and most of the remainder, being children, were playing in the streets. When I left, next morning, by post for the nearest railway station, beyond the Golden Mead, I was the only passenger. But the place is well built, and has an air of contentment and comfort.

I was here on the southern side of the mountain ridge which is crowned by the Kyffhäuser, and determined to cross to Kelbra, in the Golden Mead, at its northern base. The valley was draped in the silver mists of the morning as I set out; and through them rose the spire of Jechaburg, still bearing the name of the Druid divinity there overthrown by the apostle Winfried. But there was another point in the landscape where my fancy settled — the Trauenberg, at the foot of which was fought the first great *Hunnenschlacht* (battle of the Huns). When that gallant emperor, Henry the Bird-Snarer, sent a mangy dog to Hungary, instead of the usual tribute, he knew and prepared for the consequences of his act. The Huns burst into Germany; he met and defeated them, first here, and then near Merseburg (A. D. 933), so utterly that they never again attempted invasion. Kaulbach's finest cartoon represents one or the other of these battles. Those fierce groups of warriors, struggling in a weird atmosphere, made the airy picture which I saw. One involuntarily tries to vivify history, and the imagination holds fast to any help.

After an hour and a half among the hills, I saw the Golden Mead, — so bright, so beautiful, that I comprehended the love which the German emperors, for centuries, manifested for it. I looked across a level valley, five or six miles wide, meadows green as May interrupting the bands of autumnal gold, groves and winding lines of trees marking the watercourses, stately towns planted at intervals, broad, ascending slopes of forest beyond, and the summit of the Brocken crowning all. East and west, the Mead faded out of sight in shining haze. It is a favored region. Its bounteous soil lies low and warm, sheltered by the Hartz; it has an earlier spring and a later summer than any other part of Northern Germany. This I knew, but I was not prepared to find it, also, a delight to the eye. Towards Nordhausen the green was dazzling, and there was a blaze of sunshine upon it which recalled the plain of Damascus.

At Kelbra, I looked in vain for the Kyffhäuser, though so near it; an intervening summit hides the tower. On the nearest headland of the range, however, there is a ruined castle called the Rothenburg, which has no history worth repeating, but is always visited by the few who find their way hither. I procured a small boy as guide, and commenced my proper pilgrimage on foot. An avenue of cherry-trees gave but scanty shade from the fierce sun, while crossing the level of the Golden Mead; but, on reaching the mountain, I found a path buried in forests. It was steep, and hard to climb; and I soon found reason for congratulation in the fact that the summit has an altitude of only fifteen hundred feet. It was attained at last;

the woods, which had been nearly impenetrable, ceased, and I found myself in front of a curious cottage, with a thatched roof, built against the foot of a tall round tower of other days. There were benches and tables under the adjoining trees; and a solid figure, with a great white beard, was moving about in a semi-subterranean apartment, inserted among the foundations of the castle.

Had it been the Kyffhäuser, I should have taken him for Barbarossa. The face reminded me of Walt Whitman, and, verily, the man proved to be a poet. I soon discovered the fact; and when he had given us bread and beer, he brought forth, for my purchase, the third edition of "Poems by the Hermit of the Rothenburg," published by Brockhaus, Leipzig. His name is Friedrich Beyer. His parents kept an inn on ground which became the battle-field of Jena, three or four years after he was born. His first recollection is of cannon, fire, and pillage. This is all that I learned of his history; his face suggests a great deal more. The traces of old passions, ambitions, struggles, and disappointments have grown faint from the exercise of a cheerful philosophy. He is proud to be called a poet, yet serves refreshments with as much alacrity as any ordinary *kellner*.

After a time he brought an album, saying: "I keep this for such poets as happen to come, but there are only two names, perhaps, that you have ever heard — Ludwig Storch and Müller von der Werra. Uhland was once in the Hartz, but he never came here. Rückert and a great many others have written about the Kyffhäuser and Barbarossa; but the poets, you know, depend on their fancies, rather than on what they see. I can't go about and visit them, so I can only become acquainted with the few who travel this way."

He then took an immense tin speaking-trumpet, stationed himself on a rock, pointed the trumpet at an opposite ridge of the mountain, and bellowed forth four notes which sounded like the voice of a dying bull. But, after a pause of silence, angels replied. Tones of supernatural sweetness filled the distant air, fading slowly upwards, until the blue, which seemed to vibrate like a string that has been struck, trembled into quiet again. It was wonderful! I have heard many echoes, but no other which so marvelously translates the sounds of earth into the language of heaven. "Do you notice," said the poet, "how one tone grows out of the others, and silences them? Whatever sound I make, that same tone is produced — not at first, but it comes presently from somewhere else, and makes itself heard. I call it *reconciliation* — atonement; the principle in which all human experience must terminate. You will find a poem about it in my book."

The Rothenburg has been a ruin for about three hundred years. It was a small castle, but of much more elegant and symmetrical architecture than most of its crumbling brethren. The trees which have grown up in court-yard and hall have here and there overthrown portions of the walls, but a number of handsome Gothic portals and windows remain. The round tower appears to have belonged to a much earlier structure. The present picturesque beauty of the place compensates for the lack of history and tradition. Its position is such that it overlooks nearly the whole extent of the Golden Mead and the southern slope of the Hartz — a hemisphere of gold and azure at the time of my visit. It was a day which had strayed into September out of midsummer. Intense, breathless heat filled the earth and sky, and there was scarcely a wave of air, even upon that summit.

The Kyffhäuser is two or three miles further eastward, upon the last headland of the range, in that direction. The road connecting the two castles runs along the crest, through forests of the German oak, as is most fit. Taking leave of the poet, and with his volume in my pack, I plodded forward in the shade, attended by " spirits twain," invisible to my young guide. Poetry walked on my right hand, Tradition on my left. History respectfully declined to join the party; the dim, vapory, dreamful atmosphere did not suit her. Besides, in regard to the two points concerning which I desired to be enlightened she could have given me little assistance. Why was the dead Barbarossa supposed to be enchanted in a vault under the Kyffhäuser, a castle which he had never made his residence? Fifteen years ago, at the foot of the Taurus, in Asia Minor, I had stood on the banks of the river in which he was drowned; and in Tyre I saw the chapel in which, according to such history as we possess, his body was laid. Then, why should he, of all the German emperors, be chosen as the symbol of a political resurrection? He defied the power of the popes, and was placed under the ban of the Church; he gained some battles and lost others; he commenced a crusade, but never returned from it; he did something towards the creation of a middle class, but in advance of the time when such a work could have been appreciated. He was evidently a man of genius and energy, of a noble personal presence, and probably possessed that individual magnetism, the effect of which survives so long among the people; yet all these things did not seem to constitute a sufficient explanation.

The popularity of the Barbarossa legend, however, is not to be ascribed to anything in the Emperor's history. In whatever way it may have been created, it soon became the most picturesque expression of the dream of German unity — a dream to which the people held fast, while the princes were doing their best to make its fulfillment impossible. Barbarossa was not the first, nor the last, nor the best of the great Emperors; but the legend, ever willful in its nature, fastened upon him, and Art and Literature are forced to accept what they find already accepted by the people. This seemed to me, then, to be the natural explanation, and I am glad to find it confirmed in the main points by one of the best living writers of Germany. The substance of the popular tradition is embodied in this little song of Rückert:—

"The Ancient Barbarossa,
    Friedrich, the Kaiser great,
Within the castle-cavern
    Sits in enchanted state.

"He did not die; but ever
    Waits in the chamber deep,
Where, hidden under the castle,
    He sat himself, to sleep.

"The splendor of the Empire
    He took with him away,
And back to earth will bring it
    When dawns the chosen day.

"The chair is ivory purest
    Whereof he makes his bed;
The table is of marble
    Whereon he props his head.

"His beard, not flax, but burning
    With fierce and fiery glow,
Right through the marble table
    Beneath his chin doth grow.

"He nods in dreams, and winketh
    With dull, half-open eye,
And, once an age, he beckons
    A page that standeth by.

"He bids the boy in slumber:
    'O dwarf, go up this hour,
And see if still the ravens
    Are flying round the tower.

"'And if the ancient ravens
    Still wheel above me here,
Then must I sleep enchanted
    For many a hundred year.'"

Half-way from the Rothenburg, after passing a curious

pyramid of petrified wood, I caught sight of the tower of the Kyffhäuser, a square dark-red mass, looming over the oak woods. The path dwindled to a rude forest road, and the crest of the mountain, on the left, hid from view the glimmering level of the Golden Mead. I saw nothing but the wooded heights on the right, until, after climbing a space, I found myself suddenly in the midst of angular mounds of buried masonry. The "Kaiser Friedrich's tower," eighty feet high and about thirty feet square, appeared to be all that remained of the castle. But the extensive mounds over which I stumbled were evidently formed from the *débris* of roofs and walls, and something in their arrangement suggested the existence of vaults under them. The summit of the mountain, four or five hundred feet in length, is entirely covered with the ruins. A cottage in the midst, occupied by three wild women, is built over an ancient gateway, the level of which is considerably below the mounds; and I felt sure, although the women denied it, that there must be subterranean chambers. They permitted me, in consideration of the payment of three cents, to look through a glass in the wall, and behold a hideous picture of the sleeping Emperor. Like Macbeth's witches, they cried in chorus:—

> "Show! show!
> Show his eyes and grieve his heart;
> Take his money, and let him depart!"

That, and a bottle of bad beer, which my small boy drank with extraordinary facility, was all the service they were willing to render me. But the storied peak was deserted; the vast ring of landscape basked in the splendid day; the ravens were flying around the tower; and there were seats at various points where I could rest at will and undisturbed. The Kyffhäuser was so lonely that its gnomes might have allowed the wonder-flower to grow for me, and have opened their vaults without the chance of a profane foot following. I first sketched the tower, to satisfy Duty; and then gave myself up to the guidance of Fancy, whose face, on this occasion was not to be distinguished from that of Indolence. There was not a great deal to see, and no discoveries to make; but the position of the castle was so lordly, the view of the Golden Mead so broad and beautiful, that I could have asked nothing more. I remembered, as I looked down, the meadows of Tarsus, and pictured to myself, in the haze beyond the Brocken, the snowy summits of the Taurus. "What avails the truth of history?" I reflected; "I know that Barbarossa never lived here, yet I cannot banish his shadowy figure from my thoughts. Nay, I find myself on the point of believing the legend."

The word "Kyffhäuser" means, simply, "houses on the peak" (*kippe* or *kuppe*). The people, however, have a derivation of their own. They say that, after Julius Cæsar had conquered the Thüringian land, he built a castle for his prætor on this mountain, and called it *Confusio*, to signify the state to which he had reduced the ancient monarchy. Long afterwards, they add, a stag was found in the forest, with a golden collar around its neck, on which were the words: "Let no one hurt me; Julius gave me my liberty." The date of the foundation of the castle cannot be determined. It was probably a residence, alternately, of the Thüringians and Franks, in the early Christian centuries; the German emperors afterwards occasionally inhabited it; but it was ruined in the year 1189, just before the departure of Barbarossa for the Orient. Afterwards rebuilt, it appears to have been finally overthrown and deserted in the fourteenth century. It is a very slender history which I have to relate; but, as I said before, History did not accompany me on the pilgrimage.

The Saga, however, — whose word is often as good as the written record, — had a great deal to say. She told me, first, that the images and ideas of a religion live among the people for ages after the creed is overthrown; that the half of a faith is simply *transferred*, not changed. Here is the thread by which the legend of the Kyffhäuser may be unraveled. The gods of the old Scandinavian and Teutonic mythology retreated into the heart of certain sacred mountains during the winter, and there remained until the leaves began to put forth in the forests, when the people celebrated their reappearance by a spring festival, the Druid Pentecost. When Christianity was forced upon the land, and the names of the gods were prohibited, the prominent chiefs and rulers took their place. Charlemagne sat with his paladins in the Untersberg, near Salzburg, under the fortress of Nuremberg, and in various other mountains. Two centuries later, Otto the Great was, in like manner, invested with a subterranean court; then, after an equal space of time, came Barbarossa's turn. Gustav Freytag,[1] to whom I am indebted for some interesting information on this point, read to me, from a Latin chronicle of the year 1050, the following passage: "This year there was great excitement among the people, from the report that a ruler would come forth and lead them to war. Many believed that it would be Charlemagne; but many also believed that it would be another, whose name cannot be mentioned." This other was Wuotan (Odin), whose name the people whispered three centuries after they had renounced his worship.

This explanation fits every particular of the legend. The Teutonic tribes always commenced their wars in the spring, after the return of the gods to the surface of the earth. The ravens flying around the tower are the well-known birds of Odin. When Barbarossa comes forth, he will first hang his shield on the barren tree, which will then burst into leaf. The mediæval legend sprang naturally from the grave of the dead religion. Afterwards, —

[1] The well-known author of *Debit and Credit*, and *Pictures of the German Past*.

probably during the terrible depression which followed the Thirty Years' War, — another transfer took place. The gods were at last forgotten; but the aspirations of the people, connecting Past and Future, found a new meaning in the story, which the poets, giving it back to them in a glorified form, fixed forever.

We have only two things to assume, and they will give us little trouble. The Kyffhäuser must have been one of those sacred mountains of the Teutons in which the gods took up their winter habitation. Its character corresponds with that of other mountains which were thus selected. It is a projecting headland, partly isolated from the rest of the range, — like Tabor, "a mountain apart." This would account for the location of the legend. The choice of Barbarossa may be explained partly by the impression which his personal presence and character made upon the people (an effect totally independent of his place in history), and partly from the circumstance, mysterious to them, that he went to the Holy Land, and never returned. Although they called him the "Heretic Emperor," on account of his quarrel with the Pope, this does not appear to have diminished the power of his name among them. The first form of the legend, as we find it in a fragment of poetry from the fourteenth century, says that he disappeared, but is not dead; that hunters or peasants sometimes meet him as a pilgrim, whereupon he discovers himself to them, saying that he will yet punish the priests, and restore the Holy Roman Empire. A history, published in the year 1519, says: "He was a man of great deeds, marvelously courageous, lovable, severe, and with the gift of speech, — renowned in many things as was no one before him save Carolus the Great, — and is at last lost, so that no man knows what is become of him."

I know not where to look for another tradition made up of such picturesque elements. Although it may be told in a few words, it contains the quintessence of the history of two thousand years. Based on the grand Northern mythology, we read in it the foundation of Christianity, the Crusades, that hatred of priestcraft which made the Reformation possible, the crumbling to pieces of the old German Empire, and finally that passionate longing of the race which is now conducting it to a new national unity and power. For twenty years the Germans have been collecting funds to raise a monument to Herrmann, the Cheruskian chief, the destroyer of Varus and his legions in the Teutoburger Forest; yet Germany, after all, grew great from subjection to the laws and learning of Rome. The Kyffhäuser better deserves a monument, not specially to Barbarossa, but to that story which for centuries symbolized the political faith of the people.

The local traditions which have grown up around the national one are very numerous. Some have been transplanted hither from other places, — as, for instance, that of the key-flower, — but others, very naïve and original, belong exclusively here. It is possible, however, that they may also be found in other lands; the recent researches in fairy lore teach us that scarcely anything of what we possess is new. Here is one which suggests some passages in Wieland's "Oberon."

In Tilleda, a village at the foot of the Kyffhäuser, some lads and lasses were met, one evening, for social diversion. Among them was a girl whom they were accustomed to make the butt of their fun — whom none of them liked, although she was honest and industrious. By a secret understanding, a play of pawns was proposed; and when this girl's turn came to redeem hers, she was ordered to go up to the castle and bring back three hairs from the sleeping Emperor's beard. She set out on the instant, while the others made themselves merry over her simplicity. To their great surprise, however, she returned in an hour, bringing with her three hairs, fiery-red in color and of astonishing length. She related that, having entered the subterranean chambers, she was conducted by a dwarf to the Emperor's presence, where, after having drained a goblet of wine to his health, and that of the Frau Empress, she received permission to pluck three hairs from the imperial beard, on condition that she would neither give them away nor destroy them. She faithfully kept the promise. The hairs were laid away among her trinkets; and a year afterwards she found them changed into rods of gold, an inch in diameter. Of course the former Cinderella then became the queen.

There are several stories, somewhat similar in character, of which musicians or piping herdsmen are the heroes. Now it is a company of singers or performers, who, passing the Kyffhäuser late at night, give the sleeping Emperor a serenade; now it is a shepherd, who saying to himself, "This is for the Kaiser Friedrich" plays a simple melody upon his flute. In each case an entrance opens into the mountain. Either a princess comes forth with wine, or a page conducts the musicians into the Emperor's presence. Sometimes they each receive a green bough in payment, sometimes a horse's head, a stick, or a bunch of flax. All are either dissatisfied with their presents, or grow tired of carrying them, and throw them away, — except one (generally the poorest and silliest of the company), who takes his home with him as a souvenir of the adventure, or as an ironical present to his wife, and finds it, next morning, changed into solid gold. How faithful are all these legends to the idea of compensation! It is always the poor, the simple, the persecuted to whom luck comes.

I have two more stories, of a different character, to repeat. A poor laborer in Tilleda had an only daughter, who was betrothed to a young man equally poor, but good and honest. It was the evening before the wedding-day; the guests were already invited, and the father suddenly remembered with dismay that there was only one pot, one dish, and two plates in the house. "What shall we do?"

he cried. "You must go up to the Kyffhäuser, and ask the Princess to lend us some dishes." Hand in hand the lovers climbed the mountain, and at the door of the cavern found the Princess, who smiled upon them as they came. They made their request timidly and with fear; but she bade them take heart, gave them to eat and drink, and filled a large basket with dishes, spoons, and everything necessary for a wedding feast. When they returned to the village with their burden, it was day. All things were strange; they recognized neither house nor garden: the people were unknown to them, and wore a costume they had never before seen. Full of distress and anxiety, they sought the priest, who, after hearing their story, turned over the church-books, and found that they had been absent just two hundred years.

The other legend is that of Peter Klaus, the source from which Irving drew his Rip Van Winkle. I had read it before (as have, no doubt, many of my readers), but was not acquainted with its local habitation until my visit to the Kyffhäuser. It was first printed, so far as I can learn, in a collection made by Otmar, and published in Bremen in the year 1800. Given in the briefest outline, it is as follows: Peter Klaus, a shepherd of Sittendorf, pastured his herd on the Kyffhäuser, and was in the habit of collecting the animals at the foot of an old ruined wall. He noticed that one of his goats regularly disappeared for some hours every day; and, finding that she went into an opening between two of the stones, he followed her. She led him into a vault, where she began eating grains of oats which fell from the ceiling. Over his head he heard the stamping and neighing of horses. Presently a squire in ancient armor appeared, and beckoned to him without speaking. He was led up stairs, across a court-yard, and into an open space in the mountain, sunken deep between rocky walls, where a company of knights, stern and silent were playing at bowls. Peter Klaus was directed by gestures to set up the pins, which he did in mortal fear, until the quality of a can of wine, placed at his elbow, stimulated his courage. Finally, after long service and many deep potations, he slept. When he awoke, he found himself lying among tall weeds, at the foot of the ruined wall. Herd and dog had disappeared; his clothes were in tatters, and a long beard hung upon his breast. He wandered back to the village, seeking his goats, and marveling that he saw none but strange faces. The people gathered around him, and answered his questions, but each name he named was that upon a stone in the church-yard. Finally, a woman who seemed to be his wife pressed through the crowd, leading a wild-looking boy, and with a baby in her arms. " What is your name?" he asked.

" Maria."

" And your father?"

" He was Peter Klaus, God rest his soul! who went up the Kyffhäuser with his herd, twenty years ago, and has never been seen since."

Irving has taken almost every feature of his story from this legend; but his happy translation of it to the Catskills, and the grace and humor which he has added to it, have made it a new creation. Peter Klaus is simply a puppet of the people's fancy, but Rip Van Winkle has an immortal vitality of his own. Few, however, who look into the wild little glen, on climbing to the Catskill Mountain House, suspect from what a distance was wafted the thistle-down which there dropped and grew into a new plant, with the richest flavor and color of the soil. Here, on the Kyffhäuser, I find the stalk whence it was blown by some fortunate wind.

No doubt some interesting discoveries might be made, if the ruins were cleared and explored. At the eastern end of the crest are the remains of another tower, from which I detected masses of masonry rising through the oaks, on a lower platform of the mountain. The three wild women informed me that there was a chapel down there; but my small boy had never heard of it, and didn't know the way.

"Where do you come from, boy?" the woman asked.

"From Kelbra."

"O! ah! To be sure you don't know! The Kelbra people are blockheads and asses, every one of 'em. They think their Rothenburg is everything, when the good Lord knows that the Kaiser Red-beard never lived there a day of his life. From Kelbra, indeed! It's the Tilleda people that know how to guide strangers; you've made a nice mess of it, Herr, taking a Kelbra boy!"

Perhaps I had; but it wasn't pleasant to be told of it in that way. So I took my boy, said farewell to Barbarossa's tower, and climbed down the steep of slippery grass and stones to the ruins of the lower castle. The scrubby oaks and alder thickets were almost impenetrable; a single path wound among them, leading me through three ancient gateways, but avoiding several chambers, the walls of which are still partially standing. However, I finally reached the chapel — a structure more Byzantine than Gothic, about fifty feet in length. It stands alone, at the end of a courtyard, and is less ruined than any other part of the castle. The windows remain, and a great part of the semicircular chancel, but I could find no traces of sculpture. The floor had been dug up in search of buried treasure. Looking through an aperture in the wall, I saw another inclosure of ruins on a platform further below. The castle of Kyffhäuser, then, embraced three separate stages of buildings, all connected, and forming a pile nearly a quarter of a mile in length. Before its fall it must have been one of the stateliest fortresses in Germany.

I descended the mountain in the fierce, silent heat which made it seem so lonely, so far removed from the bright world of the Golden Mead. There were no flocks on the dry pasture-slopes, no farmers in the stubble-fields under them; and the village of Tilleda, lying under my eyes, bared its deserted streets to the sun. There, nevertheless, I found rest and refreshment in a decent inn. My destination was the town of Artern, on the Unstrut, at the eastern extremity of the Golden Mead; and I had counted on finding a horse and hay-cart, at least, to carry me over the intervening nine or ten miles. But no; nothing of the kind was to be had in Tilleda — even a man to shoulder my pack was an unusual fortune, for which I must be grateful. "Wait till evening." said the landlady, after describing to me the death of her husband, and her business troubles, "and then Hans Meyer will go with you."

The story being that the family of Goethe originally came from Artern, and that some of its members were still living in the neighborhood, I commenced my inquiries at Tilleda.

"Is there anybody of the name of Goethe in the village?" I asked the landlady.

"Yes," said she, "there's the blacksmith Goethe, but I believe he's the only one."

The poet's great-grandfather having been a blacksmith, and the practice of a certain trade or profession being so frequently hereditary among the Germans, I did not doubt but that this was a genuine branch of the family. All that the landlady could say of the man, in reply to my questions, was, "He's only a blacksmith."

The sun had nearly touched the tower on the Kyffhäuser when Hans Meyer and I set out for Artern; but the fields still glowed with heat, and the far blue hills, which I must reach, seemed to grow no nearer, as I plodded painfully along the field-roads. The man was talkative enough, and his singular dialect was not difficult to understand. He knew no tradition which had not already been gathered, but, like a genuine farmer, entertained me with stories of hail-storms, early and late frosts, and inundations. He was inveterately wedded to old fashions, and things of the past, had served against the Republicans in 1849, and not a glimmering idea of the present national movement had ever entered his mind. I had heard that this region was the home of conservative land-owners, and ignorant peasants who believe in them, but I am not willing to take Hans Meyer as a fair specimen of the people.

It is wearisome to tell of a weary journey. The richest fields may be monotonous, and the sweetest pastoral scenery become tame, without change. I looked over the floor of the Golden Mead, with ardent longing towards the spire of Artern in the east, and with a faint interest towards the castle of Sachsenberg, in the south, perched above a gorge through which the Unstrut breaks its way. The sun went down in a splendor of color, the moon came up like a bronze shield, grain-wagons rolled homewards, men and women flocked into the villages, with rakes and forks on their shoulders, and a cool dusk slowly settled over the great plain. Hans Meyer was silent at last, and I was in that condition of tense endurance when an unnecessary remark is almost as bad as an insult; and so we went over the remaining miles, entering the gates of Artern by moonlight.

The first thing I did in the morning, was to recommence my inquiries in regard to Goethe. "Yes," said the landlord, "his *stammhaus* (ancestral house) is here, but the family don't live in it any longer. If you want to see it, one of the boys shall go with you. There was formerly a smithy in it; but the smiths of the family left, and then it was changed."

I followed the boy through the long, roughly-paved main street, until we had nearly reached the western end of the town, when he stopped before an old yellow house, two stories high, with a steep tiled roof. Its age, I should guess, was between two and three hundred years. The street-front, above the ground floor,— which, having an arched entrance and only one small window, must have been the former smithy,— showed its framework of timber, as one sees in all old German houses. Before the closely ranged windows of the second story there were shelves with pots of gilliflowers and carnations in blossom. It was a genuine mechanic's house, with no peculiar feature to distinguish it particularly from the others in the street. A thin-faced man, with sharp black mustache, looked out of one of the windows, and spoke to the boy, who asked whether I wished to enter. But as there was really nothing to be seen, I declined.

According to the chronicles of Artern, the great-grandfather Goethe, the blacksmith, had a son who was apprenticed to a tailor, and who, during his *wanderschaft*, sojourned awhile in Frankfort-on-the-Main. He there captivated the fancy of a rich widow, the proprietress of the Willow-Bush Hotel (the present "Hotel Union"), and married her, — or she married him, — a fact which presupposes good looks, or talents, or both, on his part. His son, properly educated, became in time the Councillor Goethe, who begat the poet. The latter, it is said, denied that the tailor was his *grandfather*, whence it is probable that an additional generation must be interpolated; but the original blacksmith has been accepted, I believe, by the most of Goethe's biographers. A generation, more or less, makes no difference. Goethe's ancestry, like that of Shakespeare, lay in the ranks of the people, and their strong blood ran in the veins of both.

No author ever studied himself with such a serene, objective coolness as Goethe; but when he speaks to the world, one always feels that there is a slight flavor of *dichtung* infused into his *wahrheit*. Or perhaps, with the arrogance natural to every great intellect, he reasoned outward, and assumed material from spiritual facts. Fiction being only Truth seen through a different medium, the poet who can withdraw far enough from his own nature to contemplate it as an artistic study, works under a different law from that of the autobiographer. So when Goethe illustrates himself, we must not always look closely for facts. The only instance, which I can recall at this moment, wherein he speaks of his ancestors, is the poetical fragment: —

> "Stature from father, and the mood
>   Stern views of life compelling;
> From mother I take the joyous heart,
>   And the love of story-telling;
> Great-grandsire's passion was the fair —
>   What if I still reveal it?
> Great-grandam's was pomp, and gold, and show,
>   And in my bones I feel it."

It is quite as possible, here, that Goethe deduced the character of his ancestors from his own, as that he sought an explanation of the latter in their peculiarities. The great-grandsire may have been Textor, of his mother's line; it is not likely that he knew much of his father's family-tree. The burghers of Frankfurt were as proud, in their day, as the nobility of other lands; and Goethe, at least in his tastes and habits, was a natural aristocrat. It is not known that he ever visited Artern.

Concerning the other members of the original family, the landlord said: "Not one of them lives here now. The last Goethe in the neighborhood was a farmer, who had a lease of the *scharfrichterei*" (an isolated property, set apart for the use of the government executioner), "but he left here some six or eight years ago, and emigrated to America." "Was he the executioner?" I asked. "O, by no means!" the landlord answered; "he only leased the farm; but it was not a comfortable place to live upon, and, besides, he didn't succeed very well." So the blacksmith in Tilleda and the American Goethe are the only representatives left. What if a great poet for our hemisphere should, in time, spring from the loins of the latter?

I ordered a horse and carriage with no compunctions of conscience, for I was really unable to make a second day's journey on foot. The golden weather had lasted just long enough to complete my legendary pilgrimage. The morning at Artern came on with cloud and distant gray sweeps of rain, which soon blotted out the dim headland of the Kyffhäuser. I followed the course of the Unstrut, which here reaches the northern limit of his wanderings, and winds southward to seek the Saale. The valley of the river is as beautiful as it is secluded, and every hour brings a fresh historical field to the traveller. No highway enters it; only rude country roads lead from village to village, and rude inns supply plain cheer. Tourists are here an unknown variety of the human race.

I passed the ruins of Castle Wendelstein, battered during the Thirty Years' War, — a manufactory of beet-sugar now peacefully smokes in the midst of its gray vaults and buttresses, — and then Memleben, where Henry the Bird-Snarer lived when he was elected Emperor, and Otto II. founded a grand monastery. Other ruins and ancient battle-fields followed, and finally Nebra, where, in 531, the Thuringians fought with the Franks three days, and lost their kingdom. On entering Nebra, I passed an inn with the curious sign of "Care" (*Sorge*), — represented by a man with a most dismal face, and his head resting hopelessly upon his hand. An inn of evilest omen; and, assuredly, I did not stop there.

Further down the valley, green vineyards took the place of the oak forests, and the landscapes resembled those of the Main and the Neckar. There were still towns, and ruined castles, and battle-fields, but I will not ask the reader to explore the labyrinthine paths of German history. The atmosphere of the legend had faded, and I looked with an indifferent eye on the storied scenes which the windings of the river unfolded. At sunset, I saw it pour its waters into those of the Saale, not far from the railway station of Naumburg, where I came back to the highways of travel.

A WEEK ON CAPRI.

Looking seaward from Naples, the island of Capri lies across the throat of the bay like a vast natural breakwater, grand in all its proportions, and marvelously picturesque in outline. The fancy is at once excited, and seeks to find some definite figure therein. Long ago, an English traveller compared it to a couchant lion; Jean Paul, on the strength of some picture he had seen, pronounced it to be a sphinx; while Gregorovius, most imaginative of all, finds that it is "an antique sarcophagus, with bas-reliefs of snaky-haired Eumenides, and the figure of Tiberius lying upon it."

Capri is not strictly a by-way of travel, inasmuch as most of the tourists who come to Naples take the little bay-steamer, visit the Blue Grotto, touch an hour at the *marina*, or landing-place, and return the same evening *via* Sorrento. But this is like reading a title-page, instead of the volume behind it. The few who climb the rock, and set themselves quietly down to study the life and scenery of the island, find an entire poem, to which no element of beauty or interest is wanting, opened for their perusal. Like Venice, Capri is a permanent island in the traveller's experience — detached from the mainland of Italian character and associations. It is not a grand dramatic epic, to which light waves keep time, tinkling on the marble steps; but a bright, breezy pastoral of the sea, with a hollow, rumbling undertone of the Past, like that of the billows in its caverns. Venice has her generations, her ages of heroic forms: here one sole figure, supremely fierce and abominable, usurps the historic background. Not only that: its shadow is projected over the life of the island, now and for all time to come. Here, where Nature has placed terror and beauty side by side, the tragedy of one man is inextricably blended with the idyllic annals of a simple, innocent people. To feel this, one must live a little while on Capri.

It was nearly the end of January, when Antonio, our boatman, announced that we had the "one day out of a dozen," for crossing the ten miles of sea between Sorrento and the island. I had my doubts, placing my own weather-instinct against the boatman's need of making a good fare in a dull season; but we embarked, nevertheless. The ripple of a sirocco could even then be seen far out on the bay, and a cloudy wall of rain seemed to be rising from the sea. "*Non c'è paura*," said the sailors; "we have a god-mother at the marina of Capri, and we are going to burn a lamp for her to-night. She will give us good weather." They pulled gayly, and we soon passed the headland of Sorrento, beyond which the mouth of the Bay of Naples opened broadly to view. Across the water, Ischia was already dim with rain; and right in front towered Capri, huge, threatening, and to the eye inaccessible but for the faint glimmer of houses at the landing-place.

Here we met the heavy swell rolling in from the sea. The men bent to their oars, with cries of "*Hal-li! maccheroni à Capri!*" The spray of the coming rain struck us, but it was light and warm. Antonio set the sail, and we steered directly across the strait, the sky becoming darker and wilder every minute. The bold Cape of Minerva, with its Odyssean memories, and the Leap of Tiberius, on Capri, were the dim landmarks by which we set our course. It was nearly two hours before we came to windward of the latter, and I said to Antonio: "It is one day out of a dozen for cold and wet." He was silent, and made an attempt to look melancholy. However, the rocks already overhung us; in front was a great curving sweep of gardens, mounting higher and ever higher in the twilight; and the only boat we had seen on the deserted bay drew in towards us, and made for the roadstead.

The row of fishermen's houses on the beach beckoned welcome after the dreary voyage. At first I saw no human being, but presently some women and children appeared, hurrying to the strand. A few more lifts on the dying swell, and our keel struck the shore. The sailors jumped into the water; one of the women planted a tall bench against the bow, and over this bridge we were landed. There was already a crowd surrounding us with clamors for gifts and service. The woman with the bench was the noisiest: "It is mine!" she continually cried, — "*I* brought it!" I gave her a copper coin, expecting, after my Neapolitan experiences to hear wilder cries for more; but she only uttered, "*Eh? due bajocchi!*" in an indescribable tone, shouldered her bench, and walked away. Antonio picked out two maidens, piled our baggage upon their heads, and we set off for the town of Capri. The clamorous crowd dissolved at once; there was neither insult nor pursuit. It was a good-humored demonstration of welcome — nothing more.

It was but a single step from the strand — the only little fragment of beach on ten miles of inaccessible shore — to the steep and stony pathway leading up the height. It still rained, and the night was rapidly falling. High garden walls further darkened the way, which was barely wide enough to allow two persons to pass, and the bed of which, collecting the rain from the steeps on either side, was like that of a mountain torrent. Before us marched the bare-legged porteresses, with astonishing lightness and swiftness, while we plodded after, through the rattling waters, often slipping on the wet stones, and compelled to pause at every corner to regain our breath. The bright houses on the ridge overhead shone as if by their own light, crowning the dusky gardens, and beckoning us upwards.

After nearly half an hour of such climbing, we emerged from between the walls. A vast, hollow view opened dimly down to the sea for a moment; then we passed under an arch, and found ourselves in the little square of the town, which is planted on the crest of the island, at its lowest point. There are not forty feet of level ground; the pavement falls to both shores. A few paces down the southern slope brought us to a large white mansion, beside which the crown of a magnificent palm-tree rustled in the wind. This was the hostelry of Don Michele Pagano, known to all artists who have visited Capri for the last twenty years. A stately entrance, an ample staircase, and lofty, vaulted chambers, gave the house a palatial air, as we came into it out of the stormy night. The two maidens, who had carried forty pounds apiece on their heads, were not in the least flushed by their labor. The fee I gave seemed to me very small, but they were so well pleased that Antonio's voice, demanding, " Why don't you thank the Signore ? " made them start out of a dream, — perhaps of pork and macaroni. At once, like children saying their lessons, they dipped a deep courtesy, side by side, saying, " *Grazie, Signore!* " I then first saw how pretty they were, how bright their eyes, how dazzling their teeth, and how their smiles flashed as they said " Good-night ! " Meanwhile, Don Michele's daughter had kindled a fire on the hearth, there was a promise of immediate dinner, and we began to like Capri from that moment.

My first walk satisfied me that no one can make acquaintance with the island, from a boat. Its sea-walls of rock are so enormous, that they hide almost its entire habitable portion from view. In order to make any description of its scenery clear to the reader, the prominent topographical features must be first sketched. Capri lies due south of Naples, its longer diameter running east and west, so that it presents its full-broadside to the capital. Its outline, on the ground plan, is that of a short, broad-topped boot, the toe pointing towards the Sorrentine headland. The breadth, across the top, or western end, is two miles, and the length of the island is about four miles. The town of Capri lies just at the top of the instep, where the ankle is narrowest, occupying also the crest between the northern and southern shores. Immediately to the west of it rises a tremendous mountain-wall, only to be scaled at one point. All the island beyond this wall is elevated considerably above the eastern half, the division being also municipal and social. The eastern part, however, possesses the only landing-places on both shores, whence it is the most animated and populous, claiming at least two thirds of the entire number of five thousand souls on the island. The most elevated points are the Salto (leap) di Tiberio, the extreme eastern cape, which rises nearly a thousand feet above the sea; and Monte Solaro, a part of the dividing wall which I have just mentioned, about double the height of the Salto. In addition to the landing-place on the northern shore, there is a little cove just opposite, below the town, where boats can land in still weather. Elsewhere, the rocks descend to the water in a sheer wall, from one to eight hundred feet in height. Although so near Naples, the winds from the mountains of the Peninsula are somewhat softened in crossing the bay, and the winter temperature is about ten degrees higher in consequence.

When we crossed the little square of the town to the entrance-gate, on the morning after our arrival, there was a furious *tramontana* blowing. The whole circuit of the Bay of Naples was visible, drawn in hard, sharp outlines, and the blue basin of water was freckled with thousands of shifting white-caps. The resemblance of the bay to a vast volcanic crater struck my fancy: the shores and islands seem to be the ruins of its rim. Such a wind, in Naples, would have been intolerable: here it was only strong at exposed points, and its keen edge was gone. We turned eastward, along the narrow, dirty street, to get into the country. In a hundred yards the town ceased, and the heavy walls gave place to enormous hedges of cactus. A boy, walking the same way, asked: "Are you going to

Timberio" (Tiberius)? The ruins of the Villa Jovis, the principal palace of the Emperor, were already to be seen, on the summit of the eastern headland of the island. Along a roughly paved lane, under the shade of carob and olive trees, we finally came to a large country-house in a most picturesque state of ruin. A crumbling archway, overhung by a fringe of aloes, which had thrust their roots between the stones, attracted my attention, and I began to sketch it. Not many minutes elapsed before five or six boys came out, and watched me from the arch. They would have been good accessories, but, whenever I looked at one, he got out of the way. Presently they brought an aloe, and set it upon the rocks; but, seeing that I paid no attention to it, one of them remarked with a grimace, "No butiglia," — meaning that he expected no gratuity from me. They were lively, good-natured imps, and so it was a pleasure to disappoint them agreeably.

We went also down the southern slope of the island, and came at random into the Val Tragara, — a peaceful solitude, where twenty-five centuries of labor have turned the hostile rocks into tiers of ever-yielding gardens. One range of these is supported upon arches of masonry that formerly upheld the highway which Tiberius constructed between his palaces. I afterwards found other traces of the road, leading in easy zigzags to the site of the fourth palace on San Michele. Descending deeper in the Val Tragara we missed the main path, and stumbled down the channels of the rain between clumps of myrtle and banks whereon the red anemone had just begun to open its blossoms. The olive-trees, sheltered from the wind, were silent, and their gray shadows covered the suggestive mystery of the spot. For here Tiberius is supposed to have hidden those rites of the insane Venus to which Suetonius and Tacitus so darkly allude.

"Non ragioniam di lor, ma guarda e passa."

A single almond-tree, in flower, made its own sunshine

in the silvery gloom; and the secluded beauties of the place tempted us on, until the path dropped into a ravine, which fell towards the sea. Following the line of the ancient arches there is another path — the only level walk on the island — leading to a terrace above the three pointed rocks off the southern coast, called the Faraglioni. In the afternoon, when all the gardens and vineyards from the edge of the white cliffs to the town along the ridge lie in light, and the huge red and gray walls beyond, literally piled against the sky, are in hazy shadow, the views from this path are poems written in landscape forms. One does not need to remember that here once was Rome; that beyond the sea lie Sicily and Carthage; that Augustus consecrated the barren rock below to one of his favorites, and jested with Thrasyllus at one of his last feasts. The delight of the eye fills you too completely; and Capri, as you gaze, is released from its associations, classic and diabolic. If Nature was here profaned by man, she has long ago washed away the profanation. Her pure air and healthy breezes tolerate no moral diseases. Such were brought hither; but they took no root, and have left no trace, except in the half-fabulous "Timberio" of the people.

It is time to visit the Villa Jovis, the Emperor's chief residence. The *tramontana* still blew when we set out; but, as I said, it had lost its sharp edge in coming over the bay, and was deliciously bracing. As the gulf opened below us, after passing Monte San Michele, we paused to look at the dazzling panorama. Naples was fair in sight; and the smoke of Vesuvius. following the new lava, seemed nearly to have reached Torre del Greco. While we were studying the volcano through a glass, a tall man in Scotch cap and flannel shirt came up, stopped, and addressed us in Italian.

"You see that white house yonder on the cliff?" said he; "a Signore Inglese lives there. It's a nice place, a beautiful situation. There's the place for the cows, and there are the columbaria, and all sorts of things. It's what they call a *quinta* in Portugal."

"Is the Englishman married?" I asked.

"I don't know," he replied; "I believe there's a certain woman in the house."

I handed him the glass, which he held to his eyes for five minutes, without saying a word. Suddenly he broke out in English: "Yes, as you say, the powdery appearance — the — ah, the sudden change! Boreal weather, you know; but the indications seem to me, having watched and kept the thing in view, quite — ah — *quite* of *your* opinion!"

I was speechless, as may easily be imagined; and, before I could guess what to reply, he handed me the glass, took off his cap, said: "Here's hoping — ah, wishing that we may meet again — *perhaps!*" and went off with tremendous strides.

"Who is that, Augusto?" I asked of the small Caprese boy who carried our books and umbrellas.

"*Un Signo' Inglese.*"

"Is anything the matter with him?"

"*È un po' pazzo*" (a little cracked).

"Where does he live?"

"Yonder!" said Augusto, pointing to the very house, and place for the cows, and the columbaria, to which the gentleman himself had called my attention. It was his own house! The "certain woman," I afterwards learned, was his legal wife, a girl of Capri. As for himself, he bears a name noted in literature, and is the near relative of three authors.

Two pleasant girls kept us company a little further, and then we went on alone, by a steep, slippery path, paved with stone, between the poor little fields of fig and olive. The patches of wheat were scarcely bigger than cottage flower-beds, and in many places a laborious terrace supported only ground enough to produce a half-peck of grain.

Lupines and horse-beans are the commonest crop at this season. Along our path bloomed "the daisy-star that never sets," with anemone and golden broom. The Villa Jovis was full in view, and not distant; but the way first led us to the edge of the cliffs on the southeastern side of the island. From a rough pulpit of masonry we looked down on the wrinkled sea near a thousand feet below. The white-caps were but the tiniest sprinkles of silver on its deep-blue ground.

As we mounted towards the eastern headland, the tremendous walls of the western half of Capri rose bold and bright against the sky; but the arcs of the sea horizon, on either side, were so widely extended that they nearly clasped behind Monte Solaro. It was a wonderful, an indescribable view; how can I give it in words? Here I met an old man, in a long surtout, who stopped and conversed a minute in French. He was a soldier of Napoleon, now the keeper of a little restaurant at the Salto di Tiberio, and had just been made happy by the cross and a pension. The restaurant was opened by a peasant, and we passed through it to the Salto. A protecting rampart of masonry enables you to walk to the very brink. The rock falls a thousand feet, and so precipitously that the victims flung hence must have dropped into the waves. We looked directly across the strait to the Cape of Minerva, and towards Salerno as well as Naples. The snow-crowned Monte Sant' Angelo, rising in the centre, gave the peninsula a broad pyramidal form, buttressed by the headlands on either side. The Isles of the Sirens were full in view; and, beyond them, the whole curve of the Salernic gulf, to the far Calabrian cape of Licosa. The distance was bathed in a flood of airy gold, and the gradations in the color of the sea, from pale amethyst to the darkest sapphire below us, gave astonishing breadth and depth to the immense perspective. But the wind, tearing round the point in furious gusts, seemed trying to snatch us over the rampart, and the horror of the height became insupportable.

Much of the plan of the Villa Jovis may still be traced. As we approached the ruins, which commence a few paces beyond the Salto, a woman made her appearance, and assumed the office of guide. "Here lived Timberio," said she; "he was a great man, a beautiful man, but O, he was a devil! Down there are seven chambers, which you can only see by a torch-light; and here are the *piscine*, one for salt water and one for fresh; and now I'll show you the mosaic pavement — all made by Timberio. O, the devil that he was!" Timberio is the favorite demon of the people of Capri. I suspect they would not give him up for any consideration. A wine of the island is called the "Tears of Tiberius" (when did he ever shed any, I wonder?), just as the wine of Vesuvius is called the Tears of Christ. When I pointed to the distant volcano, whose plume of silver smoke was the sign of the active eruption, and said to the woman, "Timberio is at work yonder!" she nodded her head, and answered: "Ah, the devil! to be sure he is."

We picked our way through the ruins, tracing three stories of the palace, which must have been four, if not five stories high on the land side. Some drums of marble columns are scattered about, bits of stucco remain at the bases of the walls; there is a corridor paved with mosaic, descending, curiously enough, in an inclined plane, and the ground-plan of a small theatre; but the rubbish left does not even hint of the former splendor. It is not one of those pathetic ruins which seem to appeal to men for preservation; it rather tries to hide itself from view, welcoming the broom, the myrtle, and the caper-shrub to root-hold in its masses of brick and mortar.

On the topmost platform of ruin is the little chapel of Santa Maria del Soccorso, together with the hermitage of a good-natured friar, who brings you a chair, offers you bits of Tiberian marble, and expects a modest alms. Here I found the wild Englishman, sitting on a stone bench beside the chapel. He pointed over the parapet to the awful precipice, and asked me: "Did you ever go over there? *I* did once — to get some jonquils. You know the rock-jonquils are the finest." Then he took my glass, looked through it at the distant shores, and began to laugh. "This reminds me," said he, "of a man who was blown up with his house several hundred feet into the air. He was immensely frightened, when, all at once, he saw his neighbor's house beside him — blown up too. And the neighbor called out: 'How long do you think it will take us to get down again?' Cool — wasn't it?" Thereupon he went to the ladies of the party, whom he advised to go to the *marina*, and see the people catch shrimps. "It's a beautiful sight," he said. "The girls are so fresh and rosy — but, then, so are the shrimps!"

It is no lost time, if you sit down upon a block of marble in the Villa Jovis, and dream a long, bewildering day-dream. Here it is almost as much a riot for the imagination to restore what once was, as to create what might be. The temples of Minerva and Apollo, across the strait, were both visible from this point. Looking over Capri, you place the second palace of Tiberius on the summit of Monte Tuoro, which rises against the sea on your right; the third on the southern side of the island, a little further; the fourth on Monte San Michele; the fifth and sixth beyond the town of Capri, near the base of the mountain wall. Roads connecting these piles of splendor cross the valleys on high arches, and climb the peaks in laborious curves. Beyond the bay, the headland of Misenum and the shores of Baiæ are one long glitter of marble. Villas and temples crown the heights of Puteoli, and stretch in an unbroken line to Neapolis. Here the vision grows dim, but you know what magnificence fills the whole sweep of the shore — Portici and Pompeii and Stabiæ, growing visible again as the palaces shine above the rocks of Surrentum!

After the wonder that such things were, the next greatest wonder is that they have so utterly vanished. What is preserved is so fresh and solid that Time seems to have done the least towards their destruction. The masonry of Capri can scarcely have been carried away, while such quarries — still unexhausted — were supplied by the mainland; and the tradition is probably correct, that the palaces of Tiberius were razed to the ground immediately after his fall. The charms of the island were first discovered by Augustus. Its people were still Greek, in his day; and it belonged to the Greek Neapolis, to which he gave the larger and richer Ischia in exchange for it. The ruins of the Villa Jovis are supposed to represent, also, the site of his palace; and Tiberius, who learned diplomacy from the cunning Emperor, and crime from the Empress, his own mother, first came hither with him. A period of twenty or thirty years saw the splendors of Capri rise and fall. After Tiberius, the island ceased to have a history.

Every walk on these heights, whence you look out far over bays, seas, and shores, is unlike anything else in the world. It is surprising what varieties of scenery are embraced in this little realm. In the afternoon we saw another phase of it on the southern shore, at a point called the Marina Piccola. After passing below the town and the terraced fields, we came upon a wild slope, grown with broom and mastic and arbutus, among which cows were feeding. Here the island shelves down rapidly between two near precipices. The wind was not felt; the air was still and warm, and the vast, glittering sea basked in the sun. At the bottom we found three fishers' houses stuck among the rocks, more like rough natural accretions than the work of human hand; a dozen boats hauled up on the stones in a cove about forty feet in diameter; and one solitary man. Silence and savage solitude mark the spot. Eastward, the Faraglioni rise in gray-red, inaccessible cones; the ramparts of the Castello make sharp, crenelated zigzags on the sky, a thousand feet above one's head; and only a few olive-groves, where Monte Tuoro falls into the Val

Tragara, speak of cultivation. One might fancy himself to be upon some lone Pacific island. The fisher told us that in tempests the waves are hurled entirely over the houses, and boats in the cove are then dashed to pieces. But in May, the quails, weary with their flight from Africa, land on the slope above, and are caught in nets by hundreds and thousands.

We had not yet exhausted the lower, or eastern half of the island. Another morning was devoted to the Arco Naturale, on the southern coast, between Monte Tuoro and the Salto. Scrambling along a stony lane, between the laborious terraces of the Capri farmers, we soon reached the base of the former peak, where, completely hidden from view, lay a rich circular basin of level soil, not more than a hundred yards in diameter. Only two or three houses were visible; some boys, hoeing in a field at a distance, cried out, "*Signo', un baioc'!*" with needless iteration, as if the words were a greeting. Presently we came upon a white farmhouse, out of which issued an old woman and four wild, frouzy girls — all of whom attached themselves to us, and would not be shaken off.

We were already on the verge of the coast. Over the jagged walls of rock we saw the plain of Pæstum beyond the sea, which opened deeper and bluer beneath us with every step. The rich garden-basin and the amphitheatre of terraced fields on Monte Tuoro were suddenly shut from view. A perpendicular cliff of white rock arose on the right; and below some rough shelves wrought into fields stood the Natural Arch, like the front of a shattered Gothic cathedral. Its background was the sea, which shone through the open arch. High up on the left, over the pointed crags, stood a single rock shaped like a Rhine-wine beaker, holding its rounded cup to the sky. There is scarcely a wilder view on Capri.

Following the rough path by which the people reach their little fields, we clambered down the rocks, along the brink of steeps which threatened danger whenever the gusts of wind came around the point. The frouzy girls were at hand, and eager to help. When we declined, they claimed money for having given us their company, and we found it prudent to settle the bill at once. The slope was so steep that every brink of rock, from above, seemed to be the last between us and the sea. Our two boy-attendants went down somewhere, out of sight; and their song came up through the roar of the wind like some wild strain of the Sirens whose isles we saw in the distance. The rock is grandly arched, with a main portal seventy or eighty feet high, and two open windows at the sides.

Half-way down the cliff on the right is the grotto of Mitromania — a name which the people, of course, have changed into "Matrimonio," as if the latter word had an application to Tiberius! There were some two hundred steps to descend, to a little platform of earth, under the overhanging cliffs. Here the path dropped suddenly into a yawning crevice, the floor of which was traversed with cracks, as if ready to plunge into the sea which glimmered up through them. Passing under the gloomy arch, we came upon a chamber of reticulated Roman masonry, built in a side cavity of the rock, which forms part of the main grotto or temple of Mithras. The latter is about one hundred feet deep and fifty wide, and opens directly towards the sunrise.

Antiquarians derive the name of the grotto from *Magnum Mithræ Antrum*. There seems to be no doubt as to its character: one can still perceive the exact spot where the statue of the god was placed, to catch the first beams of his own luminary, coming from Persia to be welcomed and worshipped on the steeps of Capri. It is difficult to say what changes time and earthquakes may not have wrought; but it seems probable that the ancient temple extended to the front of the cliffs, and terminated in a platform hanging over the sea. A Greek inscription found in this grotto associates it both with the superstition and the cruelty of

Tiberius. I have not seen the original, which is in the Museum at Naples, but here repeat it from the translation of Gregorovius: —

> "Ye who inhabit the Stygian land, beneficent demons,
> Me, the unfortunate, take ye also now to your Hades, —
> Me, whom not the will of the gods, but the power of the Ruler,
> Suddenly smote with death, which, guiltless, I never suspected.
> Crowned with so many a gift, enjoying the favor of Cæsar,
> Now he destroyeth my hopes and the hopes of my parents.
> Not fifteen have I reached, not twenty the years I have numbered,
> Ah! and no more I behold the light of the beautiful heavens.
> Hypatos am I by name: to thee I appeal, O my brother, —
> Parents, also, I pray you, unfortunate, mourn me no longer!"

A human sacrifice is here clearly indicated. This mysterious cavern, with its diabolical associations, the giddy horror of the Salto, and the traces of more than one concealed way of escape, denoting the fear which is always allied with cruelty, leave an impression which the efforts of those historiasters who endeavor to whitewash Tiberius cannot weaken with all their arguments. Napoleon was one of his admirers, but his opinion on such matters is of no great weight. When Dr. Adolf Stahr, however, devotes a volume to the work of proving Tiberius to have been a good and much-abused man, we turn to the pages of Suetonius and the Spintrian medals, and are not convinced. The comment of the old woman at the Villa Jovis will always express the general judgment of mankind, — "*O, che diavolo era Timberio!*"

If you stand at the gate of the town, and look eastward towards the great dividing wall, you can detect, on the corner nearest the sea, the zigzag line of the only path which leads up to Anacapri and the western part of the island. One morning when the boy Manfred, as he brought our coffee, told us that the *tramontana* had ceased blowing, we sent for horses, to make the ascent. We had been awakened by volleys of musketry; the church-bells were chiming, and there were signs of a festa, — but Felice, the owner of the horses, explained the matter. Two young men, mariners of Capri, had recently suffered shipwreck on the coast of Calabria. Their vessel was lost, and they only saved their lives because they happened, at the critical moment, to call on the Madonna del Carmine. She heard and helped them: they reached home in safety, and on this day they burned a lamp before her shrine, had a mass said in their names, and invited their families and friends to share in the thanksgiving. I heard the bells with delight, for they expressed the poetry of superstition based on truth.

We set out, in

"The halcyon morn
To hoar February born."

Indeed, such a day makes one forget *tramontana*, sirocco, and all the other weather-evils of the Italian winter. Words cannot describe the luxury of the air, the perfect stillness and beauty of the day, and the far, illuminated shores of the bay as they opened before us. We saw that the season had turned, in the crocusses and violets which blossomed beside the path — the former a lovely pale-purple flower, with fire-tinted stamens. With Felice came two little girls, Luigia and Serafina, the former of whom urged on a horse, while the other carried on her head the basket of provisions. Our small factotum, Augusto, took charge of the bottles of wine, and Felice himself bore the shawls and books. Beyond the town, the path wound between clumps of myrtle, arbutus, and the delicate white erica, already in bud. Under us lay the amphitheatre of vineyards and orange-groves; and the town of Capri, behind, stretching from San Michele to the foot of the Castello, seemed a fortified city of the Middle Ages. Over the glassy sea rose Vesuvius, apparently peaceful, yet with a demon at work under that silvery cloud; Monte St. Angelo, snowy and bleak; and the rich slopes of Sorrento and Massa.

One of the *giumente* (as Felice called his horses) turned on seeing the rocky staircase, and tried to escape. But it was a sign of protest, not of hope. They were small, unshod, very peaceful creatures, doomed to a sorry fate, but they never had known anything better. Their horse-ideal was derived from the hundred yards of *un*stony path below Capri, and the few fresh turnips and carrots which they get on holidays. It was, perhaps, a waste of sympathy to pity them; yet one inclines to pity beasts more readily than men.

At the foot of the staircase we dismounted, and prepared to climb the giddy steep. There are five hundred and sixty steps, and they will average more than a foot in height. It is a fatiguing but not dangerous ascent, the overhanging side being protected by a parapet, while the frequent landings afford secure resting-places. On the white precipices grew the blue "flower of spring" (*fiore della primavera*), and the air was sweet with odors of unknown buds. Up and still up, we turned at each angle to enjoy the wonderful aerial view, which, on such a morning, made me feel half-fledged, with sprouting wings which erelong might avail to bear me across the hollow gulf. We met a fellow with a splendid Roman head, whereon he was carrying down to the *marina* the huge oaken knee of some future vessel. Surprised at the size of the timber, I asked Felice whether it really grew upon the island, and he said there were large oaks about and beyond Anacapri.

Half-way up, the chapel of Sant' Antonio stands on a little spur, projecting from the awful precipices. Looking down, you see the ruins of the Palazzo a' Mare of Tiberius, the bright turquoise patches where the water is shallow, and its purple tint in shadow. White sails were stretching across from the headland of Sorrento, making for the Blue Grotto. There were two more very long and steep flights of steps, and then we saw the gate on the summit, arched against the sky. Hanging from the rocks, but inaccessible, were starry bunches of daffodils. It had seemed to me, on looking at the rocky walls from Capri, that an easier point of ascent might have been chosen, and I believe it is settled that Tiberius visited his four western palaces by a different path; but I now saw that the islanders (not possessing despotic power) have really chosen the most accessible point. The table-land beyond does not, as I had imagined, commence at the summit of the cliffs, but far below them, and this staircase strikes the easiest level.

There are few equal surprises on Capri. Not many more steps, and we found ourselves on a rich garden-plain, bounded on the left by stony mountains, but elsewhere stretching away to sky and sea, without a hint of the tremendous cliffs below. Indeed, but for the luminous, trembling haze around the base of the sky, one would not surmise the nearness of the sea, but rather think himself to be in some inland region. The different properties are walled, but there is no need of terraces. Shining white houses, with domed roofs, stand in the peaceful fields. The fruit-trees grow rank, huge oaks and elms with ivied trunks rise above them, and the landscape breathes a sweet, idyllic air. I noticed many cherry-trees of great size. The oaks, though deciduous, still wore the green leaves of last summer, which will only be pushed from the twigs when this year's buds open. High over this pleasant land, on a bare rock, are the towers of a mediæval castle, now named after Barbarossa — the corsair, not the Emperor.

Presently we came to Anacapri, cleanest, most picturesque and delightful of Italian villages. How those white houses, with their airy *loggias*, their pillared *pergolas*, and their trim gardens, wooed us to stay, and taste the delight of rest, among a simple, beautiful, ignorant, and honest people! The streets were as narrow and shady as those of any oriental city, and the houses mostly presented a blank side to them; but there were many arches, each opening on a sunny picture of slim, dark-haired beauties spinning silk, or grandams regulating the frolics of children. The latter, seeing us, begged for *bajocchi;* and even the girls did the same, but laughingly, with a cheerful mimicry of mendicancy. The piazza of the village is about as large as the dining-room of a hotel. A bright little church occupies one side; and, as there was said to be a view from the roof, we sent for the key, which was brought by three girls. I made out the conjectured location of the ninth, tenth, eleventh, and twelfth palaces of Tiberius, whereof only a few stones remain, and then found that the best view was that of the three girls. They had the low brow, straight nose, short upper lip, and rounded chin which belongs to the Caprese type of beauty, and is rather Hellenic than Roman. Their complexion was dark, sunburnt rather than olive, and there was a rich flush of blood on their cheeks; the eyes long and large, and the teeth white as the kernels of fresh filberts. Their bare feet and hands, spoiled by much tramping and hard work, were out of keeping with their graceful, statuesque beauty. A more cheerful picture of Poverty (for they are all miserably poor), it would be difficult to find.

It was but a mile further to the headland of Damecuta. Felice, however, advised us rather to visit the tower of Lima, above the Punta della Carena, the northwestern extremity of the island, and his advice proved to be good in the end. We descended a stony steep into a little valley, shaded by superb olive-groves, under which the crops of lupines were already beginning to blossom. The dell fell deeper as we advanced; the grass was starred with red anemones, and there were odors of concealed violets. A mile further, we came upon a monastery, with a square, crenelated tower, beyond which the fields gave place to a narrow strip of stony down. All at once the shore yawned beneath us, disclosing the extremity of the island, with three deserted batteries on as many points of rock, a new light-house, and the little cove where the troops of Murat landed, when they surprised the English and recaptured

Capri, in 1808. Westward, there was a wide sweep of sunny sea; northward, Ischia, Procida with its bright town, Baiæ and Pozzuoli. Here, at the foot of an old martello tower, we made our noon halt, relieving Serafina of the weight of her basket, and Augusto of his bottles.

The children and young girls, going out to their work in the fields, begged rather pertinaciously. "We are very poor," they cried; "and you are so grand and beautiful you can surely give us something." On the return, we met a group of lively maidens coming up from Capri, who said, when I told them there were no more *bajocchi* in my pockets: "Well, then, give us a franc, and we will divide it among us!" Nevertheless, begging is not the nuisance on Capri that it is on the main-land. It is always good-humored, and refusal is never followed by maledictions. The poor are positively and certainly poor, and they seem to think it no shame to take what they can get over and above their hard earnings. When one sees how very industrious and contented they are, it is rather a pleasure to add a few coppers to the little store laid aside for their holidays.

With every day, every hour, of our residence, we more fully realized the grandeur and variety of the landscapes of Capri. The week which I thought sufficient to enable us to see the island thoroughly drew towards its close; and although we had gone from end to end of the rocky shores, climbed all the principal peaks, and descended into every dell and ravine, our enjoyment was only whetted, not exhausted. The same scenes grow with every repetition. There is not a path or crooked lane among the old houses, which does not keep a surprise in reserve. The little town, with only here and there a stone to show for the Past, with no architectural interest whatever, is nevertheless a labyrinth of picturesque effects. In the houses, all the upper chambers are vaulted, and the roofs domed above them as in the Orient; while on one or more sides there is a *loggia* or arched veranda, overhung with cornice of grapevines, or gay with vases of blooming plants. Thick walls, narrow windows, external staircases, palm-trees in the gardens, and raised platforms of masonry placed so as to catch the breezes of summer nights, increase the resemblance to the Orient. Living there, Syria seems to be nearer than Naples.

In the Val Tragara, near the sea, there is a large deserted monastery, the Certosa, dating from the fourteenth century. Here, as elsewhere, the monks have either picked out the choicest spot for their abode or have made it beautiful by their labor. The Certosa is still stately and imposing in its ruin. In the church the plaster is peeling off, leaving patches of gay fresco on the walls and ceiling. The sacristy and an adjoining chapel are riddled with cannon-balls; and two recumbent marble statues of the founders, resting on their sarcophagi, look at each other from opposite sides, and seem to wonder what the desolation means. The noble court-yard, surrounded with arched corridors, is dug up for a garden; there is straw and litter in the crumbling cells; and the prior's apartment, with its wonderful sea and coast views, is without an occupant. The garden only has not forgotten its former luxury. Its vines and fig-trees equal those of Crete and Syria; and its cactuses have become veritable trees, twenty feet in height. The monks succeeded in getting hold of the best land on the island; yet I have no doubt that the very people they impoverished wish them back again.

The Caprese are very devout and superstitious. They have two devils ("Timberio" being one), and a variety of saints. The beautiful little church in the town, externally so much like a mosque, is filled with votive offerings, painted or modeled in wax, each of which has its own story of miraculous interposition and escape. On one side of the nave sits in state the Madonna del Carmine, — a life-sized doll, with fair complexion, blue eyes, and a profusion of long curling tresses of real blonde hair. In her lap she holds a dwarfish man, with hair of nearly equal length. A dozen wax-candles were burning before her, in anticipation of her coming *festa*, which took place before we left Capri. She is the patron saint of the coral-fishers, none of whom neglected to perform their share of the celebration.

The day was ushered in with volleys of musketry, and the sounds, or rather cries, of the worst brass band I ever heard, which went from house to house, blowing, and collecting coppers. After the forenoon mass, the procession was arranged in the church, and then set out to make the tour of the town. First came the members of a confraternity, mostly grizzly old men, in white gowns, with black capes, lined with red; then followed a number of small boys, behind whom marched the coral-fishers, forty or fifty in number — brown, weather-beaten faces, burned by the summers of the African coast. They were dressed with unusual care, and their throats seemed ill at ease inside of collar and cravat. Every one in the procession carried a taper, which he shielded from the wind with the hollow left hand, while his right managed also to collect the melted wax. Next appeared the Madonna, on her litter of state, followed by six men, who bore her silken canopy. In her train were the priests, and about a hundred women and girls brought up the rear.

Among the latter there were some remarkably lovely faces. The mixture of yellow, blue, and scarlet colors which they delight to wear contrasted brilliantly with the glossy blackness of their hair and the sunny richness of their complexion. The island costume, however, is beginning to disappear. Only a few girls wore the *mucadore*, or folded handkerchief, on the head, while several were grand in wide silk skirts and crinolines. The people are not envious, but many a longing glance followed these progressive maidens.

In so small a domain as Capri, all that happens is known to everybody. A private romance is not possible; and so, on this occasion, the crowd on the little piazza were moved by a curiosity which had no relation to the Madonna del Carmine. The story, as I received it, is this: Nearly a year ago, the aunt of a beautiful girl who was betrothed to one of the young coral-fishers was visited by an Englishman then staying at the Hotel Tiberio, who declared to her his violent love for the niece, and solicited her good offices to have the previous engagement broken off. Soon after this the Englishman left; the aunt informed the girl's father of the matter, the betrothal with the coral-fisher was suspended, and the father spent most of his time in frequenting the hotels to ascertain whether a rich young Englishman had arrived. A few days before our visit to Capri, the girl received presents from her unseen and unknown wooer, with a message requesting her not to appear in the procession of the Madonna del Carmine. The Englishman stated that he was at the Hotel Tiberio, and only waited the arrival of certain papers in order to claim her as his bride. Thereupon the father came to the hotel, but failed to discover the mysterious stranger. Two artists, and several ladies who were there, offered to assist him; but the mystery still remained unsolved. Other letters and presents came to the girl; but no young, rich Englishman could be found on the island. The artists and ladies took up the matter (determined, I am very glad to say, to drive away the Englishman, if there were one, and marry the girl to the coral-fisher), but I have not yet heard of any *dénoûement.* The young fisher appeared in the procession, but the girl did not; consequently, everybody knew that the mysterious letters and presents had made her faithless. For my part, I hope the coral-fisher — a bright, stalwart, handsome young fellow — will find a truer sweetheart.

After making the complete tour of the town, which occupied about half an hour, the procession returned to the church. The coral-fishers were grave and devout; one could not question their sincerity. I was beginning to find the scene touching, and to let my sympathy go forth with the people, when the sight of them dropping on their knees before the great, staring doll of a Madonna, as she bobbed along on the shoulders of her bearers, turned all my softness into granite. The small boys, carrying the tapers before her, were employed in trying to set fire to each other's shocks of uncombed hair. Two of them succeeded, and the unconscious victims marched at least a dozen steps with blazing heads, and would probably have been burned to the scalp had not a humane by-stander extinguished the unfragrant torches. Then everybody laughed; the victims slapped those who had set fire to them; and a ridiculous comedy was enacted in the very presence of the Madonna, who, for a moment, was the only dignified personage. The girls in the rear struck up a hymn without the least regard to unison, and joked and laughed together in the midst of it. The procession dissolved at the church door, and not a moment too soon, for it had already lost its significance.

I have purposely left the Blue Grotto to the last, as for me it was subordinate in interest to almost all else that I saw. Still it was part of the inevitable programme. One calm day we had spent in the trip to Anacapri, and another, at this season, was not to be immediately expected. Nevertheless, when we arose on the second morning afterwards, the palm-leaves hung silent, the olives twinkled without motion, and the southern sea glimmered with the veiled light of a calm. Vesuvius had but a single peaceful plume of smoke, the snows of the Apulian Mountains gleamed rosily behind his cone, and the fair headland of Sorrento shone in those soft, elusive, aerial grays, which must be the despair of a painter. It was a day for the Blue Grotto, and so we descended to the *marina*.

On the strand, girls with disordered hair and beautiful teeth offered shells and coral. We found mariners readily and, after a little hesitation, pushed off in a large boat, leaving a little one to follow. The *tramontana* had left a faint swell behind it, but four oars carried us at a lively speed along the shore. We passed the ruins of the baths of Tiberius (the *Palazzo a' Mare*), and then slid into the purple shadows of the cliffs, which rose in a sheer wall five hundred feet above the water. Two men sat on a rock, fishing with poles; and the boats further off the shore were sinking their nets, the ends of which were buoyed up with gourds. Pulling along in the shadows, in less than half an hour we saw the tower of Damecuta shining aloft, above a slope of olives which descended steeply to the sea. Here, under a rough, round bastion of masonry, was the entrance to the Blue Grotto.

We were now transshipped to the little shell of a boat which had followed us. The swell rolled rather heavily into the mouth of the cave, and the adventure seemed a little perilous, had the boatmen been less experienced. We lay flat in the bottom; the oars were taken in, and we had just reached the entrance, when a high wave, rolling up, threatened to dash us against the iron portals. "Look out!" cried the old man. The young sailor held the boat back with his hands, while the wave rolled under us into the darkness beyond; then, seizing the moment, we shot in after it, and were safe under the expanding roof. At first, all was tolerably dark: I only saw that the water near the entrance was intensely and luminously blue. Gradually, as the eye grew accustomed to the obscurity, the irregular vault of the roof became visible, tinted by a faint reflection from the water. The effect increased, the longer we remained; but the rock nowhere repeated the dazzling sapphire of the sea. It was rather a blue-gray, very beautiful, but far from presenting the effect given in the pictures sold at Naples. The silvery, starry radiance of foam or bubbles on the shining blue ground was the loveliest phenomenon of the grotto. To dip one's hand in the sea, and scatter the water, was to create sprays of wonderful, phosphorescent blossoms, jewels of the Sirens, flashing and vanishing garlands of the Undines.

A chamber, and the commencement of a gallery leading somewhere, — probably to the twelfth palace of Tiberius, on the headland of Damecuta, — were to be distinguished near the rear of the cavern. But rather than explore further mysteries, we watched our chance and shot out, after a full-throated wave, into the flood of white daylight Keeping on our course around the island, we passed the point of Damecuta, — making a chord to the arc of the shore, — to the first battery, beyond which the Anacapri territory opened fairly to view. From the northern to the northwestern cape the coast sinks, like the side of an amphitheatre, in a succession of curving terraces, gray with the abundant olive. Two deep, winding ravines, like the *wadies* of Arabia, have been worn by the rainfall of thousands of years, until they have split the shore-wall down to the sea. Looking up them, we could guess the green banks where the violets and anemones grew, and the clumps of myrtle that perfumed the sea-breeze.

Broad and grand as was this view, it was far surpassed by the coast scenery to come. No sooner had we passed the pharos, and turned eastward along the southern shore of the island, than every sign of life and laborious industry ceased. The central mountain-wall, suddenly broken off as it reached the sea, presented a face of precipice a thousand feet high, not in a smooth escarpment, as on the northern side, but cut into pyramids and pinnacles of ever-changing form. Our necks ached with gazing at the far summits, piercing the keen blue deeps of air. In one place the vast gable of the mountain was hollowed into arches and grottos, from the caves of which depended fringes of stalactite; it resembled a Titanic cathedral in ruins. Above the orange and dove-colored facets of the cliff, the jagged topmost crest wore an ashen tint which no longer suggested the texture of rock. It seemed rather a soft, mealy substance, which one might crumble between the fingers. The critics of the realistic school would damn the painter who should represent this effect truly.

Under these amazing crags, over a smooth, sunny sea, we sped along towards a point where the boatman said we should find the Green Grotto. It lies inside a short, projecting cape of the perpendicular shore, and our approach to it was denoted by a streak of emerald fire flashing along the shaded water at the base of the rocks. A few more strokes on the oars carried us under an arch twenty feet high, which opened into a rocky cove beyond. The water being shallow, the white bottom shone like silver; and the pure green hue of the waves, filled and flooded with the splendor of the sun, was thrown upon the interior facings of the rocks, making the cavern gleam like transparent glass. The dance of the waves, the reflex of the "netted sunbeams," threw ripples of shifting gold all over this green ground; and the walls and roof of the cavern, so magically illuminated, seemed to fluctuate in unison with the tide. It was a marvelous surprise, making truth of Undine and the Sirens, Proteus and the foam-born Aphrodite. The brightness of the day increased the illusion, and made the incredible beauty of the cavern all the more startling, because devoid of gloom and mystery. It was an idyl of the sea, born of the god-lore of Greece. To the light, lisping whisper of the waves, — the sound nearest to that of a kiss, — there was added a deep, dim, subdued undertone of the swell caught in lower arches beyond; and the commencement of that fine posthumous sonnet of Keats chimed thenceforward in my ears: —

> "It keeps eternal whisperings around
> Desolate shores, and with its mighty swell
> Gluts twice ten thousand caverns, till the spell
> Of Hecate leaves them *their old shadowy sound.*"

After this, although the same enormous piles of rock

overhung us, there were no new surprises. The sublimity and the beauty of this southern coast had reached their climax; and we turned from it to lean over the gunwale of the boat, and watch the purple growth of sponges through the heaving crystal, as we drew into the cove of the *piccola marina*. There Augusto was waiting our arrival, the old fisher was ready with a bench, and we took the upper side of Capri.

My pen lingers on the subject, yet it is time to leave. When the day of our departure came, I wished for a *tramontana*, that we might be detained until the morrow; but no, it was a mild sirocco, setting directly towards Sorrento, and Antonio had come over, although, this time, without any prediction of a fine day. At the last fatal and prosaic moment, when the joys that are over must be paid for, we found Don Michele and Manfred as honest as they had been kind and attentive. Would we not come back some time? asked the Don. Certainly we will.

When the sail was set, and our foamy track pointed to the dear isle we were leaving, I, at least, was conscious of a slight heart-ache. So I turned once more and cried out, "*Addio, Capri!*" but the stern Tiberian rocks did not respond, "*Ritornate!*" and so Capri passed into memory.

A TRIP TO ISCHIA.

The island of Ischia, rising like a loftier Salamis at the northern entrance of the Bay of Naples, is so unlike its opposite sentinel, Capri, that the landscape-painter, to whom the peculiarities of mountain forms are as familiar as to the geologist, would pronounce as readily on the diversity of its origin. The latter might say: "This island is Plutonic, that Neptunic;" and the former: "Here are long, finely broken outlines, and sharp, serrated summits; yonder, broad masses and sudden, bold escarpments;" but both would express the same fact in different dialects. The two islands are equidistant from the main land; they occupy the same relative position to the bay and to the central Vesuvian peak; they are equally noble land-marks to the mariners coming from the Tyrrhene or the Ionian Sea. Here the resemblance ends. Capri is the resort of artists, Ischia of invalids. Tiberius and the Blue Grotto belong to the litany of travel; but Ischia — larger, richer, more accessible than Capri — has no such special attractions to commend it. It must be sought for its own sake.

The little steamer upon which I embarked at Naples was called the *Tifeo*, from Typhœus, the Titan who lies buried under Epomeo, like Enceladus under Etna. The decks were crowded; but every face was Italian, and every tongue uttered the broad, barbaric dialect of Southern Italy. Priests, peasant-women, small traders, sailors, and fishermen were mingled in a motley mass, setting their faces together in earnest gossip, and turning their backs upon sea, shore, and sky. As we passed Castell' dell' Ovo, the signs of the recent terrible land-slide on the rock of Pizzofalcone drew their attention for a minute; and I, too, looked with a shudder at the masses of rock under which I had lived, unsuspectingly, until within three days of the catastrophe. The house wherein we had chosen quarters was crushed to atoms; and, although nearly a month had elapsed, the great pile of ruin was not yet cleared away.

Onward over the bright blue sea, — past the shores of Posilippo, the marine villa of Lucullus, and the terraced steep, yonder, where the poet Silius Italicus kept sacred the tomb of his master, Virgil, — past the burnt-out crater of Nisida, and the high, white houses of Pozzuoli, until the bay of Baiæ opens to the right, and we fetch a compass for the ancient Cape Misenum. How these names stir the blood! Yet my fellow-voyagers never lifted their eyes to the shores; and if they mentioned the names, it was, perhaps, to say, "I bought some pigs at Baiæ the other day," or, "What is land worth about Lake Avernus?" or, "Do you raise pumpkins at Cumæ?"

Between Cape Misenum and the island of Procida there is a strait two or three miles in width. The town of Procida rests on the water like a long, white wedge, the butt of which bears up the immense old fortress. Approaching from Naples, the whole island lies before the loftier Ischia like Imbros before Samothrace, and seems to belong to it, as ancient geographers declare that it once did. The town is like a seaport of the Grecian Archipelago, and, as seen from the water, one could not wish it cleaner or less irregular. Fronting the sea, it presents a crescent of tall white houses, broken with arched balconies, and deep, scattered windows, and stained with patches of gray and moss-green. Over the domed roofs rises here and there a palm. The castle to the left, on its rock, rejoices in its ancient strength, and seems to command the Bay of Gaeta as well as that of Naples.

I tried to recall something of the history of Procida, and struck in the middle of the thirteenth century on the famous Giovanni, — "John of Procida," — before and after whom there was a blank. The island once belonged to him *in toto*, and must have been a goodly possession. I believe he lost it for a time, on account of the part which he took in the Sicilian Vespers. Meanwhile the steamer came to a stop in the little port, and boats crowded about the gangways. I determined to go the length of the island towards Ischia by land, and so scrambled down with the rest.

I landed on a narrow quay, so filthy and malodorous that I made haste to accept the guidance of the first boy who offered his services. He led me into a street just as bad; but, as we mounted towards the castle, the aspect of the town improved. This is the only place in Italy where the holiday costume is Greek, and one might therefore expect to find faces of the Hellenic type; yet such are fewer than on Capri. The costume disappears more and more, and only on grand festas do the women appear in bodices embroidered with gold, and gowns edged with the ancient labyrinth pattern. They have splendid eyes, like all the islanders; but I saw no beauties in my rapid march across Procida.

After the view from the castle, there is really nothing of interest in the little town. The island is low and nearly level, so that the high walls which inclose the road shut out all view of its vineyards and gardens. The eastern shore, near which my path led, is formed by three neighboring craters, the rims of which are broken down on the seaside, and boats anchor on the lava of the bottoms. The road was almost a continuous street, the suburb of Procida running into that of the large village of L' Olmo. A crowd of wayfarers went to and fro, and in all the open arches women sat spinning in the sun. There were no beggars; one of the women, indeed, called across the road to another, as I passed, "Ask him for a bajocco!" but the latter laughed, and turned her head aside. Although so little of the island was to be seen, there was no end to the pictures made by the windings of the road, the walls draped with fern and ivy, the deep arches of shade with bright, sunlit court-yards behind them, and the quaint terraces overhung with vines.

A walk of two miles brought me to the western shore, where the road descended to the fishing hamlet of Chiaiolella. The place seemed to be deserted; I walked between the silent old houses, and had nearly reached the beach, when a brown old mariner glided out from the shadow of a buttress, and followed me. Some boats lay on the sand in the little land-locked crater-bay; and presently three other men, who had been sleeping somewhere in the corners, came forward, scenting a fee. Of course they asked too much; but, to my surprise, they gradually abated the demand, although there was no competition. The old man said, very frankly, "If you give us a franc apiece, we shall only make ten sous, and we should like to earn a little more." We thereupon soon came to terms; two of them carried me into the boat, and we set off for Ischia.

Just beyond the last point of Procida rises the rocky island of Vivara, which is nothing but a fragment left from the ruin of a volcanic crater. Its one slanting side is covered with olive-trees, and a single house stands on the summit. The landing-place is a rocky shelf a yard or so in width, only accessible when the sea is quite smooth. The island belongs to Signor Scotti, of Procida, so the boatmen told me, but he is too shrewd to live upon it. As we floated past it into the open strait, the Bay of Gaeta opened broadly on the right, stretching away to the far Cape of Circe, beyond Terracina. In front Ischia, grand in its nearness, possessed the sea. One is here still in Odyssean waters. Here Homer once sailed, so sure as there ever was a Homer, and heard Typhœus groaning under Inarime. What Kinglake so finely says of the Troad is here equally true. The theories of scholars go to the winds; one learns to believe in Homer, no less than in Moses.

The picture of Ischia, from the sea, is superb. In front

towers the castle, on a thrice bolder and broader wedge of rock than that of Procida; withdrawn behind it, as if for protection, the white crescent of the town sweeps along the water; garden-groves rise in the rear, then great, climbing slopes of vine, and, high over all, Monte Epomeo converges the broken outlines of the island, and binds them together in his knotted peak. The main features are grandly broad and simple, yet there is an exquisite grace and harmony in the minor forms of the landscape. As we ran under the shadows of the castle-rock, whereon the Marquis Pescara was born, my thoughts were involuntarily directed to two women, — his sister, the heroic Costanza, whose defense of the castle gave the governorship of Ischia to her family for two hundred and fifty years; and his wife, Vittoria Colonna. Her, however, we remember less as the Marchesa Pescara than as the friend of Michael Angelo, in whose arms she died. Theirs was the only friendship between man and woman, which the breath of that corrupt age did not dare to stain, — noble on both sides, and based on the taste and energy and intellect of both. Vittoria, of whom Ariosto says, —

> "Vittoria è 'l nome; e ben conviensi a nata
> Fra le vittorie,"

retired to this castle of Ischia to mourn her husband's death. Strange that her sorrow excites in us so little sympathy; while, at this distance of time, the picture of Michael Angelo after her death gives us a pang. Moral, — it is better to be the friend of a great artist than the wife of a great general.

The landing at Ischia is as attractive as that at Procida is repulsive. The town comes down to the bright, sunny quay in a broad, clean street; the houses are massive, and suggestive of comfort, and there are glimpses of the richest gardens among them. "You must go to the *locanda nobile*," said the sailors; and to make sure they went with me. It is, in fact, the only tolerable inn in the place; yet my first impression was not encouraging. The locanda consisted of a large hall, filled with mattresses, a single bare bedroom, and the landlord's private quarters. The only person I saw was a one-eyed youth, who came every five minutes, while I sat watching the splendid sunset illumination of the castle and sea, to ask, " Shall I make your soup with rice or macaroni?" " Will you have your fish fried or *in umido* ?" Notwithstanding all this attention, it was a most meagre dinner which he finally served, and I longed for the fleshpots of Capri. In spite of Murray, artists are not stoics, and where they go the fare is wont to be good. The English guide says, very complacently : " Such or such an hotel is third-rate, *patronized by artists!*" or, " The accommodations are poor ; *but artists may find them sufficient!* " — as if " artists " had no finer habits of palate or nerves ! When I contrasted Pagano's table in Capri with that of the *nobile locanda* of Ischia, I regretted that artists had not been staying at the latter.

In walking through the two cold and barren rooms of the hotel I had caught a glimpse, through an open door, of a man lying in bed, and an old Franciscan friar, in a brown gaberdine, hanging over him. Now, when my Lenten dinner (although it was Carnival) was finished, the *padrona* came to me, and said: " Won't you walk in and see Don Michele ? He's in bed, sick, but he can talk, and it will pass away the time for him."

" But the Frate " — here I hesitated, thinking of extreme unction.

" O, never mind the Frate," said the *padrona ;* " Don Michele knows you are here, and he wants to have a talk with you."

The invalid landlord was a man of fifty, who lay in bed, groaning with a fearful lumbago, as he informed me. At the foot of the bed sat the old friar, gray-headed, with a snuffy upper lip, and an expression of amiable imbecility on his countenance. The one-eyed servant was the landlord's son; and there were two little daughters, one of whom, Filomena, carried the other, Maria Teresa. There was also a son, a sailor, absent in Egypt. "Four left out of twelve," said Don Michele; "but you notice there will soon be thirteen; so I shall have five, if the Lord wills it."

"And so you are from America," he continued; "my son was there, but, whether in North or South, I don't know. They say there is cholera in Africa, and I hope the saints will protect him from it. Here on Ischia — as perhaps you don't know — we never had the cholera; we have a saint who keeps it away from the island. It was San Giuseppe della Croce, and nobody can tell how many miracles he has wrought for us. He left a miraculous plant, — it's inside the castle, — and there it grows to this day, with wonderful powers of healing; but no one dares to touch it. If you were to so much as break a leaf, all Ischia would rise in revolution."

"What a benefit for the island!" I remarked.

"Ah, you may well say that!" exclaimed Don Michele. "Here everything is good, — the fish, the wine, the people. There are no robbers among us, — no, indeed! You may go where you like, and without fear, as the Frate will tell you. This is my brother" (pointing to the friar). "I am affiliated with the Franciscans, and so he comes to keep me company."

The friar nodded, took a pinch of snuff, and smiled in the vague, silly way of a man who don't know what to say.

"I have met many of your brethren in the Holy Land," I said, to the latter.

"Gran Dio! you have been there?" both exclaimed.

I must needs tell them of Jerusalem and Jericho, of Nazareth and Tiberias; but Don Michele soon came back to America. "You are one of the nobility, I suppose?" he said.

"What!" I answered, affecting a slight indignation; "don't you know that we have no nobility? All are equal before the law, and the poorest man may become the highest ruler, if he has the right degree of intelligence." (I was about to add, *and honesty*, but checked myself in time.)

"Do you hear that?" cried Don Michele to the friar. "I call that a fine thing."

"*Che bella cosa!*" repeated the friar, as he took a fresh pinch of snuff.

"What good is your nobility?" I continued. "They monopolize the offices, they are poor and proud, and they won't work. The men who do the most for Italy are not nobles."

"True! true! listen to that!" said Don Michele. "And so, in America, all have an equal chance?"

"If you were living there," I answered, "your son, if he had talents, might become the governor of a State, or a minister to a foreign court. Could he be that here, whatever might be his intellect?"

"*Gran Dio! Che bella cosa!*" said the friar.

"It is the balance of Astræa!" cried Don Michele, forgetting his lumbago, and sitting up in bed. I was rather astonished at this classical allusion; but it satisfied me that I was not improvidently wasting my eloquence; so I went on: —

"What is a title? Is a man any the more a man for having it? He may be a duke and a thief, and, if so, I put him far below an honest fisherman. Are there titles in heaven?" Here I turned to the friar.

"Behold! A noble — a beautiful word!" cried the Don again. The friar lifted his hands to heaven, shook his head in a melancholy way, and took another pinch of snuff.

We were in a fair way to establish the universal fraternal republic, when a knock at the door interrupted us. It was Don Michele's sister, accompanied by an old man, and a young one, with a handsome but taciturn face.

"Ah, here is my *figliuccio!*" said Don Michele, beckoning forward the latter. "He will furnish a donkey, and guide you all over Ischia — up to the top of Epomeo, to Fori', and Casamich'."

Now I had particularly requested a young and jovial fellow, not one of your silent guides, who always hurry you forward when you want to pause, and seem to consider you as a bad job, to be gotten rid of as soon as possible. Giovanni's was not the face I desired, but Don Michele insisted stoutly that he was the very man for me; and so the arrangement was concluded.

I went to bed, feeling more like a guest of the family than a stranger; and, before sleeping, determined that I would make an experiment. The rule in Italy is, that the man who does not bargain in advance is inevitably cheated; here, however, it seemed that I had stumbled on an unsophisticated region. I would make no bargains, ask no mistrustful questions, and test the natural honesty of the people.

Mounted on the ass, and accompanied by Giovanni, I left the *locanda nobile* the next morning to make the tour of the island. "Be sure and show him everything and tell him everything!" cried Don Michele, from his bed; whereat Giovanni, with a short "Yes!" which promised nothing to my ear, led the way out of the town.

We ascended the low hill on which the town is built, under high garden walls, overhung by the most luxuriant foliage of orange and olive. There were fine cypresses, — a tree rare in Southern Italy, — and occasional palms. We very soon emerged into the country, where Epomeo towered darkly above us, in the shadow of clouds which the sirocco had blown from the sea. The road was not blinded by walls, as on Procida, but open and broad, winding forward between vineyards of astonishing growth. Here the threefold crops raised on the same soil, about Naples and Sorrento, would be impossible. In that rich volcanic earth wheat is only the *parterre* or ground-floor of cultivation. The thin shade of the olive, or the young leaves of vine, do not intercept sun enough to hinder its proper maturity; and thus oil or wine (or sometimes both) becomes a higher crop, a *bel étage;* while the umbrella-pines, towering far above all, constitute an upper story for the production of lumber and firewood. Ischia has the same soil, but the vine, on account of the superior quality of its juice, is suffered to monopolize it. Stems of the thickness of a man's leg are trained back and forth on poles thirty feet high. The usual evergreen growths of this region, which make a mimicry of summer, have no place here; far and wide, high and low, the landscape is gray with vines and poles. I can only guess what a Bacchic labyrinth it must be in the season of vintage.

The few trees allowed to stand were generally fig or walnut. There are no orange-groves, as about Sorrento, for the reason that the wine of Ischia, being specially imported to mix with and give fire and temper to other Italian wines, is a very profitable production. The little island has a population of about thirty thousand, very few of whom are poor, like the inhabitants of Capri. During my trip I encountered but a single beggar, who was an old woman on crutches. Yet, although the fields were gray, the banks beside the road were bright with young grass, and gay with violets, anemones, and the golden blossoms of the broom.

On our left lay the long slopes of Monte Campagnano, which presents a rocky front to the sea. Between this mountain and Epomeo the road traversed a circular valley, nearly a mile in diameter, as superbly rich as any of the favored gardens of Syria. The aqueduct which brings water from the mountains to the town of Ischia crosses it on lofty stone arches. Beyond this valley, the path entered a singular winding ravine thirty or forty feet in depth, and barely wide enough for two asses to pass each other. Its walls of rock were completely hidden in mosses and ferns, and old oak-trees, with ivied trunks, threw their arms across it. The country people, in scarlet caps and velvet jackets, on their way to enjoy the *festa* (the Carnival) at the villages, greeted me with a friendly "*buon dì!*" I was constantly reminded of those exquisitely picturesque passes of Arcadia, which seem still to be the haunts of Pan and the Nymphs.

Bishop Berkeley, whose happiest summer (not even excepting that he passed at Newport) was spent on Ischia, must have frequently travelled that path; and, without having seen more of the island, I was quite willing to accept his eulogies of its scenery. I had some difficulty, however, in adjusting to the reality Jean Paul's imaginary description, which it is conventional to praise, in Germany. The mere enumeration of orange-trees, olives, rocks, chestnut woods, vines, and blue sea, blended into a glimmering whole, with no distinct outlines, does not constitute description of scenery. An author ventures upon dangerous ground, when he attempts to paint landscapes which he has never seen. Jean Paul had the clairvoyant faculty of the poet, and was sometimes able to "make out" (to use Charlotte Brontë's expression) Italian atmospheres and a tolerable dream of scenery; but he would have described Ischia very differently if he had ever visited the island.

Winding on and upward through the ravine, I emerged at last on the sunny hillside, whence there was a view of the sea beyond Monte Campagnano. A little further, we reached the village of Barano, on the southeastern slope of Epomeo — a deep, gray gorge below it, and another village beyond, sparkling in the sun. The people were congregated on the little piazza, enjoying the day in the completest idleness. The place was a picture in itself, and I should have stopped to sketch it, but Giovanni pointed to the clouds which were hovering over Epomeo, and predicted rain. So I pushed on to Moropano, the next village, the southern side of the island opening more clearly and broadly to view. A succession of vine-terraces mounted from the sea to a height of two thousand feet, ceasing only under the topmost crags. At intervals, however, the slopes were divided by tremendous fissures, worn hundreds of feet deep through the ashen soil and volcanic rock. Wherever a little platform of shelving soil had been left on the sides of the sheer walls, it was covered with a growth of oaks.

The road obliged me to cross the broadest of these chasms, and, after my donkey had once fallen on the steep path notched along the rock, I judged it safest to climb the opposite side on foot. A short distance further we came to another fissure, as deep but much narrower, and resembling the cracks produced by an earthquake. The rocky walls were excavated into wine-cellars, the size of which, and of the tuns within, gave good token of the Ischian vintages. Out of the last crevice we climbed to the village of Fontana, the highest on the island. A review of the National Guards was held in a narrow open space before the church. There were perhaps forty men — fishermen and vine-growers — under arms, all with military caps, although only half a dozen had full uniforms. The officers fell back to make room for me, and I passed the company slowly in review, as I rode by on the donkey. The eyes were "right," as I commenced, but they moved around to left, curiously following me, while the heads remained straight. Gallant-looking fellows they were nevertheless; and moreover, it was pleasant to see a militia system substituted for the former wholesale conscription.

At the end of the piazza, a dry laurel-bush hanging over the door, denoted a wine-shop; and Giovanni and I emptied a bottle of the Fontana vintage before going further. I ordered a dinner to be ready on our return from Epomeo, and we then set out for the hermitage of San Nicola, on the very summit. In a ravine behind the village we met a man carrying almost a stack of straw on his head, his body so concealed by it that the mass seemed to be walking upon its own feet. It stopped on approaching us, and an unintelligible voice issued from it; but Giovanni understood the sounds.

"The hermit of San Nicola is sick," he said; "this is his brother."

"Then the hermit is alone on the mountain?" I asked.

"No, he is now in Fontana. When he gets sick, he comes down, and his brother goes up in his place, to keep the lamp a-burning."

We were obliged to skirt another fissure for some distance, and then took to the open side of the mountain, climbing between fields where the diminishing vines struggled to drive back the mountain gorse and heather. In half an hour the summit was gained, and I found myself in front of a singular, sulphur-colored peak, out of which a chapel and various chambers had been hewn. A man appeared, breathless with climbing after us, and proved to be the moving principle of the straw-stack. He unlocked a door in the peak, and allowed the donkey to enter; then, conducting me by a passage cut in the living rock, he led the way through, out of the opposite side, and by a flight of rude steps, around giddy corners, to a platform about six feet square, on the very topmost pinnacle of the island, 2,700 feet above the sea.

Epomeo was an active volcano until just before Vesuvius awakened, in A. D. 79; and as late as the year 1302 there was an eruption on Ischia, at the northern base of the mountain. But the summit now scarcely retains the crater form. The ancient sides are broken in, leaving four or five jagged peaks standing apart; and these, from the platform on which I stood, formed a dark, blasted foreground, shaped like a star with irregular rays, between which I looked down and off on the island, the sea, and the Italian shores. The clouds, whose presence I had lamented during the ascent, now proved to be marvelous accessories. Swooping so low that their skirts touched me, they covered the whole vault of heaven, down to the sea horizon, with an impenetrable veil; yet, beyond their sphere, the sunshine poured full upon the water, which became a luminous under-sky, sending the reflected light *upward* on the island landscape. In all my experience, I have never beheld such a phenomenon. Looking southward, it was scarcely possible not to mistake the sea for the sky; and this illusion gave the mountain an immeasurable, an incredible height. All the base of the island — the green shores and shining towns visible in deep arcs between the sulphury rocks of the crater — basked in dazzling sunshine; and the gleam was so intense and golden under the vast, dark roof of cloud, that I know not how to describe it. From the Cape of Circe to that of Palinurus, two hundred miles of the main-land of Italy were full in view. Vesuvius may sweep a wider horizon, but the view from Epomeo, in its wondrous originality, is far more impressive.

When I descended from the dizzy pinnacle, I found Giovanni and the hermit's brother drying their shirts before a fire of brush. The latter, after receiving a fee for his services, begged for an additional fee for St. Nicholas. "What does St. Nicholas want with it?" I asked. "*You* will buy food and drink, I suppose, but the saint needs nothing." Giovanni turned away his head, and I saw that he was laughing.

"O, I can burn a lamp for the saint," was the answer.

Now, as St. Nicholas is the patron of children, sailors, and travellers, I might well have lit a lamp in his honor; but as I could not stay to see the oil purchased and the lamp lighted, with my own eyes, I did not consider that there was sufficient security in the hermit's brother for such an investment.

When I descended to Fontana the review was over, and several of the National Guards were refreshing themselves in the wine-shop. The black-bearded host, who looked like an affectionate bandit, announced that he had cooked a pig's liver for us, and straight-way prepared a table in the shop beside the counter. There was but one plate, but Giovanni, who kept me company, ate directly from the dish. I have almost a Hebrew horror of fresh pork; but since that day I confess that a pig's liver, roasted on skewers, and flavored with the smoke of burning myrtle, is not a dish to be despised. Eggs and the good Ischian wine completed the repast; and had I not been foolish enough to look at the host as he wiped out the glasses with his unwashed fingers, I should have enjoyed it the more.

The other guests were very jolly, but I could comprehend little of their jargon when they spoke to each other. The dialect of Ischia is not only different from that of Capri, but varies on different sides of the island. Many words are identical with those used on Sardinia and Majorca; they have a clear, strong ring, which — barbaric as it may be — I sometimes prefer to the pure Italian. For instance, *freddo* (with a tender lingering on the double *d*) suggests to me only a bracing, refreshing coolness, while in the Ischian *frett* one feels the sharp sting of frost. Filicaja's pathetic address to Italy, —

"Deh fossi tu men bella, o almen più forte!"

might also be applied to the language. The elision of the terminal vowels, which is almost universal in this part of Italy, roughens the language, certainly, but gives it a more masculine sound.

When the people spoke to me, they were more careful in the choice of words, and so made themselves intelligible. They were eager to talk and ask questions, and after one of them had broken the ice by pouring a bottle of wine into a glass, while he drank from the latter as fast as he poured, the Captain of the Guard, with many apologies for the liberty, begged to know where I came from.

"Now tell me, if you please," he continued, "whether your country is Catholic or Protestant?"

"Neither," said I; "it is better than being either."

The people pricked up their ears, and stared. "How do you mean?" some one presently asked.

"All religions are free. Catholics and Protestants have equal rights; and that is best of all — is it not?"

There was a unanimous response. "To be sure that is best of all!" they cried; "*avete ragione.*"

"But," said the Captain, after a while, "what religion is your government?"

"None at all," I answered.

"I don't understand," said he; "surely it is a Christian government."

It was easy to explain my meaning, and I noticed that the village magistrate, who had entered the shop, listened intently. He was cautiously quiet, but I saw that the idea of a separation of Church and State was not distasteful to the people. From religion we turned to politics, and I gave them a rough sketch of our republican system. Moreover, as a professed friend of Italian nationality, I endeavored to sound them in regard to their views of the present crisis. This was more delicate ground; yet two or three spoke their minds with tolerable plainness, and with more judgment and moderation than I expected to find. On two points all seemed to be agreed, — that the people must be educated, and must have patience.

In the midst of the discussion a mendicant friar appeared, barefooted, and with a wallet on his shoulder. He was a man of thirty, of tall and stately figure, and with a singularly noble and refined countenance. He did not beg, but a few bajocchi were handed to him, and the landlord placed a loaf of bread on the counter. As he was passing me, without asking alms, I gave him some money, which he took with a slight bow and the words, "Providence will requite you." Though so coarsely dressed, he was not one of those friars who seem to think filth necessary to their holy character. I have rarely seen a man whose features and bearing harmonized so ill with his vocation. He looked like a born teacher and leader; yet he was a useless beggar.

The rain, which had come up during dinner, now cleared away, and I resumed my journey. Giovanni, who had made one or two desperate efforts at jollity during the ascent of the mountain, was remarkably silent after the conversation in the inn, and I had no good of him thenceforth. A mistrustful Italian is like a tortoise; he shuts up his shell, and crow-bars can't open him. I have not the least doubt that Giovanni believed, in his dull way, in the temporal power of the Pope and the restoration of the Bourbons.

There were no more of the great volcanic fissures to be crossed. The road, made slippery by the rain, descended so rapidly that I was forced to walk during the remainder of the day's journey. It was a country of vines, less picturesque than I had already passed; but the sea and southwestern shore of the island were constantly in view. I first reached the little village of Serrara, on a projecting spur of Epomeo; then, after many steep and rugged descents, came upon the rich garden-plain of Panza. Here the surface of the island is nearly level, the vegetation is wonderfully luxuriant, and the large gray farm-houses have a stately and commanding air. In another hour, skirting the western base of Epomeo, the towers of Foria, my destination for the night, came into view. There were some signs of the Carnival in the lively streets — here and there a mask, followed by shouting and delighted children; but the greater part of the inhabitants contented themselves with sitting on the doorsteps and exchanging jokes with their neighbors.

The guide-book says there is no inn in Foria. Don Michele, however, assured me that Signor Scotti kept a *locanda* for travellers, and I can testify that the Don is right. I presume it is "noble," also, for the accommodations were like those in Ischia. On entering, I was received by a woman, who threw back her shoulders and lifted her head in such an independent way that I asked, "Are you the padrona?"

"No," she answered, laughing; "I'm the *modestica;* but that will do just as well." (She meant *domestica,* but I like her rendering of the word so well that I shall retain it.)

"Can you get me something for dinner?"

"Let us see," said she, counting upon her fingers; "fish, that's one; kid, that's two; potatoes, that's three; and — and — surely there's something else."

"That will do," said I; "and eggs?"

"*Sicuro!* Eggs? I should think so. And so that will suit your Excellency!"

Thereupon the *modestica* drew back her shoulders, threw out her chest, and, in a voice that half Foria might have heard, sang I know not what song of triumph as she descended to the kitchen. Signor Scotti, for whom a messenger had been sent, now arrived. He had but one eye, and I began to imagine that I was on the track of the Arabian Prince. After a few polite commonplaces, I noticed that he was growing uneasy, and said, "Pray, let me not keep you from the Carnival."

"Thanks to your Excellency," said he, rising; "my profession calls me, and with your leave I will withdraw." I supposed that he might be a city magistrate, but on questioning the *modestica,* when she came to announce dinner, I found that he was a barber.

I was conducted into a bedroom, in the floor of which the *modestica* opened a trap-door, and bade me descend a precipitous flight of steps into the kitchen. There the table was set, and I received my eggs and fish directly from the fire. The dessert was peculiar, consisting of raw stalks of anise, cut off at the root, very tough, and with a sickly sweet flavor. Seeing that I rejected them, the *modestica* exclaimed, in a strident voice, —

"Eh? What would you have? They are beautiful, — they are superb! The gentry eat them, — nay, what do I know? — the King himself, and the Pope! Behold!" And with these words she snatched a stalk from the plate, and crunched it between two rows of teeth which it was a satisfaction to see.

Half an hour afterwards, as I was in the bedroom which had been given to my use, a horribly rough voice at my back exclaimed, "What do you want?"

I turned, and beheld an old woman as broad as she was short, — a woman with fierce eyes and a gray mustache on her upper lip.

"What do *you* want?" I rejoined.

She measured me from head to foot, gave a grunt, and said, "*I'm* the padrona here."

I was a little surprised at this intrusion, and considerably more so, half an hour afterwards, as I sat smoking in the common room, at the visit of a gendarme, who demanded my passport. After explaining to him that the document had never before been required in free Italy, — that the law did not even oblige me to carry it with me, — I handed it to him.

He turned it up and down, and from side to side, with a puzzled air. "I can't read it," he said, at last.

"Of course you can't," I replied; "but there is no better passport in the world, and the Governor of Naples will tell you the same thing. Now," I added, turning to the padrona, "if you have sent for this officer through any suspicion of me, I will pay for my dinner and go on to Casamicciola, where they know how to receive travellers."

The old woman lifted up her hands, and called on the saints to witness that she did not mistrust me. The gendarme apologized for his intrusion, adding: "We are out of the way, here, and therefore I am commanded to do this duty. I cannot read your passport, but I can see that you are a *galantuomo*."

This compliment obliged me to give him a cigar, after which I felt justified in taking a little revenge. "I am a republican," I cried, " and a friend of the Italian Republicans! I don't believe in the temporal power of the Pope! I esteem Garibaldi!"

"Who doesn't esteem him?" said the old woman, but with an expression as if she didn't mean it. The gendarme twisted uneasily on his seat, but he had lighted my cigar, and did not feel free to leave.

I shall not here repeat my oration, which spared neither the Pope, nor Napoleon the Third, nor even Victor Emanuel. I was as fierce and reckless as Mazzini, and exhausted my stock of Italian in advocating freedom, education, the overthrow of priestly rule, and the abolition of the nobility. When I stopped to take breath, the gendarme made his escape, and the padrona's subdued manner showed that she began to be afraid of me.

In the evening there was quite an assemblage in the room, — two Neapolitan engineers, a spruce young Forian, a widow with an unintelligible story of grievances, and the never-failing *modestica*, who took her seat on the sofa, and made her tongue heard whenever there was a pause. I grew so tired with striving to unravel their dialect, that I fell asleep in my chair, and nearly tumbled into the brazier of coals; but the chatter went on for hours after I was in bed.

In the heavenly morning that followed I walked about the town, which is a shipping port of wine. The quay was piled with tuns, purple-stained. The situation of the place, at the foot of Epomeo, with all the broad Tyrrhene sea to the westward, is very beautiful, and, as usual, a Franciscan monastery has usurped the finest position. No gardens can be richer than those in the rear, mingling with the vineyards that rise high on the mountain slopes.

After the *modestica* had given me half a tumbler of coffee and a crust of bread for my breakfast, I mounted the donkey, and set out for Casamicciola. The road skirts the sea for a short distance, and then enters a wild dell, where I saw clumps of ilex for the first time on the island. After a mile of rugged, but very beautiful, scenery, the dell opened on the northern shore of Ischia, and I saw the bright town and sunny beach of Lacco below me. There was a sudden and surprising change in the character of the landscape. Dark, graceful carob-trees overhung the road; the near gardens were filled with almonds in light green leaf, and orange-trees covered with milky buds; but over them, afar and aloft, from the edge of the glittering sapphire to the sulphur-crags of the crowning peak, swept a broad, grand amphitheatre of villas, orchards, and vineyards. Gayly colored palaces sat on all the projecting spurs of Epomeo, rising above their piles of garden terraces; and, as I rode along the beach, the palms and cypresses in the gardens above me were exquisitely pencilled on the sky. Here everything spoke of old cultivation, of wealth and luxurious days.

In the main street of Lacco I met the gendarme of Foria, who took off his cocked hat with an air of respect, which, however, produced no effect on my donkey-man, Giovanni. We mounted silently to Casamicciola, which, as a noted watering-place, boasts of hotels with Neapolitan prices, if not comforts. I felt the need of one, and selected the Sentinella Grande on account of its lordly position. It was void of guests, and I was obliged to wait two hours for a moderate breakfast. The splendor of the day, the perfect beauty of the Ischian landscapes, and the soft humming of bees around the wall-flower blossoms, restored my lost power to enjoy the *dolce far niente*, and I had forgotten all about my breakfast when it was announced.

From Casamicciola it is little more than an hour's ride to Ischia, and my tour of the island lacked but that much of completion. The season had not commenced, and the marvelous healing fountains and baths were deserted; yet the array of stately villas, the luxury of the gardens, and the broad, well-made roads, attested the popularity of the watering-place. Such scenery as surrounds it is not surpassed by any on the Bay of Naples. I looked longingly up at the sunny mountain-slopes and shadowed glens, as I rode away. What I had seen was but the promise, the hint, of a thousand charms which I had left unvisited.

On the way to Ischia I passed the harbor, which is a deep little crater connected with the sea by an artificial channel. Beside it lies the Casino Reale, with a magnificent park, uninhabited since the Bourbons left. Beyond it I crossed the lava-fields of 1302, which are still unsubdued. Here and there a house has been built, some pines have been planted, clumps of broom have taken root, and there are a few rough, almost hopeless, beginnings of fields. Having passed this dreary tract, the castle of Ischia suddenly rose in front, and the bright town received me. I parted from the taciturn Giovanni without tears, and was most cordially welcomed by Don Michele, his wife, the one-eyed son, and the Franciscan friar. The Don's lumbago was not much better, and the friar's upper lip, it seemed to me, was more snuffy than ever.

In the evening I heard what appeared to be a furious altercation. I recognized Don Michele's voice, threatening vengeance, at its highest pitch, while another voice, equally excited, and the screams of women, gave additional breath to the tempest. But when I asked my one-eyed servitor, "What in Heaven's name has happened?" he mildly answered, "O, it's only the uncle *discoursing* with papa!"

I arose at dawn, the next day, to take the steamer for Naples. The flaming jets of Vesuvius, even against the glowing morning sky, were visible from my window, twenty-five miles distant. I was preparing to bid farewell to Ischia with a feeling of profound satisfaction. My experiment had succeeded remarkably well. I had made no bargains in advance, and had not been overcharged to the extent of more than five francs during the whole trip. But now came the one-eyed son, with a bill fifty per cent.

higher than at first, for exactly the same accommodation. This, too, after I had promised to send my friends to the *locanda nobile*, and he had written some very grotesque cards, which I was to disseminate.

Don Michele was calling me to say good-by. I went to his chamber, and laid the grotesque cards upon the bed. "Here!" I exclaimed; "I have no use for these. I shall recommend *no* friends of mine to this hotel. You ask another price now for the same service."

The Don's countenance fell. "But we kept the same room for you," he feebly urged.

"Of course you kept it," I said, "because you have no other, and nobody came to take it! This is not the balance of Astræa! You lament over the condition of Italy, — you say she has fallen behind the other nations of Europe, — and here is one of the causes! So long as you, and the people of whom you are one, are dishonest, — so long as you take advantage of strangers, — just so long will you lack the order, the security, the moral force which every people possess who are ashamed to descend to such petty arts of cheating!"

"*Ma — Signore!*" pleaded Don Michele.

"It is true!" I continued; "I, who am a friend of Italy, say it to you. You talk of corruption in high places, — begin your reforms at home! Learn to practice common honesty; teach your children to do it; respect yourselves sufficiently to be above such meanness, and others will respect you. What were my fine, my beautiful words worth to you? I thought I was sowing seed on good ground" —

"Signore, Signore, hear me!" cried the Don.

"I have only one word more to say, and that is *Addio!* and not *a rivederci!* I am going, and I shall not come back again."

Don Michele jumped up in bed, but I was already at the door. I threw it open, closed it behind me, and dashed down the stairs. A faint cry of "Signore!" followed me.

In two minutes more I was on the pier, waiting for the steamer to come around the point from Casamicciola. The sweet morning air cooled my excitement, and disposed me to gentler thoughts. I fancied Don Michele in his bed, mortified and repentant, and almost regretted that I had not given him a last chance to right himself in my eyes. Moreover, reviewing the incidents of my trip, I was amused at the part which I had played in it. Without the least intent or premeditation, I had assumed the character of a missionary of religious freedom, education, and the Universal Republic. But does the reader suppose that I imagine any word thus uttered will take root, and bring forth fruit, — that any idea thus accidentally planted will propagate itself further?

No, indeed!

THE LAND OF PAOLI.

The Leghorn steamer slid smoothly over the glassy Tyrrhene strait, and sometime during the night came to anchor in the harbor of Bastia. I sat up in my berth at sunrise, and looked out of the bull's eye to catch my first near glimpse of Corsican scenery; but, instead of that, a pair of questioning eyes, set in a brown, weather-beaten face, met my own. It was a boatman waiting on the gangway, determined to secure the only fare which the steamer had brought that morning. Such persistence always succeeds, and in this case justly; for when we were landed upon the quay, shortly afterwards, the man took the proffered coin with thanks, and asked for no more.

Tall, massive houses surrounded the little circular port. An old bastion on the left, — perhaps that from which the place originally took its name, — a church in front, and suburban villas and gardens on the shoulders of the steep mountain in the rear, made a certain impression of pride and stateliness, notwithstanding the cramped situation of the city. The Corsican coast is here very bold and abrupt, and the first advantage of defense interferes with the present necessity of growth.

At that early hour few persons were stirring in the streets. A languid officer permitted us to pass the *douane* and sanitary line; a large-limbed boy from the mountains became a porter for the nonce; and a waiter, not fully awake, admitted us into the "Hôtel d'Europe," a building with more space than cleanliness, more antiquated furniture than comfort. It resembled a dismantled palace — huge, echoing, dusty. The only tenants we saw then, or later, were the waiter aforesaid, who had not yet learned the ordinary wants of a traveller, and a hideous old woman, who twice a day deposited certain oily and indescribable dishes upon a table in a room which deserved the name of *manger*, in the English sense of the word.

However, I did not propose to remain long in Bastia; Corte, the old capital of Paoli, in the heart of the island, was my destination. After ascertaining that a diligence left for the latter place at noon, we devoted an hour or two to Bastia. The breadth and grandeur of the principal streets, the spacious new *place* with a statue of Napoleon in a Roman toga, the ample harbor in process of construction to the northward, and the fine coast-views from the upper part of the city, were matters of surprise. The place has grown rapidly within the past fifteen years, and now contains twenty-five thousand inhabitants. Its geographical situation is good. The dagger-shaped Cape Corso, rich with fruit and vines, extends forty miles to the northward; westward, beyond the mountains, lie the fortunate lands of Nebbio and the Balagna, while the coast southward has no other harbor for a distance of seventy or eighty miles. The rocky island of Capraja, once a menace of the Genoese, rises over the sea in the direction of Leghorn; directly eastward, and nearer, is Elba, and far to the southeast, faintly seen, Monte Cristo, — the three representing mediæval and modern history and romance, and repeating the triple interest which clings around the name of Corsica.

The growth of Bastia seems to have produced but little effect, as yet, on the character of the inhabitants. They have rather the primitive air of mountaineers; one looks in vain for the keenness, sharpness, and, alas! the dishonesty, of an Italian seaport town. Since the time of Seneca, who, soured by exile, reported of them, —

> "Prima est ulcisci lex, altera vivere raptu,
> Tertia mentiri, quarta negare Deos," —

the Corsicans have not been held in good repute. Yet our

first experience of them was by no means unprepossessing. We entered a bookstore, to get a map of the island. While I was examining it, an old gentleman, with the Legion of Honor in his button-hole, rose from his seat, took the sheet from my hands, and said: "What's this? what's this?" After satisfying his curiosity, he handed it back to me, and began a running fire of questions: "Your first visit to Corsica? You are English? Do you speak Italian? your wife also? Do you like Bastia? does she also? How long will you stay? Will she accompany you?" etc. I answered with equal rapidity, as there was nothing obtrusive in the old man's manner. The questions soon came to an end, and then followed a chapter of information and advice, which was very welcome.

The same naïve curiosity met us at every turn. Even the rough boy who acted as porter plied me with questions, yet was just as ready to answer as to ask. I learned much more about his situation and prospects than was really necessary, but the sum of all showed that he was a fellow determined to push his way in the world. Self-confidence is a common Corsican trait, which Napoleon only shared with his fellow-islanders. The other men of his time who were either born upon Corsica or lived there for a while — Pozzo di Borgo, Bernadotte, Massena, Murat, Sebastiani — seem to have caught the infection of this energetic, self-reliant spirit.

In Bastia there is neither art nor architecture. It is a well-built, well-regulated, bustling place, and has risen in latter years quite as much from the growth of Italian commerce as from the favor of the French government. From the quantity of small coasting craft in the harbor, I should judge that its trade is principally with the neighboring shores. In the two book-shops I found many devotional works and Renucci's History, but only one copy of the *Storiche Corse*, which I was glad to secure.

When the hour of departure came, we found the inquisitive old gentleman at the diligence office. He was our companion in the *coupé*, and apparently a personage of some note, as at least a score of friends came to bid him adieu. To each of these he announced in turn: "These are my travelling companions — an American gentleman and his wife. They speak French and Italian; they have never been in Corsica before; they are going to Corte; they travel for pleasure and information." Then there were reciprocal salutations and remarks; and if the postilion had not finally given the signal to take our places, we should soon have been on speaking terms with half Bastia.

The road ran due south, along the base of the mountains. As we passed the luxuriant garden-suburbs, our companion pointed out the dusky glitter of the orange-trees, and exclaimed: "You see what the Corsican soil produces. But this is nothing to the Balagna. There you will find the finest olive culture of the Mediterranean. I was prefect of the Balagna in 1836, and in that year the exportation of oil amounted to six millions of francs, while an equal quantity was kept for consumption in the island."

Brown old villages nestled high up in the ravines on our right; but on the left the plain stretched far away to the salt lake of Biguglia, the waters of which sparkled between the clumps of poplars and elms studding the meadows. The beds of the mountain streams were already nearly dry, and the summer malaria was beginning to gather on the low fields through which they wandered. A few peasants were cutting and tedding hay here and there, or lazily hauling it homewards. Many of the fields were given up to myrtle and other wild and fragrant shrubs; but there were far too few workers abroad for even the partial cultivation.

Beyond the lake of Biguglia, and near the mouth of the Golo River, is the site of Mariana, founded by Marius. Except a scattering of hewn stones, there are no remains of the Roman town; but the walls of a church and chapel of the Middle Ages are still to be seen. The only other Roman colony on Corsica — Aleria, at the mouth of the Tavignano — was a restoration of the more ancient Alalia, which tradition ascribes to the Phoceans. Notwithstanding the nearness of the island to the Italian coast, and its complete subjection to the Empire, its resources were imperfectly developed by the Romans, and the accounts of it given by the ancient writers are few and contradictory. Strabo says of the people: "Those who inhabit the mountains live from plunder, and are more untamable than wild beasts. When the Roman commanders undertake an expedition against the island, and possess themselves of the strongholds, they bring back to Rome many slaves; and then one sees with astonishment the savage animal nature of the people. For they either take their own lives violently, or tire out their masters by their stubbornness and stupidity; whence, no matter how cheaply they are purchased, it is always a bad bargain in the end."

Here we have the key to that fierce, indomitable spirit of independence which made the Genoese occupation one long story of warfare; which produced such heroes as Sambucuccio, Sampieri, and Paoli; and which exalted Corsica, in the last century, to be the embodiment of the democratic ideas of Europe, and the marvelous forerunner of the American Republic. Verily, Nature is "careful of the type." After the Romans, the Vandals possessed Corsica; then the Byzantine Greeks; then, in succession, the Tuscan Barons, the Pisans, and the Genoese — yet scarcely one of the political forms planted among them took root in the character of the islanders. The origin of the Corsican Republic lies back of all our history; it was a natural growth, which came to light after the suppression of two thousand years.

As we approached the gorge through which the Golo breaks its way to the sea, the town of Borgo, crowning a mountain summit, recalled to memory the last Corsican victory, when Clement Paoli, on the 1st of October, 1768, defeated and drove back to Bastia a French force much greater than his own. Clement, the brooding monk in his cloister, the fiery leader of desperate battle, is even a nobler figure than his brother Pascal in the story of those days.

We changed horses at an inn under the mountain of Borgo, and then entered the valley of the Golo, leaving the main road, which creeps onward to Bonifacio through lonely and malarious lands. The scenery now assumed a new aspect. No more the blue Tyrrhene Sea, with its dreams of islands; a valley wilder than any infolded among the Appenines opened before us. Slopes covered with chestnut groves rose on either side; slant ravines mounted between steep escarpments of rock; a village or two, on the nearer heights, had the appearance of refuge and defense, rather than of quiet habitation, and the brown summits in the distance held out no promise of softer scenes beyond.

Our companion, the prefect, pointed to the chestnut groves. "There," said he, "is the main support of our people in the winter. Our Corsican name for it is 'the bread tree.' The nuts are ground, and the cakes of chestnut-flour, baked on the hearth, and eaten while fresh, are really delicious. We could not live without the chestnut and the olive."

The steep upper slopes of the mountains were covered with the *macchia* — a word of special significance on the island. It is equivalent to "jungle" or "chaparral"; but the Corsican *macchia* has a character and a use of its own. Fancy an interminable thicket of myrtle, arbutus, wild laurel, lentisk, box, and heather, eight or twelve feet in height, interlaced with powerful and luxuriant vines, and with an undergrowth of rosemary, lavender, and sage. Between the rigid, stubby stems the wild boar can scarcely make his way; thorns and dagger-like branches meet above — yet the richest balm breathes from this impenetrable wilderness. When the people say of a man, "he has taken to the macchia," every one understands that he has committed a murder. Formerly, those who indulged in the fierce luxury of the *vendetta* sometimes made their home for years in the thickets, communicating privately, from time to time, with their families. But there is now no scent of blood lurking under that of the myrtle and lavender. Napoleon, who neglected Corsica during his years of empire (in fact, he seemed to dislike all mention of the island), remembered the odors of the macchia upon St. Helena.

Our second station was at a saw-mill beside the river. Here the prefect left us, saying: "I am going to La Porta, in the country of Morosaglia. It is a beautiful place, and you must come and see it. I have a ride of three hours, on horseback across the mountains, to get there."

His place in the *coupé* was taken by a young physician bound for Pontenuovo, further up the valley. I was struck by the singular loneliness of the country, as we advanced further into the interior. Neither in the grain-fields below, nor the olive-orchards above, was any laborer to be seen. Mile after mile passed by, and the diligence was alone on the highway. "The valley of the Golo is so unhealthy," said the physician, "that the people only come down to their fields at the time for ploughing, sowing, and reaping. If a man from the mountains spends a single night below here, he is likely to have an attack of fever."

"But the Golo is a rapid mountain stream," I remarked; "there are no marshes in the valley, and the air seems to me pure and bracing. Would not the country become healthy through more thorough cultivation?"

"I can only explain it," he answered, "by the constant variation of temperature. During the day there is a close heat, such as we feel now, while at night the air becomes suddenly chill and damp. As to agriculture, it don't seem to be the natural business of the Corsican. He will range the mountains all day, with a gun on his shoulder, but he hates work in the fields. Most of the harvesting on the eastern coast of the island, and in the Balagna, is done by the Lucchese peasants, who come over from the mainland every year. Were it not for them, the grain would rot where it stands."

This man's statement may have been exaggerated, but further observation convinced me that there was truth in it. Yet the people are naturally active and of a lively temperament, and their repugnance to labor is only one of the many consequences of the vendetta. When Paoli suppressed the custom with an iron hand, industry revived in Corsica; and now that the French government has succeeded in doing the same thing, the waste and pestilent lands will no doubt be gradually reclaimed.

The annals of the Corsican vendetta are truly something terrible. Filippini (armed to the teeth and protected by a stone wall, as he wrote) and other native historians estimate the number of murders from revenge in the three and a half centuries preceding the year 1729 at three hundred and thirty-three thousand, and the number of persons wounded in family feuds at an equal figure! Three times the population of the island killed or wounded in three hundred and fifty years! Gregorovius says: "If this island of Corsica could vomit back all the blood of battle and vendetta which it has drunk during the past ages, its cities and towns would be overwhelmed, its population drowned, and the sea be incarnadined as far as Genoa Verily, here the red Death planted his kingdom." France has at last, by two simple, practical measures, stayed the deluge. First, the population was disarmed; then the bandits and blood-outlaws were formed into a body of *Voltigeurs Corses*, who, knowing all the hiding-places in the macchia, easily track the fugitives. A few executions tamed the thirst for blood, and within the past ten years the vendetta has ceased to exist.

While we were discussing these matters with the physician, the diligence rolled steadily onwards, up the valley of the Golo. With every mile the scenery became wilder, browner, and more lonely. There were no longer villages on the hill-summits, and the few farm-houses perched beside the chestnut-orchards appeared to be untenanted. As the road crossed by a lofty stone arch to the southern bank of the river, the physician said: "This is Pontenuovo, and it is just a hundred years to-day since the battle was fought." He was mistaken; the battle of Pontenuovo, fatal to Paoli and to the independence of Corsica, took place on the 9th of May, 1769. It was the end of a struggle all the more heroic because it was hopeless from the start. The stony slopes on either side of the bridge are holy ground; for the Corsicans did not fight in vain. A stronger people beyond the sea took up the torch as it fell from their hands, and fed it with fresh oil. History (as it has hitherto been written) deals only with events, not with popular sympathies and enthusiasms; and we can therefore scarcely guess how profoundly the heart of the world was stirred by the name of Corsica, between the years 1755 and 1769. To Catharine of Russia as to Rousseau, to Alfieri as to Dr. Johnson, Paoli was one of the heroes of the century.

Beyond Pontenuovo the valley widens, and a level road carried us speedily to Ponte alla Leccia, at the junction of the Golo with its principal affluent, the Tartaglia. *Pontelech* and *Tartatch* are the Corsican words. Here the scenery assumes a grand Alpine character. High over the nearer mountains rose the broken summits of Monte Padro and Capo Bianco, the snow-filled ravines glittering between their dark pinnacles of rock. On the south, a by-road wandered away through the chestnut-woods to Morosaglia; villages with picturesque belfries overlooked the valley, and the savage macchia gave place to orchards of olive. Yet the character of the scenery was sombre, almost melancholy. Though the myrtle flowered snowily among the rocks, and the woodbine hung from the banks, and the river filled the air with the incessant mellow sound of its motion, these cheerful features lost their wonted effect beside the sternness and solitude of the mountains.

Towards the end of this stage the road left the Golo, and ascended a narrow lateral valley to the village of Omessa, where we changed horses. Still following the stream to its sources, we reached a spur from the central chain, and slowly climbed its sides to a higher region — a land of rocks and green pasture-slopes, from the level of which a wide sweep of mountains was visible. The summit of the pass was at least two thousand feet above the sea. On attaining it, a new and surprising vista opened to the southward, into the very heart of the island. The valley before us dropped in many windings into that of the Tavignano, the second river of Corsica, which we overlooked for an extent of thirty miles. Eastward the mountains sank into hills of gentle undulation, robed with orchards and vineyards, and crowned with villages; westward they towered into dark, forbidding ranges, and the snows of the great central peaks of Monte Rotondo and Monte d' Oro, nearly ten thousand feet in height, stood gray against the sunset. Generally, the landscapes of an island have a diminished, contracted character; but here the vales were as amply spread, the mountains as grandly planted, as if a continent lay behind them.

For two leagues the road descended, following the bays and forelands of the hills. The diligence sped downward so rapidly that before it was quite dusk we saw the houses and high rock fortress of Corte before us. A broad avenue of sycamores, up and down which groups of people were strolling, led into the town. We were set down at a hotel of primitive fashion, where we took quarters for the night, leaving the diligence, which would have carried us to Ajaccio by the next morning. Several French officials had possession of the best rooms, so that we were but indifferently lodged; but the mountain trout on the dinner-table were excellent, and the wine of Corte was equal to that of Tuscany.

While the moon, risen over the eastern mountains, steeps the valley in misty silver, and a breeze from the Alpine heights deliciously tempers the air, let us briefly recall that wonderful episode of Corsican history of which Pascal Paoli is the principal figure. My interest in the name dates from the earliest recollections of childhood. Near my birthplace there is an inn and cluster of houses named Paoli — or, as the people pronounce it, Peōli. Here twenty-three American soldiers were murdered in cold blood by the British troops, in September, 1777. Wayne's battle-cry at the storming of Stony Point was, "Remember Paoli!" The old tavern-sign was the half-length portrait of an officer (in a red coat, I think), whom, I was told, was "General Paoli," but I knew nothing further of him, until, some years later, I stumbled on Boswell's work; my principal authority, however, is a recent volume,[1] and the collection of Paoli's letters published by Tommasco.

It is unnecessary to review the long struggle of the Corsicans to shake off the yoke of Genoa; I need only allude to the fact. Pascal, born in 1724 or 1725, was the son of Hyacinth Paoli, who was chosen one of the chiefs of the people in 1734, and in connection with the other chiefs, Ceccaldi and Giaffori, carried on the war for independence with the greatest bravery and resolution, but with little success, for two years. In March, 1736, when the Corsicans were reduced to the last extremity, the Westphalian adventurer, Theodore von Neuhoff, suddenly made his appearance. The story of this man, who came ashore in a caftan of scarlet silk, Turkish trousers, yellow shoes, a

[1] *Histoire de Pascal Paoli*, par M. Bartoli. Largentiere, 1866.

Spanish hat and feather, and a sceptre in his right hand, and coolly announced to the people that he had come to be their king, is so fantastic as to be scarcely credible; but we cannot dwell upon it. His supplies of money and munitions of war, and still more his magnificent promises, beguiled those sturdy republicans into accepting the cheat of a crown. The fellow was not without ability, and but for a silly vanity, which led him to ape the state and show of other European courts, might have kept his place. His reign of eight months was the cause of Genoa calling in the aid of France; and, after three years of varying fortunes, the Corsicans were obliged to submit to the conditions imposed upon them by the French commander, Maillebois.

Hyacinth Paoli went into exile, and found a refuge at the court of Naples with his son Pascal. The latter was carefully educated in the school of Genovesi, the first Italian political-economist of the last century, and then entered the army, where he distinguished himself during campaigns in Sicily and Calabria. Thus sixteen years passed away.

The Corsicans, meanwhile, had continued their struggle under the leadership of Giaffori, another of the many heroes of the island. When, in 1753, he was assassinated, the whole population met together to celebrate his obsequies, and renewed the oath of resistance to death against the Genoese rule. Five chiefs (one of whom was Clement Paoli, Pascal's elder brother) were chosen to organize a provisional government and carry on the war. But at the end of two years it was found prudent to adopt a more practical system, and to give the direction of affairs into the hands of a single competent man. It was no doubt Clement Paoli who first suggested his brother's name. The military experience of the latter gave him the confidence of the people, and their unanimous voice called him to be their leader.

In April, 1755, Pascal Paoli, then thirty years old, landed at Aleria, the very spot where King Theodore had made his theatrical entry into Corsica nineteen years before. Unlike him, Paoli came alone, poor, bringing only his noble presence, his cultivated intelligence, and his fame as a soldier, to the help of his countrymen. "It was a singular problem," says one of the historians of Corsica; "it was a new experiment in history, and how it might succeed at a time when similar experiments failed in the most civilized lands would be to Europe an evidence that the rude simplicity of nature is more capable of adapting itself to democratic liberty than the refined corruption of culture can possibly be."

Paoli, at first reluctant to accept so important a post, finally yielded to the solicitations of the people, and on the 15th of July was solemnly invested with the Presidency of Corsica. His first step shows at once his judgment and his boldness. He declared that the vendetta must instantly cease; whoever committed blood-revenge was to be branded with infamy, and given up to the headsman. He traversed the island, persuading hostile families to bury their feuds, and relentlessly enforced the new law, although one of his relatives was the first victim. But he was not allowed to enter upon his government without resistance. Matra, one of the Corsican chiefs, was ambitious of Paoli's place, and for a year the island was disturbed with civil war. Matra claimed and received assistance from Genoa, and Paoli, defeated and besieged in the monastery of Bozio, was almost in the hands of his rival, when reinforcements appeared, headed by Clement and by Carnoni, a blood-enemy of the Paolis, forced by his noble mother to forswear the family enmity, and deliver instead of slay. Matra was killed, and thenceforth Paoli was the undisputed chief of Corsica.

It was not difficult for the people, once united, to withstand the weakened power of Genoa. That republic possessed only Bastia, Ajaccio, and Calvi; the garrisoning of which fortresses, by a treaty with France in 1756, was transferred to the latter power, in order to prevent them from falling into the hands of the Corsicans. The French proclaimed a neutrality which Paoli perforce was obliged to respect. He therefore directed his attention to the thorough political organization of the island, the development of its resources, and the proper education of its people. He had found the country in a lamentable condition when he returned from his exile. The greater part of the people had relapsed into semi-barbarism in the long course of war; agriculture was neglected, laws had fallen into disuse, the vendetta raged everywhere, and the only element from which order and industry could be evolved was the passionate thirst for independence, which had only been increased by defeat and suffering.

Paoli made the completest use of this element, bending it all to the purposes of government, and his success was truly astonishing. The new seaport of Isola Rossa was built in order to meet the necessity of immediate commerce; manufactories of all kinds, even powder-mills were established; orchards of chestnut, olive, and orange trees were planted, the culture of maize introduced, and plans made for draining the marshes and covering the island with a network of substantial highways. An educational system far in advance of the times was adopted. All children received at least the rudiments of education, and in the year 1765 the University of Corsica was founded at Corte. One provision of its charter was the education of poor scholars, who showed more than average capacity, at the public expense.

Paoli was obliged to base his scheme of government on the existing forms. He retained the old provincial and municipal divisions, with their magistrates and elders, making only such changes as were necessary to bind the scattered local jurisdictions into one consistent whole, to which he gave a *national* power and character. He declared the people to be the sole source of law and authority; that his office was a trust from their hands, and to be exercised according to their will and for their general good; and that the central government must be a house of glass, allowing each citizen to watch over its action. "Secrecy and mystery in governments," he said, "not only make a people mistrustful, but favor the growth of an absolute irresponsible power."

All citizens above the age of twenty-five years were entitled to the right of suffrage. Each community elected its own magistrates, but the voters were obliged to swear before the officials already in power, that they would nominate only the worthiest and most capable men as their successors. These local elections were held annually, but the magistrates were not eligible to immediate reëlection. A representative from each thousand of the population was elected to the General Assembly, which in its turn chose a Supreme Executive Council of nine members — one from each province of the island. The latter were required to be thirty-five years of age, and to have served as governors of their respective provinces. A majority of two thirds gave the decisions of the General Assembly the force of law; but the Council, in certain cases, had the right of veto, and the question was then referred for final decision to the next Assembly. Paoli was President of the Council and General-in-chief of the army. Both he and the members of the Council, however, were responsible to the nation, and liable to impeachment, removal, and punishment by the General Assembly.

Paoli, while enforcing a general militia system, took the strongest ground against the establishment of a standing army. "In a free land," he said, "every citizen must be a soldier, and ready to arm at any moment in defense of his rights. But standing armies have always served Despotism rather than Liberty." He only gave way that a limited number should be enrolled to garrison the fortified places. As soon as the people were sufficiently organized to resist the attempts which Genoa made from time to time to recover her lost dominion, he devoted his energies wholly to the material development of the island. The Assembly, at his suggestion, appointed two commissioners of agriculture for each province. The vendetta was completely suppressed; with order and security came a new prosperity, and the cities held by the *neutral* French began to stir with desires to come under Paoli's paternal rule.

The resemblance in certain forms as in the general spirit and character of the Constitution of the Corsican Republic to that of the United States, which was framed more than thirty years afterwards, is very evident. Indeed, we may say that the latter is simply an adaptation of the same political principles to the circumstances of a more advanced race and a broader field of action. But if we justly venerate the courage which won our independence and the wisdom which gave us our institutions, how shall we sufficiently honor the man and the handful of half-barbarous people who so splendidly anticipated the same great work! Is there anything nobler in history than the Corsican episode? No wonder that the sluggish soul of Europe, then beginning to stir with the presentiment of coming changes, was kindled and thrilled as not for centuries before. What effect the example of Corsica had upon the American Colonies is something which we cannot now measure. I like to think, however, that the country tavern-sign of " General Paoli," put up *before* the Revolution, signified more than the mere admiration of the landlord for a foreign hero.

At the end of ten years the Genoese Senate became convinced that the recovery of Corsica was hopeless; and when Paoli succeeded in creating a small fleet, under the command of Perez, Knight of Malta, they saw their Mediterranean commerce threatened with destruction. In the year 1767 the island of Capraja was captured by the Corsicans; then Genoa set the example which Austria has recently followed in the case of Venetia. A treaty was signed at Versailles on the 15th of May, 1768, between the French Minister, the Duke de Choiseul, and the Genoese Ambassador, whereby Genoa transferred to France all her right and title to the island of Corsica. This was a deathblow to the Republic; but the people armed and organized, determined to resist to the end. The splendid victory at Borgo gave them hope. They asked and expected the assistance of England; but when did England ever help a weak and struggling people? The battle of Pontenuovo, on the 9th of May, 1769, sealed the fate of the island. A month afterwards Paoli went into exile with three hundred of his countrymen. Among those who fled, after the battle, to the wild Alpine fastnesses of Monte Rotondo, was his secretary, Carlo Bonaparte, and the latter's wife, Letitia Ramolino, then seven months *enceinte* with the boy who afterwards made Genoa and France suffer the blood-revenge of Corsica. Living in caves and forests, drenched with rain, and almost washed away by the mountain torrents, Letitia bore her burden to Ajaccio, and Napoleon Bonaparte was one of the first Corsicans who were born Frenchmen.

Paoli's journey through Italy and Germany to England was a march of triumph. On reaching London he was received by the king in private audience; all parties joined in rendering him honor. A pension of two thousand pounds a year was granted to him (the greater part of which he divided among his fellow exiles), and he took up his residence in the country from which he still hoped the liberation of Corsica. For twenty years we hear of him as a member of that society which included Burke, Reynolds, Johnson, Garrick, and Goldsmith; keeping clear of parties, yet, we may be sure, following with an interest he hardly dared betray the events of the American struggle.

But the French revolution did not forget him. The Corsicans, in November, 1789, carried away by the republican movement in France, had voted that their island should be an integral part of the French nation. There was a general cry for Paoli, and in April 1790, he reached Paris. Lafayette was his friend and guide; the National Assembly received him with every mark of respect; the club of the *Amis de la Constitution* seated him beside its President — Robespierre; Louis XVI. gave him an audience, and he was styled by the enthusiastic populace "the Washington of Europe." At Marseilles he was met by a Corsican deputation, two of the members of which were Joseph and Napoleon Bonaparte, who sailed with him to their native island. On landing at Cape Corso, he knelt and kissed the earth, exclaiming, " O my country, I left thee enslaved and I find thee free ! " All the land rose to receive him ; *Te Deums* were chanted in the churches, and the mountain villages were depopulated to swell his triumphal march. In September of the same year the representatives of the people elected him President of the Council and General of the troops of the island.

Many things had been changed during his twenty years' absence, under the rule of France. It was not long before the people divided themselves into two parties — one French and ultra-republican ; the other Corsican, working secretly for the independence of the island. The failure of the expedition against Sardinia was charged to Paoli, and he was summoned by the Convention to appear and answer the charges against him. Had he complied, his head would probably have fallen under the all-devouring guillotine ; he refused, and his refusal brought the two Corsican parties into open collision. Paoli was charged with being ambitious, corrupt, and plotting to deliver Corsica to England. His most zealous defender was the young Napoleon Bonaparte, who wrote a fiery, indignant address, which I should like to quote. Among other things he says, " We owe *all* to him — even the fortune of being a republic ! "

The story now becomes one of intrigue and deception, and its heroic atmosphere gradually vanishes. Pozzo di Borgo, the blood-enemy of Napoleon, alienated Paoli from the latter. A fresh, cunning, daring intellect, he acquired a mischievous influence over the gray-haired, simple-hearted patriot. That which Paoli's enemies charged against him came to pass; he asked the help of England, and in 1794 the people accepted the sovereignty of that nation, on condition of preserving their institutions, and being governed by a viceroy, who it was presumed would be none other than Pascal Paoli. The English fleet, under Admiral Hood, speedily took possession of Bastia, Calvi, Ajaccio, and the other seaports. But the English government, contemptuously ignoring Paoli's services and claims, sent out Sir Gilbert Elliott as viceroy; and he, jealous of Paoli's popularity, demanded the latter's recall to England. George III. wrote a command under the form of an invitation; and in 1795, Paoli, disappointed in all his hopes, disgusted with the treatment he had received, and recognizing the hopelessness of healing the new dissensions among the people, left Corsica for the last time. He returned to his former home in London, where he died in 1807, at the age of eighty-two years. What little property he had saved was left to found a school at Stretta, his native village; and another at Corte, for fifteen years his capital. Within a year after his departure the English were driven out of Corsica.

Paoli rejoiced, as a Corsican, at Napoleon's ascendency in France. He illuminated his house in London when the latter was declared Consul for life, yet he was never recalled. During his last days on St. Helena, Napoleon regretted his neglect or jealousy of the old hero; his lame apology was, "I was so governed by political considerations, that it was impossible for me to obey my personal impulses!"

Our first object, on the morning after our arrival in

Corte, was to visit the places with which Paoli's name is associated. The main street conducted us to the public square, where stands his bronze statue, with the inscription on the pedestal: "À PASCAL PAOLI LA CORSE RECONNAISSANTE." On one side of the square is the Palazza, or Hall of Government; and there they show you his room, the window-shutters of which still keep their lining of cork, as in the days of assassination, when he founded the Republic. Adjoining it is a chamber where the Executive Council met to deliberate. Paoli's school, which still flourishes, is his best monument.

High over the town rises the battered citadel, seated on a rock which on the western side falls several hundred feet sheer down to the Tavignano. The high houses of brown stone climb and cling to the eastern slope, rough masses of browner rock thrust out among them; and the place thus has an irregular pyramidal form, which is wonderfully picturesque. The citadel was last captured from the Genoese by Paoli's forerunner, Giaffori, in the year 1745. The Corsican cannon were beginning to breach the walls, when the Genoese commander ordered Giaffori's son, who had previously been taken prisoner, to be suspended from the ramparts. For a moment — but only for a moment — Giaffori shuddered, and turned away his head; then he commanded the gunners, who had ceased firing, to renew the attack. The breach was effected, and the citadel taken by storm; the boy, unhurt amidst the terrible cannonade, was restored to his father.

We climbed towards the top of the rock by streets which resembled staircases. At last the path came to an end in some unsavory back-yards, if piles of shattered rock behind the houses can be so called. I asked a young fellow who was standing in the doorway, watching us, whether any view was to be had by going further.

"Yes," said he, "but there is a better prospect from the other house — yonder, where you see the old woman."

We clambered across the intervening rocks, and found the woman engaged in shearing a goat, which a boy held by the horns. "Certainly," she said, when I repeated the question; "Come into the house, and you shall look from the windows."

She led us through the kitchen into a bright, plainly furnished room, where four women were sewing. They all greeted us smilingly, rose, pushed away their chairs, and then opened the southern window. "Now look!" said the old woman.

We were dazzled by the brightness and beauty of the picture. The house was perched upon the outer angle of the rock, and the valley of the Tavignano, with the gorge through which its affluent, the Restonica, issues from the mountains, lay below us. Gardens, clumps of walnut and groves of chestnut trees, made the valley green; the dark hues of the mountains were softened to purple in the morning air, and the upper snows shone with a brilliancy which I have rarely seen among the Alps. The breeze came down to us with freshness on its wings, and the subdued voices of the twin rivers.

"Now the other window!" the women said.

It opened eastward. There were, first, the roofs of Corte, dropping away to the water-side; then a wide, bounteous valley, green, flecked with harvest gold; then village-crowned hills, and, behind all, the misty outlines of mountains that slope to the eastern shore. It is a fair land, this Corsica, and the friendly women were delighted when I told them so.

The people looked at us with a natural curiosity as we descended the hill. Old women, invariably dressed in black, gossiped or spun at the doors, girls carried water on their heads from the fountains below, children tumbled about on the warm stones, and a young mother, beside her cradle, sang the Corsican lullaby: —

"Ninni ninni, ninna nanna,
Ninni ninni, ninni nolu,
Allegrezza di la mamma,
Addormentati, o figliolu!"

There is another Corsican cradle song which has a singular resemblance to Tennyson's, yet it is quite unlikely that he ever saw it. One verse runs: —

"A little pearl-laden ship, my darling,
Thou carriest silken stores,
And with the silken sails all set
Com'st from the Indian shores,
And wrought with the finest workmanship
Are all thy golden oars.
Sleep, my little one, sleep a little while,
Ninni nauna, sleep!"

The green waters of the Tavignano, plunging and foaming down their rocky bed, freshened the warm summer air. Beyond the bridge a vein of the river, led underground, gushes forth as a profuse fountain under an arch of masonry; and here a number of people were collected to wash and to draw water. One of the girls, who gave us to drink, refused to accept a proffered coin, until a countryman who was looking on said, "You should take it, since the lady wishes it." A few paces further a second bridge crosses the Restonica, which has its source in some small lakes near the summit of Monte Rotondo. Its volume of water appeared to me to be quite equal to that of the Tavignano.

The two rivers meet in a rocky glen a quarter of a mile below the town; and thither we wandered in the afternoon, through the shade of superb chestnut-trees. From this, as from every other point in the neighborhood, the views are charming. There is no threat of malaria in the pure mountain air; the trees are of richest foliage, the water is transparent beryl, and the pleasant, communicative people one meets impress one with a sense of their honest simplicity. We wandered around Corte, surrendering ourselves to the influences of the scenery and its associations, and entirely satisfied with both.

Towards evening we climbed the hill by an easier path, which brought us upon the crest of a ridge connecting the citadel-rock with the nearest mountains. Directly before us opened the gorge of the Tavignano, with a bridle-path notched along its almost precipitous sides. A man who had been sitting idly on a rock, with a pipe in his mouth, came up, and stood beside me. "Yonder," said he, pointing to the bridle-path, — "yonder is the road to the land of Niolo. If you follow that, you will come to a forest that is four hours long. The old General Arrighi — the Duke of Padua, you know — travelled it some years ago, and I was his guide. I see you are strangers; you ought to see the land of Niolo. It is not so rich as Corte here; but then the forests and the lakes, — ah, they are fine!"

Presently the man's wife joined us, and we sat down together, and gossiped for half an hour. They gave us the recipe for making *broccio*, a kind of Corsican curd, or junket, which we had tasted at the hotel, and found delicious. I also learned from them many details of the country life of the island. They, like all the Corsicans with whom I came in contact, were quite as ready to answer questions as to ask them. They are not so lively as the Italians, but more earnestly communicative, quick of apprehension, and gifted with a rude humor of their own. In Bastia I bought a volume of *Pruverbj Corse*, which contains more than three thousand proverbs peculiar to the island, many of them exceedingly witty and clever. I quote a single one as a specimen of the dialect: —

"Da gattivu calzu un ne piglià magliolu,
Male u babbu e pegghiu u figliolu."

During our talk I asked the pair, "Do you still have the vendetta in this neigborhood?"

They both professed not to know what I meant by "vendetta," but I saw plainly enough that they understood the question. Finally the man said, rather impatiently, "There are a great many kinds of vendetta."

"I mean blood-revenge — assassination — murder."

His hesitation to speak about the matter disappeared as mysteriously as it came. (Was there, perhaps, a stain upon his own hand?) "O," he answered, "that is all at an end. I can remember when five persons were killed in a day in Corte, and when a man could not travel from here to Ajaccio without risking his life. But now we have neither murders nor robberies; all the roads are safe, the people live quietly, and the country everywhere is better than it was."

I noticed that the Corsicans are proud of the present Emperor on account of his parentage; but they have also some reason to be grateful to his government. He has done much to repair the neglect of his uncle. The work of Paoli has been performed over again; law and order prevail from the sea-shore to the highest herdsman's hut on Monte Rotondo; admirable roads traverse the island, schools have been established in all the villages, and the national spirit of the people is satisfied by having a semi-Corsican on the throne of France. I saw no evidence of discontent anywhere, nor need there be; for Europe has nearly reached the Corsican ideal of the last century, and the pride of the people may well repose for a while upon the annals of their heroic past.

It was a serious disappointment that we were unable to visit Ajaccio and the Balagna. We could only fix the inspiring scenery of Corte in our memories, and so make its historical associations vital and enduring. There was no other direct way of returning to Bastia than the road by which we came; but it kept a fresh interest for us. The conductor of the diligence was one of the liveliest fellows living, and entertained us with innumerable stories; and at the station of Omessa we met with a character so original that I wish I could record every word he said.

The man looked more like a Yankee than any Italian I had seen for six months. He presented the conductor with what appeared to be a bank-note for one thousand francs; but it proved to be issued by the "Bank of Content," and entitled the holder to live a thousand years. Happiness was the president, and Temperance the cashier.

"I am a director of the bank," said the disseminator of the notes, addressing the passengers and a group of countrymen, "and I can put you all in the way of being stockholders. But you must first bring testimonials. Four are required — one religious, one medical, one legal, and one domestic. What must they be? Listen, and I will tell. Religious — from a priest, vouching for four things: that you have never been baptized, never preached, don't believe in the Pope, and are not afraid of the Devil. Medical — from a doctor, that you have had the measles, that your teeth are sound, that you are not flatulent, and that he has never given you medicine. Legal — from a lawyer, that you have never been accused of theft, that you mind your own business, and that you have never employed him. Domestic — from your wife, that you don't lift the lids of the kitchen pots, walk in your sleep, or lose the keyhole of your door! There! can any one of you bring me these certificates?"

The auditors, who had roared with laughter during the speech, became suddenly grave — which emboldened the man to ply them with other and sharper questions. Our departure cut short the scene; but I heard the conductor laughing on his box for a league further.

At Ponte alla Leccia we breakfasted on trout, and, speeding down the grand and lonely valley of the Golo, reached Bastia towards evening. As we steamed out of the little harbor the next day, we took the words of our friend Gregorovius, and made them ours: —

"Year after year, thy slopes of olives hoar
 Give oil, thy vineyards still their bounty pour!
 Thy maize on golden meadows ripen well,
 And let the sun thy curse of blood dispel,
 Till down each vale and on each mountain-side
 The stains of thy heroic blood be dried!
 Thy sons be like their fathers, strong and sure,
 Thy daughters as thy mountain rivers pure,
 And still thy granite crags between them stand
 And all corruptions of the older land.
 Fair isle, farewell! thy virtues shall not sleep;
 Thy fathers' valor shall their children keep,
 That ne'er this taunt to thee the stranger cast, —
 Thy heroes were but fables of the Past!"

THE ISLAND OF MADDALENA.
WITH A DISTANT VIEW OF CAPRERA.

BEFORE leaving Florence for the trip to Corsica, in which I intended to include, if possible, the island of Sardinia, I noticed that the Rubattino steamers touched at Maddalena, on their way from Bastia to Porto Torres. The island of Maddalena, I knew, lay directly over against Caprera, separated by a strait not more than two or three miles in breadth, and thus a convenient opportunity was offered of visiting the owner and resident of the latter island, the illustrious General Giuseppe Garibaldi. I have no special passion for making the personal acquaintance of distinguished men, unless it happens that there is some point of mutual interest concerning which intelligence may be given or received. In this case, I imagined there was such a point of contact. Having followed the fortunes of Italy for the past twenty years, with the keen sympathy which springs from a love for the land, and having been so near the events of the last unfortunate expedition against Rome as to feel from day to day the reflection of those events in the temper of the Italian people, I had learned, during a subsequent residence in Rome, certain facts which added to the interest of the question, while they seemed still more to complicate its solution. There were some things, I felt, an explanation of which (so far as he would be able to give it) might be asked of Garibaldi without impropriety, and which he could communicate without any necessity of reserve.

Another and natural sentiment was mingled with my desire to meet the hero of Italian unity. I knew how shamefully he had been deceived in certain respects, before undertaking the expedition which terminated so fruitlessly at Mentana, and could, therefore, guess the mortification which accompanied him in his imprisonment (for such it virtually is) at Caprera. While, therefore, I should not have sought an interview after the glorious Sicilian and Calabrian campaign, or when the still excited world was reading Nélaton's bulletins from Spezzia, — so confounding myself with the multitude who always admire the hero of the day, and risk their necks to shake hands with him, — I felt a strong desire to testify such respect as the visit of a stranger implies, in Garibaldi's day of defeat and neglect.

> "I did not praise thee, when the crowd,
> Witched with the moment's inspiration,
> Vexed thy still ether with hosannas loud,
> And stamped their dusty adoration." [1]

Of all the people who crowded to see him at Spezzia in such throngs that a false Garibaldi, with bandaged foot, was arranged to receive the most of them, there is no trace now. The same Americans who come from Paris chanting pæans to Napoleon III., go to Rome and are instantly stricken with sympathy for Pius IX., and a certain respect for the Papacy, temporal power included. They give Caprera a wide berth. Two or three steadfast English friends do what they can to make the hero's solitude pleasant, and he has still, as always, the small troop of Italian followers, who never forsake him, because they live from his substance.

Before deciding to visit Caprera, I asked the candid advice of some of the General's most intimate friends in Florence. They assured me that scarcely any one had gone to see him for months past; that a visit from an American, who sympathized with the great and generous aims to which he has devoted his life, could not be otherwise than welcome; and, while offering me cordial letters of introduction, declared that this formality was really unnecessary. It was pleasant to hear him spoken of as a

[1] Lowell, *Ode to Lamartine*.

man whose refined amiability of manner was equal to his unselfish patriotism, and who was as simple, unpretending, and accessible personally, as he was rigorously democratic in his political utterances.

I purposely shortened my tour in Corsica, in order to take the Italian steamer which touches at Bastia, on its way to Maddalena. Half smothered in the sultry heat, we watched the distant smoke rounding the rocks of Capraja, and the steamer had no sooner anchored outside the mole, than we made haste to embark. The cloth was already spread over the skylight on the quarterdeck, and seven plates denoted six fellow-passengers. Two of these were ladies, two Italians, with an old gentleman, who proved to English, although he looked the least like it, and an unmistakable Garibaldian, in a red shirt. The latter was my *vis-à-vis* at table, and it was not long before he startled the company by exclaiming: "In fifty years we shall have the Universal Republic!"

After looking around the table, he fixed his eyes on me, as if challenging assent.

"In five hundred years, perhaps," I said.

"But the priests will go down soon!" he shouted; "and as for that brute" (pointing with his fork towards Corsica), "who rules there, his time is soon up."

As nobody seemed inclined to reply, he continued: "Since the coming of the second Jesus Christ, Garibaldi, the work goes on like lightning. As soon as the priests are down, the Republic will come."

This man, so one of the passengers informed me, had come on board *en bourgeois*, but as the steamer approached Corsica, he suddenly appeared on deck in his red shirt. After we left Bastia, he resumed his former costume. In the capacity to swagger, he surpassed any man I had seen since leaving home. His hair hung about his ears, his nose was long, his beard thick and black, and he had the air of a priest rather than a soldier,— but it was an air which pompously announced to everybody: "Garibaldi is the Second Christ, and I am his Prophet!"

Over the smooth sea we sped down the picturesque Corsican coast. An indentation in the grand mountain chain showed us the valley of the Golo; then came the heights of Vescovato, where Filippini wrote the history of the island, and Murat took refuge after losing his Neapolitan kingdom; then, Cervione, where the fantastic King Theodore, the First and Last, held his capital; after which night fell upon the shores, and we saw only mountain phantoms in the moonlight.

At sunrise the steward called me.

"We are passing the *bocca*," — the Straits of Bonifacio, — said he, "and will soon be at Maddalena."

It was an archipelago of rocks in which the steamer was entangled. All around us, huge gray masses, with scarcely a trace of vegetation, rose from the wave; in front, the lofty, dark blue, serrated mountains of Sardinia pierced the sky, and far to the right faded the southern shores of Corsica. But, bleak and forsaken as was the scene, it had a curious historical interest. As an opening between the islands disclosed the white rocks, citadel, and town of Bonifacio, some fifteen miles distant, I remembered the first important episode in the life of Napoleon. It was in the year 1792, while Pascal Paoli was still President of Corsica. An expedition against Sardinia having been determined upon by the Republic, Napoleon, after, perhaps, the severest struggle of his life, was elected second in command of the battalion of Ajaccio. A work[1] written by M. Nasica, of the latter place, gives a singular picture of the fierce family feuds which preceded the election. It was the commencement of that truly Corsican *vendetta* between Pozzo di Borgo and the future emperor, which only terminated when the former was able to say, after Waterloo: "I have not killed Napoleon, but I have thrown the last shovelful of earth upon him."

[1] *Mémoires sur l'Enfance et la Jeunesse de Napoléon.* Ajaccio, 1853.

The first attempt of the expedition was to be directed against the island of Maddalena. A battery was planted on the uninhabited rock of Santa Teresa (beside which we passed), and Maddalena was bombarded, but without effect. Napoleon prepared a plan for its capture, but Colonna, the first in command, refused to allow him to make the attempt. A heated discussion took place in the presence of the other officers, and Napoleon, becoming at last indignant and impatient, turned to the latter, and said: " He doesn't know what I mean."

" You are an insolent fellow," retorted Colonna.

Napoleon muttered, as he turned away: " We have only a *cheval de parade* for commander."

At Bonifacio, afterwards, his career came near being suddenly terminated. Some Marseilles marines who landed there provoked a quarrel with the soldiers of the Corsican battalion. Napoleon interfered to restore order, whereupon he was seized by the fierce Marseillaise, who would have hung him to a lamp-post, but for the timely aid of the civil authorities. The disfavor of Paoli, who was at that time under the control of Pozzo di Borgo, finally drove Napoleon from Corsica; so that the machinations of his bitterest enemy really forced him into the field where he was so suddenly and splendidly successful.

While we were recalling this fateful fragment of history, the steamer entered the narrow strait between Maddalena and the main land of Sardinia, and at the same moment two stately French vessels made their appearance, crossing tracks on the route between Marseilles and the Orient. The rocky island of San Stefano, lying opposite Maddalena, forms a sheltered harbor, which Caprera, rising eastward against the sea, renders completely landlocked. But what a wild, torn, distorted, desolate panorama! A thin sprinkling of lavender, rosemary, and myrtle serves but to set off the cold gray of the granite rocks; the summits rise in natural bastions, or thrust out huge fangs or twisted horns. There is nowhere any softening of these violent outlines. They print themselves on the farthest distance, and one is not surprised that the little village of Maddalena, the white house on Caprera, and two or three fishing-huts on the Sardinian shore, are the only signs of human habitation.

Beside the village, however, there was a little valley, near the head of which a cool, white villa, perched on a mass of rocks, shone against the rugged background.

"That is my place," said the old Englishman, "and I shall be happy to see you there."

"I shall certainly come, if we have time enough after visiting Caprera," I replied.

The Englishman, an entire stranger, was very kind in his offers of service; the Garibaldian was so pompous and arrogant in his manner, that I soon perceived that no assistance could be expected from him. Nevertheless, chance threw us into the same boat, on landing in the little harbor. I had ascertained that there was a hotel, kept by one Remigio, in Maddalena; and although one of "our mutual friends" had advised me to go directly to Caprera, — Garibaldi's hospitality being as certain as sunrise, or the change of the tide, — I determined to stop with Remigio, and forward my letters. When the Prophet of the Second Coming stepped on shore, he was accosted by an old veteran, who wore a red shirt and blue goggles. They embraced and kissed each other, and presently came up another weather-beaten person, with an unmistakably honest and amiable face, who was hailed with the name of "Basso!"

I knew the name as that of one of Garibaldi's most faithful followers, and as the boat, meanwhile, had been retained to convey the party to Caprera, I stepped up to Basso and the Prophet and asked: "Will one of you be good enough to take these letters to General Garibaldi, and let the boatman bring me word when it will be convenient for him to receive me?"

"Certainly," said the Prophet, taking the letters, and remarking, as he pointed to Basso, "*this* is the General's secretary."

The latter made a modest gesture, disclaiming the honor, and said: "No; *you know* that you are really his secretary."

The boat shoved off with them. "It is a queer company," I said to myself, "and perhaps I ought not to have intrusted the letters to their care." One letter was from a gentleman in a high diplomatic position, whose reputation as a scholar is world-wide, and who possesses the most generous, and at the same time the most intelligent, sympathy with the aspirations of the Italian people. The other was from a noble woman, who has given the best energies of her life to the cause, — who shared the campaigns of Sicily and Calabria, and even went under fire at Monte Rotondo and Mentana to succor the wounded. Probably no two persons had a better right to claim the courtesy of Garibaldi in favor of one, who, though a stranger, was yet an ardent friend.

The Hotel Remigio directly fronted the quay. No sign announced its character, but the first room we entered had a billiard-table, beyond which was a kitchen. Here we found La Remigia, who conducted us up a sumptuous staircase of black and white marble (unwashed) into a shabby dining-room, and then left us to prepare coffee. A door into an adjoining apartment stood half-open. I looked in, but seeing a naked leg stretched out upon a dirty blanket, made a speedy retreat. In a quarter of an hour coffee came, without milk, but with a bottle of rum instead. The servitress was a little girl, whose hands were of so questionable a complexion, that we turned away lest we should see her touch the cups. I need not say that the beverage was vile; the reader will have already guessed that.

We summoned La Remigia, to ascertain whether a breakfast was possible. "*Eh, che vuole?*" ("What can you expect?") said she. "This is a poor little island. What would you like to have?"

Limiting our wishes to the probabilities of the place, we modestly suggested eggs and fish, whereat La Remigia looked relieved, and promised that we should have both. Then, although the heat was furious, I went forth for a stroll along the shore. A number of bronze boys had pulled off their tow shirts, and were either sitting naked on the rocks, or standing in the shallow coves, and splashing each other with scallop-shells. Two or three fishing-boats were lazily pulling about the strait, but the greater part of the population of Maddalena sat in the shade and did nothing.

The place contains about fifteen hundred inhabitants, but scarcely one half that number were at home. The others were sailors, or coral fishers, who are always absent during the summer months. The low, bright-colored houses are scattered along the shore, in such order as the huge, upheaved masses of granite will allow, and each street terminates in a stony path. In the scanty garden-inclosures, bristling masses of the fruit-bearing cactus overhang the walls, repellant as the rocks from which they spring. Evidently the place supplies nothing except the article of fish; all other necessaries of life must be brought from Sardinia. The men are principally pensioned veterans of the Italian navy, who are satisfied with the sight of blue water and passing vessels; the women (rock-widows, one might call them), having the very simplest household duties to perform, usually sit at their doors, with some kind of knitting or netting, and chatter with their nearest neighbors. I had scarcely walked a quarter of a mile before the sleepy spirit of the place took hold of my feet, and I found myself contemplating the shadowy spots among the rocks, much more than the wild and rugged island scenery across the strait.

Garibaldi's house on Caprera flashed in the sun, and

after a while I saw a boat pulling away from the landing-place below it. I returned to the harbor to meet the boatman, and receive the answer which my letters required. It was a red-headed fellow, with a face rather Scotch than Italian, and a blunt, direct manner of speech which corresponded thereto.

"The General says he is not well, and can't see you," said he.

"Have you a letter?" I asked.

"No; but he told me so."

"He is sick, then?"

"No," said the boatman, "he is not sick."

"Where did you see him?"

"Out of doors. He went down to the sea this morning and took a bath. Then he worked in the garden."

The first sensation of a man who receives an unexpected blow is incredulity, and not exasperation. It required a slight effort to believe the boatman's words, and the next impression was that there was certainly some misunderstanding. If Garibaldi were well enough to walk about his fields, he was able to receive a visitor; if he had read the letters I forwarded, a decent regard for the writers would have withheld him from sending a rude verbal answer by the mouth of a boatman. The whole proceeding was so utterly at variance with all I had heard of his personal refinement and courtesy, that I was driven to the suspicion that his followers had suppressed the letters, and represented me, perhaps, as a stranger of not very reputable appearance.

Seeing that we were stranded for three days upon Maddalena, — until the steamer returned from Porto Torres, — I determined to assure myself whether the suspicion was just. I could, at least, give the General a chance to correct any misunderstanding. I therefore wrote a note, mentioning the letters and the answer I had received through the boatman; referring to other friends of his in

America and Italy, whom I knew; assuring him that I had had no intention of thrusting myself upon his hospitality, but had only meant to desire a brief personal interview. I abstained, of course, from repeating the request, as he would thus be able to grant it more gracefully, if a misrepresentation had really been made. Summoning the red-headed boatman, I gave him the note, with the express command that he should give it into Garibaldi's own hands, and not into those of any of the persons about him.

La Remigia gave us as good a breakfast as the house could furnish. The wine was acutely sour, but the fish were fresh and delicate. Moreover, the room had been swept, and the hands of the little servant subjected to a thorough washing. There was a dessert of cherries, brought all the way from Genoa, and then the hostess, as she brought the coffee, asked: " When will your Excellencies go to Caprera? "

" If the General is sick," I remarked, " we shall probably not be able to see him."

" He was not well two or three weeks ago," said she; " he had the rheumatism in his hands. But now he goes about his fields the same as before."

A second suspicion came into my head. What if the boatman should not go to Caprera with my letter, but merely sleep two or three hours in the shade, and then come back to me with an invented verbal answer? It was now high noon, and a truly African sun beat down on the unsheltered shores. The veterans had been chased from their seats on the quay, and sat in dozing, silent rows on the shady sides of the houses. A single boat, with sail spread, hardly moved over the dazzling blue of the harbor. There was no sign of active life anywhere, except in the fleas.

Leaving my wife in La Remigia's care, I took one of the rough paths behind the town, and climbed to a bold mass of rocks, which commanded a view of the strait from Ca-

prera to Sardinia. Far off, beyond the singular horns and
needles of rock, cresting the mountains of the latter island,
a thunder-gust was brewing; but the dark, cool shadows
there only served, by contrast, to make the breathless heat
on Maddalena more intense. Nevertheless, a light wind
finally came from somewhere, and I stretched myself out
on the granite, with Caprera before my eyes, and reflected
on the absurdity of any one human being taking pains to
make the acquaintance of any other particular human
being, while I watched the few boats visible on the surface
of the water below. One, rowing and sailing, rounded the
point of San Stefano, and disappeared; another crept
along the nearer shore, looking for fish, coral, or sponges;
and a third, at last, making a long tack, advanced into the
channel of La Moneta, in front of Garibaldi's residence.
It was Red-head, honestly doing his duty. Two or three
hours went by, and he did not return. When the air had
been somewhat cooled by the distant thunder, we set forth
to seek the English recluse. The path followed the coast,
winding between rocks and clumps of myrtle in blossom,
until the villa looked down upon us from the head of a
stony dell. On three sides, the naked granite rose in irregular piles against the sky, while huge blocks, tumbled
from above, lay scattered over the scanty vineyards below.
In sheltered places there were a few pines and cedars, of
stunted growth. The house, perched upon a mass of rock
forty or fifty feet high, resembled a small fortress. As we
approached it, over the dry, stony soil, the bushes rustling
as the lizards darted through them, the place assumed an
air of savage loneliness. No other human dwelling was
visible on any of the distant shores, and no sail brightened
the intervening water.

The Englishman came forth and welcomed us with a
pleasant, old-fashioned courtesy. A dark-eyed Sardinian
lady, whom he introduced to us as his daughter-in-law, and
her father, were his temporary guests. The people after-

wards told me, in Maddalena, that he had adopted and educated a Neapolitan boy, who, however, had turned out to be a *mauvais sujet*. We were ushered into a large vaulted room, the walls of which, to my astonishment, were covered with admirable paintings — genuine works of the Flemish and Italian masters. There was a Cuyp, a Paul Potter, a Ruysdael, a Massimo, and several excellent pictures of the school of Corregio. A splendid library filled the adjoining hall, and recent English and Italian newspapers lay upon the table. I soon perceived that our host was a man of unusual taste and culture, who had studied much and travelled much, before burying himself in this remote corner of the Mediterranean. For more than twenty years, he informed us, the island had been his home. He first went thither accidentally, in his search for health, and remained because he found it among those piles of granite and cactus. One hardly knows whether to admire or commiserate such a life.

Our host, however, had long outlived his yearning for the busy world of men. His little plantation, wrung from Nature with immense labor and apparently great expense, now absorbed all his interest. He had bought foreign trees — Mexican, African, and Australian — and set them in sheltered places, built great walls to break the sweep of the wind which draws through the Straits of Bonifacio, constructed tanks for collecting the rains, terraces for vineyards, and so fought himself into the possession of a little productive soil. But the winds kept down the growth of his pines, the islanders cut his choicest trees and carried them off for fire-wood, and it was clear that the scanty beginnings we saw were the utmost he would be able to keep and hold against so many hostile influences.

After we had inspected the costly picture-gallery, and partaken of refreshments, he took us to his orange-garden, a square inclosure, with walls twenty feet high, at the foot of the rocks. The interior was divided by high ramparts of woven brushwood into compartments about thirty feet square, each of which contained half a dozen squat, battered-looking trees, I should have imagined the outer walls high enough to break the strongest wind, but our host informed me that they merely changed its character, giving to the current a spiral motion which almost pulled the trees out of the earth. The interior divisions of brushwood were a necessity. Above the house there was a similar inclosure for pear and apple trees. The vines, kept close to the earth, and tied to strong stakes, were more easily tended. But the same amount of labor and expense would have created a little paradise on the shores of Sorrento, or the Riviera di Ponente; in fact, as many oranges might have been raised in Minnesota, with less trouble.

According to the traditions of the people, the whole island was wooded a hundred and fifty years ago. But, as savage tribes worship trees, so the first inclination of the civilized man is to destroy them. I still hold to the belief that the disforested Levant might be reclothed in fifty years, if the people could be prevented from interfering with the young growth.

When we reached Maddalena, the boatman had returned from Caprera. This time he brought me a note, in Garibaldi's handwriting, containing two or three lines, which, however, were not more satisfactory than the previous message. "*Per motivo de' miei incomodi*" (on account of my ailments), said the General, he could not receive me. This was an equivocation, but no explanation. His motive for slighting the letters of two such friends, and refusing to see one who had come to Maddalena to testify a sympathy and respect which had nothing in common with the curiosity of the crowd, remained a mystery. In the little fishing-village, where nothing could long be kept secret, the people seemed to be aware of all that had occurred. They possessed too much natural tact and delicacy to question us, but it was easy to see that they were much surprised. Red-head made quite a long face when I told him, after reading the letter, that I should not need his boat for a trip to Caprera.

After allowing all possible latitude to a man's individual right to choose his visitors, the manner in which my application had been received still appeared to me very rude and boorish. Perhaps one's first experience of the kind is always a little more annoying than is necessary; but the reader must consider that we had no escape from the burning rocks of Maddalena until the third day afterwards, and the white house on Caprera before our eyes was a constant reminder of the manner or mood of its inmate. Questions of courtesy are nearly as difficult to discuss as questions of taste, each man having his own private standard; yet, I think, few persons will censure me for having then and there determined that, for the future, I would take no particular pains to seek the acquaintance of a distinguished man.

We were fast on Maddalena, as I have said, and the most we could make of it did not seem to be much. I sketched a little the next morning, until the heat drove me indoors. Towards evening, following La Remigia's counsel, we set forth on a climb to the Guardia Vecchia, a deserted fortress on the highest point of the island. Thunder-storms, as before, growled along the mountains of Sardinia, without overshadowing or cooling the rocks of the desert archipelago. The masses of granite, among which we clambered, still radiated the noonday heat, and the clumps of lentisk and arbutus were scarcely less arid in appearance than the soil from which they grew. Over the summit, however, blew a light breeze. We pushed open the door of the fort, mounted to a stone platform with ramparts pierced for six cannon, and sat down in the shade of the watch-tower. The view embraced the whole Strait of Bonifacio and its shores, from the peak of Incudine in Corsica, to the headland of Terranova, on the eastern coast of

Sardinia. Two or three villages, high up on the mountains of the latter island, the little fishing-town at our feet, the far-off citadel of Bonifacio, and — still persistently visible — the house on Caprera, rather increased than removed the loneliness and desolation of the scenery. Island rising behind island thrust up new distortions of rock of red or hot-gray hues which became purple in the distance, and the dark-blue reaches of sea dividing them were hard and lifeless as plains of glass. Perhaps the savage and sterile forms of the foreground impressed their character upon every part of the panorama, since we knew that they were everywhere repeated. In this monotony lay something sublime, and yet profoundly melancholy.

As we have now the whole island of Caprera full and fair before us, let us see what sort of a spot the hero of Italian Unity has chosen for his home. I may at the same time, without impropriety, add such details of his life and habits, and such illustrations of his character, as were freely communicated by persons familiar with both, during our stay in Maddalena.

Caprera, as seen from the Guardia Vecchia, is a little less forbidding than its neighbor island. It is a mass of reddish-gray rock, three to four miles in length and not more than a mile in breadth, its axis lying at a right angle to the course of the Sardinian coast. The shores rise steeply from the water to a central crest of naked rock, some twelve hundred feet above the sea. The wild shrubbery of the Mediterranean — myrtle, arbutus, lentisk, and box — is sprinkled over the lower slopes, and three or four lines of bright, even green, betray the existence of terraced grain-fields. The house, a plain white quadrang'e, two stories in height, is seated on the slope, a quarter of a mile from the landing-place. Behind it there are fields and vineyards, and a fertile garden-valley called the Fontanaccia, which are not visible from Maddalena. The house, in its present commodious form, was built by Victor

Emanuel, during Garibaldi's absence from the island, and without his knowledge. The latter has spent a great deal of money in wresting a few fields from the unwilling rock, and his possession, even yet, has but a moderate value. The greater part of the island can only be used as a range for cattle, and will nourish about a hundred head.

Garibaldi, however, has a great advantage over all the political personages of our day, in the rugged simplicity of his habits. He has no single expensive taste. Whether he sleeps on a spring-mattress or a rock, eats *filet* or fish and macaroni, is all the same to him — nay, he prefers the simpler fare. The persons whom he employs eat at the same table with him, and his guests, whatever their character or title, are no better served. An Englishman who went to Caprera as the representative of certain societies, and took with him, as a present, a dozen of the finest hams, and four dozen bottles of the choicest Château Margaux, was horrified to find, the next day, that each gardener, herdsman, and fisherman at the table had a generous lump of ham on his plate and a bottle of Château Margaux beside it! Whatever delicacy comes to Garibaldi is served in the same way; and of the large sums of money contributed by his friends and admirers, he has retained scarcely anything. All is given to " The Cause."

Garibaldi's three prominent traits of character — honesty, unselfishness, and independence — are so marked, and have been so variously illustrated, that no one in Italy (probably not even Pius IX. or Antonelli) dares to dispute his just claim to them. Add the element of a rare and inextinguishable enthusiasm, and we have the qualities which have made the man. He is wonderfully adapted to be the leader of an impulsive and imaginative people, during those periods when the rush and swell of popular sentiment overbears alike diplomacy and armed force. Such a time came to him in 1860, and the Sicilian and Calabrian campaign will always stand as the climax of his achievements. I do not speak of Aspromonte or Mentana now. The history of those attempts cannot be written until Garibaldi's private knowledge of them may be safely made known to the world.

It occurred to me, as I looked upon Caprera, that only an enthusiastic, imaginative nature could be content to live in such an isolation. It is hardly alone disgust with the present state of Italy which keeps him from that seat in the Italian Parliament, to which he is regularly reëlected. He can neither use the tact of the politician, nor employ the expedients of the statesman. He has no patience with adverse opinion, no clear, objective perception of character, no skill to calculate the reciprocal action and cumulative force of political ideas. He simply sees *an end*, and strikes a bee-line for it. As a military commander he is admirable, so long as operations can be conducted under his immediate personal control. In short, he belongs to that small class of great men, whose achievements, fame, and influence rest upon excellence of character and a certain magnetic, infectious warmth of purpose, rather than on high intellectual ability. There may be wiser Italian patriots than he; but there is none so pure and devoted.

From all that was related to me of Garibaldi, I should judge that his weak points are, an incapacity to distinguish between the steady aspirations of his life and those sudden impulses which come to every ardent and passionate nature, and an amiable weakness (perhaps not disconnected from vanity) which enables a certain class of adventurers to misuse and mislead him. His impatience of contrary views naturally subjects him to the influence of the latter class, whose cue it is to flatter and encourage. I know an American general whose reputation has been much damaged in the same way. The three men who were his companions on Caprera during my stay in Maddalena were Basso, who occasionally acts as secretary; he whom I termed the Prophet, a certain Dr. Occhipinti

(Painted-Eyes), a maker of salves and pomatums, and Guzmaroli, formerly a priest, and ignominiously expelled from Garibaldi's own corps. There are other hangers-on, whose presence from time to time in Caprera is a source of anxiety to the General's true friends.

Caprera formerly belonged to an English gentleman, a passionate sportsman, who settled there thirty years ago on account of the proximity of the island to the rich game regions of Sardinia. Garibaldi, dining with this gentleman at Maddalena in 1856, expressed his desire to procure a small island on the coast for his permanent home, whereupon the former offered to sell him a part of Caprera at cost. The remainder was purchased by a subscription made in England, and headed by the Duke of Sutherland. I was informed that Garibaldi's faithful and noble-hearted friends, Colonel and Mrs. Chambers of Scotland, had done much towards making the island productive and habitable, but I doubt whether its rocks yet yield enough for the support of the family.

The General's oldest son, Menotti, his daughter Teresa, her husband Major Canzio, and their five children, Mameli, Anzani, Lincoln, Anita, and John Brown, have their home at Caprera. Menotti is reported to be a good soldier and sailor, but without his father's abilities. The younger son, Ricciotti, spends most of his time in England. Teresa, however, is a female Garibaldi, full of spirit, courage, and enthusiasm. She has great musical talent, and a voice which would give her, were there need, a prima donna's station in any theatre. Her father, also, is an excellent singer, and the two are fond of making the rocks of Caprera resound with his *Inno ai Romani*.

Garibaldi was born at Nice in 1807, and is therefore now sixty-one years old. His simple habits of life have preserved his physical vigor, but he suffers from frequent severe attacks of rheumatism. The wound received at Aspromonte, I was told, no longer occasions him inconvenience.

In features and complexion he shows his Lombard and German descent. His name is simply the Italian for *Heribald*, "bold in war." In the tenth century Garibald I. and II. were kings of Bavaria. In fact much of the best blood of Italy is German, however reluctant the Italians may be to acknowledge the fact. The Marquis D'Azeglio, whose memoirs have recently been published, says in his autobiographical sketch, " Educated in the hatred of the *Tedeschi* (Germans), I was greatly astonished to find from my historical studies, that I was myself a *Tedesco*." The "pride of race" really is one of the absurdest of human vanities. I have heard half-breed Mexicans boast of their "Gothic blood," born Englishmen who settled in Virginia talk of their "Southern blood," and all the changes rung on Cavalier, Norman, or Roman ancestry. The Slavic Greeks of Athens call themselves "Hellenes," and Theodore of Abyssinia claimed a direct descent from Solomon. Garibaldi might have become purely Italian in name, as Duca di Calatafimi, if he had chosen. His refusal was scarcely a virtue, because the offer of the title was no temptation.

The strait opening eastward to the sea was not wholly in sight from the Guardia Vecchia, but we saw enough of it to enable us to track the path of Garibaldi's escape, the previous October. An intervening point hid the cove of Stagnatello, where he embarked in his little boat called "The Snipe" (*beccacino*) : yet its position was shown by the Punta dell' Arcaccio beyond. On the Maddalena shore we saw the gardens and cottage of the English lady, the "Hermitess of La Moneta," who received him after his passage of the strait, and concealed him the following day. While he was thus concealed, he wrote an account of the adventure for his daughter Teresa, yet so evidently with an eye to its future publication, that its style unconsciously reflects the vein of vanity which runs through his character. Before leaving his imprisonment at Varignano, he gave permission to the Frau von S——, an intimate friend, to publish a

German translation, from which I take the chief part of the narrative. The Italian original has not yet been published.

Garibaldi, who speaks of himself in the third person, as "The Solitary," left his house on the evening of the 14th of October (1867), accompanied by two friends, Froscianti and Barberini, and a boatman whom he calls Giovanni. They descended through the valley of the Fontanaccia to the cove of Stagnatello, off which, in the strait, the Italian war-steamers lay at anchor. What followed must be given in his own words: —

"Having reached the wall" (at the bottom of the cultivated fields of the Fontanaccia), "the Solitary took off his poncho, and exchanged his white hat for a cap of his son, Menotti. He gave the garments, which he had removed, to Barberini, and after he had convinced himself that there was no one on the other side of the wall, he climbed upon it, and sprang down, with an astonishing activity.

"A memory of his adventurous youth inspired him, and he felt himself twenty years younger. Besides, were not his sons and his companions in arms already fighting the mercenaries of the priestly power? Could he keep quiet? — content himself with the pruning of his trees, and lead the shameful life of the *moderati*? When the Solitary was fortunately over the wall, he said to Barberini: 'It is still too bright; we will wait a little while here, and smoke half a cigar.' Thereupon he drew a match-box — it was a treasured souvenir of the amiable Lady S. — out of his left pocket, used it, and then offered his lighted 'cavour' to his companion, who had a cigarette in readiness. The Solitary is accustomed to cut these long, black Tuscan cigars through the middle, and only smoke half a one at a time.

"Soon the nightly shadows began to obscure the atmosphere, but in the east a faint gleam made itself seen as the herald of the approaching queen of night.

"'Within three-quarters of an hour the moon will have risen behind the mountains,' remarked the Solitary; 'we dare not longer delay.'

"Both men arose and betook themselves to the little harbor. Giovanni was there at his post, and with his and Barberini's help, the *beccacino* was soon launched upon the water. This is our smallest boat, designed for duck-shooting, and so flat that the one person who has room therein must lie upon the bottom and propel it with a paddle. In a moment the Solitary took his place, lying flat upon his poncho. After Giovanni had pushed the light vessel into the sea, and convinced himself that everything was properly arranged, he himself got into the *becca*, a boat built exactly like the *beccacino*, only of greater dimensions, and rowed, singing loudly, in the direction of the yacht.

"'Halt! who goes there?' called out the marines of the war-vessels, degraded to *alguazils*, to police-servants, hailing the boat of the Sardinian, who, meanwhile, did not allow himself to be disturbed either in his song or his journey.

"But when a third challenge came to his ears he answered: 'I am going on board!' for, however without result the musket-shots might be in the darkness, they never fail to strike an inexperienced man with terror. The Solitary, now propelling his *beccacino* with strokes, now with a small paddle, as is customary with the American canoes, followed his course along the shore of Paviano, between the cove of Stagnatello and the cape of Arcaccio; and verily the humming-bird, fluttering around the fragrant flowers of the torrid zone, and sipping their honey in the manner of the industrious bee, is more noisy than was the light *beccacino*, as it rapidly shot over the bosom of the Tyrrhene sea. Arrived at the Punta dell' Arcaccio, the Solitary recognized the faithful Froscianti among the lofty masses of stone. 'Nothing new as far as the rocks of Arcaccio,' whispered the latter from a distance.

Then I am safe!' replied the Solitary, directing his boat with increasing swiftness past the steep cliffs, until he reached a point whence he could see the little Rabbit Isle (the southernmost of three which inclose the harbor of Stagnatello) and then struck out boldly on the sea, in a northwestern direction.

"As the Solitary perceived how fast the moonlight increased, he paddled more rapidly, and, driven by the sirocco, his boat passed the Strait de la Moneta with a swiftness which a steamer might have envied.

"By moonlight and seen at a certain distance, each rock rising out of the sea more or less resembles a vessel, and since the commander of the Ratazzi squadron had laid a requisition upon all the barks of Maddalena in order to increase the number of boats with which he besieged Caprera, it appeared as if the little archipelago of Moneta swarmed with shallops and boats, all for the purpose of hindering *one* man in the performance of his duty.

"As soon as the Solitary had reached the little island of Giardinelli, off the northeastern coast of Maddalena, he turned the *beccacino* into the labyrinth of rocky reefs, which lift themselves like a bulwark along the shore, and from out this secure concealment he sharply inspected the coast, stretching before him in the light of the moon.

"When the Solitary found himself near the island of Giardinelli, he saw that there were three different ways by which he could reach the channel separating it from Maddalena : by water, paddling around it either on the northern or the southern side, or by landing and crossing the island on foot. After full consideration, he determined to try the latter plan.

"Whether it was owing to the skill of the boatman of the *beccacino*, or the neglect of the unsuspicious, sleeping sentinels, I will not discuss; but this is certain, that the Solitary landed upon Giardinelli, not only with a whole skin, but without being disturbed by a single 'Who goes there?'

Yet he had scarcely hauled his skiff ashore before he noticed that there were many impediments in his way to the channel; since the island, which serves as a pasture to the cattle of Maddalena, is divided into several fields, all of which are inclosed by high walls, covered with thorny shrubs.

"When, after many detours and much break-neck climbing, the Solitary was about to pass the last of these walls, he imagined that he saw on the other side a row of crouching sailors. If this were no optical delusion, it would not have surprised him in the least, since it had been reported to him on Caprera, that several seamen and soldiers had landed on the island in the course of the day. The loss of time, which this circumstance occasioned to the Solitary explained also to him, why two of his friends, whom he should have found near the channel, were not at their posts.

"It was not until ten o'clock, and after he had looked very sharply about him, that the Solitary undertook to cross the shallow arm of the sea which divides Giardinelli from Maddalena. He had not taken ten steps when loud calls from the watching war-vessels, accompanied with musket-shots, were heard — but this did not disconcert the Solitary in his zealous passage through the salt flood. He soon had the critical passage behind him, and set foot upon Maddalena. But a very fatiguing way was still before him, for his boots, filled with water, creaked and incommoded him on the uneven ground.

"When, finally, the sight of the house of Mrs. C. showed the Solitary the vicinity of a hospitable refuge, he strode more cautiously forward, through fear that the villa might be surrounded by spies; and only when a cloud covered the moon, did he dare to knock lightly upon one of the windows with his Scotch stick. Mrs. C., however, had had faith in the Solitary's lucky star. Advised in advance of his plan, she had been keenly listening to his footsteps, so that at the first tap on the window, she hurried from the door, and welcomed her old neighbor with her accustomed gracious smile."

All the next day Garibaldi remained concealed in the English lady's cottage. The following night he crossed from the northern shore of Maddalena to Sardinia, where his friends had a sloop in readiness. In three or four days more he was in Tuscany, and the Italian Government was astounded at his appearance in Florence before his escape from Caprera had been discovered by the blockading squadron.

While upon the rocky summits of Maddalena, we made search for the former dwellings of the inhabitants, but became bewildered in the granite labyrinth, and failed to find them. The present village on the shore owes its existence to Nelson. Previous to his day those waters were swept by Barbary corsairs, and the people of the island, being without protection, lived almost like troglodytes, in rude hovels constructed among the rocks. Nelson, while in the Mediterranean, at the end of the last century, made Maddalena one of his stations, and encouraged the inhabitants to come forth from their hiding-places. On the altar of the church in the town which they then began to build there are still the silver candlesticks which he presented. This, and Napoleon's previous attempt to gain possession of the island, are the two incidents which connect Maddalena with history.

We made a few other scrambles during our stay, but they simply repeated the barren pictures we already knew by heart. Although, little by little, an interest in the island was awakened, the day which was to bring the steamer from Porto Torres was hailed by us almost as a festival. But the comedy (for such it began to seem) was not yet at an end. I had procured the return tickets to Leghorn, and was standing in Remigia's door, watching the pensioners as they dozed in the shade, when two figures appeared at the end of the little street. One was Painted-Eyes, the maker of salves, and I was edified by seeing him suddenly turn when he perceived me, and retrace his steps. The other, who came forward, proved to be one of Garibaldi's stanchest veterans, — a man who had been in his service twenty-five years, in Montevideo, Rome, America, China, and finally in the Tyrol.

"Where is the man who was with you?" I asked.

"He was coming to the locanda," said he; "but when he saw you, he left me without explaining why."

The veteran knew so much of what had happened that I told him the rest. He was no less grieved than surprised. His general, he said, had never acted so before; he had never refused to see any stranger, even though he came without letters, and he was at a loss to account for it.

There was a stir among the idlers on the quay; a thread of smoke arose above the rocky point to the westward, and — welcome sight! — the steamer swept up and anchored in the roadstead. La Remigia, who had been unremitting in her attentions, presented a modest bill, shook hands with us heartily, and Red-head, who was in waiting with his boat, carried us speedily on board. The steamer was not to leave for two hours more, but now the certainty of escape was a consolation. The few islanders we had known parted from us like friends, and even the boatman returned to the deck on purpose to shake hands, and wish us a pleasant voyage. I found myself softening towards Maddalena, after all.

In one of the last boats came the same Occhipinti again, accompanied by Guzmaroli, the ex-priest. The former was bound for Leghorn, and the prospect of having him for a fellow-passenger was not agreeable. He avoided meeting us, went below, and kept very quiet during the passage. I felt sure, although the supposition was disparaging to Garibaldi, that this man was partly responsible for the answer I had received.

A fresh breeze blew through the Strait of Bonifacio, and we soon lost sight of the rocks which had been the scene of our three days' Robinsoniad. The only other passenger, by a singular coincidence, proved to be "the Hermitess of La Moneta," as she is called on Maddalena, — the widow of the gentleman who sold Caprera to Garibaldi, and herself one of the General's most trusted friends. Through her, the island acquired a new interest. In the outmost house on the spur which forms the harbor lay an English captain, eighty years old, and ill; in the sterile glen to the north lived another Englishman alone among his books and rare pictures; and under a great rock, two miles to the eastward, was a lonely cottage, opposite Caprera, where this lady has lived for thirty years.

In the long twilight, as the coast of Corsica sped by, we heard the story of those thirty years. They had not dulled the keen, clear intellect of the lady, nor made less warm one human feeling in her large heart. We heard of travels in Corsica on horseback nearly forty years ago; of lunching with bandits in the mountains; of fording the floods and sleeping in the caves of Sardinia; of farm-life (if it can be so called) on Caprera, and of twenty years passed in the cottage of La Moneta, without even a journey to the fishing-village. Then came other confidences, which must not be repeated, but as romantic as anything in the stories of the Middle Ages — yet in all, there was no trace of morbid feeling, of unused affection, of regret for the years that seemed lost to us. Verily, though these words should reach her eyes, I must say, since the chances of life will scarcely bring us together again, that the freshness and sweetness with which she had preserved so many noble womanly qualities in solitude, was to me a cheering revelation of the innate excellence of human nature.

"Yet," she said, at the close, "I would never advise any one to attempt the life I have led. Such a seclusion is neither natural nor healthy. One may read, and one may think; but the knowledge lies in one's mind like an inert mass, and only becomes vital when it is actively communicated or compared. This mental inertness or deadness is even harder to bear than the absence of society. But there always comes a time when we need the face of a friend — the time that comes to all. No, it is not good to be alone."

After all, we had not come to Maddalena in vain. We had made the acquaintance of a rare and estimable nature — which is always a lasting gain, in the renewed faith it awakens. The journey, which had seemed so wearisome in anticipation, came rapidly to an end, and there was scarcely a regret left for Caprera when we parted with the Hermitess of Maddalena at Leghorn, the next afternoon. A few days afterwards she sent me the original manuscript of Garibaldi's "Hymn to the Romans," which he had presented to her. I shall value it as much for the giver's, as for the writer's sake.

Our friends in Florence received the news of our adventure with astonishment and mortification; but, up to the time of this present writing, the matter remains a mystery. One conjecture was made, yet it seemed scarcely credible, — that Garibaldi was getting up a new expedition against Rome.

A short time after my trip to Maddalena, a German professor of note, who had a special interest in communicating personally with Garibaldi, made the journey from Germany for that sole purpose, and was similarly repelled.

IN THE TEUTOBURGER FOREST.

No part of Germany is so monotonous and unlovely as that plain which the receding waves of the North Sea left behind them. The stranger who lands at Bremen or Hamburg enters upon a dead, sandy level, where fields of lean and starveling cereals interchange with heathery moorlands and woods of dwarfish pine. Each squat, ugly farmhouse looks as lonely as if there were no others in sight; the villages are collections of similar houses, huddled around a church-tower so thick and massive that it seems to be the lookout of a fortress. The patient industry of the people is here manifested in its plainest and sturdiest forms, and one cannot look for the external embellishments of life, where life itself is so much of an achievement.

As we advance southward the scenery slowly improves. The soil deepens and the trees rise; the purple heather clings only to the occasional sandy ridges, between which greenest meadows gladden our eyes. Groves of oak make their appearance; brooks wind and sparkle among alder thickets; the low undulations swell into broad, gently rounded hills, and at last there is a wavy blue line along the horizon. If you are travelling from Hanover to Minden, some one will point out a notch, or gap, in that rising mountain outline, and tell you that it is the Porta Westphalica — the gateway by which the river Weser issues from the Teutoburger Forest.

I had already explored nearly every nook of Middle Germany, from the Hartz to the Odenwald; yet this — the storied ground of the race — was still an unknown region. Although so accessible, especially from the celebrated watering-place of Pyrmont, whence any of its many points of interest may be reached in a day's drive, I found little about it in the guide-books, and less in books of travel. Yet here, one may say, is the starting-point of German history. Hermann and Wittekind are the two great representatives of the race, in its struggles against Roman and Christian civilization; and the fact that it adopted both the one and the other, and through them developed into its later eminence, does not lessen the value of those names. Indeed, the power of resistance measures the power of acceptance and assimilation.

It was harvest-time as I sped by rail towards Minden, along the northern base of the mountains. Weeks of drought and heat had forced the fields into premature ripeness, and the lush green meadows were already waiting for the aftermath. About Bückeburg the rye-fields were full of reapers, in an almost extinct costume, — the men in heavy fur caps, loose white over-shirts, and boots reaching to the knee; the women with black head-dress, bodice, and bright scarlet petticoat. These tints of white, scarlet, and black shone splendidly among the sheaves, and the pictures I saw made me keenly regret that progress has rendered mankind so commonplace in costume. When I first tramped through Germany, in 1845, every province had its distinctive dress, and the stamp of the country people was impressed upon the landscapes of their homes; but now a great leveling wave has swept over the country, washing out all these picturesque characteristics, and leaving the universal modern commonplace in their stead. If the latter were graceful, or cheap, or practically convenient, we might accept the change; but it is none of these. Fashion has at last combined ugliness and discomfort in our clothing, and the human race is satisfied.

Soon after leaving Minden the road bends sharply southwards, and enters the Porta Westphalica — a break in the Weser mountains which is abrupt and lofty enough to possess a certain grandeur. The eastern bank rises from the water in a broken, rocky wall to the height of near five hundred feet; the western slants sufficiently to allow foothold for trees, and its summit is two hundred feet higher. The latter is called "Wittekind's Mount," from a tradition that the famous Saxon king once had a fortress upon it. Somewhere in the valley which lies within this Westphalian Gate is the scene of the last battle between Hermann and Germanicus. Although the field of action of both these leaders extended over the greater part of Northern Germany, the chief events which decided their fortunes took place within the narrow circle of these mountains.

I passed through Oeynhausen, — a bright, cheerful watering-place, named after the enterprising baron who drove an artesian shaft to the depth of two thousand feet, and brought a rich saline stream to the surface, — and at Herford, the next station, left the line of rail. I looked in vain for the towers of Enger, a league or so to the west, where Wittekind died as a Christian prince, and where his bones still rest. Before turning aside for Detmold and the hills of the Teutoburger Forest, let me very briefly recall the career of that spiritual successor of Hermann.

Nothing certain is known of Wittekind's descent or early history. We first hear of him as one of the leaders of the Saxons in the invasion of Westphalia, which they undertook in the year 774, while Charlemagne was occupied in subduing the Lombards. Three years later, when this movement was suppressed and the greater part of the Saxon chiefs took the oath of fidelity to the Emperor at Paderborn, Wittekind fled to the court of his brother-in-law, King Siegfried of Jutland. He returned in 778, while Charlemagne was in Spain, driving back the Saracens, and devastated the lands of the Rhine. After carrying on the war with varying success for four years, he finally surprised and almost annihilated the Frank army at the Süntelberg, not far from Hameln, on the Weser. Enraged at his defeat, Charlemagne took a horrible revenge: he executed forty-five hundred Saxons, who were in his hands. All the tribes rose in revolt, acknowledged Wittekind as their king, and for three years more continued the desperate struggle, the end of which was a compromise. Wittekind received Christian baptism, was made duke of Saxony, and, according to tradition, governed the people twenty years longer, from his seat at Enger, as a just and humane prince. The Emperor Karl IV. there built him a monument in the year 1377.

At Herford I took my place in the diligence for Detmold, with a horse-dealer for company on the way. It was a journey of three hours, through a very pleasant and beautiful country, lying broad and warm in the shelter of circling mountains, veined with clear, many-branched streams, and wooded with scattered groves of oak and beech. If there was any prominent feature of the scenery, as distinguished from that of other parts of Germany, it was these groves, dividing the bright meadows and the golden slopes of harvest, with their dark, rounded masses of foliage, as in the midland landscapes of England. The hills to the south, entirely clothed with forests, increased in height as we followed their course in a parallel line, and long before we reached Detmold I saw the monument to Hermann, crowning the Grotenburg, a summit more than a thousand feet above the valley.

The little capital was holding its annual horse-fair, yet I had no trouble in finding lodgings at one of its three inns, and should have thought the streets deserted if I had not been told that they were unusually lively. The principality of Lippe has a population of a little more than a hundred thousand, yet none of the appurtenances of a court and state are wanting. There is an old ancestral castle, a modern palace, a theatre, barracks and government buildings — not so large as in Berlin, to be sure, but just as important in the eyes of the people. A stream which comes down from the mountains feeds a broad, still moat, encompassing three sides of the old castle and park, beyond which the fairest meadows stretch away to the setting sun. Ducks and geese on the water, children paddling in the shallows, cows coming home from the pastures, and men and women carrying hay or vegetables, suggested a quiet country village rather than a stately *residenz;* but I was very careful not to say so to any Detmolder. The repose and seclusion of the place took hold of my fancy: I walked back and forth, through the same streets and linden-shaded avenues in the long summer evening, finding idyls at every turn; but alas! they floated formlessly by and faded in the sunset.

Detmold is the birthplace of the poet Freiligrath, and I went into the two bookstores to see if they kept his poems — which they did not. Fifty years hence, perhaps, they will have a statue of him. As I sat in my lonely room at the inn, waiting for bedtime, my thoughts went back to that morning by the lake of Zurich, when I first met the banished poet; to pleasant evenings at his house in Hackney; and to the triumphant reception which, at Cologne, a few days before, had welcomed him back to Germany. This was the end of twenty-three years of exile, the beginning of which I remembered. Noble, unselfish, and consistent as his political course had been, had he followed it to his detriment as a poet, or had he bridged the gulf which separates the Muses from party conflicts? That was the question, and it was not so easy to resolve. Poesy will cheer as a friend, but she will not *serve.* She will not be driven from that broad field of humanity, wherein the noise of parties is swallowed up, and the colors of their banners are scarcely to be distinguished. Freiligrath has written the best political poems in the German language, and his life has been the brilliant illustration of his principles; yet I doubt whether "The Dead to the Living" will outlive the "Lion-Ride."

I picked up, however, a description of the Teutoburger Forest, written by the Cantor Sauerländer of Detmold — a little book which no one but a full-blooded Teuton could have written. Fatiguingly minute, conscientious to the last degree, overflowing with love for the subject, exhaustive on all points, whether important or not, the style — or, rather, utter lack of style — so placed the unsuspecting author before the reader's mind, that it was impossible to mistake him, — a mild, industrious, harmless egotist, who talks on and on, and never once heeds whether you are listening to his chatter.

I took him with me, but engaged, in addition, a young gardener of the town, and we set out in the bright, hot morning. My plan for the day embraced the monument to Hermann on the Grotenburg, the conjectured field of the defeat of Varus, and the celebrated Extern Rocks. Cool paths through groves of oak led from the town to the foot of the mountain, having reached which I took out the Cantor, and read: " From this point to the near forest the foot-path mounts by a very palpable grade, wherefore the wanderer will find himself somewhat fatigued, besides suffering (frequently) from the burning rays of the sun, against which, however, it is possible to screen one's self by an umbrella, *for which reason* I would venture to suggest a moderate gait, and observant pauses at various points!" Verily, if his book had been specially prepared for the reigning prince, Paul Friedrich Emil Leopold, he could not have been more considerate.

The fatiguing passage, nevertheless, was surmounted in ten minutes, and thenceforth we were in the shade of the forest. At about two thirds of the height the path came upon a *Hünenring*, or Druid circle, one of the largest in Germany. It is nearly five hundred feet in diameter, with openings on the north and south, and the walls of rough stones are in some places twenty feet high. Large trees are growing upon them. There was another and greater ring around the crest of the mountain, but it has been thrown down and almost obliterated. German antiquarians consider these remains as a sufficient evidence to prove that this is the genuine *Teutoburg*, — the fortress of Teut, or Tuisco, the chief personage of the original Teutonic mythology. They also derive the name of Detmold from "Theotmalle," the place of Teut. There can be no doubt as to the character of the circles, or their great antiquity; and, moreover, to locate the Teutoburg here explains the desperate resistance of the tribes of this region both to Rome and to Charlemagne.

Near the summit I found some traces of the greater circle, many of the stones of which were used, very appropriately, for the foundation of the monument to Hermann. This structure stands in an open, grassy space, inclosed by a young growth of fir-trees. It is still incomplete; but we, who long ago stopped work on the colossal Washington obelisk, have no right to reproach the German people. Thirty years ago the Bavarian sculptor Von Bandel exhibited the design of a statue to Hermann. The idea appealed to that longing for German unity the realization of which seemed then so far distant; societies were formed, collections made, fairs held for the object, and the temple-shaped pedestal, commenced in 1841, was finished in 1846, at a cost of forty thousand thalers. The colossal statue which should crown it demanded an equal sum — two thirds of which, I am told, has been contributed. Parts of the figure have been already cast, and the sculptor, now nearly seventy years old, still hopes to see the dream of his life fulfilled. But the impression has gone abroad that the strength of the winds, sweeping unchecked from the Rhine and from Norway across the Northern Sea, is so great upon this Teutoburger height, that the statue would probably be thrown down, if erected. A committee of architects and engineers has declared that, with proper anchorage, the figure will stand; yet the contributions have ceased.

The design of the temple-base is very simple and massive. On a circular foundation, sixty feet in diameter by eleven in height, stands a structure composed of ten clustered pillars, connected by pointed arches, the outer spans of which are cut to represent stems of oak, while heavy garlands of oak-leaves are set in the triangular interspaces. The first rude beginning of Gothic art is here suggested, not as a growth from the Byzantine and Saracenic schools, but as an autochthonous product. Over the cornice, which is fifty feet above the base, rises a solid hemisphere of masonry, terminating in a ring twenty-five feet in diameter, which is to receive the metal base of the colossus. The latter will be ninety feet in height to the point of the sword, making the entire height of the monument a hundred and eighty-two feet.

I mounted to the summit, and looked over the tops of the forest upon a broad and beautiful panoramic ring of landscape. The well-wooded mountains of the region divided the rich valleys and harvest lands which they inclosed. On all sides except the west they melted away in the summer haze; there, they sank into the tawny Westphalian plain, once the land of marshes, traversed by the legions of Varus. While yonder, beyond the ring of the forest sacred to Teut, the fields were withering and the crops wasting in the sun, here they gave their fullest bounty; here the streams were full, the meadows green, and the land laughed with its abundance. From this point I overlooked all the great battle-fields of Hermann and Wittekind. The mountains do not constitute, as I had supposed, a natural stronghold; but in their heart lies the warmest and most fertile region of Northern Germany.

In the neighboring hostelry there is a plaster model of the waiting statue. Hermann, with the winged helmet upon his head, and clad in a close leathern coat reaching nearly to the knee, is represented as addressing his warriors. The action of the uplifted arm is good, but the left hand rests rather idly upon the shield, instead of unconsciously repeating in the grip of the fingers the energy of the rest of the figure. The face — ideal, of course — is quite as much Roman as Teuton, the nose being aquiline, the eyebrows straight, and the lips very clearly and regularly cut. To me the physiognomy would indicate *dark* hair and beard. I found the body somewhat heavy and ungraceful; but as it was to be seen from below, and in very different dimensions, the effect may be all that is designed.

In the Hall of Busts in the Museum of the Capitol, in Rome, there is a head which has recently attracted the interest of German archæologists. It stands alone among the severe Roman and the exquisitely balanced Grecian heads, like a genial phenomenon of character totally distinct from theirs. When I stood before it, a little puzzled, and wondering at the absurd label of " Cecrops?" affixed to the pedestal, I had not learned the grounds for conjecturing that it may be a portrait of him whom Tacitus calls Arminius; yet I felt that here was a hero, of whom history *must* have some knowledge. It is certainly a blonde head, with abundant locks, a beard sprouting thinly and later than in the South, strong cheek-bones, a nose straight but not Grecian, and lips which somehow express good fellowship, vanity, and the habit of command. The sculptor Bandel made a great mistake in not boldly accepting the conjecture as fact, and giving Hermann this head. Dr. Emil Braun considers that it is undoubtedly a bust of one of the young German chiefs who were educated at the court of Augustus; and he adds, very truly, "If this can be proven, it will be of great importance as a testimony of the intellectual development of the German race, even in those early times."

Hermann, who was born in the year 16 B. C., must have gone to Rome as a boy, during the campaigns of Drusus and Tiberius in Northern Germany. He became not only a citizen, but a Roman knight, was intrusted with the command of a German legion, and fought in Pannonia. He acquired the Latin tongue, and acquainted himself with the military and civil science of the Romans. Had the wise and cautious policy of Tiberius been followed, he might have died as a Consul of the Empire; but the brutal rule of Varus provoked the tribes to resistance, and Hermann became a German again. He turned against Rome the tactics he had learned in her service, enticed Varus away from the fortified line of the Rhine, across the marshes of the Lippe, and on the southern slope of the Teutoburger Forest, in a three days' battle fought amid the autumn storms, annihilated the Roman army of fifty thousand men. Well might the Imperial city tremble, and the old Augustus cry out to the shade of the slain commander, "Varus, Varus, give me back my legions!"

For five years the sovereignty of Hermann and the independence of his people were not disturbed. But after the death of Augustus, in the year 14 A. D., Germanicus determined to restore the prestige of the Roman arms. In the mean time Hermann had married Thusnelda, daughter of Segestus, another chief of the Cheruski, who had reclaimed her by force in consequence of a quarrel, and was then besieged by his son-in-law. Segestus called the Romans to his aid, and delivered Thusnelda into their hands to grace, two years later, the triumph decreed to Germanicus. Hermann, infuriated by the loss of a wife whom he loved, summoned the tribes to war, and the Roman commander collected an army of eighty thousand men. The latter succeeded in burying the bones of Varus and his legions, and was then driven back with great loss. Returning in the year 16 with a still larger army, he met the undaunted Hermann on the Weser, near Hameln. The terrible battle fought there, and a second near the Porta Westphalica, were claimed as victories by the

Romans, yet were followed by a retreat to the fortresses on the Rhine. Germanicus was preparing a third campaign when he was recalled by the jealous Tiberius. The Romans never again penetrated into this part of Germany.

Hermann might have founded a nation but for the fierce jealousy of the other chieftains of his race. He was victorious in the civil wars which ensued, but was waylaid and murdered by members of his own family in the year 21. His short life of thirty-seven years is an unbroken story of heroism. Even Tacitus, to whom we are indebted for these particulars, says of him: "He was undoubtedly the liberator of Germany, having dared to grapple with the Roman power, not in its beginnings, like other kings and commanders, but in the maturity of its strength. He was not always victorious in battle, but in war he was never subdued. He still lives in the songs of the Barbarians, unknown to the annals of the Greeks, who only admire that which belongs to themselves — nor celebrated as he deserves by the Romans, who, in praising the olden times, neglect the events of the later years."

Leaving the monument, my path followed the crest of the mountain for two or three miles, under a continuous roof of beech. Between the smooth, clean boles I looked down upon the hot and shining valley, where the leaves hung motionless on the trees, but up on the shaded ridge of the hills there was a steady, grateful breeze. The gardener was not a very skillful guide, and only brought me to the *Winnefeld* (Winfield) after a roundabout ramble. I found myself at the head of a long, bare slope, falling to the southwest, where it terminated in three dells, divided by spurs of the range. The town of Lippspringe, in the distance, marked the site of the fountains mentioned by Tacitus. The *Winnefeld* lies on the course which an army would take, marching from those springs to assault the Teutoburg, and the three dells, wooded then as now, would offer rare chances of ambuscade and attack. There is no difficulty in here locating the defeat of Varus. That the Teuton victory was not solely the result of Hermann's military skill is proven by the desperate bravery with which his warriors confronted the legions of Germanicus five years later.

Standing upon this famous battle-field, one cannot but recall the subsequent relations of Germany and Rome, which not only determined the history of the Middle Ages, but set in action many of the forces which shape the present life of the world. The seat of power was transplanted, it was exercised by another race, but its elements were not changed. Hermann, a knight of Rome, learned in her service how to resist her, and it was still the Roman mind which governed Italy while she was a defiant dependency of the German Empire. Charlemagne took up the uncompleted work of Germanicus, and was the true avenger of Varus after nearly eight hundred years. The career of Hermann, though so splendidly heroic, does not mark the beginning of Germany; the race only began to develop after its complete subjection to the laws and arts and ideas of Rome. Thus the marvelous Empire triumphed at last.

I descended the bare and burning slopes of the mountain into a little valley, plunged into a steep forest beyond, and, after plodding wearily for an hour or more, found myself, as nearly as I could guess, on the banks of a brook that descends to the town of Horn. The gardener seemed at fault, yet insisted on leading me contrary to my instinct of the proper course. We had not gone far, however, when a mass of rock, rising like a square tower above the wooded ridge to the eastward, signaled our destination; and my discomfited guide turned about silently, and made towards it, I following, through thickets and across swamps, until we reached the highway.

The Extern Rocks (*Externsteine*) have a double interest for the traveller. They consist of five detached masses of gray sandstone, one hundred and twenty-five feet in height, irregularly square in form, and with diameters varying from thirty to fifty feet. They are planted on a grassy slope, across the mouth of a glen opening from the mountains. Only a few tough shrubs hang from the crevices in their sides, but the birch-trees on the summits shoot high into the air and print their sprinkled leaves on the sky. The hills of the Teutoburger Forest are rounded and cliffless, and the same formation, it is said, does not reappear elsewhere.

In the base of the most northern of these rocks a chapel, thirty-six feet long, has been hewn — but when, or by whom, are matters of conjecture. Some very imaginative antiquaries insist that the Romans captured by Hermann were here sacrificed to the pagan gods; others find evidence that the place was once dedicated to the worship of Mithras (the sun); but the work must probably be ascribed to the early Teutonic Christians. The rocks are first mentioned in a document of the year 1093. On the outer wall of the chapel there is a tablet of sculpture, in high relief, sixteen feet by twelve, which is undoubtedly the earliest work of the kind in Germany. Its Byzantine character is not to be mistaken, and, judging by the early Christian sculptures and mosaics in Italy, it may be as old as the ninth or tenth century. The tablet is in three compartments, the lower one representing the Fall of Man, the centre the Descent from the Cross, while at the top the Almighty receives the soul of the Son in his arms, and holds forth the Banner of the Cross. Although mutilated, weather-beaten, and partly veiled in obscuring moss, the pathos of the sculpture makes itself felt through all the grotesqueness of its forms. Goethe, who saw it, says: "The head of the sinking Saviour leans against the countenance of the mother, and is gently supported by her hand — a beautiful, reverent touch of expression which we find in no other representation of the subject." The drapery also, though stiff, has yet the simplicity and dignity which we so rarely find in modern art.

Two of the rocks may be ascended by means of winding stairways cut in their sides. On the summit of the first there is a level platform, with a stone table in the centre — probably the work of the monks, to whom the place belonged in the Middle Ages. By climbing the central rock, and crossing a bridge to the next, one reaches a second chapel, eighteen feet in length, with a rock-altar at the further end. It is singular that there is no record of the origin of this remarkable work. We know that the spirit of the Teutonic mythology lived long after the introduction of Christianity, and the monks may have here found and appropriated one of its sacred places.

By the time I reached the town of Horn, a mile or so from the base of the mountains, I was too scorched and weary to go further afoot, and, while waiting dinner in the guests'-room of the inn, looked about for a means of conveyance. Three or four stout *Philister*, drinking beer at an adjoining table, were bound for Steinheim, which was on my way; and the landlord said, "An 'extra post' will be expensive, but these gentlemen might make room for you in their carriage."

They looked at each other and at me. "We are already *seven*," said one, "and must be squeezed as it is."

"By no means," I replied to the landlord; "get me an extra post."

Both vehicles were ready at the same time. In the meantime I had entered into conversation with one of the party, — a bright, cheerful young man, — and told him that I should be glad to have company on the way.

"Why did you engage an extra post?" they all exclaimed. "It is expensive! we are only *five*; you might have gone with us, — we could easily make room for you!"

Yet, while making these exclamations, they picked out

the oldest and least companionable of their party, and bundled him into my "expensive" carriage! I never saw anything more coolly done. I had meant to have the agreeable, not the stupid member, but was caught, and could not help myself. However, I managed to extract a little amusement from my companion as we went along. He was a Detmolder, after confessing which he remarked, —

"Now I knew where *you* came from before you had spoken ten words."

"Indeed! Where, then?"

"Why, from Bielefeld!"

My laughter satisfied the old fellow that he had guessed correctly, and thenceforth he talked so much about Bielefeld that it finally became impossible to conceal my ignorance of the place. I set him down in Steinheim, dismissed the extra post, and, as the evening was so bright and balmy, determined to go another stage on foot. I had a letter to a young nobleman, whose estate lay near a village some four or five miles further on the road to Höxter. The small boy whom I took as guide was communicative; the scenery was of the sweetest pastoral character; the mellow light of sunset struck athwart the golden hills of harvest, the lines of alder hedge, and the meadows of winding streams, and I loitered along the road full of delight in the renewal of my old pedestrian freedom.

It was dusk when I reached the village. The one cottage inn did not promise much comfort; but the baron's castle was beyond, and I was too tired to go further. The landlord was a petty magistrate, evidently one of the pillars of the simple village society; and he talked well and intelligently, while his daughter cooked my supper. The bare rooms were clean and orderly, and the night was so warm that no harm was done when the huge globe of feathers under which I was expected to sleep rolled off the bed and lay upon the floor until morning.

Sending my letter to the castle, I presently received word that the young baron was absent from home, but that his mother would receive me. As I emerged from the shadows of the narrow village street into the breezeless, burning air of the morning, the whole estate lay full and fair in view — a thousand acres of the finest harvest land, lying in the lap of a bowl-shaped valley, beyond which rose a wooded mountain range. In the centre of the landscape a group of immemorial oaks and lindens hid the castle from view, but a broad and stately linden avenue connected it with the highway. There were scores of reapers in the fields, and their dwellings, with the barns and stables, almost formed a second village. The castle — a square mass of building, with a paved court-yard in the centre — was about three hundred years old; but it had risen upon the foundations of a much older edifice.

The baroness met me at the door with her two daughters, and ushered me into a spacious room, the ceiling of which, low and traversed by huge beams of oak, was supported by a massive pillar in the centre. The bare oaken floor was brightly polished; a gallery of ancestral portraits decked the walls, but the furniture was modern and luxurious. After a friendly scolding for not claiming the castle's hospitality the night before, one of the daughters brought refreshments, just as a *Burgfräulein* of the Middle Ages might have done, except that she did not taste the goblet of wine before offering it. The ladies then conducted me through a range of apartments, every one of which contained some picturesque record of the past. The old building was pervaded with a mellow atmosphere of age and use; although it was not the original seat of the family, their own ancestral heirlooms had adapted themselves to its physiognomy, and seemed to continue its traditions. Just enough of modern taste was visible to suggest home comforts and conveniences; all else seemed as old as the Thirty Years' War.

After inspecting the house, we issued upon the *pleas-aunce* — a high bosky space resting on the outer wall of the castle, and looking down upon the old moat, still partially full of water. It was a labyrinth of shady paths, of arbors, with leaf-enframed windows opening towards the mountains, and of open, sunny spaces rich with flowers. The baroness called my attention to two splendid magnolia-trees, and a clump of the large Japanese *polygonum*. "This," she said, pointing to the latter, "was given to my husband by Dr. von Siebold, who brought it from Japan; the magnolias came from seeds planted forty years ago." They were the most northern specimens of the trees I had found upon the continent of Europe. But the oaks and lindens around the castle were more wonderful than these exotic growths. Each one was "a forest waving on a single stem."

The young baron was not expected to return before the evening, and I was obliged to continue my journey, though every feature of the place wooed me to stay. "But at least," urged the hostess, "you must visit my husband's twin brother, who is still living at the old *burg*. We were going to send for him to-day, and we will send you along." This was a lift on my way; and, moreover, it was a pleasure to meet a gentleman of whom I had heard so much — a thinker, a man of scientific culture, and a poet, yet unknown to the world in either of these characters.

The youngest daughter of the house made ready to accompany me, and presently a light open wagon, drawn by a span of ponies, came to the door. After my yesterday's tramp in the forest it was a delightful change. The young lady possessed as much intelligence as refinement, and with her as a guide the rich scenery through which we passed assumed a softer life, a more gracious sentiment. From the ridge before us rose the lofty towers of a church attached to an extinct monastery, the massive buildings of which are now but half tenanted by some farmers; on the right a warm land of grain stretched away to the Teutoburger Forest; on the left, mountains clothed with beech and oak basked in the sun. We passed the monastery, crossed a wood, and dropped into a wild, lonely valley among the hills. Here the *Oldenburg*, as it is called, already towered above us, perched upon the bluff edge of a mountain cape. It was a single square mass of the brownest masonry, seventy or eighty feet high, with a huge, steep, and barn-like roof. It dominated alone over the beech woods; no other human habitation was in sight.

When we reached the summit, however, I found that the old building was no longer tenanted. Behind it lay a pond, around which were some buildings connected with the estate, and my fair guide led the way to the further door of a house in which the laboring people lived. She went to seek her uncle, while I waited in a room so plainly furnished that an American farmer would have apologized for it. Presently I was summoned up stairs, where the old baron caught me by both hands, and pressed me down into his own arm-chair before it was possible to say a word. His room was as simple as the first; but books and water-color drawings showed the tastes of its occupant.

It was truly the head of a poet upon which I looked. Deep-set, spiritual eyes shone under an expansive brow, over which fell some thin locks of silky gray hair; the nose was straight and fine, with delicate, sensitive nostrils, and there was a rare expression of sweetness and purity in the lines of the mouth. It needed no second glance to see that the old man was good and wise and noble and perfectly lovable. My impulse was to sit on a stool at his feet, as I have seen a young English poet sitting at the feet of good Barry Cornwall, and talk to him with my arms resting upon his knees. But he drew his chair close beside me, and took my hand from time to time, as he talked; so that it was not long before our thoughts ran together, and each anticipated the words of the other.

"Now tell me about my friend," said he. "We were inseparable as students, and as long as our paths lay near each other. They say that three are too many for friendship, but we twin-brothers only counted as one in the bond. We had but one heart and one mind, except in matters of science, and there it was curious to see how far apart we sometimes were. Ah, what rambles we had together, in Germany and on the Alps! I remember once we were merry in the Thüringian Forest, for there was wine enough and to spare; so we buried a bottle deep among the rocks. We had forgotten all about it when, a year or two afterwards, we happened all three to come back to the spot, and there we dug up the bottle, and drank what seemed to be the best wine in the world. I wonder if he remembers that I wrote a poem about it."

Then we walked out through the beech woods to a point of the mountain whence there was a view of the monastery across the wild valley. "It was but yesterday," said the old baron, "since I stood here with my brother — both little boys — and listened to the chimes of vesper. There were monks in the old building then. What is life, after all? I don't understand it. My brother was a part of myself. We had but one life; he married and his home was mine; his children are mine still. We were born together; three years ago he died, and I should have died at the same time. How is it that I live?"

He turned to me with tears in his eyes, and a sad, mysterious wonder in his voice. I could only shake my head, for he who could have answered the question would be able to solve all the enigmas of life. The man seemed to me like a semi-ghost, attached to the earth by only half the relation of other men. "I live here as you see," he continued; "but I am not lonely. All my life of seventy-three years I have been laying aside interest for this season. I have still my thoughts and questions, as well as my memories. I am part of the great design which I have always found in the world and in man, and I have learned enough to accept what I cannot fathom."

These were brave and wise words, and they led on to others, as we walked in the shadows of the beech woods, until summoned to dinner. The baron's niece superintended the meal, and a farmer's daughter waited at the table. I was forced to decline a kind invitation to return to the castle with the old man, and spend the night there — for I could take but a brief holiday in the Teutoburger Forest. Then they proposed taking me to the town of Höxter, on the Weser, whither I was bound; but while I was trying to dissuade the young lady from a further drive of ten miles, the sound of a horn suddenly broke the solitude of the woods. A post-carriage came in sight, drove to the door, and from it descended the *Kreisrichter* (District Judge), on a visit to the old baron. As I noticed that he intended remaining for the night, I proposed taking the carriage by which he had arrived, though I should have preferred making the journey on foot.

It was so arranged, and half an hour afterwards I took leave of the noble old man, with the promise — which all the battle-fields of Hermann and Wittekind would not have suggested to me — of some day returning to the Teutoburger Forest. Leaving the mountains behind me, I followed a road which slowly descended to the Weser through the fairest winding valleys, and before sunset reached Höxter. A mile further, at the bend of the river, is the ancient Abbey of Corvey, where, in the year 1515, the first six books of the Annals of Tacitus, up to that time lost, were discovered. The region which that great historian has alone described, thus preserved and gave back to the world a portion of his works.

www.ingramcontent.com/pod-product-compliance
Lightning Source LLC
Chambersburg PA
CBHW022109300426
44117CB00007B/652